Devil Make a Third

D1520928

The Library of Alabama Classics,

reprint editions of works important

to the history, literature and culture of

Alabama, is dedicated to the memory of

Rucker Agee

whose pioneering work in the fields

of Alabama history and historical geography

continues to be the standard of

scholarly achievement.

DEVIL MAKE A THIRD

DOUGLAS FIELDS BAILEY

with an Introduction by
Alan T. Belsches

THE UNIVERSITY OF ALABAMA PRESS
Tuscaloosa and London

Copyright 1948 by E. P. Dutton & Co., Inc.

Copyright renewed 1976 by Louie H. Bailey

Introduction Copyright © 1989 by
The University of Alabama Press
Tuscaloosa, Alabama 35487–2877
All Rights Reserved
Manufactured in the United States of America

LIBRARY OF CONGRESS
Library of Congress Cataloging-in-Publication Data

Bailey, Douglas Fields, 1912–1987.
Devil make a third / by Douglas Fields Bailey ; with an
introduction by Alan T. Belsches.
p.   cm. — (The Library of Alabama classics)
Reprint. Originally published: New York : Dutton, 1948.
Bibliography: p.
ISBN 0-8173-0420-7 (pbk. : alk. paper)
I. Title.   II. Series
PS3503.A4175D4 1989
813'.54—dc19   88-17678
                                                    CIP

British Cataloguing-in-Publication Data available

To my wife and to my mother

All of the characters, all of the
events and all of the places in
this book are fictitious

FOREWORD

As the *town is the nation in seed, so is a strong man the kernel of the town.*

The life of the strong man is the beam from which the vigor of the town is projected, and, since the progress of man is by nature episodic, so a town may leap one year and stumble another. Robust in peak times, bloodless in the valleys, the commonwealth ebbs and flows with the temper of its men.

The lusty, always greedy, sometimes fumbling fingers of the strong man enrich the country in spite of his motives, as the earthworm's blind and selfish groping mellows the soil.

Those other men, those who grovel and hesitate, live only within the boundary of their fears, in a dusty husk of a world, until the strong man comes, saying,

"I will build for myself, and if the public harvest follows my private vice, then join me at the board and leave it gratified."

Devil Make a Third

INTRODUCTION

Alan T. Belsches

IN 1912 SOUTHEASTERN Alabama was an agricultural region fighting the devastation caused by the boll weevil and hoping for progress and prosperity with the expansion of the railroad. In that same year, William Fields Bailey was born in Dothan, Alabama. According to Wendell and Pamela Stepp's history, in the early 1800s Dothan was no more than a crossroads known as Poplar Spring. The site offered a major source of water for settlers coming from Charleston, Savannah, and Jacksonville along trails first used by Indians of the Creek Confederacy. By the 1840s, the trails intersecting at Poplar Spring were safe enough from Indian attack to become major stagecoach routes between the small but thriving towns of Columbia and Gordon in the east and Geneva, Daleville, and Newton to the west. Saint Andrews Street and Main Street in Dothan today, which Bailey calls St. Simon and Basin in his novel *Devil Make a Third*, were built over these original routes.

Because the area's sandy soil was largely unproductive, few travelers remained long enough at Poplar Spring to establish a settlement. Occasionally turpentine gatherers from Georgia would tap the pine trees in the area, but not until 1880, with the establishment of a church at Poplar Spring, did the settlement really begin to thrive. By 1885, the community of nearly two hundred citizens became incorporated and took the name of Dothan. In 1889, the railroad came to town on its way from Bainbridge, Georgia, to the state's capital in Montgomery, providing an easier access to markets for the area's chief agricultural products of turpentine, lumber, and cotton than the old water routes on the Chattahoochee River.[1]

By 1912, the town's population had reached 7,500.[2] Its mayor was Joe "Buck" Baker, Jr., the uncle of William Fields Bailey. Buck had been the oldest in a family of fourteen children and had moved to Dothan from the country in 1887. That move from farm to city, from the intense physical labor behind the plow to a more intellectually demanding job behind a store counter was a transition reenacted countless times throughout the rural South, and was to become the theme of Bailey's *Devil Make a Third*.

Bailey exhibited a strong interest in writing in his youth, often recounting stories about his mother's family. After growing up in one of the houses his Grandmother Baker had his Uncle Buck build for her three youngest daughters on what is now Crawford Street in Dothan, Bailey attended first the University of Alabama at Tuscaloosa and then the University of Missouri in the early 1930s. His financial support came from the large holdings of rental property and farmlands owned by the Baker family.

Upon returning to the area, Bailey worked for local newspapers both in Marianna, Florida, and in Dothan. However, through his studies at Tuscaloosa he came under the influence of Hudson Strode, a professor of English who taught courses in Shakespeare and creative writing. He submitted to Strode drafts of short stories he was writing and, through their close association, Bailey was encouraged to attempt a novel that would incorporate knowledge of his hometown, insights into members of his mother's family, and that would also provide a historical look at the South of the turn of the century. He would write under the pseudonym Douglas Fields Bailey.

In 1945, once the threat of being drafted into World War II was over, Bailey outlined some scenes and began his novel. Writing mostly in the evenings, after working for an insurance business during the day, Bailey would typically envision the details of various scenes in the novel and then write them down. Usually he made few changes to his first drafts because he had spent hours depicting the events in his mind. This process produced a novel composed of a series of dramatic scenes loosely strung together by interludes that serve to account for the passage of time between the chapters. About every six weeks during this writing period, Bailey carried his manuscript to Tuscaloosa to read his chapters to Strode's creative writing classes. And when the New York publisher E. P. Dutton contacted Strode for manuscripts from promising Southern writers, Strode sent Bailey's *Devil Make a Third*.

In his Foreword to the novel Bailey suggests that his subject is "The lusty, always greedy, sometimes fumbling fingers of the strong man [who] enrich[es] the country in spite of his motives, as the earthworm's blind and selfish groping mellows the soil." This type of ruthless, striving individual when explored in a political setting is like the Willie Stark of Robert Penn Warren's *All the King's Men* (1946). Historically set a generation of Southerners later than that of *Devil Make a Third*, Warren's novel asks how much corruption is tolerable in a politician who does help his economically depressed constituency. Even though Willie Stark uses his political power to further his own ends, he also aids the citizens of Louisiana by building roads, schools, and hospitals. Although Warren's narrator, Jack Burden, is forced to voice his admiration, he finally rejects Willie's actions.

In *Devil Make a Third*, Bailey asks a similar question but without the aid of a first person narrator. How should Aven's citizens feel about Buck Bannon, the leader of their community whose actions have brought growth and development to a burgeoning town as well as thousands of dollars to his own pocket? And even more important, how should Buck Bannon, the main character of the novel, feel about himself?

But here we find Bailey exploring more than the single question that Warren explored—and perhaps better. Bailey describes, through the story of the Bannon family, that great migration of Southern men from family farms to towns in order to improve their economic standing—a sociological change still occurring today. What are the familial and personal conflicts to be encountered in such a change? These are precisely the questions that *Devil Make a Third* explores so well.

When the novel opens, Buck Bannon, age eighteen and the oldest of fourteen children, has decided to leave the family farm in southeast Alabama to seek his own fortune in the little town of Aven, which has recently developed along a railroad spur. He leaves home determined that his own body will not become as bent and broken to the plow as his father's.

On his arrival in the town of Aven, young Buck perceives both the positive and negative aspects of town life. The people who live in town look " 'like bees in a hive,' " but Buck believes that even their monotonous existence can lead to riches. Buck vows to take the shortest route possible to achieve financial success because he believes " 'The place a man starts at ain't the thing—it's where he ends up that counts.' "

The morning after his arrival, Buck's first successful attempt at bargaining for a job (that would not be a "tool job") wins him a salary as a salesman and a place to live in the back of the store. From this beginning his fortunes improve quickly. His later financial success comes through the personal loans he makes, reminiscent of Jason Compson's in William Faulkner's *The Sound and the Fury* (1929).

Each week railroad men in Aven seek out Buck, offering their watches as collateral for the cash they need to enjoy the women, liquor, and gambling available in the town. Even though Buck initially wishes to lend money at no interest, he decides that loan-sharking will be his shortcut to becoming a rich man. Within a year, just when his boss, the store's owner, needs cash for his wife's medical expenses, Buck is ready to buy a partnership in the store.

As Buck's financial success continues, Bailey shows his desire to share his wealth with his family as a way of saving them from the debilitating work of farming. After two years in Aven he returns home, and Bailey portrays Buck's hidden longing to return to the sights, smells, and tastes of life on the farm. " 'Two years ago when I was hasslin' to leave it,' " he admits to himself, " 'I never would have figured dirt could smell so good.' " Now these images flood his mind, but Bailey also describes here an even deeper sense of Buck's wanting to belong.

Throughout history, many Southerners who have left the farm question whether their social move has meant a forsaking of their roots, their heritage. Louis D. Rubin, Jr. writes of this identity crisis in his essay "Fugitives as Agrarians: The Impulse Behind *I'll Take My Stand*." Rubin discusses how even Southern writers and intellectuals in contemporary society struggle against the sense of severing their roots when they receive an education or move out of the South where the ties to the land remain so strong. In his essay, Rubin uses as examples his literary colleagues who, when they get together, drink, smoke, and swap tales as a way of remembering their youth among the common folk and as a way of reaffirming to each other and to themselves that they still can be accepted as part of the Southern rural classes.[3]

Buck is certainly no writer or intellectual, but like the modern Southerners in Rubin's essay, Buck misses the sense of community that he once shared as a member of the Bannon family on the farm. Over a century earlier, young Robin Molineux in Nathaniel Hawthorne's short story "My Kinsman, Major Molineux" experienced the same feeling of loss. As young farm boys coming to the big city, both choose to relinquish their rural innocence. For Robin the result is acceptance as a member of the town's community. For Buck the loss of innocence is more severe. He must reject the town's railroad men as friends and equals and accept the isolation of the moneylender in the hope of bettering his lot. But during his stay at home, Buck begins to question whether his move was the right decision after all. He begins to realize that he has only substituted one kind of "grubbing" on the farm for another in the town. And what he has gained by it pales in contrast to the pleasant memories of his youth. Although his mind will now always be that of the businessman, his heart will remain forever on the farm.

This desire to refrain from psychologically breaking with farm life and all it represents is especially evident in Buck's parents. When Buck's father, Joe Bannon, sees the new house his son has built for the family in town, his vision is drawn first to the land around the house. " 'Somethin' ought to grow there' " he says to Buck. Even the excellent price they received for the family farm, he believes, came from the good crops growing on it.

In contrast to his son, the conservative financial practices that Joe Bannon developed as a farmer continue when he becomes a store clerk. When Buck suggests his parents should borrow money to buy land ahead of the railroad, Joe's cautious response is that they should wait and build up their cash supplies first. Buck accuses him of " 'thinkin' like a poor man.' " And even after Joe is persuaded, he dislikes Buck's tactic of using alcohol to trick the railroad land agent. When Joe Bannon dies, Bailey shows, in the final conversation between son and father, the older generation's fear of individuals who put money ahead of moral principles. Joe Bannon leaves his entire estate to his wife. She must monitor Buck's management of the family assets because, as Joe tells Buck, " ' . . . I been worried sometimes that you'd let a dollar outshine what it'll buy.' "

Although Joe Bannon consented to move into town and to work for his son in a store as a way of saving his health, his wife, Jeanie Bannon, retains her ties to the land. She leaves the farm with the family to assure financial security for her numerous offspring, but at her approaching death she prefers to return to the country. Because Buck senses his mother's true leanings, he buys her a farm and builds a new house for her there. Yet when she feels death's approach, Jeanie prefers to lie in a bed in her tenants' dilapidated house. Even when Buck argues that she deserves more expensive accommodation, Bailey has Jeanie's response mark their difference in attitude toward money and life: " 'There ain't no stylish way to die.' "

[5]

For Buck Bannon, his mother is the primary controlling force in his life, and through their relationship Bailey dramatizes the changes in the family that come with the move from farm to town. Throughout the novel, Buck is willing to break accepted mores if it brings him personal gain. Jeanie Bannon is not. Soon after the family's arrival in town, she finds Buck sleeping with Vic, a young school teacher who boards with the family. Jeanie forces the teacher to leave and even changes the name of the youngest Bannon child from Vic to Christina to emphasize her rejection of any new town morality.

The biggest family conflict concerns Jeanie's struggle to control the family's assets and to assure a house in town for her daughters. When Buck denies Jeanie's wishes to send his younger sisters to school in Tennessee, to deed them business property, and to provide them with a house, she admits that his business sense " 'comes straight from me.' " But unlike Buck, Jeanie's reasons for trying to undermine his financial authority are unselfish. It is for her other children, not for herself. When Buck eventually consents to his mother's requests, both gain what they desire, she a house and financial security for her daughters and he the knowledge that no one, not even his mother, can dominate him. In real life, Bailey grew up in Dothan in one of these houses built by his Uncle Buck Baker for his mother who was one of the Baker daughters.

By the time of Jeanie Bannon's death, Buck has achieved financial success as Aven's mayor, a hotel owner, and a prominent businessman, achievements equaled in reality by Bailey's own Uncle Buck Baker. But Jeanie's illness causes Buck to reassess his own life. He found friendship with Tobe Parody, Aven's sheriff, but Tobe (modelled after the real Tobe Domingus, Dothan's early marshall and chief of police, who was wounded in a gun battle on Main Street over cotton gin taxes) is killed when saving Buck's life. Buck married the daughter of his chief business competitor and fathered a child, but his first wife leaves him before his son's birth because of his visits to the town's prostitutes. And when the doctor tells him that his mother has less than one year to live because of cancer, Buck reflects:

"Time. There's never enough of it to go around . . . when a man's young time stretches out in front forever. Then by God, he stoops

down one day to pick up a kid's ball and he comes back up panting a
little and dizzy and he'd meant to holler and throw hell out of it,
limber as hickory. He just rolls it back and stands there and wonders
what went with time. And there's not a thing he can do but mumble
in his head that it went too fast and he didn't have any warning.
Warnings come every day, though. Somebody dies and another one's
born."

He perceives now the fleetingness of life, but Buck's response is not
remorse. He even acknowledges that at his father's death and at
Tobe's death he had thought chiefly of himself and of his own sur-
vival. Now he can admit:

"Why lie about it. It takes something like this to make a man take
stock, but I reckon I been knowing that what I've done wasn't for the
next generation, and it wasn't because I couldn't do it different. It
was because I was scared . . . that I couldn't stand a life time of
plowing, chopping cotton, praying for rain or screaming at a freeze.
Scared . . . that if I didn't get it one way I wouldn't be man enough
to get it the other way."

We see Buck at his best here and at his most honest self. He will not
condemn what he has done nor try to rationalize it. His admissions
reveal his inner fear of being unable to achieve his ideal of himself.

His conversation with his second wife Lota reveals how the words
of his mother's doctor have haunted him. He admits that often he
has wondered if he has " 'swapped years for minutes. What I had
thought was rich was poor and what I'd felt was good was bad and it
began to eat in me like a shanker. . . . ' " He confesses that he has
never had time to think of higher things. He has always been forced
to face one problem after another with little time to worry over ef-
fects or larger issues. But his mother's death forces him to ask those
larger questions and to attempt to achieve some good with his new
wealth and power. His solution is to build an opera house for Aven.
In real life an opera house was completed in Dothan in 1915, during
the administration of Mayor Buck Baker. Like the hospital built by
Willie Stark in *All the King's Men*, Buck Bannon's new opera house
will be a monument to the people. And even though the money for
it comes from gambling, Buck is determined to use it for the good of
others.

With his vision of the opera house ever before him, Buck diverts his grief at his mother's death into its construction. But his attempts to achieve this goodness are unsuccessful. Buck extorts the contractor who uses illegal convict labor, the contractor dupes Buck by using a faulty mixture of mortar, and finally the entire opera house is destroyed by fire during its opening. These disastrous events cause the reader to wonder about Bailey's final assessment of Buck and his life. He has us admire Buck's courage and heroism in directing the citizens out of the burning building and in saving his friend Virgil's life, but why has Bailey not allowed Buck to achieve his goal?

At the end of the novel, Buck and Lota argue over how successful Buck has been in life. All of his graft and corrupt dealings have resulted in some good, Buck thinks, and all of his positive acts have ended in disaster. But Lota wonders whether " 'it makes much difference after all what a man's reasons are, if good comes from a bad motive.' " She, who has the last word in the novel, affirms that " 'no matter what happens, the good you've done is done and can't be undone. . . . ' "

When Buck considers if he should stop attempting to do good, Lota affirms: " 'I don't believe . . . anybody can live without trouble if he has brains and a heart. And you've got plenty of both.' " Her opinion seems to reflect Bailey's. Good and bad always come together in this life if one has the courage to live it. As the title, taken from Shakespeare's *Henry VI*, Part II suggests, the third component of Buck's life, in addition to his brains and heart, is the devil or evil. Goodness does not exist without evil in this world.

Bailey's original, unpublished ending for the novel, however, was quite different. Included for the first time at the end of this facsimile printing of the 1948 edition, Bailey's intended ending has Buck die in the opera house fire. The editors at Dutton asked Bailey to end the novel on a happy note, and he complied with the request even though he felt it weakened the novel.

Bailey's original ending concludes with Buck pushing Virgil, his guitar-playing friend, to safety from the crumbling wall before crashing to the pavement. Buck remains conscious long enough to recognize a spectator's shoe and to speak his last thoughts: " 'It don't hurt. God, I wonder if this is all folks are scared of.' " His final wondering about death is answered positively in the narrator's comment: "He didn't think, or feel, or taste anything else."

This naturalistic ending, reminiscent of the conclusion of Frank Norris's 1899 novel *McTeague*, is a stark negative answer to the questions of life that Bailey poses in his account of Buck Bannon's life. Of course, all the fears of death that Buck once had are destroyed, but then so is the good that he tried to accomplish for the community. Because his final attempt to achieve goodness has failed, his life seems of little merit, of little purpose.

The romanticism of the published happy ending may seem contrived for today's readers, but Lota's ability to crystalize Bailey's message in her final comments avoids any confusion over Bailey's attitude toward his hero. He admires, through Lota's eyes, Buck's accomplishments and admits that good and evil always exist together. Bailey does not condone the evil that Buck does, but emphasizes strongly that without that evil and the good that accompanied it, neither the Bannon family nor the town of Aven would have prospered.

Reviews of the novel in 1948 were mixed. Virginia Bennett in *Commonweal* admired Bailey's "real feeling for the land and people about which he writes," but suggested he remain with newspapers because he was "not yet regulated to literary form".[4] Peggy Thomson's review in the *New York Herald Tribune Weekly Book Review* praised Bailey's "painstaking, obviously sincere interest in the craft of word-arranging" in his descriptions, although she felt that he lost a sense of objectivity toward Buck.[5] But *The Saturday Review*'s comments by Edwin S. Mills, Jr., entitled "Machiavelli in Alabama" brought to light the lasting merits of the book, Bailey's novel as an invaluable description of the changes that occurred in the South as it entered the industrial age and the heavy toll suffered by the family unit as a result of that transition.[6]

William Fields Bailey died on November 2, 1987, in Dothan, Alabama, the town whose early years he accurately immortalized in this novel. The population of Dothan has grown to over 54,000. Light industry competes with agriculture as the major employer of the area's citizens, and Buck Baker's opera house, which did not burn, has become a Historic Landmark. But the move from farm to city that Bailey chronicled in *Devil Make a Third* still continues, and the moral and social dilemmas faced by Buck Bannon are still relevant to many Southerners today.

CHAPTER ONE

Buck left the farm when he was eighteen.

He was plowing one day, plowing east with the sun blinding him and the lines galling the back of his neck. Suddenly, he decided that it didn't make much difference if his eyes hurt and the ropes scrubbed sweat salt into his neck. He was eighteen and he was following a mule for the last time. He struck a new course, sighting between his mule's ears at his mother, who was rocking determinedly on the front porch. Buck laughed to himself at the thought of her rocking.

"She's shore mastered that chair," he told his mule.

Buck's new furrow was cutting across fresh-plowed dirt, but he didn't notice it. He kept his eyes on his mother and felt good all over with a feeling like power making his chest too full. He lifted his head so he could see his mother better, over the bobbing head of the mule. Each step brought another detail out in sharper pattern. She was wearing the shapeless dress she always wore when she was going to have another baby. Buck felt a sudden lurch under his ribs as he remembered that he was the first of twelve children. He could call back to mind the births of the last eight.

His mother was leaning forward now and Buck could see the sun glinting on the jar of Maccaboy snuff at her feet and picking out the first solid streaks of grey in her hair. He pushed his mule faster, cursing it softly, until his plow point was zooming out of the dirt and skittering a few paces before he could jam it into a deeper bite. He was close enough to see how the sun threw little ragged shadows over the chicken-foot patterns in the yard, but he only shifted his eyes to his mother's face. It was swollen a little, around the jaw, but the chin was pushed forward like it always was. Again Buck felt a loose upsetting inside him. He could tell how she felt by the tired puffiness around her eyes. He saw them shine, though, right out of the swelling and he thought about a treed possum, how you couldn't be sure the dim lump in the branches was a possum until the moon glinted in his eyes. As if it were something solid, the thought formed that he could always find his mother in her eyes, no matter what happened to the rest of her.

His plow point curled out of soft dirt and began to labor in hard-caked clay and he took his eyes off his mother for the first time. He jerked hard on one line and drew his mule into a tight circle around the sanded yard, and the fullness in his chest began to choke up into his throat. The sense of power swelling up made him feel reckless all over and swingy in the hips like a dirt-road sport.

There was more to the ache in his chest than the drumming power. There was something like a gay release from pressure working up inside and the feeling was like a young bull feels when he goes in the pasture and plunges again and again into a springy sapling, testing his strength. Suddenly, Buck could stand the fullness no longer. He jerked the lines from around his neck and slapped his straining mule with the looped ends.

"Git agoin'," he yelled, and tried to say more words but the powerful brightness kept boiling so fast he couldn't cut words with his mind. He was just yelling. It was a good feeling. He kept on plowing in tight circles that grew smaller with each round and bellowed as he went. He was showing off now and throwing his feet out to one side or the other and popping his heels. He felt the words come sharp now and they tasted good.

"ROUND AND ROUND," he hollered. "Swing yore partner and do it again." Any words that bubbled up, he could yell. They eased his chest.

The circles were getting smaller and Buck was having to swing the plow stocks wide, stepping loose-ankled on slabs of baked earth the plow had turned, and it was hard to kick up his heels.

Now his head was back and the bellowing had rasped his throat until the pain made his voice go higher, but he wouldn't stop yelling. He kept on until words wanted to come out, but his throat wouldn't wait for his lips to say them. So he hollered on awhile, just because it had to rise up and he bobbed his head up and down like the mule did. That was funny, so he began to punch his head forward as the mule lunged into a smaller circle, and he threw his head up and back like the mule did when they struck a soft spot.

His face was pokeberry red when the mule balked, stuttering

four clumsy feet in a turn too short to make, and he was standing on the rim of the smallest circle, facing his mother. He stopped yelling and tried to swallow past the burn in his throat and watched carefully while a dun-colored bantam hen walked with tight legs out from under the house and curiously tested the new softness of the dirt. His eyes roved slowly until they found his mother again. He cocked his head on one side as his eyes met hers. He didn't say anything.

She moved now for the first time. She leaned forward in her hide-bottomed rocker and spat delicately into the syrup bucket flowerpot at her feet. She watched Buck while she did it, with no expression on her face.

"Son," she said, mildly, "you act like you've plowed up a snake."

Buck felt the hard clutch go out of his throat and chest then. He laughed out loud. He straightened up, quickly, and jerked the plow point out of the dirt. He tossed the handles slightly higher to point the plowshare straight down and drove it deep into the last unplowed spot. Then he lowered his head a little and looked upwards at his mother.

"Mother," he said, "this is the last time I'll ever follow a mule. I got twenty dollars and I'm headin' for town."

Her face changed then.

Buck walked closer and watched her eyes as he reached up and caught the porch railing and shook it with both hands. He wondered why the jaw didn't soften, retreat a little. The eyes looked out at him like he was still a back-porch yearling. The jaw still pushed forward and pulled down the corners of her full lips until they trailed off into deepening wrinkles. She shook her head at him, full of gentle warning.

"Them pickpockets'll fight over you," she said.

They gathered around Buck that day after dinner. The big ones did, anyhow. The creepers and the crawlers just looked up at Buck big-eyed and fell down all the time.

Coke was big enough to hang onto Buck and it looked like he wouldn't turn him loose. "For God's sake, Coke," Buck suddenly said, "let go o' my leg and do somethin' else. Suck a meat skin."

The sudden sharpness in his mother's voice cut through the

bumble of words, and Buck looked across the room. She was sitting on the hand-hewn bench that had been soaped and scrubbed until little soft splinters stuck up now and then, even against the grain.

"I say you ain't to use the Lord's name while you're in the house, Buck."

Her rough hand closed tighter on the arm of Buck's father, who began to push his big frame up from the bench. He was a tall man, with red hair that curled a little and a full red beard that he had chopped off straight across at his neck line. His eyes were kind and most of the time they beamed with something that seemed to say he was happy. The eyes shone some now as he shook his head slowly.

"I ain't goin' to do nothin', Mother," he said.

He turned away from her and walked, shambling a little, over to help his oldest son twist a baling wire around a small wooden box full of clothes.

His voice was roughly shy as he spoke to Buck. It joked beneath the shyness. "Don't you go sparkin' in them jeans o' mine, son. Them Aven folks'll think it's me."

Buck laughed and pulled his father closer to stand beside him. The big children squealed some and got excited because they were measuring again. Jeff and Hearn, just under Buck in the boys, turned tail and backed up against each other like the men did, pushing their round heads back together and watching Buck and their father do the same. Little Coke got excited, too, but didn't know why and rolled under the table in a gust of his own laughter that didn't stop until he began to lick at a spot of spilled syrup. The men strained to grow taller, watching for judgment from the mother.

"If we count cowlicks, he's as big as you, Joe," she said, raising her voice and smiling a bit with her eyes alone because that might hide the proudness.

Joe Bannon looked at his son. He studied his face first, then turned to the tired woman on the bench. He shook his head.

"He's my size," he said, slowly, "but he's you all over, Jeanie. You kin see the McPherson stock ashinin' from fetlock to forelock."

Buck's mother seemed to grow shy and her face reddened

[14]

spottily through the swelling. She was trying to keep sheer pleasure from her voice when she spoke.

"His eyes're grey," she said, "and my nose ain't got no hump."

Buck rubbed his nose with a crooked forefinger.

"That comes o' rootin' for vittles in this here sorry clay," he said, and felt the words lay out one beside the other in the sudden quiet. He wished he had them back.

Joe Bannon walked slowly away from Buck. His shamble was a little stiff now, bringing the hunch back to his shoulders, as if he were still thrusting hard against a plow stock. He rubbed his hand on the table top, polishing.

"We made vittles out o' that clay, Buck," he said and held his voice low. "And you et 'em. Don't run the land down."

"We like it, son," his mother said, and there was a lift and a point to the start of her words.

Buck felt the awkwardness grow as he looked at his parents and couldn't say what he felt. He scratched his leg and looked at the floor. He turned quickly, when the words wouldn't come, and picked up his box and tucked it under his arm.

"Reckon it didn't kill me," he mumbled, and took a small step towards the door, watching his parents.

They rose and moved with him, tentatively, and Buck smiled a little as he took a longer step and saw them follow. He felt the quick tension leave the room as his mother suddenly leaned down and cuffed little Coke away from his syrup lick under the table.

They followed him outside. They were all laughing as they crowded around the flat-bed wagon in the yard, and Buck felt the excitement rise up to choke him again. He threw his box into the bed of the wagon and caught Jeff under the arms and tossed him up on the seat.

"Here, rooster," he said, "it's high time you'uz learnin' the way to Aven. You'll all have to be comin' in town to see me, and Jeff can drive you."

Buck's mother caught him by the arm. "He's too little, son. He'll get lost."

Buck looked down at his mother and smiled without saying anything for a while, then he shook his head.

"When I was twelve I went to mill and back and made the trade. That was near as far as Aven." He looked out of the corner of his eyes at his father and laughed fast and low in his throat, like he was nervous. "Besides," he went on, "Papa ought to be here with you. There'll be a good moon tonight and if Jeff don't go to sleep he'll get back."

He turned away from them and climbed quickly in the wagon. He punched Jeff in the ribs with a rough elbow. "Asleep already?"

He didn't look at the little knot of mother and father and sisters and brothers when Jeff flicked the lines and pulled the mule sharply around to avoid a peach tree. He didn't look back, but his throat hurt a little from tightness and he listened carefully to the smooth whispering grind of the iron-rimmed wheels on hard sand. He didn't want ever to forget that sound.

One corner of the wagon bed suddenly bucked, riding high on a front wheel because Jeff had cut too sharply, and it bumped back to level as they straightened out, but Buck didn't look back.

They didn't talk on the way, because Buck didn't feel like it. The power and the excitement were still bubbling inside, but it was like he'd left something behind that made him want to use the power as he would a tool. There was a deadness in him now that he'd felt before, when he'd fought at school and won and had some fight left and nowhere for it to go.

School was something to cramp him inside. He remembered the small room with the bed pushed over in the corner and the cotton quilt with the funny frocking on the edges. The steady crunch of the wagon wheels lulled him until the picture of the schoolroom was a jumble of his first day and his last day—that time when he was eleven and had to quit school to help in the fields—and his Blue Back speller that cost a quarter bushel of meal —pitch pine popping and sparking and scorching some while the others froze—swapping seats and wishing spring would come— sudden bursts of temper from being too close together—and the Peters boy that got somebody else's lunch bucket and they had to open it to prove it wasn't his—little Doshie Evans crying and ashamed to claim it when they saw that all she had was fatback, syrup, and corn bread—and all the rest of them being real quiet because they didn't want anybody to see what they had.

It was dark when Jeff yelled suddenly and grabbed the lines to his chest. The mule had lunged downhill and pulled the wagon, three wheels awry and one spinning off the ground, into a narrow creek bed. Buck lifted his head quickly as the mule's unshod feet fumbled in the darkness for a foothold on the other bank.

"Whoa, here, boy," he said, quietly, and held Jeff's arm to keep him from rattling the lines. He stood up in the wagon and looked around in the night. The moon had not risen and the darkness was like something he could feel between his fingers. The sun had gone and dusk had come and gone, too, and he'd hardly known it. Little night sounds crowded in around them after they were quiet for a few moments, and a frog thumped a tub near the bank of the creek.

Buck felt Jeff's shivery movement closer and looked down to see the boy's eyes watching him, big and shining.

"Scared?" he said, softly.

"Who, me?" Jeff's voice was low and it shook.

Buck reached out and patted him on his thin shoulder that was shaking a little from a chill in the air that came out of the wet bottom.

"Reckon you can turn around, here," he said, "and get started back. Moon'll be up pretty soon and it'll get you home."

Jeff nodded in the dark. He wrapped the lines around his wrist.

"How 'bout you?" he asked, shaking a little more.

Buck felt around in the back for his box and pulled it up under his right arm.

"I'll get there," he said, "it ain't much further."

He reached out with a foot and tested his weight on the shaft. He placed his left hand on the mule's rump and began to walk out the shaft, sliding his hand along the rough sweaty ridge of backbone until he felt the up-curved end of the shaft with his foot. He pushed off, dividing his shove between his hand on the mule's collar and his foot on the shaft, and jumped clear of creek water. He turned around as he reached solid ground and was trying to see Jeff to say good-bye when the first moonlight sidled over his shoulder into the boy's face.

Jeff smiled, then, a little brighter. "It's up," he said, and his voice didn't shake any more. Buck smiled at him, but Jeff couldn't see his face, and Buck rubbed his hand hard up and down the mule's bony face.

"Don't let Papa make you plow the big mule, boy," he said,

[17]

"Big John'll pure pull yore arms out at the sockets. But you got to quit sleepin' in the cotton rows when you ought to be choppin'."

He backed off a little, and waved his hand just a small wave from side to side.

"Well, I'm gone," he said, and turned around and walked off. He didn't look back.

Even when he could barely hear Jeff struggling to turn his mule in the narrow road, Buck didn't look back. He walked in the moonlight, knowing he was half a mile from Aven and a new kind of living and working and being. He walked and felt the power rise again and the gayness that he'd had in the yard that morning came back and put a tiptoe feeling in the calves of his legs. The night felt good now and he suddenly was hungry. He wondered, walking faster, if he'd be able to spend some of his twenty dollars on food in Aven after dark. Food was something he could stand right now, he thought, and laughed out loud. Even some of his mother's cush he could take and eat out of the palm of his hand like it was a bowl. He'd nuzzle into that Thanksgiving cush like a hound.

Thanksgiving Day was something to think about, when his mother would have one turkey for thirteen eaters and she would make all the kids fill up on cush before they got to turkey. Corn meal and onions and meat stock were cheaper than turkey. The thought of Thanksgiving at home was bringing back cold emptiness inside, when the first shining finger of railroad glinted suddenly ahead of him and his feet began to crunch on a new roadbed. Cinders.

New smells rose up around him—smell of fresh-cut fat pine ties and tar and oil and smoke that coughed shudderingly out of the belled stack of a small switch engine whose firebox glowed like a woodsfire. And the new odors told him, like the clean green breezes had told him of spring on the farm, that a small corner of Alabama wasn't lying fallow any longer, but was heavy with the germ of a town.

Buck was walking into the moon and looking it in the face and he could almost feel it as he crossed the tracks. The feeling inside him was good, but he didn't know what it was. It wasn't the surge of power or the excitement of reaching Aven. Buck didn't know what it was, but he knew he was too full to hold it. He stared straight at the low-hanging moon and walked into Aven's first row of tin-roofed shacks with a swing to his copper-toed shoes and a roll to his shoulders.

As he walked, he made up a song.

> "Moon, oh moon, if I couldn't get no fuller'n you,
> I wouldn't try to shine."

A brakeman in the new ACL yards heard him and came from the shadow of the switch engine to watch. He grinned at the swagger.

"Damned if you ain't somethin'," he said to Buck's back.

CHAPTER TWO

THERE WAS a smoky chill in the air when Buck found his bed. He lay on his back and pioneered with his shoulder blades until they settled on a spot that wasn't a knot and wasn't a wide crack. Then he inched his body along on the baggage truck to accommodate his shoulder blades. He was comfortable all over. The baggage truck was new, so new that the big iron-rimmed wheels were hardly scratched, and little fat half globes of red paint still pouted where the sun had blistered.

Buck lay very still for a few minutes until he thought about something, then he laughed and his stomach tightened until his heels lifted slightly off the truck and dropped back.

"It's better'n wakin' up with Hearn rootin' from one side and Jeff from the other till they prize me up off the pallet."

He could see them then in his mind—Jeff stumbling through a shy and secretive world, in a constant inner quarrel because he could never bring himself to feel a part of anything, family or farm, work in the fields or games in the yard. And Hearn just the opposite, quick and sure, full of a sly humor that often hurt, fast to learn and just as fast to lose interest. Strangers liked him first and he knew that they liked him. And girls—already he was the one curious older girls took behind the privy after school, and already his eyes would glide over one girl without quickening, to suddenly narrow sleepily at first sight of her sister.

The two of them he saw plainly, then the thought slid easily along a familiar track until it brought back the picture of his mother. She was sitting on the front porch pleating and unpleating her skirt, while she talked to him about leaving. His eyes closed tightly at thought of her words.

"Shirt sleeves to shirt sleeves," she had said, and rocked a little as if to lay a weight on her words to make them stick. "We got rid o' downright *hard* shirt sleeves, son, when we bought land and we don't want no more for us or ours."

When we bought land!

The words came again and again and somehow Buck felt a squirming sense of helplessness and a queer rush of pride for his folks.

[20]

When we bought land!

There was nothing before they bought land, nothing but Joe Bannon and their first little shack near the edge of raw red dirt that fought the green peep of young cotton. Nothing but virgin pine and scrub oak pushing from behind and the cleared ground in front squeezing to choke thinner and thinner the strip she called her yard. There was nothing but that and a live creek meandering the year round through the bottom and playing a rushing night harmony between the high and the low of tree frogs and katydids.

Buck rolled a little on the baggage truck, helplessly trying to forget the look on his mother's face as she talked.

"Nothing much else," she had said.

There was nothing but those things and the clay floor in the little cabin, with the sloppy wetness of one corner never completely drying. That corner where they stripped and shivered, each washing all over while the other was careful to be busy at the fireplace, lifting the lid off a mess of greens and fatback.

Nothing else? Only the things she didn't want to say!

There was the simple peace of the fireplace—little and made of field stone and strong with a gusty draught. There were the wishes they made on the fire—wishes sent to ride the coattails of charred leaves that sucked up the chimney and went out over the roof like baby comets. Wishes, and laughing out loud when the wishes she made couldn't come true because the leaves she threw sometimes didn't rise. There was the gentle comfort of being alone together and having only each other; and there was the quick gladdening in the blood that came of sharing small tasks; and the quickening pride in his strength that rose when she washed Joe Bannon's back; and the pity of the awkward arm that would be strong and limber but for the rifle at Chickamauga Gap and slippery ellum bark for dressing.

Buck was uncomfortable thinking in the dark, remembering how his mother had bitten her lips telling him about the good things. He strained inwardly, trying to help her in his thoughts, knowing that she needed help over the shame of showing her feelings.

"One more thing," she had said, rocking slowly and shading

her eyes. Only one more thing—a wish that came true on a leaf that didn't rise.

That was Joe's first holiday.

She'd started to ease out of bed so the rustling of the shucks wouldn't wake Joe, when he'd walked in the door, already dressed, smiling fit to ruffle his young beard and toting a bucket of sand. He'd grinned big and poked his head at the fireplace where he'd built her fire and where hot smells of side meat and chicory coffee bellied out of the chimney's draught. He'd been glad to see the sleepy smile on her face and poured his sand out in the middle of the room. He'd cut a step or two, laughing, and kicked at the sand, and watched the tinka-bell reflections from bright little flakes in the sand. He'd put his hands on his hips and winked when he told her what the sand was for. Floorin'. Floorin' to cover the clay and drain off their bath water. Floorin' that was something to make your feet smile. And he'd pulled her out of bed and hugged her so she couldn't squeal with the happiness that was in her.

That was one more day.

All day long he toted sand, bucket after bucket, swinging up the little trail, dragging down his good arm. All day long she'd swept it smooth over the floor until the creek-bottom sand had made the little room look bigger with cleanness and brightness. And at night, they had walked over it barefooted, and had a good time together as they picked out the rocks that hurt their feet. Those were the good things, the things she could rock to her bosom and hoard for remembering, but they weren't the things she could say. All she could say was, "That's shirt sleeves, son, and we got this land between us and them."

And now Buck lay on his baggage truck and slept, but only half of him was in Aven—the rest of him staggered on unsteady feet while he tried to scoop the raw red dirt back with one hand and fight off virgin pine and scrub oak with the other.

Then a bawling voice was in Buck's ears and he was shuddering himself awake in a greyish dawn and rubbing hard on his face with hands that didn't seem to belong to him.

"God's bottom!" the red-faced man was roaring. "A hobo on a baggage truck I never thought to see."

Buck blinked hard and tried to swing his mind back to Aven and finally smiled sheepishly at the freight clerk. He laughed and scrambled down, jerking his wooden box towards him.

"Who's boss here?" he said, before he turned around.

"I ain't," the red-faced man said quickly, "but if you're any kind o' hand with a pick, we'll take you."

Buck shook his head and hefted the box under his arm.

"Much obliged," he said, slowly, "but I ain't aimin' to dig in no more dirt."

He hitched at his jeans with his free hand, then waved it briefly back at the clerk as he went out into the sunlight. He lifted his knees high for two or three steps, trying to work out early morning stiffness, then he looked up and saw Aven. He saw a row of tin-roofed store buildings lining the street nearest the railroad and his eyes narrowed a little, wondering who owned them. He felt excitement yeasting inside at sight of a small neat buggy with new harness, as it drove right up to a hog in the middle of a mud puddle and then had to back up and go around because the hog wouldn't move. He saw a few unpainted houses, clinging like children to the skirts of the one business street. The washlines of the unpainted houses ballooned with overalls and Buck tightened up, knowing that the houses were jammed with railroading boarders.

"Like bees in a hive," he muttered, and his eyes strayed on, following the careless streets that branched off from the row of stores. It seemed to Buck that the streets ran of their own free will in any direction, wandering aside sometimes, but always leading to richer homes that wore paint. Some streets were shorter than others.

"Them short ones," Buck thought, "look like they just can't make it past them painted houses."

He walked on, looking as he went. He saw the doors of the stores yawn the town awake and felt a crowding sense of something like fear inside. He glanced out of the corner of his eyes at the few people he passed, hoping every time that it would be a countryman and his wife. He could tell them because the woman always walked slightly behind and to the left of the husband and they wouldn't be talking. Buck could smile in greeting to them, but he'd only look at the others, feeling his neck stiffen as he did and quarreling with himself because he felt a need to prove on sight that he was just as good as anybody.

He shook that thought off and looked at the town again.

"It ain't much," he said to himself, "but God knows it ain't no older'n little Coke. It'll grow, but right now it looks like somebody just flung it out there because they didn't have no use for it."

He went on down the street, looking for a place to eat, and thinking.

"Food comes first. Then I got to get me a job—job where a man don't have to use a tool. Tool jobs make corns on a man's hands and when he gets through he's so tired he ain't got sense enough to spend his money right. Now, I got to lay onto the right job, but I don't know what it is. It oughtn't to make so much difference, long as it ain't a tool job. I hate to sweat. The place a man starts at ain't the thing—it's where he ends up that counts. If he just keeps pushin', a fellow'd plow a mighty long furrow and get somewheres, but a man that stops because he don't want to walk through a horse lot is apt to stay right at the lot. Reckon I'll just go at it like guttin' a hog and take the first job somebody offers me, long as it ain't handlin' a tool."

Buck was so busy thinking he nearly walked into a small towheaded boy holding the tie rope to a heifer in front of a good-sized general store. Buck scuffled his palm over the boy's head and cocked his eye to the side so he could spell out the name of the store.

"Green's General Mdse," he said, slowly, then looked down at the boy. "Looks like I'll eat counter vittles, boy. Shore ain't no other place."

He went inside and looked around. There was a crowd of folks and there was a little fattish man without much hair hurrying around and trying to wait on all of them at one time. Buck figured he'd best wait, so he sat down on a big sack of salt standing up on one end, and screwed around on it until it fitted him. He felt big lumps of salt in the bag crumble until his seat was soft and yielding. He put his clothes box down beside him and took off his hat. He ran his fingers around the sweat band, drying it, and put his hat carefully on the box. Then he got to watching the fat man and the customers and forgot his empty stomach. He was wondering if he couldn't ask for work here when he noticed a couple standing near the door, talking quietly. The woman was building small mounds with pointed tops in the garden seed bin, and flattening them out again with the palm of her rough hand. Buck wondered if she wanted some garden seeds, the way she was fondling them. Seemed like she couldn't keep her hands off them, especially the peas. They kept running through her fingers when she'd pick up a handful, and she'd turn them loose like she hated to do it—like she couldn't just reach down and pick them up again. She'd throw the last two or three in the box one at a time, looking sideways at her husband all the while.

Buck heard the fat little man hurry his words out to a rawboned man standing near the meat block.

"What can I do for you?" he said, and ran the words together. The big man mumbled something and Buck stopped listening. He muttered under his breath.

"What the hell? Reckon I'll start guttin' that hog."

He got up and walked over to the couple near the seed bins. He looked back and saw Mr. Green rubbing his hands together and looking the other way. Buck rubbed his hands together and smiled at the woman.

"What can I do for you, ma'am?" he said, and hoped he didn't sound like a kid boy.

The woman looked up at him with eyes that wouldn't stay still. They wandered all over the store and her face took on a look that Buck had seen on his mother's face when she was criticizing another woman's quilting.

"We was lookin' at the seeds," the woman said, "but I don't know."

Buck spoke quickly.

"If you got the green thumb, there's a hill o' beans in every seed."

The woman pursed her lips and turned around to spit out the door, trying to hide a creeping smile.

"I got the thumb, all right," she said offhand, and cut her eyes at her husband. "What do you think, Jess?"

The man shrugged.

" 'F I git a few plugs o' tobacco, I kin git along," he said. "It ain't like that heifer was—"

He broke off and shifted his chew as his wife frowned quickly and began to examine the seed bin carefully. Buck felt a grin pulling at his lips. This was fun. He tightened his lips.

"You got a heifer to swap?" he said.

The woman nodded and the man tossed his head towards the calf the little boy was guarding out front. Buck stepped nearer the door and looked closely at the heifer. He didn't turn around when he spoke.

"The ma musta died," he said, and heard the sharp intake of breath from the woman.

"They was two dropped on the place," she said, primly, "but they both got suck."

Buck glanced at the man and winked.

"This'n got the hind tit," he said, and laughed with the man. Buck wondered if the store's owner knew what was going on. He looked back and saw the little man busily cutting meat and talking, so he reached around in the candy case and got two pieces of licorice.

"Let's go take a look," he said, and the couple followed him outside. The woman was whispering to the man, and Buck made out like he didn't know it. He walked over to the boy, and gave him the licorice sticks and scrubbed his head again, before he took the tie rope. He pulled the calf towards him.

"Why, it can walk," he said, and watched the man. The man laughed out loud. "Hell," he said, "what'll you give me?"

Buck slowly tied the calf rope to a hitching post.

"How much garden you figurin' to make?" he said.

"Couple acres," she said, and her eyes wandered again.

Buck shook his head quickly. He held up one finger.

"We'll furnish one acre," he said, then he looked at the man again. "That's so there'll be some chewin' left in the bargain."

The woman stared at the little boy sucking his licorice and spitting black. Then she looked back at her husband. She ducked her head once and smiled. Her eyes didn't wander any more.

Buck caught the man by the arm and they went back inside. Buck watched the fussy store owner busy in the back, while he hurriedly sacked up what he judged to be enough seed and tossed in two plugs of tobacco. His customers left. Then he sat down on the sack of salt again and watched the heifer and waited for the folks to thin out. He was thinking to himself about how easy it was, when the owner hurried up to him and rubbed his hands.

Buck spoke first. "Mr. Green," he said, "you got a heifer."

Green dropped his head to one side and stared at Buck. He opened his mouth but didn't say anything. Buck pointed at the heifer tied outside.

"I traded for it," he said, "I swapped seeds to plant one acre o' peas and threw in a couple plugs o' tobacco."

Mr. Green's eyes grew round and he made little chewing movements with his mouth before he could speak.

"Who in hell are you," he said, "come a'bustin' in my store, swappin' right and left?"

Buck ducked his head and swallowed. The swallow came hard.

"My name's Buck Bannon," he said, "an' I want a job tradin' for you. You needed help right bad this mornin'."

Mr. Green frowned and looked at his seed bin.

"Godamighty," he yelled suddenly. "Them seed coulda sold for two dollars."

Buck stood up quickly.

"I'll give you two dollars for the heifer." He reached in his pocket.

Mr. Green chewed emptily and looked down at Buck's copper-toed shoes for a minute. He looked back up at Buck and kept chewing. Then, suddenly, he smiled a little. He shook his head.

"Calf's worth four." He motioned with his head back towards the meat block. "Cut meat?"

Buck grinned. Swallowing came easier. He shook his head.

"I'm a trader," he said, "that's about all I do."

Mr. Green nodded and chewed some more.

"Well," he said, and shrugged his shoulders, "I c'n cut meat."

Buck stuck out his hand. "And I can swap."

They shook hands, then, and Buck breathed deep and looked around the store to see what there was to swap. The long shelves of pine, still white with newness, were held up by walls that were wide apart up near the front but seemed to narrow in the darkness of the rear, where smoke from the winter's wood stove had blackened what it touched. The shelves on the right didn't have much on them; they seemed to be waiting for stock. The ones on the left had fewer empty spaces, since they carried the burden of overalls, jumpers, bolts of cloth, piece goods and work shoes. The counters looked as if they had been tumbled out of a huge box and left where they stopped rolling. They held sparse offerings of candy, chewing and smoking tobacco, sewing thread and needles, button cards, and almanacs. Buck saw it all and his eyes flared again with yesterday's excitement as they swung around the store. His mouth quirked when he saw the seed bins, pushed up to hold the swinging shutters back off the front, but he stopped smiling when he saw the two bunches of bananas hanging above them.

He was still hungry.

Buck had finished his breakfast of bananas, when Mr. Green mentioned salary. He chewed a long time before he spoke.

"Reckon five dollars a week'll be about right," he said, hopefully, "since you ain't no meat cutter."

Buck sat still on the sack of salt and looked down at Mr. Green's feet. He didn't speak. He was thinking, "Five dollars is a lot of money. And it ain't what a man starts at that counts. Five dollars. That's a lot, but if I'm a trader, I ought to argue for my own money, so he'll know I'll holler for his. I can always come down." He looked up at Mr. Green and shook his head, slowly.

"Oughta get more," he said.

Mr. Green pursed his lips and carefully inspected the greasy apron to indicate that he knew a trade was on.

"You don't have to open up but ever' other mornin'," he said softly.

Buck stood up and polished at a glass casing with his sleeve. He thought about opening up. He thought about that and getting up out of bed at daylight—if he had a bed. The two thoughts suddenly coupled and bore a full thought. He didn't look up when he spoke.

" 'F I get seven," he said, "I'll move out of where I'm at now, and sleep in the store. I'll watch it at night and open up ever' day."

Mr. Green wiped off his hands and stuck one out again. He beamed.

"It's a bargain," he said, and acted like he was going to bustle without moving. "Now, reckon you can move in pretty soon?"

Buck pursed his lips and nodded soberly.

"Tonight," he said.

Green's eyes opened wide.

"Where you stayin'?" he said, suspiciously.

Buck twisted his head around in his soft collar.

"At the freight depot," he said, and held back the laugh that wanted to come out.

Mr. Green moaned. He struck his hands together and shook his head violently.

"If I hadn't a shook on it," he said, "I'd throw you out in the streets."

But his eyes were kind when he said it.

INTERLUDE

THEY WERE *walking down Aven's muddy business street. Both were short and both had red faces and both wore the long billed railroad man's striped cap. One shook his head.*

"Payday," *he said, bitterly.* "Payday, Bascom, an' I oughta cut my throat."

The other nodded and stepped around a puddle too deep to wade.

"Why, hell, Jake," *he said,* "I'm the damned fool that started it all. 'F I hadn't borrowed the first dollar from Buck Bannon, he'd never o' made a loan. I was itchin' to get to Mabe's place and didn't have a copper. By God, I had to tell him how much interest to charge, and I offered to put up my watch."

They walked in silence for a moment, until Jake suddenly grinned.

"What the hell," *he said,* "it's pretty good to have a place to go, though. When you got to have it, I mean."

The other pushed up the bill of his cap.

"It'd be all right," *he admitted,* "if the danged fool hadn't learnt us railroadin' men can't work unless we got our watches. Someday, by God, I'm a'goin' to leave him stuck with mine and buy me another'n."

"He'd just sell it for a profit," *his friend said.* "Nope," *he went on,* "we're stuck. Borrow two dollars and pay fifty cents interest ever' week. Why, he don't even want the two dollars. Just that damned fifty cents."

The moon was riding high and shining halfway through the length of Green's store when they got to the shuttered doors, and looked through the small windows.

They could see the light in the back, and by it, the quiet figure, leaning against a counter making marks in a little book, and scuffling his feet at mice that were no longer afraid of him.

Jake suddenly laughed.

"Son of a gun's figurin' how much all us railroaders owe him," he said. "Been there ever' payday for over a year."

He tapped on the glass and saw the figure push away from the counter, still looking at the book, and walk slowly towards the front.

Jake punched his friend in the ribs.

"Look at him," he said, "he don't look much like he did that night we took him down to Mabe's."

"Remember how he goggled at them curtains and couldn' keep from lookin' at hisself in them mirrors? Until the girls come in."

They laughed and slapped each other on their backs and Jake hollered.

"Jake, them's white girls," he said, mocking Buck's slow tones and his breath exploded.

They were still laughing when Buck Bannon opened the shutters and smiled at them.

CHAPTER THREE

BUCK STOOD still and listened to the frantic screaming of the engine as it breasted Tate's Hill. He couldn't hear it, but he could see it in his mind—the rocking whip of the drive shaft as it churned the big wheels around in a shower of sparks. He could see the shuddering jerk of each loaded car as sand was dropped and the wheels bit into a few inches of traction. He leaned forward unconsciously, somehow finding inside a small pulling for the little engine, and he listened again for the urgent howl. It came, different this time, riding towards him in triumph, trumpeting the news that the rise had been topped and the hollows of Aven lay at the foot of the grade.

"That's Jernigan on the cord," he said to himself. "Many times as I've heard it, the last sixteen months, I won't never forget the way he gives it that laughin', wheedlin' twist."

He pulled his shoulders straight, abruptly, and tried to settle them more comfortably into the too-tight black coat that showed so little wear it no longer matched the trousers.

"Couldn't forget Jernigan." His mouth twisted wryly. "Or Bascom Wooten." Wooten coming that night so many months ago and tapping on the small window at the back of Green's store. His great raw slab of a face screwed up with embarrassment as he held out his heavy railroading watch, and his coarse rumble. "You kin hold this watch for the two dollars an' git three back on payday." Buck felt again the quick urge to be generous, to say, "Keep your watch and just pay me back the two," because Wooten was a friend. Then, again, came the quick knowledge and the awe that he had found the short cut; and again he knew the bite of shame as he had known it when he carried the watch slowly back towards the lamp that sat on the goods box at one end of his cot.

He closed his lips tightly, remembering, and trying not to remember, as he faced around to the big white house up the precise gravel walkway that parted two squares of green lawn. "No time to drag around," he muttered, and took two steps towards Amos Longshore's home. Then, he stopped again, staring with a puzzled frown at the lawn. "More and more folks here lettin' grass grow in their yards." He shrugged slightly. "Mother wouldn't have it." His eyes wandered back over towards the body of Aven, where the homes and stores and blacksmith shops and lumber yards nudged each other. It was built too tightly and he knew it. It didn't matter now, but the time would come when store fronts would have to be pushed back to widen the streets. "It's growin' crazy as a gourd vine," he said softly, "flingin' out a creeper now and then and stores and houses hitchin' on whenever they feel like it." It was all wrong, growing without plan or system, and he could feel it with a helpless pain inside. He tightened his grip on the neck of the plain paper bag in his hand, and held it closer against his leg, scowling uselessly at the small clump of stores that had volunteered in the last year. "Half a mile from the rail-road," he thought, "just to get closer to the spring and the distillery." He shook his head to clear it and started up the walk, swinging his arms and hitting the gravel good solid licks with his heels. "By God, business may leave where I am now, but it'll find me where it's going when it gets there."

He heard the train whistle again, two short bragging whoops, and knew it was in the yards.

"It keeps comin'," he thought. "Bringin' me somethin' to sell and a man to buy it. And he's got to borrow money from me to pay for it so I get the interest and part of the profit. It's brought me here to see Amos Longshore with a sack of money and dressed up like a travelin' dentist. That's part of it, but mostly, I reckon, it's bein' willin' to live like a hog in the back of Green's store, and stayin' lonesome because you can't make money by lendin' to friends. God, I'd like to see the homefolks."

He drew a deep breath, trying to calm the flurry of excitement as he reached out to knock on the front door with the butt of his pocketknife, but it wouldn't stop. His blood thrummed in his veins like a covey of quail flushing up and out. He heard light footsteps in the hall beyond the door and his mind quirked, suddenly.

"A year ago, I'd have been scared to come after Amos Long-shore, but a year ago I wouldn't have tried to take Green's store away from him."

The door opened and Buck forgot trains and Longshore and Green and stores. He just stood still and looked at the girl in front of him. Far off, he heard the rustle as his hand twisted the neck

[32]

of his paper bag. He wanted to speak but he didn't. He just looked. She was small, with square shoulders thrown far back. Her face wasn't square, but a high forehead and a long full mouth made it look as if it were. Buck had the clear thought that there wasn't a thing about her that would be pretty by itself, but if you saw her like a scope of timber or a sunset, she was right good to look at. He liked her mouth and watched it move, but at first he didn't hear what she said.

"Well, give it to me," she said, again, impatiently, and held out her hand. Buck grasped the sack tighter.

"It ain't yours yet," he said, and his voice wanted to rise with laughter. "I've come to see Mr. Longshore."

"Oh," she said, "Daddy?"

Buck's shoulders rose slightly. "I reckon."

She frowned at him as if she wanted to figure something out, standing very still for a moment; then she started to turn away.

"Wait," Buck said, quickly, without thinking. She stopped and waited with her eyebrows questioning and her throat was smooth and slim coming out of the simple neck of her pale-green dress. "Do you live here all the time?" Buck felt his words clumsy in his throat.

"I do now." Her voice was smooth and matter-of-fact, yet her eyes still were on his face with their puzzled query.

"I never saw you before," Buck explained, soberly; "around town, I mean."

Her brow drew suddenly into two sharp lines over her straight nose, as if he had come too close.

"I've been away," she said, with her voice still smooth, but flat. Her head came up an inch. "To finishing school."

Buck's teeth flashed white against the dark brown of his skin. "Are you finished?" he asked, softly.

Her face was quickly expressionless and she turned away from him. "I'll get my father," she said, coolly and walked back down the hall, leaving the front door open.

Buck leaned closer to the opening, watching carefully, wondering if her hips swung free, trying to imagine what was going on under her full skirt. The hips had to swing free because her shoulders and head didn't move and she walked like a colored woman with a bundle on her head. He wondered and measured her in

[33]

his mind. She'd be light against his darkness, slim against his thickening chest and heavy shoulders; her eyes would be blue against his grey. She'd be soft against his hard solidness and her mouth would be warm, moving against his.

"Mmmm," he said, "like findin' rock candy in the syrup bucket." He shook his head hard and breathed in deep, trying to throw the film off his mind. "Business, business, business." He unbuttoned his coat so his new white shirt would show more, and spread his legs wide apart waiting and watching the hall until he saw Amos Longshore coming towards him. He was a slight man, and short. He moved with jerky steps and his mouth worked nervously all the time. His face and hair were grey and looked like they were dusty with old dust and not with fine particles from the red dirt of the country. His nose was long and two knobs of flesh made the tip look blunt and brutal.

Buck saw Longshore with one part of his mind, but the other part watched over her father's shoulder to see if the girl would come all the way back. She didn't, but turned slowly off into one of the rooms on either side of the hall. She glanced back once, quickly, then jerked her head around as she saw him watching.

Longshore turned to follow Buck's eyes to his daughter, then he looked back at Buck out of eyes that seemed to shrink into pockets made by wrinkled, veined lids. He cleared his throat.

"What do you want?"

Buck stood away from the door so Longshore could come out. "Got some business to talk over with you."

Longshore's eyebrows rose, then his mouth pinched tight. He let his eyes travel slowly from Buck's rough, capped shoes up to the narrow black string tie that was tightly knotted in the hard collar. Buck flushed and his teeth came hard together.

"It ain't no little somethin'," he said, grimly, and opened the neck of his paper bag. He held it out for Longshore to see. Longshore's eyebrows raised some more and his mouth unpinched.

"Never saw a man carry money in a paper sack before," he said, dryly, and motioned with his head towards the porch chairs. Buck's lips relaxed a little but his eyes stayed cold and watchful. "Bastard'll bite all right," he thought, then he smiled widely, purposely showing his teeth.

"Nobody ever knocked a man in the head for a sack of candy," he said. A short laugh rustled in Longshore's throat as he let himself carefully down into one of the rockers. Then Buck saw the corners of his mouth pull down and watched the hard eyes grow secretive, deliberately filmy like the eyes of a chicken who wants to cut out some light. He could feel the old excitement of a trade coming on, and it was a relief to finally face Longshore with his hands gripping his knees and the old paper bag on his lap.

"My name's Buck Bannon," he said, bluntly, holding his voice toneless and clipping his words. "I've been workin' for Titus Green for a year. He'll sell out now, cheap, and I want to buy. I've got five hundred in this sack and it'll take eleven hundred more. I'll put up mine. You furnish the rest and I'll mortgage the whole thing to you, payable in a year."

Longshore's eyes nearly closed and he rocked steadily. Buck leaned back in his chair and crossed his legs.

"Is Green losing money since you started with him?" Longshore's voice was soft.

Buck's face didn't change.

"It's easier to make it than steal it," he said, wryly. "Besides, a man that watches everything as close as you do, will know I made this money on short loans."

"Green's is worth more than sixteen hundred," Longshore said. "How come it's so cheap?"

Buck flushed and his strong fingers closed tighter around the neck of his paper bag.

"His wife's sick. He needs money right now for some doctorin', up in Atlanta."

Longshore stopped rocking and pursed his lips. "So?" Buck's jaw muscles bulged as he clinched his teeth, then slowly they relaxed again. "So, we'd better get it in a hurry. He won't need it if she dies or gets well."

Longshore's eyes closed all the way for a second, then he reached into his pocket and pulled out his knife. He flicked the blade open with quick, almost angry fingers, and began to pare his nails. Buck watched the deliberate movements of the blade and saw little curls fall, whiter than the nails they left.

"What makes you think I'd rob a man because I had him where the hair is short?"

[35]

Buck moved his feet further apart. His voice was coarser, rasping a little in his throat.

"I asked questions. You like to make a dollar."

Longshore's knife hovered, hesitating a trifle over another nail, then cut calmly and neatly.

"What's to stop me going down and buying Green out? I could cut you out of the deal!" He spoke sharply. Buck drew in a deep breath before he answered. His mouth turned down at one corner and he patted his sack.

"You want my five hundred," he said, bluntly, and held his breath. He wondered if Longshore would rise at that. Longshore rocked twice, quickly, with his eyes on Buck's face, then suddenly he snapped the knife blade shut. He stood up and dropped the knife back in his pocket.

"You're right," he said, and his voice was low and curiously gentle, "and I think I'm going to get it. Come back tomorrow and I'll have the money and the papers ready."

Buck let his breath out slowly and stood up to face Longshore, then he nodded. He didn't hold out his hand to bind the bargain and somehow way inside he wondered dully why he couldn't, or why Longshore carefully put both his hands in his pockets. They looked at each other as the emptiness of dusk slowly filled with cricket sounds and the little noises of night. Buck's mouth finally pulled down in a rueful kind of smile and his voice came dead and flat, with no excitement.

"I ain't got time to stop and build bridges when I come to a creek. I've got to jump to stay on schedule."

Longshore's upper lip curled slightly.

"Don't whine," he said, sharply; "a thief's a thief."

Buck felt blood forcing itself up past his collar. He nodded.

"Good evenin'," he said, awkwardly.

Longshore's head jerked downwards once, and he turned back towards the front door.

CHAPTER FOUR

BUCK TWIRLED a shot glass between his fingers and stared across the plain pine counter that served as a bar in Aven's only saloon. He stared hard and tried again to conjure up a picture of the blonde girl at Longshore's home. He wanted to see her as she had been that afternoon. He frowned and sometimes he closed his eyes and once he got a clear sight of her, leaning against something with a long, slow smile on her lips and her eyes looking upwards with the lids moving sleepily. Then, she was gone in a second, leaving him with the frown on his face, staring at a dirty apron hanging on a peg.

She wouldn't come back, and Buck was listening again to the noises of the saloon.

They came as if they were part of a crowded sleep. There was the jangle of the banjo, played day and night behind the thin partition that separated the whites from the colored folks' side. The banjo was supposed to have a happy whang to draw trade, but this time of night it was about played out. It was louder where Buck stood, near the curved slot through which the bartender shoved drinks to the Negro customers. There was the slow slap of cards on a damp table top, where three men played a careful hand of poker. There was always the steady thump-thump of a dog's hind foot scratching fleas under the bar.

Buck closed his eyes again to bring back the image of the girl, but it was too far gone. He shook his head and hit the bar hard.

"Godamighty!" he said. He shoved his glass across the bar. "Do it again."

The bartender was a lean man, with a loose grin that looked slippery as it squirmed around several teeth.

"It stingeth like an adder and biteth like a serpent," he said. Then he reached for the bottle of white corn whiskey which he kept filled out of the barrel under the bar.

He lurched and shook his head in a sheepish apology to Buck as he caught at the bar.

"It biteth fine, though, don't it?" he said, and poured two drinks.

[37]

Buck's drink burned good all the way down and it left something like a memory back of his nose. He didn't know whether he smelled it or tasted it, but it was something like a quick wisp of steam blown across his face from the kettle at syrup-making time.

It blazed upwards, too, burning out all thoughts of the girl.

Buck looked around the saloon, frowning, and turned his back to the bar and pawed backwards with his heel, trying to rest it on the scuffed wooden rail. He stared at the walls and the patches of turpentine oozing from the pine looked like blisters. He turned back to the bartender.

"Why don't you paint this place?" he said.

The bartender shrugged and looked down at the floor, and hiccuped softly. He shook his head, but he didn't say anything.

Buck drew a deep breath and stood up straight.

"You got my money in the safe?" he said, and nodded gravely, without an answer. "An' I got a receipt." He nodded again and felt in his pocket.

"I'm a'goin' pi'rootin'," he said, and rubbed his hands together like they felt good. "I'm a'goin' to Mabe's Place and kiss all the girls and run climb a tree an' wait for them to cut me down."

The bartender dropped a glass and didn't bother to pick it up. He just kicked it under the bar and his lips slid around his teeth.

"Wheeoo," he said, softly, blowing his breath out long and slow.

That white corn was biting good when Buck left. It was swelling up the moon and making his shadow wavy and dizzy out beside him. It was throwing the rain-washed roots of the sycamore trees up high like a sick steer's ribs. He stumbled now and then. The liquor and something else was boiling inside him and throwing off powerful big bubbles that wanted to come out in long yells. He felt good and loose-ankled and full of the devil and he needed to undo his collar.

It was shoving him when he reached Baptist Bottom.

Baptist Bottom lay between him and Mabe's Place. It crouched at night under a sullen fog, a few clapboard shacks, shrinking in the sun and swelling in the rain. Mist rose from stagnant water that drained off the higher ground of the white folks and ponded in the bottom. The fog held too long the odors of frying fish, onions, and hush puppies. It rose and dulled sights and sounds.

Even the sudden high-pitched yells from the Puddin' House were muted and sounded farther away than they really were. They always yelled in the Puddin' House. It was the only place for colored folks alone. A scuffle and a giggling laugh in the bushes near the narrow street came to Buck like an echo that had no beginning. And the preaching. There was always preaching in the Bottom and now a voice rode low through the mist, hardly mumbling beyond the crowd.

Buck was passing the preaching, just outside the Puddin' House, when the sudden bawl of the preacher caught him.

"An' this is the last word," it came, grumbling low but strong. Buck stepped closer and saw the huge figure gather itself as if to lunge at the crowd, and in the light of a kerosene lamp on a goods box he saw the muscles in the thick black throat strain for volume.

The preacher thrust his big head straight forward and glared at the crowd, holding his voice. Then he blasted out the last word.

"You got to walk the muddy streets of Aven 'fore you kin walk the golden streets of Heaven."

Slowly the preacher pulled his head back, shifting his eyes quickly from one to the other of the melting crowd. He straightened his shoulders and cleared his throat and looked down at the empty plate on the goods box. He grunted.

"God forgive 'em," he said.

Buck laughed out loud.

"Here, Big Time," he said, and held out his hand. "Preach me some hell-fire and alligator teeth."

The big head ducked out of the mist and looked at Buck.

"Ain't you kinda lit up, boss?" the preacher said.

"Like a country church," Buck said, and patted his stomach.

The preacher pursed his thick lips and smacked them once. He rolled his eyes in the direction of Mabe's Place.

"You headed down yonder, boss?" he said, and raised one eyebrow while he lowered his head slightly.

"If I hold out," Buck said.

The preacher rocked back and forth on his heels and frowned for a moment. He locked his hands behind his back and studied Buck. He smacked his lips again.

"You takin' 'em anything, boss?" he said, and his deep voice rose smoothly with the question.

Buck shook his head.

"Just my trade," he said.

The preacher shook his head slowly from side to side, discouragingly. He stooped to pick up his tin plate and lamp, then straightened again. He folded his hands on his stomach.

"Boss," he said, softly, "whore ladies likes a leetle somethin' on the side." He twiddled his blunt fingers.

Buck frowned as the thought caught his mind. He nodded slowly several times.

"Now," the preacher cleared his throat, "I got a pair o' fine billy goats, Boss, which'd make mighty pretty pets down yonder."

Buck whooped.

"What in hell'd they do—?" he started, then stopped and cocked his head on one side and looked at the preacher.

"Goats?" he said, slowly, "how much, Big Time?"

"White Cap'n," the preacher said, "I's got one more payment due on a leetle burial plot." He bowed and his eyes went soothingly over Buck. "You kin have them two goats for a dolluh each."

Buck looked down at the ground and pulled at his nose and stuck out his lower lip.

The preacher reached gently out and touched Buck's arm.

"They's right over here," he said softly, and showed the way with a sweeping left arm.

Ten minutes later Buck was leading one large white goat and following another. The front goat wanted to run but the other wanted to sit down in the mud and let his heavy horns shine in the moonlight.

"By God," Buck panted, as he jerked on a tie rope with one hand and held back with the other. "I figgered even a goat'd ruther live in a house full of ready women than lay in the road."

The backward goat fought until they neared Mabe's Place, then it suddenly began to trot and bumped into Buck's legs. Buck fell down, grabbing, and threw one arm over the front quarters of the goat. He just sat there and hollered and laughed for a few minutes and hugged his goat. Then he got up and let the goats pull him, both arms stretched out in front, walking with stiff legs and leaning backwards. He walked into the moonlight and started singing:

> "Moon, oh moon, if I couldn't get no fuller'n you,
> I wouldn't try to shine.
> You got a man in the middle o' your heart,
> But I got a gal in mine."

Mabe's Place looked dark, but Buck could see soft light under the shade of the vestibule window. He could hear music playing somewhere in the back of the house. He scraped his feet carefully on the corn-shuck mat and opened the front door. He stuck his head around the doorjamb and didn't see anyone, so he pushed the door wide open and backed in. His goats tried to hold back, but their sharp hooves couldn't get a grip on the polished floor. Buck had to drag them inside and shut the door. They were bleating softly.

Buck patted the goats to sooth them and took the tie ropes off their necks. He gazed around, gravely studying the purple velvet draperies between the dining room and the vestibule. He slapped his thigh softly as he looked at them, remembering the awed face of a young brakeman who was feeling velvet under his fingers for the first time. He caught sight of himself in one of the two full-length mirrors and tilted his head to see better, then he reached out one foot to push a goat out from between him and the mirror.

"Get away," he said, and raised his head up to holler for Mabe. "Hey, Mabe! Company."

He stared up the stairs as if he expected someone, but no one came, so his eyes drifted back down to the big peach-colored vase that held Mabe's walking sticks. He wished he had a big vase for his papa. And a newel post to put it by.

He heard a lurching footstep from the back of the house and started towards the draperies, then a sudden tapping on the floor made him turn. One of the goats was backing off from a mirror, lowering his head and pawing at the floor. His reflection was backing off and his eyes glazed, watching it.

Buck started to yell just as the goat drove forward, but no sound came. It was too late and he just stood there with his mouth open. The goat's heavy horns crashed into the glass and Buck flinched. A large triangular piece of glass began to fall outwards, seeming to float, and the goat scrambled stiff-legged beneath it, trying to get up off the floor. Buck walked slowly towards him patting the air with his hands, gentling him down and saying, "Whoa-up. Whoa-up."

He heard quickening steps behind him and turned in time to see the other goat rearing before a mirror, neck stiffened, horns lowered. He looked at one goat, then at the other, quickly, then he threw up his hands and shrugged. The crash was louder this time and the goat fell straight over onto his back. Buck rubbed his hands hard across his eyes, then walked over to the stairway and sat slowly on the lowest step and propped his elbows on his knees.

"Go to it, by God," he said.

One of the goats trotted alertly over towards Buck with his chin hairs sticking belligerently out and his neck stiffened. Buck raised his head and waited until he came closer, then he reached out and cuffed him with a half-clenched fist alongside of his head. The goat scrambled, trying to drive into Buck's knees, and Buck swiped him again, harder this time. The goat half fell and half ran into the big peach vase.

"Godamighty!" Buck said, and grabbed at the vase too late. It fell over and split into two large pieces and the walking sticks clattered. Buck snatched up one of the sticks and struck the goat sharply on the rump. The goat slipped on the floor, then caught his footing and tapped quickly away. Buck watched him, frowning, for a second, then he held his head on one side listening.

Heavy steps caused a gentle shaking of the stairs and Buck turned his head and shoulders around to look gravely up at one of the girls. She was fat and she wore a long cotton dress that clung mighty close. Her hair hung down her back and her mouth was open. She stared at the goats, then at Buck still twisted around on the bottom step, and slowly she reached up and scratched under her arm.

Suddenly she stiffened.

"Good God, girls," she screamed, "get up."

She turned and ran with her felt slippers flapping. Buck began to laugh and beat harder on the floor with the walking stick.

[42]

Then he heard a strangling sound from the dining-room doorway. He looked up and stopped laughing.

Mabe stood there, balanced on one leg, a huge man with a sagging stomach, wearing a nightshirt. His one foot was bare and his legless stump jerked in short angry circles, whipping the tail of his nightshirt around. His broad hamlike face was reddening and seemed to be swelling. His light-blue eyes squeezed shut once, then opened wide and flickered around the room.

Buck began to laugh again as one of the goats stalked over close to the hem of Mabe's nightshirt. Mabe caught at the folds of velvet drapery and waved the stump of his leg in warning to the goat. He lowered his head, then, and fastened his eyes on Buck, peering out from under heavy reddish-blond brows. Buck stopped laughing and watched, tightening inside at the expression on Mabe's face.

"Even a whore has got feelin's," Mabe rumbled, slowly, "and if a fellow can't earn the name of a gentleman in a whorehouse, he won't get it nowhere."

Buck stared silently at the big one-legged figure, knowing from the sudden cold clearness of his mind, that the liquor had worn off. He braced one hand on his knee and stood up slowly, gripping the cane so hard that the knuckles whitened on his other hand. He walked steadily over to Mabe and held out the stick. Mabe took it, wordlessly, and braced on his legless side.

"There'll be a man out here tomorrow mornin' to fix your place back," he mumbled. Then quickly he looked up into Mabe's eyes and spoke clearly, "I don't give a damn about bein' a gentleman, but, by God, I'll be payin' my debts, till I die."

INTERLUDE

JAKE WILLIS *held on to the handrail and stretched one leg out until his foot was almost dragging on the cinders beside the roadbed. When No. 54 pulled him opposite the freight depot, he eased leisurely to the ground and took two or three jolting steps.*

Then, yawning, he fumbled in his vest pocket to check his time of arrival. He muttered under his breath as his hand discovered again that he didn't have a watch.

"Hey, Jake!"

Jake looked vaguely around the yard and his eyes hurt in the noon glare, but they picked out Bascom Wooten, sitting in the shade on top of a barrel of fish.

Jake slouched across towards Bascom, taking it easy because it hurt his head to walk.

"Hell," Bascom said, when Jake got close, "I heard you was dead."

Jake laughed hollowly.

"I mout as well be," he said. "Them Albany gals got my money and Buck Bannon's got my watch."

Bascom grinned and kicked his heels against the barrel.

"Fifty-four's on time," he said, cheerfully, "but you shore lost your watch."

Jake frowned and his head hurt some more.

"Aw," he said, "Buck wouldn't keep it. I was out o' town."

Bascom laughed and rocked the barrel, jarring the rims down so hard Jake could hear dull movement from the shifting contents.

"Buck's gone," Bascom said finally. "So is your watch."

Jake groaned and his hand yearned, fluttering, towards his vest pocket.

"Wheeoo," he breathed, "watch gone, job gone."

Bascom came down off the barrel, then, and took Jake by the arm.

" 'F I didn't know how you feel," he said, shaking his head sorrowfully, "I'd keep it up. Buck's just gone home for a couple days."

Jake brightened for a second, but his smile faded almost before it had begun. He slumped.

"I don't like this," he said. "He'll lose it, or break it, or, by God, he'll swap it off for a rubber-tired buggy."

Bascom laid a hand on Jake's shoulder.

"Aw, forget it," he said. "Buck's gone to argy his folks into movin' to Aven. Told me he'd be back 'fore long with twelve head of children and his ma an' pa."

Jake's chin dropped nearer his chest.

"That's worse'n ever," he said. "Now he'll raise interest to feed all them young 'uns."

Bascom's eyes opened wide. He suddenly kicked at the cinders and a little shower of them flew up.

"Hell," he said, bitterly, "I never thought o' that."

Jake didn't answer. He just shook his head miserably from side to side and stared bleakly at the shining rails stretching east and west. Bascom was silent, too, for a long time. Then he raised his head and looked at Jake with pity in his eyes.

"He left in a rubber-tired buggy, all right," he murmured.

Jake closed his eyes.

CHAPTER FIVE

THE EARTH had mellowed after spring and now lay heavy in the early summer, as if it had finished with sucking inward the rain and the sun and was urging itself towards bearing. Buck raised his head to smell the earth as the little red mare drew his bright buggy out of the wooded draw and surged up the slight rise to land that had been newly cleared.

He breathed deeply, and like a snatch of song that could hardly be remembered, the wind carried a thread of crushed wild-plum smell, as if hogs had rooted under the thicket and wasted the juices. He breathed out slowly, hoarding the plum smell.

"That's funny," he thought. "Two years ago when I was hasslin' to leave it, I never would have figured dirt could smell so good."

Then, suddenly, he remembered other smells of the country, the damp coolness around the well housing where water had spilled over the lip of the bucket, the dry sweet bite of hayloft, and the somehow good but choky odor of cotton seed stored for planting, and sage and onions in the turkey dressing.

Food! Buck could feel his tongue wetting towards the thought of summer victuals at home. Turnip greens, not with the roots cooked in, just the small crisp salads. The sweet fresh corn on the cob with coarse salt and butter still soft from the churn. Small pones of corn bread baked dry inside and crusty brown on the top. And radishes, hot as the devil inside but cool throughout with springhouse coolness, next to bulging spring onions in a pickle dish the store had sent from Eufaula the first year Papa had bought big. And ham, baked in the oven of a stove that leaked some of its hickory to the flavor, ham sliced for men, and beside it in the center of the table the huge drumsticks and thighs and breasts of two-pound Barred Rock fryers. And, in the name of Heaven, not to be forgotten, the peas—cooked soft with a split chunk of home-cured boiling meat—the tiny white Lady Finger peas, the ones that God gave po' folks for dessert.

"Hey, Lord," Buck thought. "A little eatin' like that will make me forget the grubbin' I been doin'. Sellin' and buyin' all day and lendin' and collectin' most of the night." He chuckled to himself, then, and ran his fingers lightly over the shiny black woodwork of the buggy. "Worth it, though, ever' minute of it."

Suddenly, little muscles were tightening and quivering so with excitement around his chest and armpits that he had to shake his shoulders to stop the tingling. It was too good to be coming home —particularly with the reason he had in mind—better even than he expected. Driving onto his folks' land was something to make a man's skin nearly crawl off. And the surprise would make it better because Seab Jackson would have told them he couldn't get in until after dark.

The mare broke abruptly into a faster walk and Buck's thoughts shook back. "Smells water," he muttered, and his nostrils flared again and sucked in the country air. He reached up and settled his derby hat lower on his head, careful to touch it with the flat of his hand because he didn't want to make the nap streak the wrong way. Then he jerked the whip out of the socket and flicked it lightly over the horse's rump.

"Dinner's ready," he said out loud, and felt his stomach yearning towards his mother's table. He eased out a little more slack in the lines and felt the mare take it up in a second with a quickening step and a lunge into the collar. She came into a light trot but Buck didn't notice her. He watched over the trees that fringed the fence line until he could see smoke curling out of the chimney of the home place. Then, close and loud, he heard the bell ringing, calling the boys in from the fields. He let his horse have a little more. "Take it, you scaper." He stomped the floor board in excitement at the bell. He could see in his mind his mother with one arm shielding her eyes from the glare of noonday sun—bending rhythmically from the waist and laying her weight into steady pulls on the bell rope. She'd be singing, he knew, and he could make out like he could hear it now.

> "Oh, it rained and it poured
> And 'twas cold, stormy weather,
> In came the landlord,
> And drank up all the cider."

That would be the song, because she always sang it, trying to make the bell clapper hit when she came to what she called heavy words, like "rained" and "stormy" and "drank."

His mother was still on the back porch when Buck swung his mare in a long half circle around the side of the house. She was there near the bell like he had seen her in his mind, with a light south wind whipping her long dress and making little crackling sounds. His father was coming out of the tool shed, shading his eyes with his good arm, and some of the children were running out on the back porch. They stopped suddenly beside their mother, some of them catching at her skirt, and his father stopped dead still as Buck drove up—stylish, wheels whispering on the sand and throwing a fine golden spray.

He drove with his left hand holding the lines carelessly and his wrist drooped. His right arm was draped over the stiff leather seat back. He sat still for a moment after he stopped, then reached up with his right hand and flipped the brim of his derby so that it slipped back on his head. He leaned forward and looped his lines around the shiny whip socket, watching his mother all the time. He stayed bent over there for a long minute, fumbling needlessly at the lines. He sat up as he felt a thickness coming into his throat and began to unbutton the front of his long driving coat, so they could see his new clothes. He knew suddenly that he couldn't say what he wanted to, that they would have to speak first. He looked from the group on the porch to his father who had started walking slowly forward, peering upwards with his lips slightly parted. Buck just watched him as he came closer to lay a hand on the buggy seat and rub it, testing its quality. His father blinked at the derby.

"Well, sir," he said, "when it *does* rain, it pours, don't it?"

Buck leaned closer to catch his father's hand and shake it, then turned it loose, quickly, as if he were embarrassed, and jumped down from the buggy. He hurried over to his mother. She was waiting for him, half smiling and half trying to hide the smile, nervously wiping her hands on her dress. He came up the steps with his eyes on her face and the children stood back, shyly watching him out of big eyes. When he was close enough, his mother reached up with both hands on his shoulders and tiptoed a little to kiss him once on the cheek. She patted his shoulders with both hands.

"You've got heavier," she said, and cleared her throat. Buck nodded several times without speaking, straightening his new blue tie, until his lips began to quiver at the corners as if he had something funny on his mind.

"Mother," he said, "was you singin' 'bout the landlord and the cider when you rung that bell?"

They all began to laugh at Jeanie Bannon's down-pulled lips and little Coke ran out from behind one of the girls, all bones and red hair and raw knees, and hugged Buck around the middle, with giggles spilling out all over him. Buck knuckled his head hard and watched out of the corner of his eye as his father came up the steps, slowly pushing down with his good arm on one knee like his back was stiff. When he got on the porch, he stood up straight and his eyes were small and bright with the joke.

"When she rings," he said, "the boys start in, but when she gets to singin' it drives 'em back."

"Not all the way," Jeanie Bannon said, tartly, and pointed over Buck's shoulder. Buck turned to see Jeff and Hearn coming through the space between the tool shed and the smokehouse. He pulled loose from Coke and went out to meet them. They were shifting their eyes self-consciously as they came close in their faded hickory shirts and once-blue overalls that were growing tight on both their behinds. Hearn was limping a little but his bright brown eyes weren't as indrawn and secretive as Jeff's grey ones. Hearn would look boldly at anybody or anything. His body would be smaller than Jeff's, or Buck's, or any of the others, but it would have a finer grain, and neater bones. Jeff was growing up with an awkward knobbiness and his head seemed too large on his thin neck. His eyes didn't want to meet Buck's and kept dropping to the ground near his feet, but Hearn walked up and stuck out his hand and caught Buck's. He pulled Buck's coat open with the other hand.

"Where you preachin'?" he said, and his eyes flickered all over Buck's new clothes and then to the buggy and the mare. He pulled his hand slowly loose from Buck's and went over to the buggy. He began to rub his hand up and down on the whip socket and started to whistle softly.

When Jeff shook hands, he gave Buck only his fingers and a quick sideways shake, then he pulled his hand back and shoved it deep in his pocket.

"Good evenin'," he said, and flushed as if he knew it was the wrong thing to say. Buck shook Jeff's shoulder and turned around as Hearn came back and caught his arm. Hearn was looking up earnestly and the freckles on his forehead were puckering in tiny wrinkles.

"Look here, Buck. Take me back when you go. Maybe I can get a buggy, too."

Buck looked from one to the other and held them tightly by their thin arms. He glanced back at the porch, and frowned warningly at them before he answered.

"I got somethin' on the fire." He winked at them.

"That's a pore make-out," Buck's father said, showing his teeth through his beard. "I can put up a better splice myself, with this here puckered arm."

Buck didn't answer at first. His tongue was tight between his teeth and he was frowning in concentration as he wove a web of rawhide strips between the broken ends of a piece of harness. They were just inside the barn, on the shady side of a sharp line drawn by the shadow of the eaves. Slim lights were squeezing through cracks in the wall and he could see big dust floating in the air. Finally, he hung the harness on his knees to let his fingers rest. He thought a minute.

"Farmin' right now ain't helpin' you none." He looked directly at his father. Joe Bannon's face suddenly became expressionless and he scrubbed his right hand hard against the roughness of his blue jeans, where they stretched tight over his knee. He shook his head.

"Buck," he said, flatly, "we ain't goin' to talk about that no more. I couldn't get your ma off this place with a brush fire."

Buck leaned forward and his eyes had an eager light in them. "Mother's havin' to work like a brag mule, feedin' everybody on this place." His father shook his head again.

"We made out with less," he said, stubbornly. "Reckon she can do it with the girls' help."

Buck slapped his hand on his knee, then held up two fingers.

"Myrt and Nance," he said, "both got married as soon as somebody found out they could cook. The others ain't no help now, and if they learn, the same thing will happen." He leaned closer. "Can't you see, Papa, how Mother is fadin'? Hell, she can't stay over a stove till she dies. Get her out of it, bring her to Aven, and get a good colored woman to cook and give Mother a rest."

Joe Bannon's beard jutted out and his eyes flashed.

"By God," he said, "I'd as soon work with a circle-foot plow as eat some other woman's cookin'."

Buck threw back his head and laughed right in his father's face and couldn't stop. He kept laughing even after the old man muttered in his beard and walked stiff-legged down to the other end of the barn. Then he quieted down and watched his father piddling around for a few minutes. He eased up off the gear box and slipped out of the barn and went to the house. His mother was sitting in her hide-bottomed chair and he could see how it still bristled with brindle hairs around the edges and underneath where the thongs were tied wet and allowed to shrink to snugness. Jeanie Bannon was churning and she looked like she was seeing something so far away that nobody else would see it. She didn't notice Buck.

He walked quietly to the edge of the porch and stood there for a minute, just watching and listening to the muffled slush-thump that came from the churn dasher. He smiled, but it wasn't a glad smile when he saw big pale drops of milk fling themselves from under the churn lid and soak up into dark spots on his mother's dress. He looked at her eyes and tried to see what they saw, but all he could find was a narrow space between the smoke-house and a tool shed, and far over on a rise in the near forty he could see one of the boys chopping cotton. The figure was hazy in the sun and seemed to inch along with tiny winks of light flashing off the hoe blade. "It must be Hearn," Buck thought, "because Jeff didn't use the short stroke that was more of a scrape at the ground. Hearn cut them off at the ground, but Jeff took a good lick and chopped out root and all." He breathed deeply, then turned back towards his mother and found her eyes on him steady and unblinking, with a quizzical glint in them. He flushed and coughed and sat down awkwardly on the steps near her.

"Reckon that's Hearn?" he asked.

She nodded, churning steadily.

"Where's Jeff?"

She sniffed and one corner of her mouth curled. "Likely sittin' in the shade figurin' how he'll get around doin' his work."

[51]

Buck laughed out loud. "It'll end up with Hearn doin' the work and wonderin' how in the devil he got in such a fix."

"Ain't neither one of them too much hand to work." She didn't miss a stroke in her churning and her words were said without emphasis. Buck reached down and picked absently at a big splinter that stuck up high from the rain-warped floor. He glanced up at his mother, gauging her feelings, then looked back down again.

"They might do better at another kind o' work," he said, carelessly. "Ain't ever'body born to farm."

She glanced at him with a disturbance in her eyes, a puzzled frown between them.

"What other work?"

"I ain't farmin'."

"Hmph!" She worried the dasher around and settled the churn lid. "I'd hate to turn either one o' them loose in a town."

"They'd make out," he said, softly. "Little trainin', they'd run a store right well."

She shook her head.

"Hearn won't stay tied."

"He'll grow up."

She kept shaking her head, deliberately.

"I know my boys. An' Jeff." She stopped shaking her head and stared thoughtfully out at the field. "He might make it, but not the way you did. Somebody'd have to shove him along till he got plenty, but I reckon he could hold onto it."

Buck shrugged.

"Whatever it takes, they shore won't get it here." His mother didn't answer. "An' they won't never put out enough on this place to help Pa much," he went on. She was still silent.

"This ain't no one-horse farm," he said, carefully. "It needs good labor and lots of it."

"We make out," she said, primly. Buck noticed that her stroke on the dasher had hurried.

"Papa ain't lookin' right," he said, suddenly. "He's got a bellowsed look about him, like his breath is hard."

He saw a change then. She tightened her mouth and looked down at the floor beside the churn. Her hand gripped harder on the worn dasher handle.

[52]

"A man breaks land for forty years," she said, slowly, "but the land don't break a man but once."

Buck felt something like a paleness spreading outward from somewhere inside him. He didn't know why, but he held his breath and waited. She stopped churning and leaned forward, resting her chin on her hands, cupped on the handle of the dasher. She sat very still, staring outwards for a long time, then slowly she drew her gaze back in over the fields and into the yard and back on Buck again.

"You see his hands?" she asked, and didn't wait for an answer. "They're curled up to fit a plow stock and they don't never straighten out. It hurts me to touch them. See how his arms have got so heavy they plumb drag down his shoulders? See how close his beard is gettin' to his jumper front?"

She waited for his answer and he could feel a fierceness coming from her. He nodded but didn't speak.

"That's how land breaks a man," she said, bitterly.

Buck shook his head slowly and blinked his eyes and looked off.

"I've been tryin' to get Papa to sell out," he said, bluntly, "sell out and come to Aven with me."

Jeanie Bannon gasped. She leaned back in her chair and breathed deeply.

"Sell the land?" she said. "Sell the land?"

Buck nodded.

"Sell it, or throw it away. Do anything, but get Papa off it."

She closed her eyes. "How could we eat?" Her voice was low. Buck shifted his seat to a higher step, closer to her.

"Look," he said, "pore farmers have got to be furnished and somebody's got to furnish them."

She sniffed. "We never needed no furnishin'."

"I know," Buck said, impatiently. "You'd rather starve, but there's a lot of 'em wouldn't. See here, the man that does the furnishin' makes mor'n the farmer. You know that. Rent him his land, sell him his tools, seeds, guano, anything he wants. He'll owe you and he won't like you. He'll cuss you, but you'll have to take it. He may kick you, but take it. Then, by God, if he makes a crop, take it."

His mother closed her eyes and Buck could see her face stiffen.

[53]

She tried to rock, but it wasn't a rocking chair. "That ain't our way," she said, shortly.

Buck laughed, bitterly, and it was ugly even to his ears.

"Them that furnishes live a long time," he said. "The land don't break them."

He got up and started to walk off. He felt like he was mad at something—at himself, at the land, even at his mother. He stopped, swallowing hard, and looked back over his shoulder.

"You all muddle it out tonight," he said; "it won't hurt."

She nodded and her face was so pale Buck thought he could see the darkness of her eyes shadowing through the still-closed lids.

They talked about it in bed that night. Buck heard them. He lay on his pallet and stared up into darkness and listened to their mumbling voices through the thin wall. A word came to him now and then, strained and suddenly loud, as if Joe Bannon had turned over with an effort. Buck's body was tight, stretched between two poles, and nothing about him would go to sleep. It was like only a small part of him touched the bed and he could feel with strange surety that his mother's body was fighting sleep, too. He listened until the mumbling stopped abruptly, as if a thread had been cut, and in the quiet he could hear tiny sighing snores from the crib where little Victoria slept.

Then another sound came sifting through the cracks and he knew that his mother was crying quietly in the night and trying with her hand to smother the shuddering from her chest. He tried harder to hear, then he moved impatiently and sat quietly up on the pallet with his arms around his knees and stared straight into blackness. Carefully, he stood up and stepped over Coke's sprawling and nearly naked body. He walked softly through the kitchen and out onto the side porch. He stood for a long time out there, watching a lowering moon, and feeling with fingers that were queerly sensitive the peeled poles that supported the roof. His fingers hunted the sharp nipples that grouped in places on the smooth poles. His mind turned slowly and seemed to work to the remembered sound of his mother's crying. Then he heard bare feet padding softly through the kitchen and he knew that she was up, that she was coming out as he had, for a moment of peace and stillness, among the things that made her life.

She was shapeless in a long-sleeved nightgown with high ruffles around her neck and her feet didn't show because the gown was so long. She had one hand on her mouth as she came through the doorway, but when she saw Buck she dropped it quickly and stood still. He could hear little gulping noises from her throat. She was trying to stop crying. He turned back around and stared out over the dark fields again. He didn't want to look at her and his fingers moved faster in their nervous searching of the porch uprights. She spoke first.

"You'll get your death in this night air." Her voice shook a bit. She coughed deliberately, and went over to the narrow-gauge well housing that came up through the floor of the porch. She eased the long slim bucket noiselessly down on its rope. She didn't look at Buck as she let the bucket drop back into the water two or three times to be sure it was full. She kept her eyes away even after she had pulled it up and canted it over to drink from its cold and beaded lip. Buck wouldn't face her either. He whispered, when he spoke, and wondered far back in himself why he talked so low.

"He asleep?"

She came over beside him and touched his arm, then stood straight and very still. Buck saw her eyes, gleaming with brightness from her tears, but without their flickering lights. He started to speak again, but she shook her head.

"He sagged off to sleep," she said, dully, "like a baby or a real old man, while he was talkin' to me. It was like somethin' just went out of him, right quick."

Buck rubbed the back of his hand gently up and down against her shoulder. "What'd he say?" She turned quickly around, facing him, and stared blindly for a moment. Some of the lights came back in her eyes and she breathed faster.

"What did he say? What he said don't count. It's other things. It was him—fumblin' at the ham tonight, and hackin' it up when he used to could cut it like butter. It's me havin' to button his shirt and make out like I'm doin' it for fun."

She stopped suddenly and Buck could hear her painful swallow. He turned his face away so he wouldn't have to see her mouth trembling.

"It's them things," she went on, "them, and him turnin' over in yonder and flingin' his poor stiff hands out in his sleep. They're the things that'll move us."

Buck stood silently for a while longer, almost holding his breath, wondering if he would ever see his mother again—his mother as she used to be, all fire and full of knowing how things should be. He shook his head, finally, and touched her arm, gently. "Let's go in."

She shook her head and kept looking out over the fields. He waited a second, then left her, walking carefully over the splinters. He turned to look back when he reached the kitchen door. She was still standing there, but was looking upwards now and her back was very straight. Buck bent his head and leaned a little closer to hear her, but she wasn't talking to him.

"Please don't let me be scared of all them folks," she was saying.

INTERLUDE

THE MOON *laid a smooth wing of light over a large stack of lumber and threw sharp shadows from the raw framework of the house-to-be.*

Jake Willis hunched mournfully before the small fire, whose tired flames would gasp awhile on greying coals, then burst into startled hunger as a triangular chunk of waste pine would drop into its middle. The fire was for company, nothing else.

Jake let his head drop back once and stared up into the raveled clouds that crawled across the moon now and then like beetles on a lamp shade. When he looked back at the fire, his face was miserable.

He mumbled, "Bible says we'll always have pore folks." Then his head twisted as if it were fighting for air, and he spoke out loud, "But how come, by God, it's got to be me?"

"Hunh?"

Jake jerked around until he saw who it was, then he turned his face back to the fire, ashamed.

"Hello, Bass."

Bascom Wooten moved closer to the fire and squatted beside Jake. He flipped the long bill of his white and blue striped cap back from his eyes. He laid on the ground between them a greasy shoe box. Then, cautiously, he drew his watch from the breast pocket of his overalls and glanced at it.

"Twelve-fifty," he said.

Jake fumbled a small twig into the fire with a calloused forefinger.

"What the hell difference does it make to me? I ain't goin' nowhere."

"Well, don't blow off at me." Bass's tone was that of an injured man.

Jake took the lid off the shoe box and glanced inside.

"Fried ham again," he said, tersely, then his eyes drifted to Bass's face. "I'm like a broke-leg mule," his dull voice went on. "Ain't got but one trade an' Buck's got the only tool it takes. I cain't carpenter, nor lay brick, nor plow—cain't do a damned thing but brake on the railroad." He laid a large piece of ham on top of a slab of hoecake and bit into it. "Now I couldn't even be a night watchman if Buck wasn't buildin' his folks a house an' hired me so he could get his money back." He gulped, and stared moodily into the fire as he gnawed off another bite. Bass shifted uneasily.

"Lucky to get that, I reckon."

"No, I ain't." Jake stood up quickly and his hands shook. "Be damned if they ain't somethin' wrong when a man can lend you two dollars on a sixty-dollar watch, then in two-three year have it run up to more'n the watch cost."

"Hell." Bascom spat in the fire. "That's middle o' the night talk. When you look at Buck's little black book, you see different."

Jake sagged back down onto his hunkers. "I shoulda kept a book, too." His eyes widened in sudden hope. "Reckon that son-of-a-bitch has robbed me?" Then the hope faded. "Naw, not for less'n a hundred dollars."

"Reckon not," Bass agreed.

Suddenly, Jake slapped his hand on his knee. "Tell you one

thing right now." His voice took on strength and his chin jutted. "I could buy another'n cheaper than payin' him, but Goddammit, that's the only watch in the world to me." He shook his head solemnly up and down. "I'm a'goin' to get it back if I have to steal it."

CHAPTER SIX

THE LOCATION of the new home to cover all the Bannons was a problem that lasted only long enough for Buck to bring his dusty little buggy back in sight of Aven. It took three more days to buy the block of land, but the time wasn't badly spent and the extra hundred dollars the land had cost wasn't wasted because his store was across the street and down a little way.

"A man oughtn't to live over two hoe handles from his business," Buck had kept telling himself during the next few weeks while the foundation was being laid. "It ain't the fanciest section, but rush days in the store, we'll have plenty of hands close by," he'd mutter to himself as he watched the raw framework of the house shoulder one of its corners between the only two oak trees left on St. Simon Street.

Then, on a late afternoon in August, Buck could lean against a tree across the street from the new house, just looking—letting his mind see it again. The building of it. He had seen the first foundation stone laid for the northeast pillar. He had watched it go up piece by piece, from floor joists and sleepers to timbers and ceiling, hurrying over two vacant lots between his store and the new house, to check a load of lumber or maybe just to look and talk to the workmen.

His eyes seemed to grow smaller with the upper lids drooping as he looked at the house. "It's big," he thought, and nodded automatically to a hugely stout man who rumbled, "Howdy, Buck." Then he tipped his round-topped work hat and smiled at the small grey woman who chirped along in her husband's wake. His mind never left the house as they passed. "Big," he thought again. "Big for the time and the place, but they'd need a big one." It was square, because a square house was all he knew, but the long porch ran clear across the front and down the south side. The second story reared boxlike except for two cupolas above the porch roof, and its roof was broad, of cedar shingles that would shed many a rain. It stood there, ugly without paint, raw in the late afternoon sun, but it stood strong with heart-pine beams and a floor joist for every two feet of flooring. He frowned, seeing the turpentine patches oozing from the siding, and wished silently that he had been able to get it painted before the folks came. Then he shrugged. "Outside ain't everything." His lips moved a little as he counted the rooms in his mind, going from front to back in the house.

A slow cracking voice from behind startled him. "Plannin' to fill it up someday?" He looked back over his shoulder, and shook his head at an old man who carried a mule dealer's badge of office—a cheap walking stick whose blunt end was scuffed and stained with manure and tobacco juice.

"Won't be no time till it'll be runnin' over," he answered, "but they'll be brothers and sisters and such." He laughed. "Won't be none of mine, thank the Lord."

"Fine, fine," the old man nodded. "Well, y'all come." He turned to leave.

"Y'all come, too," Buck said, absently, and let his eyes wander back to the house, feeling a stirring in his chest when he thought of all the Bannons that were still unmarried—just two or three to the room—with places to undress without having to turn their backs. He was still staring, prouding up over the bigness of the house, when the first grinding of wagon wheels came over the tracks around the bend. He measured with his eyes between the brick pillars and chimneys until the first wagon lurched into the rutted and muddy street.

"Bought brick," he muttered. "Mother'll say it's worse'n buyin' ground coffee and Papa'll say it would be a fool to buy somethin' he could make." He chuckled inside, just as he heard the first wild whoop.

He looked up to see Coke and one of the girls running ahead of the first wagon, pointing and yelling at him and then at the house. Coke was eating a raw sweet potato and his sister's strong white teeth were sunk deep into the side of a potato that she couldn't carry in her hands because she had a bottle in one and a turnip root in the other. Buck raised his hand and took a couple of steps nearer. Little Coke came fairly close, then suddenly backed away and stood there, solemnly chewing. His sister paddled through the mud until she could stand close and look up at his face. She handed him the turnip and took the potato out of her mouth.

"We run over a cooter," she said, and he could see her bare toes curling, reaching down deeper into the cool mud. He bit into the turnip and looked seriously into her wide eyes. He nodded. "I think they eat quail eggs." He winked at them and jerked his head towards the wagon. They skipped, following Buck's long stride, but they had dropped behind to look at the house, when Buck reached the side of the wagon which held his mother and father and baby Victoria. He looked at them once, but not for long. He didn't know what made it, but he couldn't look at them. His mother braced her feet firmly against the wagon bed bottom and one corner of her mouth was pulled upwards and in, like she wanted to smile but wouldn't. She had half a sweet potato in her hand and was scraping up pulpy mouthfuls with the blunt tip of a bone-handled kitchen knife, feeding them into the pursed, old-folks mouth of Victoria.

"This'n better make haste if she's goin' to grow," she said, softly.

Buck's father still held the reins loosely in his right hand, idly whipping the ends against his legs. His eyes were going over the new place, but Buck could see that he didn't look long at the house. The eyes spent more time on the vacant land. His father spoke with relief.

"Somethin' ought to grow there." His teeth were showing through his beard, when he turned towards Buck. "Boy, you ain't never seen nothin' like the way that land was yeastin' when we sold. I figure the crop to come was what got us the price."

"It was pretty good dirt," Buck said, and wondered why his tone was defensive. He caught his mother's arm. "Get down, you ain't seen the new kitchen."

She pulled up her dress to wipe the knife off carefully on the inside of the hem. She let Buck help her down before she took Victoria, head wobbling, out of the basket on the seat and straddled her on one hip. "Let's go, Joe," she said, and began to walk firmly towards the house, studying it closely, and Buck knew she was trying to find something wrong with it. He caught her by the arm and began to hurry her towards the front steps that were so new-looking the mill marks still showed where the planes had scraped. He wouldn't let her open the front door, but slung it open himself and his voice boomed in the empty hall.

"It's a shotgun house right on," he said, "but it's got a wider hall and rooms upstairs and downstairs."

"Hmph!" His mother's eyes searched beyond him, squinting at the stairs that hugged narrowly to one wall. "Young'uns will get lost and be cryin' if they have to go out at night."

Buck pushed her elbow, taking her on down the hall, flinging doors open as he went, and pointing inside the rooms. "Parlor," he'd say, "with a big fireplace and six windows." Then he would bustle her along. "Your bedroom," and he'd be pointing, "fireplaces, too. But all the bedrooms have got fireplaces, excusin' the little attic room, and I figured any visitin' circuit riders could stay there."

"Oh, you go on," his mother said, pushing at his shoulder with her palm flattened. Her eyes were brightening, though, and she whispered up at him. "We'll put a shuck mattress up there, too."

Buck put his arm around her shoulder and hugged her lightly as they walked to the end of the hall and his proudness was about to run over when he opened the door to the dining room. "It's big," he said, and his tone was a little anxious, "but it's got to be big to feed us all at one time—and a preacher or two." His mother leaned slowly forward, peering into the room, pushing her lips out. "There'll be a table pretty soon," he went on, watching her, "with chairs to match and leather seats and arms on the one that Papa gets. That's the way they do it. There's twenty comin'."

"It'll be funny to see everybody eatin' at once," Jeanie Bannon said, "and it'll be a project to cook it in one shift."

Buck pulled her away and on down the hall a few steps. He stopped before he opened the door and looked down at his mother. "This'n took a lot of buildin'. Biggest room in the house."

He pushed the door, then, and let her go into the kitchen ahead of him. She stopped just inside and her eyes roved slowly over the room, to the pantry, to the huge woodbox, and to the cupboards, still unpainted and enormous against the wall. She looked all around, once back at Buck, then quickly to the empty chimney flue.

"There's a big stove comin' tomorrow," Buck said, quickly, before she could ask. "With warmers and a hot-water reservoir." He watched her anxiously at first. Then with his mouth slowly curving in satisfaction, he said, "I figured you'd want your old benches and table in here for breakfast."

Her eyes crinkled at the corners and she nodded soberly. "Breakfast is best in the kitchen," she said. "Thank you, son."

Buck felt his chest swell as he walked back to the other wagon, where the boys waited for someone to tell them what to do. Jeff had been driving and his face was still tight with a frown from trying not to do anything wrong. Hearn was slouched carelessly in the seat beside Jeff, looking the town over as if he had lived there before and was just back for a short visit. He was laughing as Buck came close enough to hear and he turned his head to say something to Jeff.

"Look at that bank walker's strut Buck's got." His shoulders shook. Jeff laughed, too, and all his teeth showed, but there was still something timid about it. He ducked his head at Buck and wrapped his lines carefully before he jumped off the wagon. He came close to Buck.

"It's shore somethin', ain't it?" he said, and his eyes were bigger than usual. Buck shook him gently by the shoulder, then reached up to grab Hearn by the ankle. He jerked him almost out of the seat and hollered at him.

"Get movin', you lazy hound, and let's tote some of this stuff in before dark."

He was loading Jeff and Hearn for the last trip into the house, when he heard his mother calling him from one of the front-room windows. First dark was almost upon them and he was sucking in short dry breaths and his shirt was wet. His sleeves were rolled high. He yelled back at her from the wagon and gathered up the last armload of pots and pans. He was whistling busily under his breath as he shouldered the front door open, backed in, and turned to go down the hall. His mother had lit a lamp in the kitchen and the little light made him feel like it wasn't just a house any more but was beginning to be a place for folks to live. He heard his mother's voice when he came closer, with something gay running through the tones and the words coming fast. He didn't look around until he had dumped his load with a lot of noise on the plain deal table. He stopped whistling when he turned to speak.

[63]

His mother was standing there, eyes shining brightly and some-how proudly, and she had her hand on the arm of a stranger.

She was small, the stranger was, but her hair was piled high to make her look taller, and it was so black it glinted when she moved in the lamplight. Her skin was very pale, but her lips were red against it, and her eyes were as black as her hair when she opened them wide and looked at Buck. He kept his eyes on her for a moment, puzzled, then turned towards his mother with both eyebrows raised.

"Her name's Victoria, too," Jeanie Bannon said, and nodded eagerly. Then she shook her head and made little tishing noises. "This is my boy, Buck," she told the girl, and her eyes sparkled as she patted her arm. "Big, ain't he?"

The girl laughed and her teeth showed square and white. She bit her lower lip before she spoke. "He *is* big." She made a little tapping sound with the toe of her shoe, and looked slyly sideways at Buck's mother. "Hope they're not all that size."

Buck scowled at his mother, hardly knowing why, and tried to frown at the girl, but she made him want to laugh with her. He finally shook his head and threw one leg over the corner of the table. He rubbed his hands fast up and down the wet and shiny brown muscles on his arms.

"What's goin' on here?" he said, patting his foot, too, making like he could let them go right on joking him. His mother talked excitedly, shaking the girl's arm as she told him.

"She's a schoolteacher," she said, "and she wants to live with us and teach the young'uns for room and board." She suddenly stopped and looked at Buck, drawing fast, shallow breaths. "That's how they do it," she went on, slowly, watching him and showing him with her eyes that she wanted the girl to stay. "Folks she was boardin' with had a married girl come home with a passel of kids." She seemed shy as she said it and her voice was wistful. "Her name's Victoria, too," she repeated.

The girl touched Jeanie Bannon's arm. Her voice was deep and sounded like it had laugh bubbles in it.

"I've been watching this house go up," she said, "since the first day they told me I'd have to leave." She flushed and her eyes didn't meet Buck's any longer. " 'Course, I had to wait until some of your womenfolks moved in." She waited a moment, but he didn't answer, and her shoulders began to pull back. She drew a long breath that pulled her dress tighter across her breasts. Her dress was cut square and low in front. Buck noticed that, and the way her skirt hugged tight across her hips.

"I'd teach out in the daytime," she said, quickly, and watched him rub the back of his hand on his chin, looking sideways at his mother. He finally turned both hands palm up in front of him.

"They'll need learnin'," he said, and saw his mother smile and heard the girl sigh in relief. "And maybe me, too, Miss Victoria."

The girl was quickly serious. "I'll help with things," she said, earnestly, "and I'll be around a lot, so call me Vic if you want to. All my friends call me Vic."

Buck's mother chuckled.

"Big Vic," she said. "We got a Little Vic."

CHAPTER SEVEN

Jeff reached out and caught Buck by the arm. "Wait a minute," he said. "Stand still and see if you notice somethin' I did." The words sounded loud and harsh in the night's stillness, and Jeff gulped as if he were embarrassed. His face was pale and Buck could see how the moon found angles in the boy's face that made his head look bony. Jeff was sniffing at the air.

"Smell it?" His eyes were fixed anxiously on Buck. Buck grunted. "Ham!" he said.

Jeff shook his head. "No, it's somethin' you can't smell." He sucked in a big breath. "Paint. It's worn off so the place will smell like a house now."

Buck laughed and pulled Jeff along by the arm. "Let's get on in. I'm hot, tired, and hungry."

"Me, too." They walked closer to the house. "Durned if I hadn't ruther plow than to stock shelves."

Buck suddenly stopped and stood still, not looking at Jeff, and not listening. He was frowning with concentration and staring straight ahead without seeing. Jeff started to speak but Buck held up one hand to stop him. They stood that way for a moment and it seemed as if dusk were waking up the small things that live at night and making creaking sounds.

"Damn it," Buck said, abruptly, "a man twenty-one years old that ain't got no more sense than me ought to be hung."

Jeff's eyes bugged out.

"What you done?" His voice broke and rose out of control. Buck spat in the dust as if the words to come didn't taste good.

"I could a'bought a big lot of them cheap work shoes from that drummer and undercut hell out of Mason's. Could a'sold them at cost and still made money."

Jeff screwed his thin neck around in his homemade shirt collar. "Well, if you don't make a profit, what's the sense of sellin' 'em?"

Buck kicked at the dust with his heel, hacking a hole in the walkway. "If I can get 'em in the store," he said, roughly, "I can jump prices on ever'thing we got and make a killin' while they're braggin' about gettin' shoes so cheap."

Jeff looked embarrassed again. "That's kinda slim dealin', ain't it, Buck?"

Buck stared a moment longer into the deepening darkness.

"Boy," he said, "you might as well learn now never to ask a man what to do, or tell him your plans. They'll mostly all know some reason why you oughtn't to do it and them that don't just ain't listenin'."

Jeff nodded and Buck saw his lips moving silently as if he were carefully remembering what his brother had told him. Buck snorted and the noise jarred. He pulled Jeff on towards the house.

"And don't listen so damned close to what I say. I been wrong."

Jeff looked up at him, frowning and puzzled, and the expression on his face gave Buck a kind of homesickness. It wasn't homesickness for a place or a thing, but for a day or a time, when he had looked up at his father the same way. He squirmed inwardly at his thoughts. They were more like a woman's than a full-grown man's. That started another thought.

"Somethin' else, boy," he said, still hurrying Jeff along. "Don't never tell your business to a woman. A woman is somethin' God put here to show a man that he could have been worse off."

Jeff laughed out loud, then, and grinned at Buck with his teeth shining like a coon's in the light that came from the hall through a large single pane in the front door.

"That ain't how I heard you tell it to Big Vic last night," he said, gleefully.

Buck stopped short, one foot poised on the bottom step leading up onto the front porch. He didn't speak for a slow moment, but carefully turned to face Jeff.

"Where were you?" His voice was quiet.

Jeff's laughter soaked quickly back into his chest. He swallowed hard.

"Well," he said, haltingly, "I had to go out and I stopped by them bushes close to the old wagon bed."

Buck's tone was cold. "Did you hear me leave the room?"

Jeff shook his head, miserably.

"What'd you hear at the wagon bed?"

Jeff's voice rose until he couldn't control it. "Nothin', Buck," he said, pleading a little. "Nothin'. I just knew you was goin' after her."

Buck caught him by the arm, hard this time, and shook him a little. "You heard me slip out of our room and followed me."

"No, I didn't, Buck. Honest."

"Remember, this," Buck said, slowly through his teeth, "Papa don't know yet who painted the preacher's horse green and killed it, but I do."

He pushed Jeff away from him, then, and went up the steps, hitting them hard with his heels. Jeff ran after him.

"Wait, Buck," he said, panting a little, "I didn't mean to listen. Honest to God."

Buck jerked his arm away and looked down at Jeff with his lip curling.

"Just so you won't be standin' out in the night air no more," he said, "we won't be there tonight."

They weren't in the wagon bed that night.

The moon was listing, one quarter full, and riding along easily over splotchy little clouds when Buck stopped figuring on the books in his store and hurriedly crossed the vacant lots towards the barn. He was walking quietly out of the barn with a short ladder balanced on his shoulder when he heard a muffled thump. He stopped, holding his breath for a moment and listening, then breathed easier. All he could hear was the restless feet of the cow in her stall. He didn't move for a while longer, but stood there, hardly thinking, just liking the night. The way it was. He liked to look up at the moon and feel the cool light on his face. And he liked to think about Big Vic. Big Vic! She was somethin'. And that was a hell of a name for her. She couldn't have been over five feet tall. Hair and eyes as black as a licorice stick. Plump here and there. Big Vic! He shifted the ladder more comfortably on his shoulder. "She's too little," he told himself, "but she shore don't know it."

He moved quietly towards the house, still thinking about Vic, with excitement quickening in his spine, and his smile grew broader. It was something to laugh about—her a schoolteacher and all. "Teachin' the kids for room and board and runnin' a school all her own. And teachin' me a few things on the side." He almost laughed out loud, partly because he thought it was funny,

[68]

but mostly because of the excitement that kept crowding into his chest. He smothered it, and carefully placed one end of the ladder against the window sill of Vic's room. Then he paused and listened for another full minute.

"God, it'd be hell if Mother run up on us some night," he thought. "Much as she thinks of Vic." He felt a quick surge of guilt, remembering how pleased his mother had been when she found that Vic had the same name as her youngest daughter. Little Vic—always dropping off to sleep in a second after fighting mulishly against the drug of a full stomach. Little Vic, holding everyone else awake until she slept, so he'd have to fake work at the store until it was safe to come to Big Vic.

Now, though!

He started cautiously up the ladder, but his foot scraped on the first rung. He made a soft noise in his throat and pulled his foot back and stood there, undecided for a moment. Then he knelt and took off his right shoe and stepped in stocking foot upon the rung. He removed the left shoe and dropped it beside the other on the ground. His breathing quickened as he went up, slowly and carefully. There was something unreal about it. The moon threw things out of kilter, dangled his shadow against the house before him, crooked and blobbish. Even the hint of danger curling through his mind and making the risk that much more worth taking—even it was unreal. Only one thing was real —the conjured up picture of Big Vic. He had never seen her in a bed. She'd be lying, maybe, in the big soft bed and it would be so dark he couldn't see her hair, nor her eyes except when the moon might strike tiny fires in them as it had last night. He could see in his picture, her shoulders, shining pale in the blackness and he could see her arms stretched straight up over her head and her little fists clenched tight, as she always held them.

He wondered if she would wear a nightgown.

Then his head came over the window sill and he propped his elbows on it, to rest and let his eyes get used to the total darkness of the room. Something stirred inside, close by, and he smelled her hair. He didn't know whether he heard her or felt her or saw her, but he knew that she was crouching beside the window and that she had been watching for him. He felt her then. She caught his head in her arms and pulled it close against her breast and kissed him on the back of his neck. She whispered and it was little more than a sigh.

"Hurry," she said, "hurry."

Buck's legs felt heavy as he slid over the window sill and his hand shook as Big Vic led him surely in the dark towards the big feather bed.

He lay very still and stared up into the dark. His body was dead and wonderfully far away from him, and the rest of him could go where it pleased without clumsiness.

Yet his mind lay sluggish, not moving, and the stillness was like a deep, warm, dark pool in the bend of a creek that soon would be sucked, drop by drop, back out into the current. And then would go on, alive again, a part of the hurrying water.

His first thought was that he hated to begin to think. Then, for a while, he thought about one thing, how the covers were bunched at his feet. Not thinking about straightening them out, just about them being bunched. Not even wondering how they got down there. Just thinking of them as a lump.

Then Vic stirred and another thought stung his mind. She was on his arm and it was asleep. He didn't move it, nothing moved but his mind. Thoughts started flowing, then leaping. Big Vic. Little Vic. Mother. Ladder. Jeff and having to use a ladder instead of slipping out and down the hall. Jeff and the store. Work shoes. Big Vic again. And arm asleep.

He moved carefully, pulling his arm from under her shoulders. She stirred and Buck knew that she had opened her eyes. He swung a leg off the bed and suddenly froze in that position. He wondered if he had made the noise he had heard. Then it came again and he knew it was from the window. Quickly he reached out a hand and covered Vic's mouth and quietly he slid off the bed and crouched by its side. He stared at the window with something painful in his throat, making it hard to breathe without noise.

The sound came again, a thin scraping, and Buck saw a head come weaving above the window sill. He couldn't see at first, but then the moon came out and shone on a woman's bare head. As she turned her head from side to side, searching the room, he could see her eyes glittering a little and he thought again about a possum in a tree. He knew it was his mother.

He stayed still, hardly breathing. A cold wave swept over him when she spoke.

"Buck." Her voice was soft, questioning. He didn't answer. She cleared her throat. "Buck." It came again, urgent this time, trying to persuade. He didn't move or answer, but the effort to swallow hurt his throat.

She didn't call again. She stood on the ladder, peering into the dark room for a long minute, then her head bobbed again from side to side and sank below the window sill.

Buck closed his eyes and waited until the scraping sounds had stopped. He swallowed carefully and wondered if it had made as much noise as it felt like. It was dry swallowing. He stood up and leaned close over Vic, close enough to see her frightened eyes staring up at him. He put one finger on her lips and shaped his mouth for being quiet. Quickly, then, but silently, he left the room barefooted and hurried down the long hall to his and Jeff's room, carrying his clothes under his arm. He closed the door behind him and a long shuddering breath came from somewhere deep inside him. He felt safer. But his thoughts panted.

She'd be watching the ladder, he knew, and she'd watch it for a long time. But she'd get tired and come in, and when morning came, he could brass it out and swear he was in his room. Vic could explain the ladder. Sure, it'd be all right in the morning.

Morning did make it look better. Buck felt good when he awoke. He hurried dressing and his mind felt as limber as a pine seedling as it worked over what he had better say.

"Hell," he thought, "all I got to do is just say I was at the store, then straight to my room, and stick to it. That ladder ain't none of my business and Vic can make out she didn't even know it was there. Asleep all night and didn't hear a thing. That's it."

He was almost whistling, feeling better every minute, when Jeff rattled the doorknob and came in, shivering a little as he always did in the early morning, even in the hottest weather. He had one hand behind him.

Buck tried to frown at him, but couldn't.

"Don't reckon you spent much time at the wagon bed last night," he said, laughing a little.

Jeff didn't answer. His eyes shifted from Buck's eyes all around the room and finally came to rest on Buck's bare feet. Then he looked suddenly at the floor and spoke.

"Mother sent these," he said, in a high voice, and he brought Buck's shoes around from his back and held them out.

Buck groaned and closed his eyes. His mind flickered back and he remembered kicking them off below the ladder. Something churned inside him. He tried to speak but couldn't. His mind kept yelling, "God, I must a' been crazy. Why in hell didn't I think of them shoes?" Dimly, he heard Jeff shifting from one foot to the other. Vaguely at first, he heard Jeff speak.

"She shined 'em."

Buck opened his eyes quickly and looked at them. They had been greased and polished. He suddenly reached out and grabbed them roughly away from Jeff. He sat down and began to pull them on in a hurry.

"She didn't have to do that," he said, tightening his jaw. "Now, by God, I'll just go down and man it out."

Buck walked into the kitchen with his legs stiff and his back held so straight it hurt him. All of the children were already there at the table, but he didn't look directly at anybody. Out of the corner of his eye, he saw his mother busy at the big wood range. As he sat down and began to pull the platter of fried eggs towards his plate, he glanced around the long table.

Big Vic wasn't there.

He slowly piled food on his plate and watched his mother's back. He didn't say anything. Nobody said anything. The only noise was the bubbling of water boiling and Little Vic whimpering and sucking at a sugar tit. Coke was humming as he carefully worked his finger into the side of a big biscuit, digging a hole to fill with syrup.

Buck saw that his father wasn't there. "Where's Papa?" he asked in a voice that didn't sound right to him.

"At the barn." They all spoke at once, then they stopped in confusion, as if they knew something was wrong, but couldn't fasten it down. Buck looked around again.

"Where's Big Vic?"

His mother turned to face him then. She held a long spoon in one hand and with the other she pushed her hair out of her eyes.

"She left this mornin'," she said, as if she were tired. "Early. She ain't comin' back."

Buck lowered his head slowly, watching his mother's face all the time. She turned her back quickly and began to push things around on the stove.

Jeff spoke then. "We still got Little Vic." He sounded as if he hoped they would laugh, but nobody made a sound for a moment.

Jeanie Bannon turned around deliberately and faced her children. Her eyes were as black as mulberries. Her mouth had pulled stubbornly down at the corners.

"We're goin' to call her Christina," she said. "Christina. From now on."

INTERLUDE

It was *winter and the grass that had been green was growing gold again, waiting to be burned off, or to be turned up with hairy white roots showing like veins pressed into the slick black-earth sides of a clod.*

Jake Willis drove a small wooden stake into the grass just at the spot where his end of the small-linked chain dropped. He turned around and cupped his hands.

"Come up, Bass."

Then he squatted on his heels and pulled the short collar of his overall jumper higher up on his stub of a neck. The sun felt good on his neck, but the wind robbed it of warmth almost before it could strike.

"Hey, Lord," he said, "another day, another dollar." He held his hand closer to his eye in the thin sunlight and watched a small red ant scramble frantically through and over the coarse black hairs. The ant reached his knuckle, and began to tickle. He rubbed the broad thumb of his other hand over the knuckle and killed the ant, then he smelled of his thumb. "Half to me and half to Buck Bannon," he muttered, then he looked up as he heard Bascom Wooten's feet scuffling on the hard ground.

"Ain't it time to quit?"

Bass dropped his end of the chain and the sun bounced off small patches of brightness where it had scrubbed clean of rust from being dragged. He hauled at the worn and shiny leather strap looped through the buttonhole in the breast pocket of his overalls. "Ten more minutes." He hefted his thick gold watch and grinned down until Jake looked up at him, scowling.

"Go to hell."

"Hah!" Bass made some marks in a little notebook with curled edges, using a pencil with a gnawed end. He stuffed them back in his pocket importantly and picked up the chain. "Cain't catch up, hunh?"

"Them damned young'uns must eat like boar shoats," Jake answered plaintively. "Been here six months and interest gnawin' at me like another conscience."

"I'll be glad when you get that blessed watch back," Bass said, irritably, "so you can get back on the road. I'm plumb wore out with these piddlin' jobs, helpin' you on my day off."

Jake groaned, standing up.

"That Goddamned Buck Bannon."

Bass started off, dragging the chain.

"Don't cuss him. Wasn't for him, you wouldn't even have a job helpin' to lay out the town."

Jake put his broad heavy foot on his end of the chain and threw the loop so it would slide freely.

"That's another thing, by God." He raised his voice. "How come he's big enough already to be gettin' me jobs? We got here first, but damned if he ain't got us suckin' the hind tit."

Bass trudged on with the chain winking like a hundred-foot snake behind him until it tightened, then he stooped and drove his stake. He cupped his hands.

"Come up, Jake."

Jake was panting slightly when he reached Bass, and he eased himself immediately to the ground. "Ain't it time to knock off?" he said.

Bass groaned and hauled at his watch again.

CHAPTER EIGHT

FROM WHERE Buck stopped and turned around on the corner of St. Simon and Oak Streets, the house looked solid in the sun and warm in the bite of winter's wind. His eyes narrowed and he hunched his shoulders trying to keep the wind from pocketing under the back brim of his hat.

"Lord," he said, "they fill that house up. Seems like I ain't had a minute to myself in six months."

He shook his shoulders, then swung around, sniffing at the air with his head up, and kicking his heels against the hard earth. Once he broke his long stride, to glance at one of the new markers that were laying off the town in blocks. "Layin' it out too little," he grumbled to himself. "Streets too narrow, like there wasn't enough room, and ain't nobody crowdin' us." He went on, frowning, but his eye had seemed to claim the marker, and somehow there was pride in the way his toes turned slightly out. He let his eyes pass vaguely now and then over the careless row of houses, new and old, that spotted each newly designed block of land. Some fronted the street he was on, and others backed up to it, unashamed of drying diapers and sunning mattresses.

His frown had eased slowly off and there was an eagerness in the forward jut of his chin, when he heard someone calling his name. He looked back over his left shoulder, then jerked his head back around as he heard it again.

"Mr. Bannon!"

He saw her, then, lumbering heavily off the sagging steps that led downwards directly from the kitchen of a small unpainted house. She was waving one ponderous arm, bare to the elbow and red with cold, above her bonneted head. He turned and cut across the vacant lot, stepping carefully over old bottles and cans and holes where her kids had dug caves and tunnels.

"Howdy, Miz Blissett." He touched the brim of his hat and smiled into the broad and anxious face that rose almost to a level with his own. "Yo' folks all right?"

"Well, we're livin'," she said, and twisted her lips wryly, "spite o' all we can do."

[75]

"How's Gus makin' it?"

Her small and bright blue eyes nearly disappeared in her frown.

"That's what I yelled about," she said, and looked down at the ground. She rubbed her hands over her arms fast before going on. "He still ain't workin'."

Buck touched her shoulder, just barely patted it.

"Why, Miz Blissett," he said, awkwardly, "I know when a man gets hurt, he can't—"

"That ain't it," she said, quickly, and looked up at him again. "I figured you'd keep creditin' us. It's just—" She swallowed and started again. "Don't look like he'll ever be able to brake ag'in."

"Well, Ma'am," Buck started, but she broke in.

"I figured maybe you could help him get on som'ers, at a lighter job."

"I sure will, Ma'am. I'll look around today." He tipped his hat again, and started to turn away, then he stopped and his smile was smooth and his voice lowered confidentially. "By the way, Miz Blissett, Mother's feedin' whole milk to the pigs 'cause she ain't got time to churn. Wonder if you'd run up some milkin' time and kinda spell her at the churn. Reckon, if you're bakin' any cakes, she'd be proud if you'd try some o' her butter."

"Why, I sure will, son." Her eyes were getting moist.

"Thank you, Ma'am." He turned quickly and picked his way back towards the street, and when his feet found level ground he was whistling low between his teeth and looking up to see the wind whip the last tattered sycamore leaves. "Bet they haven't tasted cake in a year," he said to himself and walked faster, as if to run away from his thoughts, until he reached the sunny side of Basin Street. He stood there a moment with his hat pushed up in front, looking carefully down and across the street at a new little brick building with a glass front. It was the only glass front on the street, but other stores, new built and old, were lining up to build a solid front, not staggering like they did up near his store. He pursed his lips thoughtfully after awhile and started off again, walking as before and paying no attention to the stores. His eyes were almost closed when he met two men in overcoats, walking bent into the wind and talking too loudly.

"Damned place needs a constable," one of them said.

The other one jerked his head up and down

"Needs it, but by God, who's goin' to work for thirty a month with things as high as they are now?"

Buck stopped and stood still, thinking hard and fast, until they were almost beside him. Then he held up his hand.

"Mr. Edgar."

Both men stopped and one of them turned a wind-bitten face and a thick fleshy nose towards Buck.

"Howdy, boy," he said, and questioned him with his round veined eyes.

"I heard what you said." Buck glanced sharply at the other man, who had snorted into the collar of his coat; then he turned slightly to face down at Mr. Edgar. "I know a man'll take that job."

"Some o' your folks, boy?"

Buck shook his head.

"Gus Blissett. He got hurt brakin', and can't go back to the road, but he's well enough to walk around and check locks and things after dark."

Edgar rubbed the back of his hand across his nose and sniffed.

"Voter, I reckon?"

"He can be made one if he ain't," Buck said, softly, then let his eyes stray over Edgar's shoulder. "An' if he gets the job, he'll vote right."

"Haw!" Mr. Edgar punched the other man with a rough elbow. "Tell you what, boy," he said, "I'll do you a favor and hire your man, but there's a leetle somethin' I want."

"Shoot."

"That thirty-five-foot piece next to your store. Reckon you could let that go at a fair price?"

"What's fair?" Buck's eyes blanked.

"I'll give three-fifty." Edgar looked over Buck's shoulder. "Cash, but not a cent more."

Buck let his eyes drift down the street and linger for a moment on a pied calf being led by a small colored boy across towards the blacksmith shop. Suddenly, he turned and smiled at Edgar.

"If Papa'll let me sell, I'll work up the papers and get them to you tomorrow."

"Bargain." Edgar stuck out his hand. "Tell Blissett to drop down pretty soon and I'll get him fixed up."

"Bargain," Buck said and stood still for a moment watching them go off up the street. "By God," he whispered to himself, "if he can make a livin' here, I can get rich."

He turned and hurried down the street towards the small colored boy who was coming out of the blacksmith shop without the calf.

"Here, boy," he said, roughly gentle, "you want some banana candy?"

The boy's huge, moist brown eyes rolled, and his tongue crept out the corner of his mouth.

"Yassuh!"

Buck took a small notebook out of his pocket and held back the stiff cardboard cover with its fertilizer advertisement. He wrote as quickly as he could. "Papa, if you can buy that thirty-five feet next to us for anything less than three hundred and fifty, do it right now. It belongs to Will J. Cumbie. Give this boy five pieces banana candy. Buck."

He folded the note carefully.

"You know where Green's store is up close to the railroad? Well, take this there and don't give it to anybody but the old man with the beard. He'll give you the candy."

"Ol' man wid de beard." The boy grabbed the note and ran between two stores, his broad dust-grey bare feet ignoring nails and broken bottles. Buck sauntered back up the street, conscious of the clutching excitement that a business deal always built inside him, but trying to push back his thoughts. He focused his eyes hard on the small building with the glass front, measuring in his mind slowly along the width of the front.

" 'Bout thirty foot," he said, softly, and began to pace it off, hoping the few people on the streets wouldn't know what he was doing. He nodded and raised his hat to some ladies, smiling, and he said, "Hey," to a little girl in a coat too big for her. He paced it once, then he came back, humming softly. He stopped when he came to the eleventh step. "Thirty-three," he said, and whistled. Abruptly, as if he had made up his mind about something, he turned around, and had to catch at the wall to steady himself.

Ivy Longshore was nearly touching him she was so close, and she was laughing at him over an armful of bundles. Buck stared at her, astonished for a moment.

"You're mighty little to be runnin' over me," he said.

She glanced up at Buck's dark hairline, then quickly looked down again.

"Well, you're mighty big to be walking around in a dream," she said, and then her words mocked him. "What can young Mr. Bannon be thinking of, walking around Aven half asleep?"

Buck flushed slightly and put one hand in his pocket.

"I was—" he started, then stopped and looked at her more closely. Her mouth was long and smooth, like he'd remembered so many times and like he'd always seen it in the last five years. Now, though, the cold had whispered color into her cheeks and lips and the flush made her eyes bluer. She was smiling and her eyes were wide. She cocked her head to one side to look up at him, waiting for him to speak.

"There's no time to tell you what I was thinkin'," he said, softly. "Not now, anyhow."

She frowned and pursed her lips.

"I'm in a hurry, too," she said, and started to turn away.

"No, wait," Buck said, quickly. "I meant that I wanted to see you again. Really see you."

She tightened her lips.

"I shouldn't have stopped," she said. "I wouldn't want you to think—" She shut her lips tight again. "I shouldn't have stopped," she repeated. Her cheeks were redder.

"It wasn't just that you stopped," Buck said. "I been meanin' to—" He looked at her for a moment before he went on.

"I was comin' to see your papa this evenin'," he went on quietly. "Maybe we could talk some after my business is over." His teeth were strong and white against the dark even brown of his face.

Ivy Longshore smiled suddenly and threw her head back again. She shifted her bundles in front of her.

"I'm sure Papa will be glad to see you," she said, and turned to leave. Then she looked back.

"Better come around six," she said. "Papa'll be at the farm till then, and he goes to bed early."

Buck smiled back at her and put on his hat again.

"The earlier the better," he said. He watched her down the street, knowing from the way she held her back straight and walked without moving her shoulders, that she could feel him watching her. He was still looking when she turned out of Basin Street up towards her home. He stood for a moment, thinking, then impatiently he turned and looked back at the little building across the street.

"I wouldn't turn down either one of 'em," he said slowly.

He slapped his hand against his thigh and walked fast back towards his old store, wondering if there weren't two things of Amos Longshore's that he'd never stand a chance of getting. The girl and the new little brick building with the shiny glass front. "Pore chance," he thought, "but I'm honin' after both of 'em." He walked faster still, with his head down, thinking until he passed the house without seeing it and reached the store.

The front to his old store was shabby beside the bright windows of the picture in his mind and the paint was peeling off the two doors that were nearly wide enough to be called shutters. He rattled the door irritably as he opened it.

"Had them damned things painted two years back and here—" He broke off thinking and nodded at a large woman whose heavy cracked milking hands yearned slowly over the yard-wide length of a bolt of stiff shiny taffeta. He saw Jeff with his back to the piece-goods counter, running his eye carefully up and down the bolts, and he noticed again how the boy's forehead wrinkled trying to remember the stock. He saw again how thin Jeff's neck was under the large square-looking head. Buck started to go help him, but stopped. "Better let him find it. He'll know himself, then."

He turned quickly as if he didn't see Jeff and the woman and glanced down the length of the store.

Hearn was there, slumped low with the back of his head riding the top rung of the cane-bottomed chair, and his feet propping him against the counter in front of the stove. His hands hung loosely, straight down from his shoulders, nearly touching the floor, and they didn't move, but his lips were puckered in a whistling that had a wild-moving flavor without much noise. His feet didn't even tap like another man's would and his eyes didn't open, only his lips moved and then slightly, in and out, low and high.

Buck's eyes wrinkled at the corners. "Damned fool," he said, inside him, "already knows the stock and's got Jeff workin' for him."

His eyes went past Hearn's chair and past the stove to where he knew Joe Bannon would be. The soft flickering of light that was lost from the old heater was kind to them, but still Joe Bannon's hands showed stiff and clumsy. The fingers never seemed limber enough to curl tightly, nor strong enough to straighten completely. They rubbed slowly over and under each other, trading placidly for the spot nearest the warmth, in movements that never varied.

Buck moved nearer the stove, not making any noise, hardly knowing that his eyes were still on his father's hands, until the hands suddenly stopped their movements and were still on Joe Bannon's knees. Then Buck looked quickly into his father's face and as quickly back down to Hearn's feet, which barred the way. He smiled at his father as he stopped and swept Hearn's legs off the fender of the stove.

"Get up front," he said, trying to keep his voice harsh. "Start earnin' enough to feed you."

Hearn said, "Aaah," and stood up slowly, stretching as he rose, and yawning into Buck's face.

"Move," Buck said. He turned Hearn around with one hand on his shoulder and bumped him from behind with his knee. Hearn bent inwards with the shove and skipped two steps before he slouched towards the front of the store.

Buck looked into the eyes above his father's beard and was suddenly glad that they could still be young at times. He glanced at the stove before he spoke and blew his breath long and slow into his cupped hands.

"Whew!" he said. "Colder'n a hound's nose."

Joe Bannon nodded and his beard split a little in the middle, showing teeth that still were strong, but slightly discolored.

"Hate to be fixin' fence on that high forty back home," he said.

"God, yes," Buck said, and shivered as if his body could still remember frost gnawing through shoes and socks.

"Get my note?" he asked casually. Joe Bannon frowned slightly and nodded.

"Cumbie's goin' to drop by the house tonight, but I can't figure how come you want that land."

[81]

"Early Edgar thinks we own it," Buck said, "and offered me three-fifty." He grinned sheepishly. "I told him I'd take it if you'd let me."

The old man rubbed the palm of his hand slowly back and forth across his mouth, but Buck could see new brightness come into his eyes and knew that he was laughing inside.

They didn't say anything more for a little while, until the father leaned forward again, putting his elbows on his knees and spreading his hands out closer to the stove. Buck watched without expression as the hands once more began to run gently over and around each other, making a dry whispering that he could hear along with the sighing of water in the little iron pan and the fast-dying sputters of fire inside the stove. Buck leaned forward, too, warming his hands, and his eyes nearly closed against the heat and the light beating fitfully through the isinglass window in the stove. Then his voice came quick and somehow rough.

"Got any money, Papa?" He leaned back and watched his father.

The old man didn't look up or stop even for a second his careful attention to his hands.

"What you want?" he said, bluntly. "You know to the dollar what I've got."

Buck felt tension leave his chest and neck and he leaned forward again, wondering why he'd hesitated, why he had felt it necessary to work up to his problem. This was his father. He was grateful for the roughness that had been in Joe Bannon's voice.

"This is how I'm fixed," Buck said, simply. He stood up slowly and spread his palms upwards and told about the new little brick building with the shiny glass front. His eyes opened wide with excitement before he got through and once he drew a picture with his hands, shaping roughly in the air before them the picture he had in his mind. "Papa," he said, "it's like you know when to plant. It ain't just knowin', it's part feelin'. Well, I got that feelin'." He didn't talk long and when he finished it was like he had been interrupted, like there was something else that might be said. He sat down again, watching his father's lips move slowly and soundlessly with thought until the old man was ready to speak.

"Boy," he said, and his still-red beard stirred, "ain't we movin' a mite fast?"

Buck shook his head stubbornly.

"Watch the barbershops," he said, "they follow the money. There ain't a one left on our street."

"Well." The red beard moved again. "Just suppose we did buy it, how come it couldn't be handled like you did this store?"

"Could be," Buck said, quickly, "but I'm short of the down payment. My money's out in loans, all good ones, and I hate to shut down on a good customer, even if the loans was due, which they ain't." He paused and wrinkled his brow. "Doubt if old Longshore'd credit me, anyhow." He smiled wryly. "I paid out too fast to suit him. He figured to get this store and keep my down payment."

He was silent for a moment, waiting for his father to speak, but the old man continued to look down at his hands.

"I don't want to borrow on this store or the house," Buck went on. Then, "They're our meat and bread, in case something goes bad wrong."

Joe Bannon grunted.

"Looks like it's cash or nothin', huh?"

Buck didn't say anything and his father was quiet for a moment longer.

"Understand, boy," he said, "this is just a horseback opinion, but right offhand I figure we'd best hold on till we pile up a little higher before we spread out." He cleared his throat and began to fumble in his coat pocket for tobacco.

"You can use my money," he went on, deliberately, "because I don't figure to last long nohow. I'm thinkin' about you—and the others. So, I reckon we'll let this thing cool some before we let out what little cash we've got."

Buck's lips pulled in further at the corners and turned down slightly. He frowned.

"Hell, Papa, our ox is gettin' belly deep in the mire. And when the ox is in the mire you get him out—"

Buck stopped suddenly, watching his father's head shake slowly from side to side. Joe Bannon's eyes stayed on his son's face. Buck started to speak, but his father shook his head quicker and raised a small neat square of tobacco between his knife blade and his thumb.

"Chew?"

Buck looked at the knife and the chew and the hand that held them, his eyes still and quiet, then he shrugged and waved it away with his hand.

"Papa," he said, "you're thinkin' like a poor man."

"A feller can do that," Joe Bannon said slowly, "when he's been as poor as I've been."

Buck didn't answer. He stood up and looked carefully at the pan on the stove for a moment, then picked it up, testing the heat of its edges. He filled it, careful not to spill any, from a wooden spigot in the bottom of an old rain barrel that stood in the corner near his father. Then he placed it back on the stove and there were tiny frying sounds as a few drops splashed on the lid. Somehow he felt clumsy, as if he'd been called down in front of strangers, and more than he had in a long time he felt that his father was his father. He fumbled to find common ground again.

"You need a haircut," he said, awkwardly, his mouth onesided. "Better hunt up one of those barbershops I told you about."

His father roughed his hand up over one side of his head where the hair was thick.

"I'll go to my regular barber," he said, smiling gently.

Buck picked up his hat off the counter and stood for a moment, turning it slowly in his hands, then he pulled it firmly down on his head.

"Reckon I'll go watch One Hundred and One come in."

He started off, not swaggering, but dragging his fingers along the top of a counter towards the front of the store and didn't look back until he heard his father clear his throat.

"I know you're goin' off to figure some more," Joe Bannon called. "By God, you're stubborn as your mama."

Two hours later, Buck went up the steps to his home in two strides and hurried into the long dim hall, slamming the door behind him. He was breathing deep and slow. His face was flushed with something besides hurrying in the cold and his eyes were narrow and glittering. He glanced down the hall and into the room to his left, then swung into the parlor on his right.

Vestasia was in the parlor, propped up high in front of the piano. She had been practicing and eating an apple, but now she was just sitting and staring at Buck, chewing slowly.

"Where's Papa?" Buck said quickly, his voice strained.

Vestasia nodded her head, still chewing, and made empty motions with her hands, trying to tell Buck to wait until she could swallow.

"Aw, hell!" Buck said impatiently and started to turn. He heard a strangling sound and looked back at his sister. She was red in the face and her eyes were running with tears.

"Kitchen," she gasped, and small bits of apple flew out of her mouth. She smiled a little, coughing, but proud that she'd got it out, and took another big bite as Buck hurried down the hall.

"Papa," Buck said, as he flung into the kitchen. Then he stopped, feeling awkward again. His father was sitting on the worn bench, straddling one end, and behind him stood Jeanie Bannon, one knee on the end of the bench and one foot on the floor. She was talking as she worked, talking with something light and young in her voice, and the flourish of her hands was a part of this work and this work alone. She was cutting Joe Bannon's hair. She'd comb carefully down one side of his head, cocking her eyes to the side, then she'd slide the neat blades of her scissors under a wild patch of hair. She'd snip and the snipping would flow into a flirt of the wrist that tossed a clump of hair off the blades onto a large square of brown butcher paper. The two movements were almost one and Buck knew, from far back, that his mother was proud that only she had cut her husband's hair since their floor was clay and sand. He watched them for a moment longer, not listening to her talking, hardly seeing with his eyes, mostly feeling the picture as it was now and as it had been in the past, always the same bench, in the same position, and with his mother always talking excitedly, as if cutting Joe Bannon's hair was like camp meeting or chicken on the ground.

Buck waited impatiently, but without speaking again, until his mother sighed and took her knee off the bench and straightened her back, groaning contentedly, and stepping backwards to inspect the haircut. She looked it over carefully, then she smiled triumphantly at Buck.

"Best in town," she said, and clicked her scissors at him.

Buck laughed.

"Countriest folks I ever saw. Whyn't you go to a regular barber?"

[85]

"Hmph!" his father said, swinging one leg stiffly across the bench and sitting up straight. "Reckon I would if I could find one to beat your mama's price."

Jeanie Bannon laughed and started to sit down when Buck came over and patted her on the arm.

"Don't sit down," he said, "I got to see Papa on some private business." He winked and smiled to soften it.

His mother stooped to herd a few stray clumps of hair onto the paper shield. She sniffed.

"Don't think it worries me," she said. "I got all the secrets I wanted to hear before you were ten."

Buck waited until his mother's footsteps sounded far down the hall, then he swung back towards his father with his eyes shining and his jaw set hard.

"I just left Ed Puckett," he said. "You know him. Used to be with the railroad here. Surveyor."

Joe Bannon nodded and crossed his legs.

"I thought I recognized a fellow gettin' off the train," Buck went on. "An' Ed told me about it. This fellow's from up North and he's the one came down to buy the land for the new spurs last year."

His father frowned and started to speak, but Buck kept talking.

"He ain't workin' for the same road no more." He leaned his head back and his lips hardly moved. His eyes were hard and dark.

Joe Bannon's expression changed slowly and he eased himself down on the bench. He reached for his pocketknife and tobacco, but kept his eyes on Buck.

"Buyin' land?" he said, calmly.

Buck nodded and took one step nearer his father. He leaned over and spoke rapidly in a voice that he tried to hold low and tight to keep from shaking.

"This is what it is. He's hired Ed to do the surveyin' and he's goin' to start pickin' his route next week. He hasn't told Ed for sure which way he's headin', but the line's runnin' from Albany to join up with the road to Mobile. Naturally, they'll hit Aven. Me and Ed figured everything and there ain't but one way for him to come."

He stopped and wiped his forehead, breathing deeply, and pushed his hair back.

"He'll cross Basin Street within two blocks of the store I wanted to buy. He'll build a depot, and a freight yard, and that section of town'll grow up crazy as a plum thicket."

Buck stopped and straightened up then with a half-smiling triumph in his eyes. Joe Bannon pulled his beard carefully out to the longest strand and looked at it curiously for a moment. He looked up and nodded.

"Buy it. I got the money."

"No, sir," Buck said, quickly. "Let's go whole hog. I'll throw in my old store and the new one as collateral so I can buy it without help." He watched silently until his father nodded. "Then," he said, "you get out this afternoon and tomorrow morning and buy, quiet-like, all the ridge land you can northeast of town. They'll hunt the ridges. Don't buy anything but poor land with a good stand of timber on it. We'll sell the timber first thing, then, by God, we'll have 'em hooked. They'll condemn at a price that'll give us a profit on the land deal, then we'll have the timber sale on top of it. Buy it right into Aven long as the price is right, then we'll sit tight and let 'em come to us."

Joe Bannon stared at his son for a moment and his eyes were puzzled, not with the business, but puzzled as if he were trying to place a stranger in his memory. He laughed low.

"I'll do it," he said, and slapped his knee. "It looks like big gamblin', but I'll do it. But how come this afternoon?"

"I sent Ed off with a gallon of whiskey," Buck said. "Told him to take half of it out to Colt Peterman's place in the country, and he could have the rest. He'll be drunk for two days and won't have a chance to tell it in town. That'll give us a two-day jump on the rest."

Joe Bannon sighed and slowly got up.

"Son," he said carefully, "if I do say it myself—" He stopped, then, and just looked at Buck. He didn't say any more, just shook his head slowly.

Buck jumped up from the bench. His chest felt loose and good inside, but bigger outside, and all his muscles were strong and limber.

"I got to light a shuck. Old Longshore'll be back from the farm

[87]

pretty soon and he can smell a deal a mile off. I got to catch him 'fore he sniffs this'n."

His father said, "Hmph! That all you're goin' after?"

Buck started unbuttoning his shirt. "He's got a lot of things I want."

The old man frowned. "Mother says ever' rose's got a thorn."

Buck started through the door into the hall, towards the room they used for bathing, holding his shirt and black string tie in one hand.

"Papa," he said, "I got a right rough thumb and a man don't get hurt unless he's gentlin' a brier."

CHAPTER NINE

THERE WAS a fire in the Longshores' parlor and Buck backed up to it and spread the tails of his coat. He leaned his shoulder blades against the high mantelpiece and turned his hands slowly behind him to keep them from getting too hot on one side.

He was impatient for Amos Longshore to finish washing off the dirt of the country. Impatient with a part of his mind. The other part saw Ivy again as she had looked when she opened their front door. There had been a question dark in her eyes, as if she wondered by the looks of him what was in his mind.

Buck remembered how she had walked down the hall, seeming to sway from her shoulders down, with the promise of liveness in her slim body. And how he had felt as he watched, standing sideways in the parlor door, knowing he was to see her alone after his business was over.

Forcing himself to breathe more slowly, Buck looked around the high-ceilinged, square box of a room with curious eyes.

The open fire and the light of an oil lamp with its rose-colored glass screen laid a soft glow over the stiff, unused furniture and shadowed a few vague pictures on the walls. The light flickered in a mirror set in an old-fashioned piece of furniture. Buck didn't know what it was, but it had hooks that were meant for hats and coats. He left the fire, rubbing his hands briskly on the seat of his pants, and stood in front of the mirror. He ducked his head and leaned backwards a little to see all of himself.

He turned around quickly. The image in the mirror had grinned back at him as if it were satisfied with the long body and the wide heavy shoulders it saw. It was pleased with the effect of dim light on his dark suit and white shirt. He felt a quick rush of something like guilt as he heard Amos Longshore's short stride coming up the hall. He hurried back to the fireplace and leaned casually against the mantel again.

"Evenin', Buck," Longshore said, hurrying to the fire and bending low over it with his hands outspread. He rubbed them leisurely, as if they could taste the warmth, then pulled a small chair up close and dropped into it with a long sigh.

"I'm a pore man to be farmin'," he said, and closed his eyes. "Wish to God I could sell you that place, Buck."

Buck laughed and moved over a little so the fire wouldn't burn his pants.

"I got a bellyful o' farmin'," he said, "but if the price is right, I'll buy anything."

Longshore sighed again, this time with pleasure, and stretched his feet out close to the fire.

"Well, sir," he said, "this is one time a man wouldn't have to furnish a down payment. Damned thing's eatin' me up."

Buck was in a hurry to get down to business, but he held back. It didn't do to rush Amos Longshore. Let him ease up on it himself, if he was in a trading mood. He'd found that out in five years of business in Aven.

"Where's it lay?" he said, carelessly, and turned to face the fire.

Longshore grunted and swore as he pulled his feet away from the fire.

"Too hot," he said, then looked up. "It's, I reckon, two-three mile northeast of here, but hell, you ain't wantin' no farm. Not this 'un, anyhow. Nothin' but tie-tie's and rock ridges that'd ruin a plowshare to ever' half acre."

Buck felt the sudden pumping of blood in his temples, and he swallowed hard. He stared at a group picture of Longshore, his wife, and Ivy, on the mantelpiece and he was glad Longshore couldn't see his face. He wanted to laugh, but he held it back.

"Papa might take it," he said, carelessly. "He's got a couple sorry tenants he'd like to place."

He turned around, then, and pulled a chair up beside Longshore. He slid far down in the chair and laid his head on the back and let his hands drop down to his sides.

"You got somethin' I want, though," he said, lazily. "I'm in the humor to do some buyin'."

Longshore looked at Buck out of the corner of his eyes for a moment, then pursed his lips and spat into the fire.

"I'll sell anything," he said, and cleared his throat, "if the price is right."

Buck didn't move his head, but he glanced quickly sideways at Longshore.

"I got a kind of a rash," he said. "I figure to put a new store downtown and get some o' that silk-stockin' trade. Let the boys run Green's. I'm gettin' tired o' handlin' blue jeans." His tone was still careless, but his bottom lip began to stick out. Longshore grunted.

"My brick store," he said bluntly. "Whyn't you come out and say it?"

Buck felt all the tension leave his body. It was out now and it could fall only one way or the other. He'd done about all he could, and the rest was up to the other man. He stirred slightly in his chair and turned his head towards Longshore.

"It'll save me buildin' across the street," he said. He waited a moment. "An' you ain't never been hurt in a trade," he said.

Longshore reached out and poked the fire with a charred straight stick.

"I own the vacant lots across the street," he said slowly. "You'll take mine or none at all. At my price."

Buck groaned, then sat up.

"All right," he said, "you got a lock on me. How much?"

Longshore's mouth shut tight for a minute and he frowned at the fire. He poked it again, hard, and turned to Buck.

"Twenty-five hundred," he said.

"My God!" Buck dropped back in his chair. He lay there a moment and the impulse to say "Yes" boiled through his head. "I'd take it in a minute," he thought, "if I didn't know the old fool'd back out when I snapped at it. I can't let him think I've run under the log with it." He shook his head, slowly.

"I'll go two thousand," he said. "And that's enough profit for anybody."

Longshore spat in the fire.

"Hell, boy," he said, "you know I ain't never come off a first price. Take it or leave it. I ain't achin' to sell."

Buck was still for a long time, then he rubbed both hands across his face as if he were tired, and nodded slowly.

"I know it," he said, wryly, "you got your price and it's plenty. But I just ain't got the cash right offhand." He let the words lie out there for a moment, then turned quickly. "But what I got is out in damned good loans."

Longshore settled back in his chair. His voice was soft and sly when he spoke.

"Cash?" he said. "Why, boy, you don't need cash to deal with me. We can deal like we did on Green's store." He paused for a while and spat again. "Except that you'll have to put up Green's along with my store as collateral," he said carefully.

Buck stood up quickly and frowned down at Longshore.

"Godamighty," he said, "I ain't plumb got to open a new store." He began to walk up and down the room, taking long quick strides. Longshore watched him over his shoulder for a turn or two, then looked back into the fire. He shrugged so Buck could see him.

Buck paced the floor a few more times, watching Longshore's back, then he sat back down. He drew a deep breath and struck his fist into his palm.

"All right, dammit," he said. "I got the itch and I reckon I'll have to pay for it."

Longshore smiled dryly.

"Son," he said, "you bought a store."

"Either that or you bought a man," Buck said, and laughed. "Danged if you won't own me yet," he said, and stuck out his hand.

"Bargain," said Longshore. His hand was hot and dry when it reached Buck's. They shook, and Longshore stood up and stretched again. He yawned and clicked his teeth together.

"Boy," he said, "when you're my age won't nobody have to tell you it's bedtime. Not after a day on the farm."

Buck put both hands in his pockets and leaned back.

"Reckon that's right," he said, "but there's somethin' else I want." Longshore's eyes opened wider and he blinked.

"Miss Ivy," Buck said. "I'd kinda like to call on her a spell. An' if she's in the back I'd count it right nice if you'd tell her I'm here."

Longshore's mouth opened and shut back quickly. He didn't say anything, just looked at Buck.

Buck frowned suddenly. "That is, if you ain't got nothin' against it."

Longshore looked puzzled. "Nothin'," he said. "No. I got nothin' against it." He clicked his teeth absently. "Maybe she has, though," he said, abruptly, and looked up at Buck with a question in his eyes.

"Maybe," Buck said, and waited.

Longshore fidgeted. "She might not be here."

Buck shook his head slowly. "She's back there. She let me in."

Longshore shrugged, as if he were suddenly too sleepy to worry about it any longer, and turned to go.

"Uh, Mr. Longshore," Buck stopped him at the door, "I'll tell Papa to see you tomorrow, too. Maybe he'd take a fancy to that little rock farm o' yore's."

Longshore's eyes brightened. He nodded. "G'night," he said.

She was there almost before Buck knew it, her step was so soft in the hall. She was standing in the doorway, looking at Buck and smiling as if there were a secret joke inside of her, and he was still flushed with the heady feeling that always followed when he'd gambled and won. He tried to bow, but it was more of a nod, and he was watching her mouth all the time.

"Good evenin'," he said, and moved to give her room at the fireplace.

She nodded but didn't say anything, just came into the room with slow steps that barely moved the hem of her long dark-blue dress. Buck stared at her, watching the glimmer of firelight on heavy silk.

"When you walk, it looks like you ain't got legs," he said, suddenly, and then looked surprised that he had said it.

She drew a quick breath and her eyes opened wide.

"Mr. Bannon," she said, "I assure you that I have limbs." She waited a moment and her mouth set tightly. "Two," she said firmly, and turned towards the fire, not looking at him.

"That's fine," he said, and bent lower to see if she would smile. "I'm glad to hear it," he said, and watched the slow creep of laughter playing about the corners of her mouth. Then he leaned back his head and laughed out loud. She turned to face him and Buck was glad to see the corners of her eyes crinkle. She bit her bottom lip to stop laughing.

"Silly, isn't it?" she said, and took the chair Buck held for her. She looked at him seriously. Then, "But that's how they teach you to walk at boarding school," she said. She stood up again, quickly, and looked backwards and down at him.

"This is how we sit down," she said. She held her hands clasped in front, and slowly sat back down in the chair, holding her back straight with no sign of strain.

Buck rubbed his chin with his hand and looked at the floor.

"Pretty good sittin'," he said, seriously. Then he cocked his head to one side and looked down at her with eyes that were dark and glinting in the firelight.

"I don't reckon you could do anything that wasn't pretty," he said, and felt his face flush. "To me, anyhow," he added quickly.

INTERLUDE

BASCOM WOOTEN *sat in the sun on an old apple crate which he had propped against the warped weatherboarding of Dean's livery stable. Over his head a wooden sign creaked a guilty message in the chill wind—"Tolerable Fair Mule Dealing." Because it was early Sunday afternoon, his stomach was full and he wore his only suit, and because it was working on towards winter, he was glad his coat was heavy.*

He was so comfortable, he was almost sorry to see Jake Willis coming slowly towards him, scuffing up the dust of the road with his best shoes. Bascom pushed away from the wall with his shoulders and stood up, groaning and yawning, as Jake went silently to the huge padlock on the front door with a key in his hand.

"What's eatin' you?" Bascom asked as Jake threw the sliding door into motion down its track.

"Nothin'." Jake suddenly stamped his feet hard on the wide floorboards, then listened with his head turned to the side. "Damned rats in the corncrib eat more'n the mules." He led Bascom down the long corridor between the stalls, talking as he went. "Nothin' wrong at all. Old Buck's give me a chance and, by God, I'm a'goin' to stick with it."

"What chance has Buck give you?"

Jake opened the half door into one stall.

"He got me this job 'cause him and old man Dean got to be big political buddies and he says if I'll pay him half my salary ever' week, he won't charge no more interest."

"Cain't even miss one week?"

"Nair one," Jake said, positively, and started leading a horse out of the stall. He looked suspiciously at Bascom. "How come?"

Bascom shrugged. "Nothin' much. I just figured— Hell, reason I needed this rig so bad, I got a gal staked out close to Gordon an' she's got a visitor."

Jake shook his head violently and started leading the horse towards the first of three buggies lined up at the rear of the stable.

"Nossir. After I get my watch back, I'm goin' to line up a row of 'em an' work my way down it, but not until—"

Bascom's eyes were outraged, glaring at Jake.

"These girls don't charge."

Jake leered over the horse's back.

"Kinfolks?"

Bascom grinned. "Go to hell." He rubbed his hand over the horse's rump. "Shore wish you'd go," he said, wistfully. "Buck's mighty busy these days, hisself, with old man Longshore's girl."

Jake looked shocked. "He ain't after that. Way he dresses up you can see he's out to marry."

Bascom got up into the buggy. "Durned if I see how he's got time to marry, messin' with ever'thing in town. Politics, now."

Jake started leading the horse out of the stable.

"Won't hurt, though," he said over his shoulder, "for me an' you to have a friend in politics that's got more sense'n we got."

"I reckon." Bascom caught up the reins as they went out into the sunlight and looked down at Jake. "Well, boy," he said, heavily, "I got to run by an' pick up a jug I got hid out an' get goin'."

Jake wet his lips.

"Wait'll I lock up," he said, in a thoughtful voice. "I'll ride a ways."

Bascom flicked the reins as Jake settled into the seat beside him. He chuckled.

"That gal's always got a sweet shrub tied in the corner of a handkerchief. Rubs her face with it."

"Dogbite it!" Jake stomped the floor board. "I always did love a sweet-smellin' woman."

Bascom glanced at him out of the corner of his eyes, then he pulled the lines hard to the right.

"Git, horse," he said. "Eight mile to Gordon."

CHAPTER TEN

In less than a year, the new railroad had burrowed its blunt nose over the hills and hollows northeast of Aven, and on through town. Its construction crew had appeared briefly on Basin Street, a shouting, brawling, drunken, working, heaving spider with many heads, and then gone on, dragging behind a straight and shining web of steel. Every day now, bigger and blacker engines brought ties and rails and spikes to throw out in front for a new railhead.

Every day now Buck's new store windows would rattle faintly with the jar of the passing trains, and as surely Buck would weigh the stock on the shelves against the cash in the drawer, then nod in satisfaction. It felt good to be twenty-seven and already a man to be reckoned with in his own town, with his own two stores, and his own growing loan business. It felt good to be all of that, but it had its drawbacks.

Buck thought of those drawbacks as he carefully counted the change in the shallow-cupped wooden money drawer and smoothed straight the wrinkled bills underneath. He frowned as he stuffed the day's receipts into a small paper bag and moved slowly towards the darkening front of his store. Somehow in him there was growing a kind of burning that was part restlessness and part being a year older, but mostly was a vague feeling that he was wasting something.

"I got money," he turned the key in the heavy front door, dropped it in his coat pocket, and leaned back against the door facing the street, "but I reckon a man's still poor if he ain't got nothin' but money. Wonder if a man's a fool to try to pile it up. Lay up nights figurin' how to make it and then lay up some more wonderin' what to buy with it. Reckon that's damned foolishness?"

He shook his head quickly and took the sack out of his pocket and looked at it, squeezing it in his hand.

"No, it'd be crazy not to make it. Money's the yardstick. Don't make no difference if you do have to throw it away on a couple o' half-grown— No, I don't reckon it's throwed away. Jeff's shapin' up right well, slow, an' maybe a mite too careful. Hearn? Hunh! Don't reckon he'll ever cut too wide a furrow, the lazy hound, but damned if it ain't worth it just to have the fool around, jokin' an' whistlin' an' makin' friends.

"Even if it wasn't spent at all, though, it's good to make it. Just ownin' it can put you where you're goin'."

He slowly put the sack back in his pocket and patted it through his coat.

"It ought to be used, though," he said to himself. "Ain't no reason for a man sourin' up and livin' like his money was boss. Money's a thing to be worked like a hired hand. It's that and it's a crop, a green thing that'll grow like hell if it's planted and make a mighty pretty stand if it's tended."

Buck took off his hat and rubbed the back of his head against the door as he looked out on the streets of Aven with a queer kind of dissatisfaction in his eyes.

"Change of weather," he said. "Change of weather'll get me to doin' this. Thinkin' and talkin' to myself! Mostly, it's hard for me to tell even Papa what's eatin' me. Damn!"

Change of weather! Buck laughed softly.

"That'n a woman, too, if I was honest. That girl's got me to where I don't know if I'm buyin' beef or beans."

He rubbed his back impatiently against the door, impatient as if he wanted to think of something else, and he frowned out onto the street. He was standing that way still, making soundless shapes with his lips, when he heard a foot scrape on the dirt beside him. He turned quickly, and looked down in the gloom at a short thin man of about his own age, a man with very bright brown eyes that sank down in a bed of wrinkles when he laughed. Buck's own eyes crinkled at the corners, remembering the times he had sold "Stylish" George Brown the high stiff collars that had named him.

Stylish George jerked his thumb suggestively towards the street.

"Figurin' to put another store in the middle of it?" His voice was held down tight and tough, low in his throat.

Buck laughed.

"Got enough troubles with drunks now, without you drivin' a mare through my store."

George hooked his thumbs in the top of his pants and screwed his neck around in the collar.

"I don't take much while I'm workin'."

"Hmph!" Buck looked down at George. "What kind of work do you do? I see you around, prancin' like a stud horse with a diamond in his halter, but I never saw you hit a lick."

George's teeth showed white and small in his neat dark face.

"I use my head," he said, and made shuffling signs, fast, with hands that had no lost motion in their movements. "Peepin' at the hole card."

"Oh!" Buck said. "Gamblin'?"

George shook his head and smiled tightly.

"Not gamblin'," he said. "Poker. Stud or draw."

"Ain't it gamblin' the way you play it?" Buck said, cocking his head down at George.

"Don't get me wrong," George said. "I just take the breaks, I don't make 'em. Not in the comp'ny I play with."

Buck's eyebrows rose. "Reckon it ain't gamblin' with them either," he said.

George Brown shook his head. "Business." He caught Buck by the arm again. "Come on up an' watch a hand or two. Maybe take a drink. It's over McPherson's where we play. Private room with a colored boy in a white coat."

Buck looked at George with a quirk on his lips.

"Might as well," he said. "Supper's been an' gone at home."

The stairway ran up on the outside of McPherson's Saloon. It was too steep and it creaked beneath Buck's weight as he felt his way cautiously along behind Stylish George's practiced steps. The small landing at the top led into a square and barely furnished room with a fireplace that was littered with cold cigar butts and half-black curled match stems.

There was an old dining table in the center of the room and two of its corners bore large oil lamps. Around the table were four men. Their eyes blinked as they looked up to see who was coming in.

Buck knew three of them. Coot Harper was thick and shorter than Buck, and his stubby fingers, when they weren't dealing, played nervously around his blunt chin. Harper didn't do any regular work.

[98]

Buck flushed slightly when he recognized Joe Manheim. It was queer to see him there. Manheim was a small slim Jewish merchant, whose store was two doors down from Buck's. His face was dark and his lips looked damp and red even in the dimness back of the lanterns.

Charlie Factor was smaller than Stylish George and already his face was settling into an approach to old age, although he was little older than Buck. He sold furniture, and when it was necessary in the community, he made coffins.

The fourth man sat very still when the others began to move their chairs around. He glanced quickly, without moving his face at all, from Buck to George, and then back at Coot Harper.

Harper caught his eye and leaned back. He jerked his thumb at the stranger.

"Tobe Parody," he said, talking around a cigar. "Friend o' mine. Buck Bannon's the tall one and George Brown's the runt." He laughed loudly. "Stylish George," he said, and hitched his chair around some more. "Used to plow in a high collar," he said.

Buck waited until the stranger stood up, then walked over and held out his hand.

"Parody?" he said. "Was that it?"

Tobe Parody was a tall man, taller than Buck, but he was built leanly, lacking the thickness that Buck was showing in the chest. His shoulders sloped down so that their width was almost hidden and his arms were long and seemed to be weighted at the ends with hands that were huge. His face was large, lumpy around the cheekbones, and his chin was so square it looked as if it had two separate bones jutting out, barely covered with flesh, and split by a deep cleft. His eyes were small, but they were friendly as he held out his hand with an awkward lifelessness that seemed to spring from fear of his own strength.

"Some o' my folks was French," he said, almost shyly, and then he grinned broadly. "An' some was as Irish as yours." Buck liked the big man as he moved over closer and pulled up a chair for him.

"George," he said, "see if you can't get me that drink you promised me, an' get the others what they want."

George almost skipped as he went to one corner of the room and reached down.

"Makes no difference what you want," he said, "corn's what you'll get."

He jerked several times on a string that led from a chair leg, where it was tied, down through a small hole in the floor. A bell jingled faintly down below.

George rubbed his hands as he came back to the table.

"Buck's as green as hell," he said, briskly. "But there ain't no better place to learn."

Buck looked around the table slowly.

"If you all don't mind," he said. "If I get to holdin' things up, I can get out."

Manheim shook his head and started to speak, but Harper broke in. "Hell, no," he said, and his mouth split in a heavy-lipped smile. "Glad to oblige."

Tobe Parody's mouth didn't smile, but his eyes did as he looked at Buck.

"Here," he said, "I'll run you through a hand or two while the drinks are comin' up. Then maybe you won't have to pay so much to learn."

Heavy footsteps were on the landing outside by the time Buck had learned that watching the other man's cards in stud poker was as important as knowing his own.

He knew enough to ride free as long as he could, by the time the colored waiter had scooped up the change he'd thrown on the table, and his drink was still burning in his throat when Coot Harper laughed and dragged in a small pot that he'd won on nothing but high cards and a mournful, twitching face.

From the crowding hurry of blood through his chest Buck knew that gambling was a good thing for him, that the smallest pot was as important to him as the largest, and that he'd finally found the tolling power that would whisper him away from his work. The shaking excitement had foamed off and left a slow-burning tenseness by the time he'd learned that he could choose draw or stud or Western if it were his deal. His fingers lost their clumsiness. He watched the others. Even when he had dropped out of a pot with bad cards, he watched the others. He saw Charlie Factor hold on until the last card, drawing to the pair he had backed up, then fade like a rose before the single quick, casual, blunt and efficient bet of Joe Manheim.

He was casual, too, and outwardly as calm as a setting hen when he shoved a bill into the pot a few minutes later and said in a crisp voice, "Cost you ten to see."

His face didn't change, but his eyes flickered, as Charlie Factor studied his hole card, then carefully folded his hand over and slid it into the discard. He turned his head to the side as he drew in the pot, trying to keep the others from seeing his eyes.

Stylish George laughed out loud and rang for the waiter.

"By God," he said, "Buck's lost forty dollars to win ten and it's about tickled him to death."

Buck looked up at him with his eyes darkening for a second. His eyebrows drew together and he looked puzzled, then his face relaxed and he laughed with them.

"Damned if I didn't forget the money," he said. "All I wanted to do was win."

Tobe Parody smiled at him. "I know that feelin'," he said.

The bar was closed for the night when Buck won his second pot, but the excitement of waiting and watching and grunting to make the right card fall was still mounting, and his eyes were too bright, flickering around with the dealer's hands. A feeling of cold recklessness spread inside him when he waited for the last bet and the turn of the bottom card. It made him forget losses and everything else to see the bright spots fall to suit him. It made him say, "Who gives a damn?" when Parody laid a hand on his shoulder and reminded him that he'd gone into his sack for the fourth time. "Next hand," the whispering inside would say, "next hand and I'll drag it all back." There was always another hand and another card to draw, until the last hand.

Buck drew to his last hand with the same quickening brightness he'd felt since he'd first bought into the game.

"Stud," Coot Harper had said, blinking fast in the smoky room, and his fingers had flicked cards from his left hand in a swooping movement that seemed to suck a card from the deck and turn it upside down in mid-air.

Buck glanced at his hole card quickly and then his eyes went back to Harper's fingers. They were something to watch in spite of their hairy-backed bluntness, moving as if they had eyes in the tips and touching the cards as if they loved them.

Buck had treys back to back on the first two cards and on the fourth card he had a pair of them showing. Charlie Factor ran out on the third card when Buck raised Harper's bet. Manheim shrugged and gently turned his cards over on Buck's next bet when the pair showed. Tobe Parody and Stylish George flicked their cards into the center of the table when Harper raised Buck and faced another raise.

As the bets mounted, Parody sat up higher in his seat to glance at Harper's cards. Harper was looking straight ahead, at nothing in particular, but his right hand tapped in a rhythmic, horse-racing ripple from little finger to forefinger over two queens and a ten showing. His mouth jerked a little at one corner and he covered it by quickly shoving his cigar into his lips.

Buck saw the quiver of Harper's mouth and a bright exulting feeling grew inside him. He knew, then. "That's what he did when he ran me out with high cards," he thought. "He shore as hell ain't got but two o' them queens an' I can beat two pair."

He suddenly tossed out another bill.

"Up twenty," he said, and felt the coldness grow inside as he heard without looking around the sudden surprised murmur from the others at the table.

Charlie Factor said, "Damn. Too rich for my blood."

Stylish George grunted. "Biggest coon walks just 'fore dawn."

Harper didn't look up, he just rippled his fingers and worried his cigar, while Buck sat very still hoping Harper would raise, so he could raise again.

Harper didn't raise.

"See you," he said, and pulled Buck's twenty from the pile. "I'm shy," he said, then he looked around the table as if all of them were still in the hand.

"Pot right?"

Buck nodded and clenched his teeth and his eyes flicked to his cards as a king floated over the table. No help. Then they swept back across the table to Harper's live fingers. Buck frowned as the card was sucked out and turned right side up on Harper's pile. The movement had been blurred a little, the fingers had made an unnecessary movement, and the card had hesitated a fraction too long. And it was another queen. Buck felt something crowding his throat.

"Wait a minute," he said, and his voice sounded hoarse in the silence. "Hold the deal."

"Deal's over," Harper said, taking his cigar out of his mouth and rolling it gently in his fingers. "I'm high," he said, and reached out to drag another bill from the pot. "Bet twenty."

Buck reached out, too, and held his hand over the pot and looked at Harper's eyes for a long moment. He shook his head slowly.

"I'm raw at this game," he said slowly, "but somebody better tell me quick if it's good poker to pull a card off the bottom."

Harper didn't change expression. He still rolled his cigar.

"What the hell?" he said, and he couldn't hold his voice as steady as his face. "A card's a card, no matter where it comes from."

Buck let his hand drop on the pot and just looked at Harper. Harper shook his head.

"Not that I'm admittin' that card came from the bottom," he said. "That's still my pot." He sat very still.

Buck looked at Charlie Factor without moving his head.

"You see it?" he said. Factor didn't speak. Buck looked at George Brown, then at Manheim, and neither of them spoke or moved. Buck turned to Parody.

"You?" he said, and lifted his eyebrows and waited.

Parody looked at Buck for what seemed a long time, then he looked around the table at each man until his eyes came to Harper. They studied Harper for a while, calmly, then they began to grow smaller until they were almost hidden. Finally, they switched back to Buck.

"I saw it," he said, and nodded. Manheim's chair scraped on the floor as Parody spoke, and they all stood up but Buck and Harper. Parody picked up one lamp and Brown grabbed the other. They held them still and high. Harper's mouth was shaking a little at the corners and he swallowed, still looking at Buck.

Buck glanced quickly at Parody, then back at Harper.

"What'll I do?" he said, quietly, and let his hand fall on the pot.

Parody shook his head.

"Nothin'," he said, softly. "Reckon he won't be aroun' much longer no matter what you do."

[103]

Buck looked back at Harper but didn't say anything. Harper watched Buck's eyes for a second, then he glanced quickly from one to the other of the men standing around. His fingers rolled the cigar faster and faster and his mouth twitched beyond control. The cigar suddenly crumbled in his hand with a soft dry sound and it was as if something had finally snapped in the room.

Harper jumped to his feet and his lips shook loosely. His voice was shrill when he spoke.

"By God," he said, "he can set there an' stare at me, but it ain't no worse'n he does ever' day. Rob a man, by God, and bed his daughter on top of it." He stopped then, suddenly, as if he wished he could get the words back, and his right hand slid slowly towards his pocket. He was watching Buck with staring eyes.

Buck was on his feet and leaning far across the table in a movement that seemed slow and studied to the part of his mind that watched, detached, while his instincts made him move faster than he ever had before.

Buck grabbed the front of Harper's shirt and jerked him face down across the table. His left hand went out in time to catch Harper's right wrist as it shook the blade out of a spring-backed knife. Buck's mind seemed to have stopped with the last words he had heard. There was no conscious thought, only a dull kind of wondering feeling, as he twisted Harper's arm up behind him. He held Harper down with his right hand on his neck. He pulled up on Harper's knife hand. There was a sudden flush of something like bull pride in his strength, as he felt resistance slowly lessen in the thick arm. There was no time and no sound in the room as he twisted the arm, carefully, almost in a way that he might have figured out before, up over Harper's shoulder blade. Then the man on the table began to writhe and yell hoarsely, face down into the pile of money and cards. Time began again when Buck heard the sudden dry snap of bone and felt Harper go limp beneath his hands. He stared at the stubby, bloodless hand, twisted so awkwardly up over the shoulder, and at the knife that barely hung in the fingers. Then he looked up at the men around him.

"He still won't drop it," he said, and his voice sounded stupid to his own ears.

Parody breathed deeply and slowly reached over. He shook Buck's hand loose from Harper's arm, and the knife fell out.

"He couldn't turn it loose," he said, softly, "long as you had him that way."

Buck looked at him, dully, then turned back to Manheim and the others. He breathed fast and jerkily.

"What he said was a lie," Buck said shakily. "I'll kill a man for sayin' that. I may not do it this way, but I'll kill a man for sayin' that."

Charlie Factor's voice croaked.

"Got to go," he said, "got to go. Open up." He started out, but Buck stopped him.

"We was scrappin' over that card," he said, watching Factor's eyes.

"Hell, man," Factor said, "I didn't hear anything else." He glared at Buck for a moment as if to ask what else he could have heard, then he went ahead of Manheim and Brown out onto the landing.

Tobe Parody stayed behind. He watched Buck curiously while he got his hat off the wall peg, but he didn't say anything until Buck started to leave.

"Ain't you goin' to get your money?" he said, nodding towards the table where Harper lay, breathing long, shuddering breaths.

Buck didn't answer. He went over to the table and pulled Harper high enough, with one hand, to scoop the money out from under him with the other. He didn't count, just crammed it in his pocket, and let Harper fall back on the table with a groan.

"Ready?" Buck asked. Parody nodded. They blew out the lamps and closed the door carefully behind them. They were on the street before Buck spoke.

"Good friend o' yours?" he said.

Parody shook his head.

"Was," he said, "but I hadn't seen him in a couple o' years."

Buck faced Parody and the moon rode over his shoulder and lighted up the face in front of him.

"Got any objections to what I did?" he said, softly.

Parody shook his head soberly.

"Nope," he said quickly, "I got a feelin' we downright gee on that matter."

Buck touched Parody on the shoulder.

[105]

"Stick around," he said, "reckon we can gee on some other matters, too."

They finished out the night in Buck's store, Parody on the piece-goods counter and Buck stretched out on a long bench.

Buck's mind swirled. "Don't reckon I could have done that if I hadn't—" His thoughts broke off for a second and then he spoke softly up at the ceiling, "Damn, I been wonderin' what it felt like to be in love."

CHAPTER ELEVEN

SUMMER LAY like a bright yellow gauze over all of Aven and up on Rose Hill the sun dappled the shiny flanks of Buck's horse with a pattern of shadows shaped like the leaves of the sycamore above them. Now and then the horse would jerk its head irritably, mouthing a tough weed, but otherwise it didn't move. The lines were looped around the whip socket.

Stiff leather creaked beneath Buck's weight as he shifted in the buggy seat and the springs whined gratefully as he stood up on the floor board. The buggy lurched and Ivy caught at his arm.

"Whoa," she said, "you're rocking the boat." Then she crowded over as far as she could on the seat.

Buck looked down at her.

"I don't like coats," he said. "I don't want anything binding me." He had to twist his body to get the sleeves started down over his arms. His face grew a little red. There wasn't enough room in the buggy, even with him standing up. When he got his coat off, Buck breathed deeply, smiling at Ivy, and laid it on the seat between them.

She picked up his coat and folded it neatly and held it on her lap. She shook her head.

"You're a big man," she said. "Too big."

Buck sat down again.

"Too big?" he said, and reached over and took his coat out of her lap. "Too big for what?"

Ivy laughed and Buck watched the lacework of shadows and sun on her throat when her head went back.

"Too big to fit in a house," she said. "Too big to take to box suppers. Too big to sit in a church pew. And way too big to be taking off your coat in a buggy."

Buck didn't answer. He was watching her lips and trying to read the little plays in her eyes. He saw a small bluish vein throb in her throat as she laughed, and he bent his head to look for another one. She stopped laughing then and just looked at Buck. His eyes left her throat and wandered up until they met hers. She looked down quickly at her lap, then over to his, where the coat lay. She reached over and pulled it into her lap again.

"I'll hold it," she said. She sat very still a moment. "I'll hold it," she said again, louder this time.

Buck watched her face, curiously, for a minute, then glanced down at his coat in her lap. She was looking straight ahead and her face was expressionless, but her hands had gathered up large folds of his coat and they held it still and tightly.

Buck's breathing was ragged. He tried to swallow and breathe slower. Then he reached out and caught both of her wrists in his hand and just held them.

"You'll be hot, holdin' it," he said, softly.

Ivy turned quickly towards him and her eyes were almost angry.

"I like to hold it," she said, and her lower lip trembled. She sat up straight.

Buck tightened his grip on her wrists. He pulled her hands away from the coat and looked at them. They were pale and they curled as if she were asleep and had no strength in them. Buck suddenly put them to his face. They were cool and soft and there was perfume on her wrists. He held them to his face a long time, then looked up at Ivy.

"How long have you been knowin' I'm in love with you?" he said.

Ivy leaned back against the cushions and her eyes closed. When she opened them again, they seemed larger and bluer. She didn't look at Buck when she spoke.

"What makes you—?" She stopped talking then and looked down at her hands, still held in Buck's.

Buck slowly put them back into her lap. He cupped her chin in one palm and turned her face up. He leaned over and kissed her softly on the corner of her mouth. Then he took her face in both hands, with his fingers spreading in the hair at her temples, and he kissed the other corner. He turned her face between his hands slowly and his lips moved wonderingly from her mouth to the little hollow below her ear, then back to her mouth.

He held his head back and looked at her. She was very still and her eyes were closed. Her lips were open a little and they moved without sound. Buck watched the vein in her temple as he let his hands drop from her face, then he felt her hand touch his side and come up until it was on his back, and now on his shoulder. Then, suddenly, she opened her eyes and looked at him. She closed them again, quickly, and her mouth trembled as she moved her head from side to side in a gentle searching for his lips.

Dimly, Buck heard the sounds of Aven in the distance. Then time died and the light wind laughed through the sycamore and the things that live in trees moved and made noises, but they didn't hear anything.

The sudden urgent stamping of the horse and the jingle of harness metal shook time awake, and Buck looked up as he heard faint voices around the bend. He didn't see anything, so he turned to Ivy again. Small white lines went out and down from the corner of his mouth. He caught her to him, quickly, almost roughly and there was nothing gentle in his kiss. There was pain in it. Buck's lips moved over hers and he felt the sudden giving in of her body as it moved closer and molded tightly against him. He strained her body to his, wanting every part of him to touch every part of her, and aching somehow to get her so close that she would be within him.

Then Ivy began to turn her head from side to side to free her lips and she made little mouthing sounds against his lips. She held her hand for a moment, light against his cheek, then pushed him and gasped, and turned her lips away.

"No," she said, "no," and she didn't look at his face when she caught his hands and pulled them away from her body. "No," she said again, and her voice was tight and strained.

Buck's breathing was long and he tried to make it slow but there was a shakiness in it and he clenched his teeth and tightened the muscles in his throat to ease his breath. He moved away from Ivy then, and shook his head hard and didn't say anything.

"A man tastes like he smells," Ivy said, and her voice couldn't be still.

Buck frowned. "A man?" he said, trying to make his words light.

She sat up straight and pushed her shoulder blades hard against the cushions. "You," she said, "just you."

Buck started to touch her again, but the wind turned and brought low voices through the tie-tie that was so choked with laurel they couldn't see around the bend. Buck gathered up the lines and clucked and when they passed the other buggy, he and

Ivy nodded as if they were bowing and he said, "Hot, ain't it?" The man in the other buggy said, "Middlin'."

They were riding slow and calm when Buck drove past the Longshore home and down into the new part of town, the edge where homes were springing up close to the business district. He drove slowly, most of the time just looking out and seeing the land and the houses with a comfortable certainty that he was a part of this place and that it was a part of him. They stopped under a chinaberry tree in full bloom and Ivy looked up into the branches and breathed deeply, trying to suck into herself more of the heavy sweetish odor.

"Hmm," she said, "I don't know whether I like them or not."

"Well," he said, "if you don't know about the tree, what about the lots?"

Ivy looked at the lots.

"Just dirt," she said, like teasing.

Buck dropped his reins and frowned at her.

"Just dirt. Just dirt, by the Lord, and I'm seein' there a white house with a low fence around it and some flowers around ever' brick pillar. An' smoke comin' out the kitchen chimney. Just dirt."

"Huh," Ivy said. "So, we're married now, and I'm cooking."

"Well, if we ain't," Buck said, "we pretty near are. I'll give you from now until I kiss you, right in front of God'n ever'body, to set a day."

He leaned closer and took her chin in his hand. Ivy tried to pull her chin loose, but he held it tighter. She closed her eyes as he came nearer and then she said, weakly:

"September the first."

Buck suddenly turned her chin loose.

"My God," he said, "I'm goin' to get married."

Ivy laughed, then quickly the laugh ended and she frowned. She faced Buck, sitting up with her shoulders high.

"Papa," she said, slowly. "Papa doesn't—Buck, you ought to know this before— He's thinking of me, but he says you drink too much, you gamble too much, and you—" She stopped for a second, then rushed on. "There are other things," she said, "mostly the things that *we* only think about."

Buck was still for a moment, then he nodded.

[110]

"I'm all of that," he said and he set his jaw. "And I'm a man that don't change. But if you're in love with the kind of a man I am now, by the Lord, I ain't goin' to change." He slapped the buggy seat. "I'm somethin' else, too," he said. "I'm the man that's marryin' you September the first and there ain't but one livin' soul that can stop me."

Ivy looked at him.

"An' that's you," he said, and breathed shallow. "By God!"

Ivy swallowed. She opened her mouth to speak, then closed it again and cocked her head on one side.

"Well, sir," she said, matter-of-factly, "after that I'd marry you if I didn't want to, just to keep somebody else from getting you."

CHAPTER TWELVE

They were married four weeks later, in the afternoon—married by old Sime Acree, who could make his tongue sweet for Sundays after driving a wagon six days a week for the express company, whose mules demanded a gamy flavor to his words.

In spite of old Sime's sugared tones, though, and in spite of the late summer flowers that banked the fireplace of the Longshore parlor, Buck was conscious of the steady hate of Ivy's father. Even with his mind on the words of the ceremony and with his eyes on Preacher Acree's plushy lips, something in him felt the uneasiness in the room, and knew that it fed out from the dry, expressionless little man who stood perfectly still and looked out the window. And he didn't wonder any more why Ivy had insisted on such a simple wedding.

"Just family," she had said, but he had tightened the muscles in his jaw. "Tobe's got to be there." Her eyes had veiled stubbornly but briefly and Tobe had been invited. In his mind, he could see them again, Tobe, Joe and Jeanie Bannon, how they had drifted together before the ceremony began and stationed themselves across the room from Amos and Mrs. Longshore. As always, Buck had been surprised at sight of Ivy's mother, so big and bony and strong, yet so meek to follow every mood of her husband.

He could know that they were there, and a part of his mind could lie heavy with the rebel thought: "All the weddin's I ever saw, folks sang an' laughed, an' some got drunk, an' they had a good time, even the old ladies that cried." Then, deliberately, he would fill his mind with Ivy like a tired man would suck his lungs full of air. "It's not her. It's that old bastard daddy of hers. She's happy."

And he'd look down at her beside him—Ivy in a light-blue dress that fell simply from a belted waist high under her breasts to her shoe tops—Ivy with her full lips parted a little and her eyes half closed, answering without hesitation as a child might who had learned its lesson well. Then a sure confidence would come flooding back and he could tell himself that it would be over in a few more words from Sime Acree, and they would be on their way to the new little house.

Then, suddenly, it was finished and he was kissing Ivy. Her lips were sweet and promising, and the only other thought working in his mind was to hurry.

"Well, boy," Joe Bannon said, when Buck turned away from Ivy, "now you just remember, it's rough going at first and might get hard to take towards the end, but marriage is shore worth it in the middle." He stepped closer to Ivy and looked down at her for a moment, with his eyes softening, then he stooped and spoke with his red beard close to her ear. "I gentled his mammy, but he might take a curb." Ivy hugged him quickly and kissed his cheek. "I'll call on you if I need help," she said, and held her hand out to Jeanie Bannon, who had moved silently up beside them.

Buck's mother took the girl's hand and came closer. She held her cheek against Ivy's and said, softly, "You'll be happy. He won't take drivin', though. You'll have to toll him."

"Thank you, ma'am," Ivy said, and then Joe Bannon caught his wife by her arm. His other hand, hard and clumsy, fumbled at Buck's shoulder. "We better get goin' or the young'uns'll have cat hairs in the butter."

Jeanie Bannon said, "Wait a minute," and tiptoed so her lips would reach Buck's ear. "Better eat breakfast with us tomorrow." Buck winked at her and his mother blushed. "Maybe," he said, and turned back towards Ivy.

She was standing very still and straight, looking up into her father's face. Suddenly there was no sound in the room. Buck was conscious that his mother and father were uncomfortable, but he couldn't turn to them. He watched Amos Longshore lay a hand on each of Ivy's shoulders, staring down at her, and saw the thin lips move soundlessly, then clamp tight again. Longshore pulled his eyes away from Ivy's face and turned to face Buck's mother and father. His mouth smiled as he bent slightly at the waist, but Buck could see the muscles ridging his temples, as he spoke to the Bannons.

"I'm glad you could come." He nodded stiffly to Tobe and to old Sime Acree, who had drawn away from the family groups over near the windows, then he walked out with his shoulders held high and straight. Mrs. Longshore made a small sound in her throat and went past Buck with her eyes on the door as if her husband could still be seen. She let her hand trail down Ivy's arm and squeezed her fingers, then she walked on to the door and looked down the long hall after Longshore. For a second, she seemed undecided, then she faced back around.

"You all come to visit with us again," she said, in a curiously soft voice. Without waiting for an answer, she went on out of sight down the hall.

For a moment, the silence that followed Mrs. Longshore's footsteps thickened in Buck's ears, then gratefully he heard old Sime Acree clear his throat.

"Thank ye, Tobe," the preacher said, and bustled up to kiss Ivy on the cheek. "You got a good boy." He caught Buck's hand. "Shame the farmers are layin' by, youngster. They'll be crowdin' your store so you cain't run home right quick."

Buck felt blood come to his face and he saw Ivy turn her head quickly away.

"Look out, there, Sime." Tobe's voice was slow and lazy. "You ain't talkin' like Sunday."

Preacher Acree clapped a huge hand over his mouth and his eyes bulged. He grabbed Joe Bannon by the arm. "Let's go, Joe. That boy's right. God don't love ugly and I got to get home and feed the mules to mortify my flesh."

Buck felt Ivy's hand touch his arm as his mother and father walked out with the preacher. He turned to find her looking up at him with something begging in her eyes. "I'm sorry about—" She stopped and looked down. "I'm going back to see them for a minute," she went on, in a low voice.

Buck knew Tobe was watching him as Ivy went quickly into the hall. Somehow, he didn't want to look around at Tobe. The feeling that came over him was new. He didn't know what it was, but something made him avoid meeting Tobe's eyes as he roughly said, "Let's get out o' here," and left the room. He could hear Tobe following as he picked up Ivy's small handbag from beside the front door and carried it out onto the front porch. He was pushing the bag under the seat of his red-wheeled buggy before either of them spoke. Then Tobe drawled from behind:

"I don't like to cuss a man's kinfolks, Buck, but you picked one hell of a daddy-in-law."

"Damn him." Buck's tone was defensive. "I never asked him for anything and I never will."

"That's what's wrong, now. You just took what you wanted without askin'. Some folks don't like that."

Buck rubbed his finger under his nose, thoughtfully, gazing down the dusty road.

"I don't know but one way to get what I want," he said, simply.

"I reckon that's right," Tobe said, with something sad stealing into his voice. "You know I'll go to the bridge with you, but it'd be a lot easier on both of us if you'd walk right up to a thing and make friends instead of fightin' it."

Buck didn't answer. He bent forward, staring intently into the sun at a figure coming up the road towards them.

"What in the hell is that?" he said, wonderingly.

Tobe shaded his eyes with one hand and peered. He snorted. "Buffalo Bill?"

"Without a horse," Buck said, and as the figure came closer, he turned to Tobe. "You know him?"

Tobe shook his head. "Stranger to me."

The figure came closer, slowly, almost sauntering down the road, little puffs of white dust gasping up from under tight, high-heeled cowboy boots. In spite of the heat, the stranger wore a woolen vest, open in front and showing a brightly checkered shirt. Over his shoulders, so it fell within easy reach across his stomach, was slung a battered guitar. As the figure drew near Buck could see under the brim of a wide black hat where sweat and dust had crusted around the thin mouth. The stranger hardly glanced at Tobe or Buck. His small vague eyes never left Buck's horse. Gently, his right hand strayed over its muzzle.

"Do you like this horse?" he asked softly.

"Well, I'll be damned," Tobe said.

Buck's puzzled eyes went to Tobe, then back to the stranger. "Not so much I wouldn't sell him."

"That's too bad," the stranger said, then coughed apologetically. "I couldn't buy a horse."

"Broke?" Tobe's voice was harsh.

The stranger patted his guitar. "I'm in the music business," he said, simply.

"Never saw you around here before."

"I just got here."

"Figurin' to stay?"

The stranger chuckled slyly.

"Not if the police make you work. I don't like work."

Buck raised his eyebrows at Tobe.

"What's your name?" he said, bluntly.

"Virgil," the stranger said. He looked down at his guitar and carefully with his thumb he plucked one string, then his eyes wandered back to Tobe. "Let's go inside and get something to eat."

For a second, they were both silent, then Buck whooped with laughter. "Take 'im in there, Tobe," he said, roughly. "Tell 'em you want some weddin' cake, Virgil."

"Buck!" Tobe's voice was sharp, carrying warning, and the word came out as if it didn't taste right. Buck's mouth shut quickly and he looked at Tobe's frowning eyes, then he swung slowly to see Virgil's face turning white around the blackened mouth. He started to speak, but dimly he heard the door slam, and was grateful for the sound of Ivy's feet on the gravel path, hurrying towards them.

"I didn't mean—" he began awkwardly.

"Forget it. Come on, Virgil, I'll stake you to supper downtown."

Buck felt helpless and a little ashamed watching them turn to leave, then Ivy called, "Tobe," and they stopped and looked back. He watched Ivy hurry out into the road and heard her accusing Tobe. "You didn't even kiss the bride." She raised herself on tiptoe with both her hands on Tobe's shoulders and held her mouth up while Tobe bent and kissed her very lightly. "That's better," she said, and patted his shoulders. She glanced curiously at Virgil who stood with his face averted, stroking the curve of his guitar with long brown fingers. Her eyes questioned Tobe, but he took her by the arm without a word and started walking back towards the buggy.

"Don't reckon you figured to, ma'am," he said, as he held her elbow while she got in the buggy, "but you got a friend, too, when you got a husband."

"Thank you, Tobe." She laid one hand on Buck's knee as he settled into the seat beside her, and touched Tobe's shoulder with the other. "Buck and I need friends," she said, simply, and caught her lower lip between her teeth.

Tobe turned away hastily and his voice was low. "Good luck." He went back down the road to Virgil, and Buck watched over his shoulder as they cut straight across the empty roll of land, towards a row of houses drawing a thin line between the town and the larger homes which were built on the outskirts without regard to streets or roads.

In silence, then, he let the slack of the reins drop on the horse's rump and drew him around in a tight circle. He let the horse go in a fast walk down a road that was bordered on the west by dark spikes of shadow thrown by coarse weeds in the late sun.

It wasn't until the horse seemed satisfied with its gait and the buggy had steadied into easy creaking motion, that Buck dropped the reins carelessly to the floor and held them down with his foot. He felt Ivy move on the seat beside him and turned to see her twist around until her knees pushed against his thigh, and clutch with her left arm the back of the seat. Her eyes were wide and dry, staring back at the solitary white house on the hill behind them. Buck pulled her knees tighter against his leg without speaking and saw tears begin to shine in the corners of her eyes.

"Just you forget everything," he said, softly. "Lay your head back an' look over to the clouds in the west. They're pilin' up like a million tons o' lint cotton."

Ivy shook her head wordlessly, but her hand felt out until it found Buck's.

" 'Course," he said, "the house you're goin' to ain't as grand, but it's all ours an' brand-new." He caught the lobe of her ear and shook it gently. "An', by God, it's just as white."

"It's not that," she said, and jerked her head around so he wouldn't see the tears begin to flow. "It's our wedding. I wanted it pretty. I wanted everything that other girls—" She made a small choking sound and bent over until her forehead touched his shoulder. "I'll never forgive Papa."

"Here, don't say that." His words were rough but his hands were tender on her arms. "We won't hold a grudge. We'll just work to make him see we was right. Why, Lord knows, can't nobody blame a man for hatin' to lose somethin' like you."

She raised her head and tried to smile at him. He kissed her cheek and then ran the tip of his tongue over his lips and tasted her tears.

[117]

"Hmm, you're salty," he said.

She wiped at her cheek with the back of her hand and looked sideways at him.

"I *can* be sweet."

He pushed her knees out of the buggy seat and pulled her close with his arm around her shoulder. "Well, start sweetenin'," he said, and picked up the reins off the floor. He slapped the lines down on his horse's back. "Git up, you!" He felt Ivy pull his hand from her shoulder around in front and hold it tight to her breast. He caught her closer to him.

"I got to get you home quick 'fore you candy."

They went on in silence, then, while the dusk grew wistful and the shadows grew darker under a heavy canopy of limbs from the huge oaks which bordered nearly every street in Aven. The limbs drooped so low they nearly knocked Buck's hat off as he got out of the buggy in front of the small new home. He straightened his hat as he stepped onto the ground and jerked his thumb up at the limbs.

"Little later on, them limbs'll get right white with the cotton they drag off the wagons comin' into town."

Ivy stooped under the limbs as she stood up in the buggy and held out her arms to Buck. She was light in his arms, light but round and firm; she kissed him on the neck under the line of his jaw as he carried her up the steps and into the darkening narrow hall of the square one-story house.

"I don't know why," she said, huskily, as he put her gently on her feet, "but it's good to be carried over your own threshold, especially when your husband let you help build and furnish it."

He let his hands drift down her body until they touched her hips and felt the slow welcome heaviness drag into his loins as she moved closer with a half-frightened, eager-sweet quickening.

"You turn the lamps on," he said, thickly, "while I'm puttin' up the horse."

He didn't move and neither did she. Her voice came low and shaky.

"We don't need lights right now."

A finger of moonlight would whisper over Ivy's hair lying there on the pillow and then be gone like a name on the tip of a

[118]

tongue. The moon would sail another inch beyond a limb of the old oak in the yard—and the little twining of light would hunt his wife's hair again.

His wife? The moon could dust silver in her yellow hair and in his mind she'd be a little girl on a bed with her arms flung out in tired content—a weary child drugged with pleasure and sweet in a sighing sleep that didn't know a husband.

Husband? The moon would shelter its beam again and he would be standing in bated darkness at the window, knowing himself. Knowing that the small breeze was cool only because he sweated. Knowing that his bare body was coarse and greedy, and ashamed to find in himself nothing of the fineness he had felt in Ivy.

Ivy? And then suddenly the little knife of moon could be a bright devil in her hair and her lips could be swollen, wanting his, and the limbs that had dreamed in childlike sleep could quiver now in need of him.

Him? Then the oak could baffle the moon again in the heavy darkness; his body could sing a subtle tone—delicate if that was the mood, hurting and demanding hurt if the harmony changed. He wouldn't know shame of his body now. He would feel pride that he was strong enough to take her again.

He moved smoothly, big and white in the moonlight, over to the bed. He put one arm under Ivy's bare knees and the other under her shoulders, then he lifted and carried her back to the window.

He held her there in the cooling breeze against his chest until she opened her eyes and raised her lips.

INTERLUDE

JAKE WILLIS *huddled on the whittled wooden seat of the wagon and cursed the rain that dripped down the collar of his old coat. It was a fine, sifting rain that seemed to fly up and from all sides as much as it came down, and it made the dusk drearier than usual, seeping through the coal dust that always lay in the air around the freight yards.*

[119]

He glared at the shiny damp backs of the mules below him, then raised his head towards the closed door of the small office.

"Come on, Bass!" he bellowed.

Bass Wooten came hurrying through the door and slammed it shut behind him. His blue overalls showed black with coal and wetness. He put one foot on the spoke of the wagon wheel and caught the seat to pull himself up.

"Now, by God," he puffed, "I'm much obliged for you comin' to take me home, but don't rush me to death."

"That soft job o' yours done made you fat," Jake said, as he rattled the lines to start his team. "If you'd work a little, it wouldn't be so hard for you to get around."

Bass dug his elbow into Jake's side.

"Like shovelin' up behind a mule, hunh?"

Jake drove on in hurt silence.

"Aw, hell, I didn't mean nothin'." Bass cleared his throat. "Does look like Buck'd let up though, now that he's married."

"Let up!" Jake yelled the words and the mules stuttered their feet in sudden fear. "How can he cut down? I didn't mind the wife, but I shore hope don't no more Bannons come along for me to feed."

Bass's tone was soothing.

"Well, Jake, any man that's married is apt to have young 'uns."

Jake groaned.

"Well, Goddammit, he'll just have to wait till I get on my feet."

Bass started to laugh, then he saw that Jake was staring miserably at the muddy street before them, and he sat in silence for a few moments.

"Jake," he said, finally, "what bothers me is, how come he can do things like he's doin' to you and you stay friends with him?"

Jake turned slowly, his eyes bitter. He jerked his head backwards, towards the bed of the wagon.

"Right when I'm hatin' him enough to cut his tripes out, he gets aholt o' me an' tells me he'll knock off two dollars if I'll take a stove out to Miz Henderson's that's a widow." He wiped water out of his eyes with the back of his hand, and when he spoke again, his voice was rough.

" 'Course, I ain't supposed to know it, but she didn't buy that stove. He just found out she needed one an' sent it out."

Bass's words were wondering.

"Now, Lord knows you cain't hate a man'll do that." He shook his head from side to side, slowly, thinking, then suddenly he stiffened.

"Jake," he said, softly, "did you come to take me home so I could help you put up that stove?"

Jake turned his large, offended eyes towards his friend.

"Why, Bass," he said.

CHAPTER THIRTEEN

IT SEEMED to Buck as he shuffled onto the sandy loam of his mother's back yard, that the thickening hedge which surrounded the house had grown a foot in the five months since he and Ivy were married.

"Likely it's due to me not livin' here an' watchin' it every day," he thought, as he bent to whip from his dark-blue trousers the dust that came from the hedge's grey-green leaves. "Can't hardly straddle it now." Sweat seeped into the corner of his eye as he straightened up. He rubbed the back of his hand across his forehead and grumbled.

"Damned jackass weather. Three days till Christmas and winter still ain't headed up."

The weather never did make up its mind in Aven. Most places in the world had four seasons of the year. In Aven, though, God had given them only two seasons, summer and winter. Spring couldn't be called a season proper because spring frolicked right into summer so sweetly it was like the twinkle in a child's eye just suddenly *being* a smile. And autumn! Autumn was a faker in a red and yellow jacket whose flaunted colors faded and ran in the first winter rain. Then winter wouldn't make up its mind until it was almost past time for it. December would come along and the calendar would say it was time for frost to sweeten the persimmons, but the soft winds from the Gulf would tell the possums to wait a little longer near the burdening tree on the fence line, and the hot sun would say there wasn't much use in hilling your sweet potatoes. The farmers would come in the store all out of heart, eyeing the meat block and growling, "By killin' time, the hogs'll 've et up all the corn an' there won't be no meal to eat with the meat."

Weather like this, part of Buck's mind would be with the farmer and himself as friends, working together to make the ground give up its goods; then another part of his mind would roll suddenly like a trout to a rain frog, and that part of his mind would whisper, "No crop, no pay." Unless you've got a note and then there're mules and tools and sometimes land itself coming back for the feed and the seed, the side meat and the salt, the copper-toed shoes and the kettle that left the store. Then he'd pull away from that thought, and he'd say to himself that the ginning was done and the crop had been good, so what the hell if the frost never came to help out for next year. The hard money was there to shake loose the big stock of heavy coats and the bolts of fancy woolens that clogged the shelves of his store. Buck would try to convince himself that the storekeeper-furnisher took a chance and that big profits ought to come from big risks; then the thought would come to make him sweat, that whichever way the farmer moved, the storeman had him going and coming. That thought came now as he crossed the yard under the familiar chinaberry tree and he deliberately shook the guilty feeling away. He was near one corner of the back porch, with his thoughts still grinding away, when he heard a slight hissing sound.

The sound seemed to come from under the house, so he stooped to peer underneath. Across the fairly narrow width of the pantry and porch which jutted out from the main body of the house, he could see a thin pair of legs, streaked with dust and sweat from the bare feet to small unbleached-sheeting drawers. The feet were squirming in the dust and the skirt that should have covered the legs was held up out of sight above the sill that bordered the under part of the house.

"What the hell?" Buck mumbled from his crouching position. "That's either Millie or Christina, but damned if I can figure —" He stood up and walked silently to the corner of the house and carefully peered around it. "Christina," he said to himself.

She was standing with an anxious frown on her face and her mouth screwed up tightly. From the hips up she was perfectly still, but her feet moved as if they were feeling the ground. She held the below-knee length skirt of her green checked cotton dress out in front of her as if to catch something, and stared with small, intent, grey eyes at the wall in front of her.

Buck's forehead wrinkled and he narrowed his eyes.

"Now, how come—" he started and then stopped.

Two apples suddenly dropped into her skirt and Christina didn't wait to take them into her hands, but clutched skirt and all to her chest and started running head down, and yellow hair straining tighter over her forehead from the painful braids behind. Buck held out his arms and she ran right into them.

[123]

"Wup!" she said, then looked up and saw who it was. Her eyes got bigger. "I ain't done nothin'." She jerked away from him and stooped quickly to pick up the apples which had fallen to the ground. "I'll put 'em back," she whispered, with her hands tight around them and her lips shaking.

"Take it easy," Buck whispered back. He caught her by one thin shoulder and pulled her closer, against the wall but around the corner and out of sight of the porch. He knuckled her chin to make her look up at him.

She wasn't crying, but her teeth were sunk into her lower lip.

"What's this all about?" Buck held his voice low.

She didn't answer.

"You goin' to tell me?"

She didn't make a sound or shake her head.

"Damn!" Buck turned her chin loose and looked down at the top of her head for a moment, then he reached and gently took one of the apples out of her tight fingers. He rubbed it on his shirt sleeves, then took a large, deliberately noisy bite out of it. Her head began to come up by itself and her eyes widened. Her teeth came away from her lip and the corners of her lips twitched. Buck caught her by the back of the head with a casual hand and jammed the apple against her mouth. "Bite," he said. She bit, then pulled her head loose from his hand and shook the braid back over her shoulder defiantly. Her lips pulled out into a full grin.

"Now," Buck said.

She pulled him lower and glanced over her shoulder, then whispered, "Millie and me. She's helpin' Mother in the kitchen and when she goes in the pantry for somethin' she rolls 'em out the cathole."

Buck's shoulders began to shake and he coughed to stop the laughter that crowded up into his chest. He bent lower.

"How'd you frame it up?"

"Been doin' it. Whoever's helpin' in the kitchen, the other one'll walk by an' say, 'Rabbit.' The other one says 'Squirrel,' an' the one that ain't helpin' comes out to the cathole."

Buck slowly straightened up and his lips twisted as if he wanted to laugh but was holding back.

He patted her on both shoulders.

"Get back to the cathole," he said, softly. "Maybe some more'll come out."

Her eyes got bigger with anticipation and she turned quickly and in a moment was standing again with her skirt up, waiting with her eyes intent on the cathole.

Buck pulled his face straight and went quickly around the corner of the house, up the steps, and onto the big screened back porch with its two big rockers and its neat stack of soft-pine boxes which his mother saved for no reason at all except that they might come in handy someday.

As his foot scuffed on the doorsill between the porch and the kitchen, his mother glanced sharply up from her bent position over the stove.

"How you makin' it, son?" she said shortly and stooped again over the huge iron pot on the wood stove.

"Common," Buck said, "just common." His eyes searched the kitchen for his sister, but Millie was out of sight. He stepped carelessly on inside the room and heard a small movement to his right. He watched his mother while he slowly turned his head towards the pantry door. She didn't look at him.

Millie was sitting on the far end of the long breakfast bench with her eyes shadowed and dropped over a clumsy narrow mixing bowl whose wooden sides were heavily floured to keep the biscuit dough from sticking. She held the bowl on the lap of a too-large dress made exactly like Christina's and from the same bolt of cloth. Her eyes came sweetly up from the bowl long enough to touch Buck's, then dropped again to her hands, which worked automatically in the dough. He watched for a sign of guilt, but it couldn't be found on her face, and her hands were steady.

Almost soundlessly, Buck tapped with his foot the end of the bench that was nearest to him and saw Millie's head come slowly, guardedly around until her blameless blue eyes saw his and twinkled. He watched his mother, then looked back to see Millie's eyes asking a question.

"Rabbit," he said, loudly. His mother glanced absently up from the stove. "Hunh?" He didn't answer, but kept watching Millie, whose fingers suddenly flexed so hard that dough squirted between each of them. She didn't look up but Buck could see

[125]

color rising above the square-cut neckline of her dress. Her hands worked busily, while her mother stared with puzzled eyes from one to the other. Then, as Jeanie Bannon shrugged and stooped to open and look inside the fire door, Millie's wide mouth suddenly jerked at the corner and she said, distinctly, "Squirrel."

Buck saw his mother slowly stand erect and place her hands on her hips. Her mouth twisted shrewdly. "Something's up," she said, and her black eyes narrowed at them. "What is it?"

Millie laughed. "Secret." She put the mixing bowl on the table beside a long flat pan whose inside had been greased with lard on a piece of brown paper. Then she jumped up and dusted the flour off her hands. "Biscuits are ready," she said and ran noisily out the door. Jeanie Bannon turned her eyes on Buck. She lifted her hands and dropped them. "Won't nobody in this family ever grow up but me."

"Let 'em be young as long as they can," Buck said, with a rueful tone to his voice.

His mother looked away from him.

"You got grown too fast," she said, gently, "but we needed a man along then more'n we needed a boy." She bit her lip and her hands fumbled a little at the large square dishcloth before she could pick it up. "I been sorry about that," she said, awkwardly.

"Aw, hell," Buck said, and felt blood rising uncomfortably into his face. "Let's take the text on somebody else."

She turned and faced him and her fingers worked small pleats into the dishcloth.

"All right," she said, simply, "we'll get onto Hearn."

"That why you called me?"

She nodded.

"He's dead set on marryin' that little Tiller girl an' she ain't right for one o' my boys."

"Godamighty!"

She nodded soberly.

"You heard somethin' bad about her?" he asked, almost hesitantly.

"Don't nobody have to tell me what's been goin' on when a girl gets out of a buggy and has to reach down inside her dress to settle herself."

Buck whistled low and his lips twisted.

"Well, if it's gone that far, how come—?"

"Don't ask me why," she broke in. "Ain't but one thing I know —he's doin' his best to ape you and can't."

"Me?"

"You know it, good as I do. He can't drink like you, but he tries. He can't work like you, but he tries. He can't gamble like you, but he tries. There's something you've got that he ain't, but he's tryin' to get it an' he wants it bad enough to ask for a railroadin' job." She shook her head. "I ain't throwin' off on you, but it'd be better all around if the others didn't have you stuck right up in front of 'em."

"Ahh," Buck's voice was disgusted. "Ain't nothin' to that. An' besides, I figure he'll squeeze out of it in the long run."

"Have you seen that Tiller girl lately?"

Buck frowned and rubbed his jaw.

"Durned if I blame him much," he muttered. "Railroadin'! Handlin' tools and sweatin'. I'd a'guessed he had more sense than that."

"He had sense once," his mother said, slowly, then she looked at him with her eyes narrowed down, "and he'll have sense again —when he gets that girl out of his mind." She nodded slowly, meaningfully, with her eyes hard and hot on his.

Buck kept rubbing his hand slowly along the line of his jaw and his eyes drifted to the floor, then back to his mother's.

"I reckon I know what you mean," he said, softly. Then his jaw hardened. "Sure you want it done?"

She nodded once.

"It'll cost."

She shook her head.

"You can't buy her off."

Buck's smile was bitter.

"I don't know about buyin' a Tiller," he said, slowly, "but I know damned well I can buy a Bannon."

His mother's eyes closed and her mouth tightened as color rose from the high neck of her dress.

"Do whatever it takes," she said, tonelessly.

The thought of Hearn and the Tiller girl hardly lasted until Buck had walked out of his mother's front yard. "I can't blame him," the one thought ran, "the way she makes it down the street with them play-pretties bouncin', but he ain't hardly old enough, and if Mother don't want it, I know damned well what I can do with him."

Because it was nearing dusk, he didn't turn towards the old store near the family home, but cut across the street and to the right towards the new little business district which was rapidly getting to be called "town."

"Chokin' a cat with cream may not be the best way," he said, softly, "but it's a good way if the cream holds out. I'll just get 'im a red buggy and a snappy little gaited horse and a couple good bird dogs. Way he loves huntin' and runnin' around, he'll be too busy to work on the railroad and too broke to get married."

Then he threw Hearn out of his mind and sauntered towards his own home, which lay on the other side of the small cluster of stores, planing mill, blacksmith shops and open saloons. He didn't attempt to think about anything and he went along with no conscious thought that his only reason for wanting the walk home was—Aven. He wanted, somewhere so deep inside him that he wouldn't have recognized it, to watch Aven and to do it in his own way as a parent might secretly watch the antics of a child. He wanted to see it at dusk when he was least likely to be stopped, walking slowly down its dusty or muddy streets, on a private boarded walk for a few feet, then down again on the public ruts and ditches and bogs. He wanted to drowse along over the sights his eyes would see and soak up the sounds his ears would hear. A new wagon, perhaps empty of household goods or work tools, but full to the sideboards with a new family, would grind slowly through the straggling streets with old eyes searching and young eyes just as big and as solemn, flaring with excitement. Or it might be an old wagon, piled high with stove and mattresses and chairs and the children walking close to the wheels. Buck always nodded his head slowly at sight of the old wagons. "That bunch has been through the mill," he'd think, "and that kind comes to stay." It never came consciously to his mind that he was proud of Aven. He never thought, "This is my town and it's a good town." They meant the same, but his words were different. "Two more bunches. One to borrow and one to buy."

And because he thought of the newcomers, the shops and the

homes, in terms of business, it was in those same terms that he saw the rutted streets and the haphazard way of building. "If it ain't planned out right and some straight streets laid, there's goin' to be killin's over land lines." As small as it still was, Aven already looked crowded. Perhaps it was *because* the streets were so narrow, but almost always during the daytime, someone was giving it movement and life. Already, with its one engineer still afraid of the steam compressor that powered the small new water system, major companies were sending in their salesmen, all hoping to break first into the blooming new Wire grass trade area. And after they came, the drummers couldn't rent buggies or horses and sat most of the day on the front porch of the old Fritter home which the family had converted into a boardinghouse after the girls had married and gone. The drummers picked their teeth and rocked and made mention of the girls who passed, but only to each other, careful to see that no Aven man could hear. And Buck saw them as good for the town, but only in terms of money for himself. "They spend," he'd say. "My God, how they throw it away, thank the Lord." He'd speak to them as he passed, hiding a tight grin for their knob-toed shoes and their tight checked trousers. Sometimes, too, he was glad he didn't know what they were saying, to laugh so loudly when he strolled by with his hands in his pockets looking up at the sky with his heavy shoes slipping in the mud.

What he liked more than anything, though, was to see the folks from the piney woods and the gallberry lowlands come shoving into every shop and store in Aven. Like now, just before Christmas. They stood shoulder to shoulder in some of them, and the Christmas decorations of small pine trees or cedars, smilax and pine cones and red paper had to be freshened every day, particularly in the saloons. Always at this time of year and on Saturdays when the farmers came in, Aven itself seemed to make a coarse rumbling sound, with now and then a high yell of laughter riding over the jumble of voices and the jangle of banjo or guitar from the swinging doors. Often there would come the yelp of a stepped-on dog, or the unmistakable whine and slap as a drunken mule driver laid on his whip, and as often came the choked-off small scream of the mule driver's wife as the mule lurched into the crowded streets.

Now and then, one of the small clots of men and women would split as Buck walked towards them, still almost unseeing, and the men would say, "Howdy, Buck," and most of the women would raise their heads so their billed calico bonnets looked like inverted sugar scoops and say, "Evenin', Mr. Bannon." He would speak, then, with his mind lingering stubbornly on Aven, but with a part of him showing the front that they wanted to see. "Colie Mellinger," he'd say, with surprise in his voice, "where you been? Know you ain't been workin', or the seat o' them pants wouldn't be shiny as a nigger's heel."

Then he'd ramble on with the laughter of Colie Mellinger's friends following and building up and blending into the sounds that were Aven near dusk on a busy day. And he'd see the long rectangles of light suddenly fling out from a doorway in front of him as someone else lit the flowered, painted china kerosene lamps which hung from each ceiling or were set in brackets on the walls of each store. And the bright lights only made him see more clearly the rough unpainted clapboard of the smaller stores crouching in the shadows of his store and the other larger ones. His own store was already flinging through the open door and the rare-glass windows enough light to flood the street and the crowd in front of it. Buck didn't even slow down as he came abreast of it, but passed on the other side of the street.

"This is one night I ain't aimin' to work," he muttered. "Tobe can close this'n, and Papa and Jeff can close the other'n."

He was shouldering his way past two small drab women who waited in patient silence under a swinging sign that read, "The Bottle," when someone called his name.

"Buck." The voice was soft and although the word was plainly spoken, a liquid something in the tone gave it a foreign sound. He turned towards the voice, feeling a protest inside that his thoughts had been broken.

"Evenin', Joe." He moved closer to the small, softly smiling man who leaned against the wall of his building as if it were a part of him. "How's your first Christmas in Aven?"

The small man jerked his thumb at the sign on the open window shutter,

"Joe Kraft, Buy or Sell."

"This is one Kraft who approves of Christmas."

Buck laughed almost silently and touched the small man's shoulder.

"Glad you're here," he said, and suddenly felt his face flush. "I mean, you'll stick it out."

Joe Kraft raised his hands palm up.

"I passed up New York, Charleston, and Savannah," he said. "This is my last stop."

Buck winked, and said, "See you later," and turned on down the street, hurrying a little now as if he didn't want anything else to stop him, but Joe Kraft's voice came again. "Wait a minute, Buck." He stopped and the little man came closer. His face was twisting as if he didn't know what to say when he caught Buck's arm and drew him into the shadows near his store.

"I sold a whole lot of sheeting today," he whispered.

Buck's eyes grew puzzled.

"Hope to hell we did, too."

Joe Kraft shook his head.

"What I sold was to men."

Unconsciously Buck's voice lowered.

"I reckon I know what you mean," he said, slowly, feeling his way, "but it's the first I've heard of it."

"They won't say anything to me," Kraft said. "You know that. But, somehow, I figured you wouldn't like it, and maybe—"

"God, no," Buck broke in. "I don't like it and never will." He laughed harshly. "Too damned many times when they might a' come after me." He punched Joe Kraft lightly in the ribs. "Don't let it worry you. Just a bunch o' drunks goin' through Baptist Bottom for some fun."

Kraft didn't smile, but his face took on a look of vast patience.

"Fun!" His voice was soft, but bitterness was in the tone.

"Forget it," Buck said. "Maybe they'll get too drunk to do anything." He watched Kraft's lips twist in a wry smile as the little man turned away and slipped back to lean against his store front.

He went home, then, hurriedly, the shortest way, across a few back acres until he came into the wider street, bordered by sycamores which shaded his home. Joe Kraft was far from his mind as he saw the first slice of moonlight angle through the trees and touch his front porch. The dragged-out feeling left him suddenly as he thought of Ivy.

[131]

"Ivy," he said, slowly, going back over the good days and the nights they had had together; then suddenly he frowned at the thought that brushed his mind. He didn't speak aloud, but he asked himself the question, "How come Mother didn't ask about her?" He didn't move for a long time while his mind plotted step by step back to the last time he had seen his mother and Ivy together. "Friendly as two—" He stopped talking to himself, then started over. "Somethin' wrong with them two," he thought. "They acted like two preachers talkin', all buttery with each other." He shook his head and went to the door. "It's a caution to behold," he said, with his hand on the latch, "how two little old bitty women can completely surround a whole family o' men." He let the door slam carelessly behind him and dropped his hat in the dark without looking to see if it fell on the small chair by the door. "One thing I know good and well, though," he muttered, "is that I ain't goin' to say a word either way if they take battlin' sticks to each other."

"Ivy," he called loudly, as he went from the small living room into the back hall. "I'm in here." Her voice came from the bedroom. He turned at the first door to the right and stopped with a hand on each door facing.

"Wheeoo!" he whistled low as he saw Ivy, lying across the bed in the light of the big lamp with her feet towards him and her head almost hanging off the other side. "This is better'n comin' home to a hot supper." Ivy's head came slowly up. Her eyes were red. "I'm catching a cold," she said, and blew her nose on a small square of unhemmed white cloth. Buck wrinkled his nose.

"Ivy, get a handkerchief," he said. "For God's sake, go down to the big store and get a bushel of handkerchiefs."

Ivy blew her nose again, defiantly.

"Papa made us use these around the house," she said, patiently, "and save our handkerchiefs for going out. He always said there wasn't any use in making money if it all went for hilarity."

Buck came and sat on the edge of the bed. He patted her thigh and left his hand where it quit patting.

"Sugar," he said, in a gentle voice that was just as patient as hers. "Old as your daddy is, it don't make no difference to him, but at my age, I'm willin' to do most anything that'll make a woman look better." He moved his hand.

[132]

Ivy stirred suddenly and sat up.

"Don't do that." She pushed his hand away.

"Hell, you don't feel that bad, do you?"

"It's not that," she said, and stood up, moving over to turn the lamp higher. "It's just that we're married now and—"

"All that means to me," Buck said, "is we got a right to do what we please."

Ivy's lips curled slightly. Her voice was prim.

"No, Buck. You don't see—" She looked at him with her head on one side, questioningly. "Don't you think that marriage brings a responsibility to act—" She stopped and her face showed that she was feeling for words.

"Like other folks act?" Buck finished it for her.

"That's part of it."

"Damn that." Buck got up and caught her close to him. He didn't touch her body with his hands, and he spoke gently. "You're pretty much of a fool, Sugar, but you're my fool. I don't see to save me how one girl could pick up so much wrong learnin' before she's twenty-one, but somehow you ought to find out that all rules don't fit all people." He held her off and looked down at her. "Now, wouldn't I be an idiot to change the kind of man a fine girl like you would marry?" He put her head down on his shoulder and whispered into her ear. "Besides, I wouldn't tell nobody I got it."

Ivy laughed abruptly.

"You fool!" She came quickly closer and reached up on tiptoe to make her lips move against his neck. He jerked away.

"Take it easy. Go fix me some supper and I'll do the best I can, but you can't put me on and off like a coat. Not on an empty stomach, anyhow."

Ivy swayed closer until she pressed against him.

"Hungry?" she whispered, smiling confidently, joking, yet with her full lips growing heavier.

He pushed her away.

"Better watch out or you'll be wakin' up again in the middle of the night half starved."

Ivy sniffled and had to turn away from him. She blew her nose on the old cloth again, then threw it into a small basket that sat beside the clumsy dresser.

"I'll be down tomorrow for some handkerchiefs," she said. "Something's wrong with me or you're older than you think."

She went out before him, switching her hips, into the kitchen and stopped at the white wooden safe. He followed her and walked around the small kitchen table, already set for two, and on past the wood stove, out onto the narrow back porch. He stripped off his shirt and flung it over one end of the wash bench that was built from the wall out to one of the porch uprights. He dipped water from a large washtub and poured it carefully into a small blue-grey pan of baked enamel. "Wish to God they'd get them water pipes out our way," he mumbled, and reached automatically to the hollowed-out spot for a large bar of turpentine soap. As his hand touched the soap, his forehead creased.

"Damned if she'll ever learn," he said, out loud, "that soap ought not to be left in a puddle."

"Hunh?" Ivy stepped to the door.

"Nothin'." He bent over to wet his face.

It was then that they heard the first call.

"Buck Bannon!" The voice came as if it were very far away.

Buck stopped splashing in the pan and listened, still bent over. Ivy didn't move. Then they heard the sound of a horse's hooves in a fast trot.

"Buck Bannon!" It came again, more urgent this time, and with it came the creak of harness and the slap of lines.

"Now, what in the devil?" Buck straightened and began to dry his face on a coarse towel that hung from a nail in the peeled-pine upright of the porch.

"Don't answer," Ivy whispered loudly. "Maybe they'll leave."

Buck jerked his thumb at the lamp on the kitchen table.

"Nobody in Aven leaves a light on if they ain't home."

He started to the door when he heard a scuffling sound to the side of the house.

"Who is it?" he said sharply and turned quickly to go down the back steps. "Wait, Buck," Ivy said in a low pressing voice. "Don't go till you know who it is." She opened the door and came out on the porch. Buck didn't answer. He stepped softly onto the sand of his back yard and had reached the corner of the house when he heard the voice again and knew it.

"Buck?" it said, questioningly.

[134]

"Virgil!" Buck's voice was loud and relieved as he watched the slight figure in its boots and big hat come slowly into the wedge of light that fell out of the kitchen door. Virgil was awkward because of his guitar and stumbled a little in the unfamiliar yard. He was pale and sweat streaked down through the dust that caked his face. His eyes were anxious and his mouth worked.

"Been lookin' everywhere," he said, breathlessly, with one hand clutching Buck's wet forearm. "Even to both o' your stores." He stopped for breath and looked over his shoulder. As he turned back to Buck, he saw Ivy standing very still in the light from the door, with her hand rubbing slowly up and down on the doorjamb. Virgil ducked his head to her, quickly. "Evenin', ma'am." He turned and whipered urgently to Buck, "Make her go inside."

"Ivy," Buck said, with his eyes still on Virgil, "better get supper quick." He didn't look at her, but he heard the door open and close softly while his eyes moved down to see Virgil's thin hand moving jerkily on his arm. He didn't know he whispered.

"What's wrong?"

"They got one o' Mabe's girls," Virgil said in a voice that rose and fell with excitement.

"Who?" Buck said roughly.

"Ku Klux. Took her to Mercy Creek."

Buck spat on the ground in disgust.

"Damn fools! There ain't no more Ku Klux. Just a bunch o' drunk bastards that don't want their womenfolks to know they're raisin' hell."

Virgil's eyes fell from Buck's face and he cleared his throat. "They ain't all bastards."

Buck felt the blood leaving his face.

"You tryin' to tell me—?"

Virgil nodded.

"Jeff and Hearn."

"Godamighty!" Buck said, slowly, then he took one long step towards the porch. "Ivy!" He stopped and turned back to Virgil. "Hitch my buggy up." Virgil shook his head. "I borrowed a rig from Mabe."

Buck reached up and took his shirt off the nail without going

[135]

onto the porch. He started pulling it over his head as Ivy opened the back door.

"What?"

"Hold supper up," he said in a muffled voice, then his head came out and he started tucking his shirt in around his trousers. "Got somethin' to 'tend to." He started to leave, but Ivy stopped him.

"Buck." He looked back over his shoulder. She opened the door and held out a long-barreled pistol. Buck just looked at her and didn't move.

"You listen?"

She jerked her head impatiently.

"Certainly I listened." She came onto the porch and let the door slam behind her. "Take this with you."

Buck shook his head.

"I don't need no gun with them two," he said, then touched Virgil's arm. "Let's go."

"Buck," Ivy called as he reached the corner. He didn't even look back at her and he didn't answer.

CHAPTER FOURTEEN

Buck was silent until he and Virgil were in the buggy and well away from his house, out in the newest little cluster of homes that had begun to spring up to the west of town. He rode in the moonlight with his hands hanging limply between his knees, hunched forward on the stiff seats of Virgil's buggy, not watching the road or even seeing the straining hindquarters of the horse. His voice was tight when he finally spoke.

"What'd the woman do?"

Virgil shrugged.

"Mabe said she stole a little bit too much—after the customer went to sleep." He slapped his reins on the horse's rump and looked sideways at Buck. "He sent me to you."

Buck glanced sharply up.

"Mabe sent you? How'd he know I'd *give* a damn?"

Virgil chuckled.

"Mabe and I get to see the side of a man that most of them keep hid. Mabe sees them drunk and gaping at a woman all wet-mouthed." His mouth closed in a wry smile. "And nobody bothers to keep covered up around a crazy man."

Buck stared straight ahead and his voice was hoarse.

"Ain't you all got nothin' better to do than sit around and watch the rest of us act like fools?"

"Nobody's all fool." Virgil looked sideways at him. "You say you've got a price for everything. Lots o' folks believe it, but Mabe and I don't. We think you'll do a lot o' things for money, but there's a heap you won't do for any price."

"Damned if that's so."

Virgil caught the reins in his hand and said, "Whoa." The horse stopped so quickly the buggy nearly bucked where the shafts joined the axle. He stared straight ahead and wet his lips. "Well, we're betting you wouldn't stand for what's going on tonight at any price." He turned towards Buck with a gentle curve to his lips. "If we're wrong, I can turn around and go back."

Buck's eyes locked with Virgil's. He shook his head.

"I ain't worried about the girl. I just damned ain't goin' to have any o' my folks doin' somebody else's dirt for nothin'."

Virgil clucked at the horse.

"Wonder if God cares what a man's reasons are if he does right." He chuckled. "I sure don't." Buck started to answer, but shook his head as they started moving again in silence towards the heavy darkness of the woods around Mercy Creek. Buck wondered dully at the heaviness that was slowly growing inside him.

"This damned diggin' around inside a man," he thought. "Makes me feel like one o' them dreams where you're runnin' around naked. Don't do no good, anyhow. Can't make no difference to anybody else what's goin' on inside me, but they talk anyhow. An' lies, my God! That don't mean much, though. All the lies any of 'em tell don't hurt as much as one friend believin' 'em. That's one thing I like about Tobe. He don't talk much an' dammit you don't need no contract with him. Most contracts got loopholes, but there ain't no loopholes in loyalty."

Virgil's low voice broke into his thoughts.

"They're right up ahead." Virgil checked the horse with a slight pull on the lines. Buck raised up slightly to see over a clump of gallberry bushes to the small clearing that surrounded a huge magnolia tree on the edge of the swamp. Leaves and limbs shattered the moonlight into small clusters of brightness on the far side of the clearing, but close to the magnolia tree, it was a solid, wide bar that glowed, and in its light, Buck could see a small group of white-covered heads.

"Ain't but a half dozen," he muttered and sank back down in the seat. "Drive right up to 'em."

"More'n that," Virgil grunted. He lifted the reins and let them fall back down lightly on the horse. They moved slowly off the narrow roadway onto the roughness of land that had never seen a plow or a saw. As they grew closer, Buck could hear the bumble of voices.

He raised up in the buggy again, trying to see, steadying himself by holding onto Virgil's shoulder. Suddenly, he heard one man laugh loudly and give a long whooping yell. He sat back down and grabbed the whip out of the socket. He struck the horse smartly and the animal jumped forward in spite of the thick underbrush. The buggy began to rock and thump over small hillocks and its wheels and stiff springs squeaked as they struck small logs and stumps and bounced over them. Virgil held the reins in one hand and clutched the small metal arm on his left with the other.

"Don't hit 'im no more," he panted.

"They hear us," Buck said. "Keep goin' steady till you get right close, then don't say a word. Just drive right up to 'em."

Over the lower, thinning brush close to the clearing, Buck saw the clot of figures in their white robes and hoods suddenly pull away from the magnolia. One of them suddenly broke from the crowd and began to run. Another of the figures caught him by the shoulder with one hand and jerked him back into the gradually forming line that angled in front of the tree. Abruptly the buggy was through the brush and riding more easily on the smooth thick grass of the clearing. Buck leaned back in the buggy and crossed his legs. He put one arm on the back of the seat around Virgil's shoulders and held the buggy whip lightly in his other hand.

"You can slow down now," he said, out of the corner of his mouth.

Virgil checked the horse's gait and the noise of the buggy springs stopped. They rode slowly forward in a silence that seemed solid. There was no sound from the trees, and no booming of frogs from the swamp, and no bird sound. Even the steady clump of the horse's hooves was muffled, made almost soundless even to Buck by the heavy carpet of grass and wind-blown pine straw.

The thick swatch of moonlight against the heavy black of the trees, the silent row of white-covered figures, and the hushed movement of the horse and buggy all made everything seem slightly out of focus to Buck. He shook his head suddenly against the feeling of unreality and clamped his jaw hard, not moving his head but staring straight at the center of the line ahead of him.

"Wheel an' turn in front of them," he said, softly, to Virgil, "and let me step out about the middle o' the line."

Virgil brought the horse around in a slow arc until they were within fifteen feet of the row of men who stood with arms crossed coming out of rough holes cut in their sheets, blank white hoods staring straight ahead. He stopped at the middle of the line.

Buck turned his head casually and glanced down the row. The quietness of the swamp seemed to grow thicker.

Slowly, Buck leaned forward and put the buggy whip back into its socket and stood up. The moonlight struck him square in the face.

"Buck!" He heard the urgent, strangling whisper from behind the rank of men. He didn't answer, but kept his eyes on the men facing him and put one foot on the step. "Buck Bannon." The voice was a woman's voice, growing louder, higher with anger. He didn't speak as he stepped lightly off onto the ground. The buggy springs squeaked as his weight came off it, then the silence was suddenly heavier than ever. Buck took two steps close to the file of hooded figures and slowly began to walk down towards one end of the line. His head was bent as if he were studying the ground at their feet. He passed two of them, then stopped. He looked carefully at the feet of the figure beside him, then brought his eyes slowly up past the crossed arms until he stared directly into the rectangular eyeholes of the hood. He looked for a long moment, then his eyes came deliberately back down to the crossed arms. He reached out suddenly and with fingers that were gentle but firm on the man's hand, he pulled one finger loose from its clasp around the upper arm. A heavy square-cut ring gleamed in the moonlight. Buck dropped the finger and took a short silent step backward. He reached out slowly and jerked the hood from the figure. Down the line, several low voices muttered, then quickly stopped.

"Get in that buggy, Hearn." Buck's voice was flat and low.

Hearn didn't move. He stood there with his face partly clouded because the moon was to his back, but he didn't move or speak. Buck hooked his fingers carefully into the loose collar of the homemade white shrouding. He tore downward and the un-hemmed neckline gave way. He carefully pulled the split covering away from Hearn's shoulders.

"In the buggy, Hearn." His words could hardly be heard.

"Goddammit!" Hearn's one word seemed to burst from him. Buck smelled cheap whiskey. Then it seemed to him that his movements were slow and awkward. He caught Hearn by the shoulders with both hands and jerked him out of the line and turned him until his back was to the buggy. He had just time enough to see Hearn's eyes staring wide in startled bewilderment before his big fist struck him on the side of the cheek under his left eye. Hearn fell backward, arms flailing and numbed, feet trying desperately to hold him. His head struck the ground near the back wheel of the buggy. His feet moved in small spasms and his hands grabbed bunches of grass and pine straw as he tried to get up. His mouth hung loose and his eyelids snapped open and shut. Buck watched him for a moment with his back to the men, then deliberately he turned and again began his slow march. There was no sound from the line. His head was down again, studying the feet that nosed out from under the robes. Behind him as he walked, he could hear muttering start and one thin whisper of a voice, but he could catch only the sound without words. Then, without warning of sound or sight, he suddenly knew that the line had broken behind him. He felt his spine stiffen and the back of his neck told him that the small scraping sounds he was hearing came from shoes on the dead pine straw. He held himself straight, moving slowly along, still staring downwards. Then the sound of quick shallow breathing was close behind him, and he started to turn quickly. As he turned, he ducked, and saw one of the silent row of figures on his right step out, whipping its hood off as it came. Before Buck could come upright again, the hood and the arm that held it swung past and slapped into the blank white covering over the head of the man who had followed him. Buck straightened to see the robed figure staggering backward a few steps. He glanced up to see Jeff's white and sober face, but Jeff didn't look at him. Jeff watched the robed figure that made one tentative step towards him and his voice came, slowly and carefully.

"Whoever you are, I didn't mean to hurt you. I'm in this damned mix-up as deep as you, but this is my brother." He stopped and carefully pulled over his head the large square of sheeting whose center-cut hole made it a robe. He folded the robe once, then hung it over his arm. "I'm ready to go, Buck." He grinned at his brother and his teeth shone big and white in the moonlight. "You ain't got to knock hell out o' me."

Buck didn't smile in answer. He turned soberly back to the line of men and stood quietly for a moment before speaking.

"I've no quarrel with any man here," he said, softly, "but one o' you bastards won't take his losses like a man." He stopped and looked down the line. Nobody spoke. "One o' you hide 'n seek heroes ain't got the guts to do his own dirt." He stopped again. The silence was heavier. "If he'll step out o' line," he went on, casually, "I'll pay double what he claims he lost." No one moved. Buck laughed harshly. "Why, the yellow hound gets the rest o' you to whip a woman for him, but I can't hire him to take a beatin' himself." He turned to Jeff and gestured towards the line.

"Which one started this?"

Jeff shook his head.

"I won't say."

Buck let his eyes sweep down the ranks.

"If there's a man in the crowd," he said, carefully, "I'm servin' warnin' through him right now that the Bannons will whip their own women if they need it but they damned shore won't ask for help." He caught a long breath. "And there won't never be another Bannon to join a bunch o' sons-o'-bitches that have to herd up to strip a whore."

He turned and started towards the buggy with Jeff following. Hearn was standing, pale and dazed near the rear wheel, and Virgil still sat in the buggy with a set small smile on his lips. Buck reached to pull himself up.

"Wait a minute, Buck." The voice had come with a low rumble from the ranks behind. Buck turned slowly. One of the figures near the middle stepped out of line, pulling its hood slowly off as it came towards the buggy. Buck clenched his teeth together until he felt the muscles straining into knobs on his jawbones, as he recognized the hulking shoulders that rolled towards him.

"You'd a'been better off shoein' mules, Hopson," he said, tightly. The big shoulders rose a little under the robe, then fell back.

"I reckon," Hopson said and stopped in front of Buck. His breathing was slow and even, but it whistled through his teeth. "Ain't you started somethin' you ought to finish?"

Buck jerked his thumb at Jeff and Hearn.

"I came after my brothers," he said, shortly.

"Is that all?" Hopson's tone mocked him slightly.

Buck nodded.

"Well, I'll tell you," Hopson said, in a consciously drawling voice, "I ain't the man that started this and I won't say who did, but if I'd a'stood an' cussed a passel o' men for yellow bastards, I reckon I'd feel better if I proved I wasn't one."

Buck glanced sharply at the eyes of the broad slug of a man who faced him so squarely. The eyes were small and black, unblinking as a terrapin's in a fold of flesh that was like a long wrinkle. Buck looked back at the line of men, then quickly his eyes swung around to see Virgil in a small shaking of soundless laughter. Virgil moved his lips without noise, making Buck see the words, "I told you so."

"Well, I'll be goddamned," Buck said, tonelessly. He stood on tiptoe and tried to see over the line of men. The robes hid the girl too well for him to see her. He touched Hopson's arm.

"I reckon she's tied up?"

"Unh-hunh." Hopson's meaty face was expressionless.

Buck held out his hand.

"Lend me a knife."

A quick murmur of protest came from the line of men, but no one voice came out of the crowd to be recognized.

Hopson shook his head.

"You're on your own."

Buck glanced back of him at a small hissing sound. Jeff pulled his hand out of his pocket and tossed something towards him. Buck knew it in the moonlight. He caught it with one hand and turned it, experimentally, feeling the familiar shagginess of the deer-foot handle, wearing off near the jaws, but still thick at the butt end. He didn't look down at it, but kept his eyes on Hopson, gauging his reaction. He flipped out the long heavy blade which tapered down to a fine point, stained with dark threads where Joe Bannon had whittled from his tobacco plug.

Hopson showed no emotion and hardly looked at the knife.

"Papa'd raise hell if he knew you had this," Buck said over his shoulder at Jeff. Jeff didn't answer. Buck stropped the knife twice against the leg of his trousers, unconsciously trying to get the tobacco stains off the blade, not deliberately thinking, but with his mind lazily, almost sleepily wondering why the girl didn't make a sound, and if the men would let him through the line. Suddenly, he drew a deep breath and let it out slowly, almost sighing, and he started forward with his lower lip sticking out

[143]

and his eyes narrowed down. He heard plainly the quick indraw-
ing of breath from the ranks ahead of him and his lip tightened,
almost twisting back and down on itself. He felt his eyelids begin
to quiver and kept walking slowly forward, staring at the blank
white forms ahead. He turned the knife in his hand until the
sharp part of the blade hooked upwards, sticking out from under his thumb, and his eyes suddenly shifted to the waistline of the
men directly in front of him. His voice came without emphasis,
soft and almost musing.

"I've gutted a'many a hog with this knife."

The knife blade almost touched the robe in front of him. Buck
stopped, but didn't raise his eyes to the white blankness of the
hood.

"I'd hate to cut a friend, not even knowing who it is," he said in
the same low voice, "but if I have to I will." His words came
quicker, then, suddenly louder, with the tone higher. "I'm goin'
through this line, by God, one way or the other. Lay a hand on
me and at least one man's goin' to die."

His long left arm shot suddenly out and pushed against the
chest of the man in front of him. The man braced his feet and
held firm for a second, but didn't raise his hands from where
they hung at his sides. Buck pushed harder, forcing the man to
stagger backwards. He caught in his clenched hand a large fold
of the robe and felt with his fingers the tug of shirt beneath it. He
held the man stiff-armed away from him and stood very still in
the breach he had made in the line. His eyes went from side to
side and the point of the knife followed the direction of his gaze
from one to the other of the two figures on either side of him.
Neither of the two moved although the hoods with their rough-
cut holes were turned towards him. After a slow moment, Buck
turned his head towards the man he was holding at arm's-length.

"Back up," he said, softly, "until I tell you to stop. If anybody
touches me I'm goin' to kill you whether I know you or not."

He pushed and the man began to back up, slowly, towards the
magnolia tree. Buck followed, in short slow steps, keeping his
eyes steadily on the chest in front of him. The knife blade stuck
straight out from the side of his right hip, on which he had braced
his fist and the shaggy handle of the knife. As they went awkwardly towards the tree, Buck could hear the men behind him

breaking out of line. For a second the chill on the back of his neck crept down to shake him inside, but he heard Jeff and Hopson yell at the same time, and Hopson's words came, carrying a quick relief. "Leave him alone." Buck didn't look back but he breathed easier.

He guided the stumbling figure slightly to the left so he could look over its shoulder and see the magnolia and the girl who was tied to its trunk. He didn't recognize her at first, even though the moon laid a wide shoal of light right over her.

She was standing erect with her head up, bound only by her wrists which strained out behind her to meet each end of a rope whose length looped on around the big magnolia's bole. Her back was pressed tightly against the thick smooth bark with its patches of velvety fungus, so tightly that her small breasts stretched almost flat on her chest. She was naked except for a pair of high-buttoned black shoes and rolled black stockings, one of which had slipped down over the shoe top. Her long brown hair was still piled neatly, held in place by two tight plaits which crossed from side to side and went on around her head to be gathered together in the back and secured by a green roach comb. Her lips were pressed together until they almost disappeared. Her nostrils flared and her eyes glared wide and straight ahead with anger but no fear. Buck saw the small black pupil and iris set in the long whites of the eyes as he maneuvered the robed figure to his left so he could reach around back of her with his knife hand, and it was then that he recognized her.

"Well, I'll be damned, Naomi," he said, as he shoved the man directly in front of her and reached back with the knife. "If I'd a'known it was you, I'd a'hurried."

Naomi's face twisted viciously but she didn't answer. She kicked out and up with her left foot and the buttoned arch of her shoe thudded into the groin of the robed figure.

"Hey, look out—" Buck said, as the man yelped. He turned loose of the robe and the man fell, doubling up and groaning, twisting on his face in the grass. Buck caught her by her bare arm and his fingers dug cruelly into her flesh. "I ain't crazy about this job," he said, harshly, "an' I can quit it any time." He shook her. "I'll be damned if I can stand a cheap thief, myself." She was silent, but her lips worked and came back from her teeth. Buck

[145]

turned her arm loose and leaned back down. He cut the ropes and stood up. "Don't make no difference what a man's done, anyhow," he muttered, "he don't deserve that."

As the ropes fell loose, Naomi kicked out again at the man on the ground. Buck caught her arm again and jerked her roughly away. "You want me to leave you here?" He pulled her around until they faced the men who had come out of line and knotted up to one side near the buggy. Hopson and Jeff and Hearn were still grouped beside the rear wheel. Buck started walking fast towards them, holding onto Naomi's arm so that she was dragged, stumbling, in her high heels across the thick pad of grass.

"Let me go—just a minute," she panted, struggling to get loose, as they neared the buggy. "I'll kick hell out o' some more o' them—"

"Here, now," Buck broke in. "Hush up that kind o' talk an' get in the buggy." He held her by the elbow and shoved upwards as she put one foot on the round metal step. She was flung almost across Virgil and her elbow thumped against his guitar. Virgil started scrambling away from her. Buck heard several snickers from behind him and one man in the crowd whooped, "Hug 'er while it's free, Virgil."

Buck started to turn and face them, but Jeff caught his arm.

"Don't push it too far," Jeff whispered.

Buck glanced down at Jeff's sober, strained face and nodded, and through his mind flashed the runaway thought that at times this cautious, time-wasting, balance-wheel of a brother earned his salt. He turned abruptly and unthinkingly pushed against Naomi's bare buttock with the flat of his hand.

"Move over."

Naomi slapped automatically at his arm.

"Window-shopper," she said bitterly.

Buck flushed.

"Goddammit," he said, roughly, "you keep your mouth shut." He turned to Jeff. "Where's her dress?"

Jeff looked vaguely over Buck's shoulder and swallowed.

"Tore up."

Buck's lips curled.

"Ain't you proud? Throw me that sheet you're savin'." He caught the sheet and tossed it into Naomi's lap. "I hope," he said, warningly, to Jeff and Hearn together, "that you boys don't ever do nothin' to make me tell Mother what you're willin' to do for excitement."

One of the men in the still-hooded group laughed. He raised his voice to mock a child's.

"Don't tell mama on me."

Buck stood up in the buggy, feeling his face darken as blood rushed up.

"Now, I wouldn't a'brought this up," he said, spacing his words so they were very distinct, "but it looks like you all still ain't satisfied." He breathed slowly, pausing a long moment while the silence grew heavier in the swamp. "Any storekeeper knows ain't a sheet in the bunch been bleached," he went on, finally. "Wasn't a one in the lot o' you had the guts to bring a sheet from home." He paused again and heard muttering in the crowd. He held up his hand. "That just means," he said, casually, "that by tomorrow noon I'll know ever' man in Aven that bought sheetin'." The muttering started again. He raised his voice above it. "So, by God, ever' one o' you toe the mark or I'll see that ever' woman in town knows the name of ever' man in the crowd." He sat down, abruptly, and faced away from them. "Let's go, Virgil." Virgil slapped the lines down on the horse's rump. The buggy lurched.

Buck heard Hopson's bellow of laughter and it brought a quick, exulting grin to his lips, a grin which melted just as quickly when he saw Jeff and Hearn sitting side by side on the little flat box that rode behind the seat. He reached around and pushed Hearn off, then shoved at Jeff. They both stumbled backward, then turned around with alarm on their faces. Hearn said, "Hell, Buck."

"You walked out here," Buck yelled back. "Throw them sheets away an' go back through the woods. Ever'body'll think you been coon huntin'." He looked back to the front, laughing to himself, and neither of them spoke until the buggy swayed out of the gallberry clumps onto the small rutted road. Then Naomi's voice came low and venomous.

"Bastards ought to have to crawl."

Buck's tone was flat and emotionless as he answered.

"You're goin' to get a little better start on them, then you start walkin'." He heard her sharp intake of breath but he didn't look at her as he went on. "Anybody who'll steal eight dollars don't ride far with me." She didn't move or say a word. Buck put his feet up on the dashboard and leaned back in the seat.

"Get where you can steal a few thousand," he said, carelessly, "an' then you can work for me." She didn't answer, but Virgil said, "Hmph!" and Buck laughed low in his chest.

Virgil leaned down and looked across the girl's lap at Buck.

"Don't a thing in this world feel as good to you as winnin', does it, Buck?"

Buck shook his head.

Virgil straightened and raised his head until he looked up to where the light small clouds scuttled like puffy beetles across the dark sky.

"I hope to the Lord I ain't around when you lose somethin' that really counts."

Buck yawned and flipped his hand out.

"Losses don't worry me. I just draw a new hand an' raise all bets."

CHAPTER FIFTEEN

BUCK RECOGNIZED Amos Longshore's rig in front of the little house on Oak Street, and walked closer. "Married seven months," he was thinking, "an' the old devil hasn't missed many days visitin'. Reckon that's one good thing you can say for him."

He stopped beside the buggy with a hand on the shaft. The horse was blowing a little, easily, but with a full pumping that made his ribs show in the bright March moonlight. Buck slapped the horse on the chest and took out a white handkerchief to wipe his hand.

"Sweatin'," he said, wonderingly. "Old man must a'been high-tailin' it, and it dark." He turned and went through his small gate and up the walkway with his feet crunching and feeling mighty live on the fresh gravel. He was on the front porch and he could hear Ivy's voice, sounding high but far away, when the door suddenly opened and Amos Longshore came out.

"Evenin'," Buck said. "What's your hurry?"

Longshore nodded, but didn't speak. He turned his face straight towards his horse and buggy and nodded again, then he went on down the path and Buck could hear the dry crispness of his feet on the walkway. He looked after the old man for a moment.

"Wonder what's stuck in his craw."

He moved towards the doorway, still looking back, then shrugged and went inside. Ivy wasn't in the parlor, but he could hear small scraping sounds from the back so he went on through. Ivy was in the bedroom, lifting a box onto the bed. Her back was to Buck and she didn't turn around when he came into the room. She stooped to pick up another box.

"Here," Buck said, quickly. "You know better'n to be liftin'. I'll do that."

He hurried over and bent to help her. Ivy straightened up, but didn't speak.

"You know what the doctor said," Buck frowned. He started to put the box down but stopped suddenly and looked at it, then back up at Ivy and his eyes narrowed. He held the box over the bed,

"This is what you brought your clothes in," he said, slowly. "Goin' somewhere?"

"Home," Ivy said, and she held her head up high and her shoulders straight.

Buck's forehead creased between his eyes. He slowly eased the box down on the bed and straightened back up.

"Sick? Anything wrong about—?"

"No." Ivy shook her head. "What's wrong is with you."

Buck held his head on one side and looked at her, questioning. Ivy's face was pale and her forehead looked high and white and cold.

"Papa's big Jersey found a calf tonight," she said. "He had to come home through Baptist Bottom." Her eyes stayed on Buck's lips.

"Oh," Buck said, drawing it out. "I see." He nodded several times, then went on. "An' he saw me at Mabe's Place and come a'runnin' to tell you. Couldn't wait."

Ivy didn't speak. She put her hands behind her.

Buck nodded again.

"And you were goin' to run home without givin' me a chance to say anything."

"What could you say?" Ivy's voice was bitter. "They don't sell but one thing at a place like that."

Buck's face got darker and his eyes smaller.

"I was at Papa's," he said, trying to speak calmly, "and Mabe sent word that Tobe Parody had got hold o' too much and was throwin' chairs. I went down to get him." He stopped a moment. "Don't reckon your papa bothered to say I was holdin' Tobe up when he saw me."

"He told me," Ivy said. "But he couldn't tell me what made Tobe Parody more important than your sick father. Or me, here like this?"

"Tobe's my friend."

"Is he?" Ivy said, quickly. "What am I?"

Buck suddenly threw his shoulders back and shook his head.

"Now, by God," he said, "don't come houndin' me with hints and whinin' and women's words. Get down to rock and say what you mean, then we can work this thing out."

"Work it out?" Ivy's voice was scornful, then mocking. "Work

[150]

it out?" Her lips grew whiter and thinner. "I don't want to work it out. All I want to do is hate you."

Buck felt the blood leave his face and he walked to the side of the bed and threw both boxes off onto the floor. He sat down and crossed his legs.

"Sit down," he said.

Ivy didn't move. Buck waited a second, looking at her.

"Ivy," he said, trying to speak patiently, "I've told you that I went to Mabe's to get Tobe. There wasn't a reason in the world I could see why I oughtn't to have gone. Looks like me sayin' that would be enough to satisfy you."

Ivy's face didn't change.

"I believe that much of it," she said. "But you can't live with a man for six months without knowing something about him."

"What does that mean?"

Ivy's lips rose slightly at one corner, half sneering and half smiling bitterly.

"You've always taken what you've wanted." She laughed a little, then. "And I know the things you want. You're a strong man, but a weak man."

Buck stood up slowly.

"You think I stayed with one o' the girls?"

"Didn't you?"

Buck lowered his head a little, bull-like, and breathed deeply.

"Ivy," he said, suddenly, loudly, "you listen a minute. If I had stayed with one of 'em it wouldn't have had a thing to do with me and you. You said you know the kind of man I am. Well, if I'd stayed with one of 'em, it would have been just part of bein' a man like me. It wouldn't have touched me and you. What I've done wrong, if I didn't do it to you, don't seem like it ought to get us all flustered." He stopped as quickly as he had started.

"Didn't you?" Ivy said, flatly.

Buck's face got white and his lips thinned and pulled down. He stood for a long moment, watching her, but he didn't answer. Ivy's lips curled again and she bent over at the waist with her fists clenched tightly, held away from her hips.

"You did," she said, spitting her words out. Then she straightened back up and held her head back again, looking him in the face. "They fluttered their hips, didn't they?" she mocked him again. "And you couldn't wait?" She put one hand on her hip and threw her head to one side. "This is how they do it. Except they don't have babies." She clenched her fist again and leaned closer and her face was reddening. "You did do it. Didn't you?"

Buck let all the breath in his lungs escape slowly and he lifted his hands and let them fall back in a small gesture.

"Didn't you?"

"Yes," Buck said, flatly, neither sorry nor defiant.

Ivy began to laugh and it wasn't pretty. It was like it hurt to get it out. She tried to talk, choking a little.

"I can see what happened," she was saying. "Those girls were women before they were fancy. And I'm a woman." Her lips curled. "Here's big old Buck Bannon," she mocked the girls. "Got married and turned into an old man. Got more'n he can take care of at home. Big Old Buck."

She laughed some more like it hurt and her eyes were shiny and hard and dry. Buck stood watching her.

"You know how they talk," he said, slowly.

"I ought to," Ivy said, still laughing, chokily. "You remember the times you've told me. In bed, bragging that it never cost you after the first time."

Buck watched her for a moment longer, then his eyes grew smaller.

"The way you talk you'd have made a good one," he said.

Ivy started to laugh again, but stopped and turned her head quickly to one side and listened. Buck heard it, then. Someone had come through their front door in a hurry. Buck left the room and as he turned into the hall, he looked over his shoulder at Ivy. She was staring at his back, making little coughing sounds in her chest.

It was Jeff and his eyes looked big in his face and his freckles stood out dark against his paleness. He was frowning uncertainly and breathing fast.

"Papa wants you," he said, when he'd come a little closer down the hall.

Buck's face whitened, and suddenly his anger was gone, leaving him with a dead feeling inside. His mouth was dry when he spoke.

"Is he—?" He felt helpless, looking at Jeff's face. He cleared his throat roughly and glanced away. "He all right?" he said, casually.

Jeff shook his head. "No, he ain't. He's took right bad since you been gone."

Buck's eyes flickered over Jeff's shoulders to some point up the hall, then back to his brother. "You got a rig out there?"

Jeff nodded and Buck turned back towards the bedroom. Ivy was still standing where he had left her, still looking as if she were listening for something.

"I'm going to Papa," he said, and waited for her to answer. "He's bad off." She didn't speak.

"I'll be back as soon as I can," he said, and she still didn't speak or move. He turned then and left with Jeff. He didn't look back again.

All the children were still up when Buck got to the big house. They were in the parlor, sitting around big-eyed on furniture that was still stiff with newness because it had not been used. Some of the little ones were yawning and some were trying not to laugh at things that wouldn't have been funny if they had felt free to laugh. Their eyes swung to Buck as he passed the door and looked inside, and all the eyes followed him, wonderingly, until they couldn't see him any more.

Then he was at the door to the big bedroom and he could see his father.

Joe Bannon's square red beard looked a little ragged. It rested on top of the covers and for a second it seemed to Buck that there was nothing to his father but his beard and the eyes that moved calmly from face to face in the room. Then he saw his father's hands, lying large and clumsy, one across the other, pale now and still against the dark woolen quilt.

His mother stirred slightly in the rocker near the small fire, and Buck glanced at her, then back to his father, and to the bulky white-haired man who stood by the side of the bed.

"Evenin', Doc."

The doctor nodded and smiled and his eyes were kind, looking deeply out from under shaggy white eyebrows. He reached out and slipped his fingers under Joe Bannon's wrist and inclined his head slightly. Joe Bannon shook his wrist until the doctor took his hand away.

"Ain't you already made up your mind?" he said.

The doctor nodded.

"Ain't nothin' else you can do?"

The doctor shook his head.

"Well," Joe Bannon said, "good night, Doc."

The doctor smiled and touched the wrist again, not feeling for the pulse but touching it as he would touch the shoulder of a friend, touching it like a handshake with light blunt fingers. Then he stooped and picked up his black bag.

"Good night, Joe," he said, and came around the bed and walked close by Buck. "I'll be in the parlor," he said, softly. Buck nodded.

Joe Bannon didn't move his head as Buck came nearer the bed, but his eyes followed him.

"He says I'm 'bout petered out, boy."

Buck didn't speak, but his eyes and his head gestured in a question towards his mother's quiet back.

The beard moved a little on the covers.

"Mother?" Joe Bannon said, raising his eyebrows. "She's been right here an' heard it all." He was quiet then, but the covers moved as if his chest had arched and his hands fumbled with each other. The clock ticked out loudly on the mantelpiece and it sounded to Buck as if it got louder with each tick.

"Heart trouble," his father said, wryly. "Huh! Ever'body dies from heart trouble."

"How long—?" Buck started, then stopped. "When does he—?"

His father moved his feet irritably and frowned against sudden pain.

"Don't reckon I'll see day."

"Aw, Papa," Buck said, swiftly, and moved closer. His mother turned and spoke sharply.

"Buck." Buck turned his head and stopped. "He's made up his mind," Jeanie Bannon said, softly. Buck looked from one to the other, breathing unevenly. The clock ticked louder.

"I better talk while I can," his father said, calmly. "You and your ma have got to do what's to be done without me." He tried to lift his head. "Sit closer, Jeanie," he said.

The mother moved, drawing her chair from near the fire, and Buck pulled over a straight-backed chair. It gave him a queer stirring inside to see his father's shoes under the edge of the bed.

They were black, with high tops and knob toes, and there was a cloth strap hanging limply out the back of each shoe. Buck wondered dully where the socks were—he'd always seen the shoes with white cotton socks laid carefully across the toes—then he remembered that his father hadn't worn the shoes for over a week.

"Buck," his father said, clearly. "Look up at me."

Buck raised his head.

"You're goin' to be the lead horse after I'm gone," the old man said, bluntly. "But your ma is goin' to hold a check rein on you. I ain't sayin' you couldn't handle what I got better'n most. It's that I been worried sometimes that you'd let a dollar outshine what it'll buy. Mother's to hold you down."

Buck didn't answer. His mother stirred in the rocker.

"Tell him how, Joe," she said. "It's best said out."

The old man nodded. "She'll own what I leave, boy," he said. "She'll own it in her lifetime for her and the rest of you. Ain't nobody to get hurt in the split and ain't no one to get more'n the other, high nor low."

Buck looked straight ahead, over the bedstead.

"Papa," he said, slowly, then his father broke in.

"I don't mean to low-rate you, son. I couldn't do that without sayin' I just did a poor job of work on you."

Buck nodded and looked at the floor in silence. The windows rattled faintly and Buck raised his head, listening with fierce concentration for the sound he knew would follow. Then it came, a far-off, lonesome, late autumn sound, a low trembling whine that belonged with the smell of burning leaves and dusk. It wasn't the sound for a March midnight. Buck felt its out-of-placeness and wondered at the way a train whistle could seem wrong mourning through the steaming bogs of Old Bay on the night his father was to die.

They sat close to him, through the night, moving occasionally for Buck to tiptoe out to shake the doctor's hand at the front door, or for Jeanie to go quietly into the parlor and send the younger children to bed. She made coffee several times, balancing the big blackened pot on the corner of the grate, and they drank it black as if they hated to leave the room for sugar. Buck rose now and then, when the winds plucked at the eaves and shook the windows. He carefully spread the ashes under the grate

[155]

to give a better draft and laid new coal on, gently because he didn't want to jar the live fire down onto the ashes.

Joe Bannon spoke once more before dawn. He spoke in a careful, rounded manner, slowly, in spite of his chest twisting under the covers.

"A for Apple," he said, feeling his way. "A-P, Ap. P-L-E, Pull. A-P-P-L-E, Appull." He finished, triumphantly, then his chest stopped heaving for a while and the old man relaxed, breathing gently.

Buck walked tiptoe over near his mother.

"What's he sayin'?"

"He's back in Louisiana. He went to parish school there for ninety days after the war. He was twenty-one then."

The two of them watched until just before false dawn, mostly in long silences, but sometimes in quick flurries of talk. Once, Jeanie Bannon eased up from her chair and stood over her husband for a moment, watching his body twist, then she leaned over him.

"Bear *to* the pain," she said, so softly that Buck could hardly hear her. "That's the way to birth a baby and it ought to help now. It'll quicken it."

Buck moved around the bed. He touched her arm.

"We don't want to quicken it."

His mother turned her head slowly and looked up at her son.

"He does, an' God knows this is one time he ought to get what he wants."

"He can't hear you."

She turned away from the bed and stood for a moment with her left hand pressed tightly against her cheek.

"I know," she said, slowly, "but he'll know I tried to help— later on."

Buck wondered at times through the night what it would be like, walking back to his own home in the dawn, thinking and knowing that his father wouldn't be there any more. Then he'd force his mind away, feeling somehow a gnawing sense of guilt that he *could* wonder how his father's death would affect him. He'd try to work his mind over what was to come, but it was sluggish and always it swung sullenly back, seeing his mother turn from the bed with a bewildered unseeing stillness in her eyes.

Then his mind would puzzle that the eyes were dry. Neither of them had been able to relax in grief. He wondered if it were hardness or strength, or weakness, or if other people, who carried on so at death, were furnished better by God for living or dying.

It seemed that folks ought to cry. Yet, *they* didn't, or wouldn't, or couldn't.

Not even when the long legs suddenly stiffened under the comfort, could his mother cry. Even when the coarse red beard suddenly jutted its last time towards the ceiling, and even when the pain-arched chest sighed limply back, Jeanie Bannon's eyes were dry. And Jeff, when Buck had gone in and turned him quietly out of bed to tell him his father had died, Jeff hadn't cried. He had dressed silently and looked once through the door at his father. Then he had gone out the back towards the barn, and Buck knew he would be worrying with his fingers the stub of a pencil in his coat pocket and wondering what to write. Jeff kept the records, and Buck knew without seeing it, how he would lean his left forearm above his head against the crib door and write, "Daddy. Died March thirteenth," and forget to put the year down. Like he would forget to put down the year for other things. It would just be "Pigs. Born August fourth," never telling which litter or what year.

Then Buck would shake his head again, beating his tired mind back from pigs and dates to seeing his mother. She went out of the room for a moment, then came quietly back to Joe Bannon's body, with her clippers and her scissors and a neat square of brown paper. She shook her head when Buck asked her to let a barber do it this time. She lifted with gentle hands the ragged ends of the red beard.

"I did it while he was alive," was all she would say.

He watched her while the fire fell low in the grate, as she bent over to sight down the line of jaw, then clipped with the old smooth flirt of her wrist, throwing whiskers off the blade onto the brown paper. He watched until she finished, until the cold full dawn was seeping through the windows, then he took the brown paper and crumpled it hard around the whisker ends and stuffed it into the grate over the greying coals. He turned around, touching her arm with his hand, and looking down into her eyes for a long moment. They were still dry.

"I'm goin' now," he said, gently. "I'll take care of whatever comes next." He held his cheek against hers for a moment, then he turned and walked out of the room.

He walked home with the sun's rays coming into his eyes across the dark line of timber far to the east. They didn't slant downwards, but cut like a fine bright spray, filtering level with the earth through trees and brush. In the small town field to his right, Buck could see the sun bouncing lightly on dead corn shucks whose blue-grey backs had been polished by frost.

His mind groped at the fact of his father's death, pawed it and turned it to look at it again, then let it lie, and caught feverishly at shallow things. "Papa's dead," he would say, dully, and try hard to think of nothing else. Then his mind would cheat him again. While he walked stiffly up the steps of his own house, it kept telling him carefully, over and over, that he had drunk too much coffee.

The house was cold when he opened the door and, unconsciously, he tiptoed in, seeing the furniture only vaguely in the half light. He went quietly on down the hall, wondering at the strangeness he felt in his own home. He stopped at the open door to the bedroom.

The room was very neat, except that in the middle of the bed was a crumpled wad of tissue paper and part of a small roach comb. Ivy wasn't there.

Buck whirled quickly around and started towards the kitchen, then stopped, and turned his head to the left, listening.

"Ivy," he called. There wasn't any answer. He went back into the bedroom and opened a drawer in a small dresser. It was empty. The clean brown paper with which Ivy had lined her new dresser drawers still looked crisp and fresh. Buck shut it carefully so it wouldn't squeak in the deadness of the house.

"Oughtn't to leave a man at a time like this," he said thickly, and stood still a moment, looking down at the little comb on the bed.

Then, slowly, he turned around and went out of the room and down the hall and out on the front porch. He locked the front door very carefully and put the key in his pocket, then he stood a moment, undecided, watching the sun bulge higher over the trees.

Suddenly, as if he had made up his mind, he started off towards Longshore's home, stumbling a little on the gravel walk.

Amos Longshore answered the door and stood there, dry and grey and stiff, neat in a clean white shirt that he kept buttoned tight around his neck without a tie. He nodded once when Buck asked to see Ivy. "I'll see," he said, and turned back down the hall, shutting the front door.

Buck stayed on the porch, not feeling the cold, but breathing deeply the crisp air, with his mind fastening sketchily on small things—how the smells came in layers on the air like warm water would lie in a layer on top of the creek when he was a boy so his feet would be cold and his head in blood-warm water. He just thought, dully, until Longshore opened the door again. Longshore's voice was brittle and certain.

"She won't see you."

Buck hardly heard him.

"Papa died," he said.

Longshore started closing the door.

"He was a good man," he said, and Buck felt more than heard the slight heaviness laid on the first word. His feet were stiff and clumsy going down the steps and something too big was in his throat, but he didn't look back.

INTERLUDE

"JAKE!"

Bascom Wooten shoved his foot out and stuck his toe into the ribs of the overalled figure. Jake Willis lay still on the bank of the wide creek whose shallow ripplings drowned the faraway sounds from the woods and from the main gravel highway to Albany.

"Jake!" Bascom kicked harder.

Jake looked up and Bass was surprised that this was the first time he had noticed the yellowish tint the past ten years had painted into the whites of Jake's eyes.

[159]

"Hunh?" Jake said, stupidly.

"It's after sun. Get your pole an' let's get on in."

"What the hell we got to go home to?" Jake rolled over, then got up on his knees. He scratched his red, wrinkling neck and yawned. He caught at Bass's belt to haul himself up. Bass stepped back.

"You'll rot there, 'fore I'll pull you up, you lazy hound."

Jake stood up alone, groaning, and prodded Bass in the stomach with his thumb.

"The last few years shore did put a belly on you."

He bent to pick up the pole that lay behind him, but his knees creaked and he didn't bend any further. He straightened up slowly without the pole.

"Ain't worth it."

Bass snorted. He shouldered his own pole and started off, balancing his tidy little belly ahead of him in its cradle of faded blue overall bib.

"Ten years might a' put guts on me," he said, over his shoulder, "but it shore took 'em out o' you."

"I ain't lazy," Jake protested, following in a stately shamble that moved his body in sections so that his head dipped with each step like a pond gannet feeding off the bottom. "I'm liverish," he said, seriously. Bass didn't answer. "I mean it," Jake went on loudly. "Durned if sometimes I don't feel like I'm fixin' to shoot the eight rock."

"What do you care?" Bass said without turning his head or slowing down. "Anybody sleeps as much as you do wouldn't lose but six hours a day if he did die."

Jake didn't answer for a long time, not until they reached Acid Plant Hill on the edge of the Negro quarters, and saw the lights of Aven beginning to blink on in the gathering dusk. He muttered then, defensively.

"By God, you're on top now, Bass, an' that's the very reason you oughtn't to kick a man that's down." He grumbled wordlessly for a moment, then said, "Besides, by granny, you got the education. I never went no further'n high four at Old Columbia."

Bass stopped on the brow of the mound that the flat land lovers of Aven called a hill.

"Neither did Buck Bannon," he said, absently, letting his eyes rove over the twinkle of lights and the haze of smoke *and the shifting odors of suppers cooking.*

"I ain't no damned hog, though," Jake said, roughly.

"Hog?" Bass pointed out at the lights below them. He's a hog an' a land-grabber, but it was the hogs that built that town." He thumped the end of his pole on the ground. "I wish to the Lord I was a hog. Men like Buck, no matter how much you hate 'em for workin' by the rule, 'do it,' are the ones who make the country grow." He spat fiercely. "You think if they'd a'left it to me an' you, we'd ever a'built a school, or a fire department, or bricked the streets downtown? Why, hell no. We'd a'been asslin' around drunk when it come time for electric lights, but one o' them hogs says to hisself, 'If I don't get that there for my wife, she's goin' to wear tears in her face big as sweet-gum balls.' So, by God, we all get lights just because some money-grabber's wife is too proud to clean a coal-oil lamp."

He stopped suddenly to catch his breath and turned his face away from the awed look in Jake's eyes.

"Hotamighty!" Jake breathed.

"Well, I mean ever' word of it," Bass snapped. "The town's boomin'. Gettin' pretty, too." He jerked his pole off the ground and used it like a pointer. "Power plant." He kept jabbing at different spots. "Our own distillery, feed mills, fertilizer factory, cotton gins, brick buildin's, an' a God-blessed courthouse so you won't have to go clean to Abbeville to get hung."

"Now, Bass," Jake said, mildly. "You know we ain't never had the money for stuff like that."

Bass sniffed loudly.

"We had more'n Buck had when he come to town, but we throwed it away on liquor or women or fancy clothes."

Jake's voice was soft.

"An' what we didn't throw away they took."

Bass glared at him in disgust.

"Sometimes, I think they ought to take it away from us. At least they know what to do with it." He frowned. "Just what would you do with a hundred dollars right now?"

"Me?" Jake looked startled. "Why, I reckon I'd—" His voice trailed off.

"I know, if you don't," Bass took it up. "You'd get your watch *back from Buck so you could take a job you're gettin' too old to handle an' then throw your pay away ever' week."*

"Well, hell," Jake said, "a man needs a watch."

"Hmph! Fellow been without a watch long as you have ought to know that how long the clock says ain't near as important as how long it felt."

Jake looked puzzled.

"You crazy?"

"I reckon," Bass said, slowly, and let his gaze drift again over Aven, growing brighter every minute. "You know what Buck'd do with a hundred dollars. He'd buy land, or furnish a farmer, or lend it out at interest."

Jake's lips twitched.

"Or buy votes?"

Bass suddenly was uncomfortable.

"I know he started that, but damned if I blame him. Wasn't no other way to beat Longshore's gang out an' he had to beat him. After that girl left, anyhow. 'Nother thing—if he had to steal the job of mayor, it was worth it to Aven because the damned town didn't have enough cash to buy one day's feed for its mules."

Jake shook his head, slowly, studying. Finally, he said,

"One thing gets me is he ain't like them other politicians. He don't never make a speech."

"Smart," Bass said. "A man makes a speech, he can't brag on hisself like the other man can brag on him."

Jake searched his teeth with a broken pine straw and his eyes grew thoughtful. "May be right," he said, "but there's somethin' else bothers me. Who in hell got him to run in the first place?"

"He did. Come to me one day an' said some o' the other fellows was after him to run, but he wouldn't feel right about it unless the Railroad Brotherhood brought him out."

Jake whooped.

"Lord," he said, "he worked you an' the Brotherhood." He shook his head admiringly. "His pa shore had his mind on it when he got Buck."

"He's one, all right." Bass teetered on his heels, reflectively. "For instance, you notice when that girl run off an' took his kid to Georgia, he didn't go out an' throw the ball over the fence

like we'd a'done. He just buried his pa, rented out his house, moved in with his ma, an' in five years he was mayor." Bass looked meaningfully at Jake. "An' he kept his mouth shut about her."

Jake slapped his thigh.

"Talkin' 'bout me wastin' on women, look at him. It was a woman made that girl clear out."

Bass looked at him with pity in his eyes.

"You fool. Buck an' them others wait till they make it 'fore they spend it." He laughed cruelly. "An' besides, they get theirs free."

Jake rubbed his dry fingers across his chin while his eyes slowly grew bitter and his mouth worked soundlessly.

"This world ain't balanced," he mumbled. "Rich man gets it throwed at him, an' us pore bastards—" He stopped and sighed deeply. "Hey, Lord, this world, then that last white shirt an' the next world."

They stood that way for a long minute and darkness seemed to creak in over them, waking up the small things in the grass and the straggling pines and putting life into the little frogs who sawed away at the night in the bottom land below them.

"Well, sir," Bass said, softly as he started down hill, "right or wrong, one thing's dead certain—Buck never done a thing yet that either one of us wouldn't like to do."

CHAPTER SIXTEEN

Buck knew who his visitor was from the shapeless shadow form on the frosted glass door. He could tell by the way she tilted her head on one side before she touched the knob and he knew the shape of the bonnet. She was the only woman in Aven still wearing bonnets.

He was frowning as if he were annoyed when she came inside, sidling a little, as if she hated to open the door too wide. He watched in silence as she turned to look back at the writing on the glass.

"Humph! Private," she said. "Many times as I've washed the rings from a May haw pond off your legs."

"That's to keep folks out," Buck said, smiling to soften it.

She came slowly forward, paying no attention to what he said, but looking around and clucking her tongue at the bright new plaster on the walls of the city hall office. When she was close enough, she rubbed her hand carefully across the top of his desk and her fingers seemed to relish the smoothness and linger on the grain. She looked for dust on her fingers when she sat down, then smoothed the bonnet back off her head so as not to muss up her white hair. She smiled before she spoke, showing her teeth just as strong and white as they ever had been.

"I don't know whether to be glad my boy's the mayor," she said, "or mad 'cause he won't come when I want him."

"Lord," Buck said, "don't get mad. Enough folks hammerin' on me as it is." He ran his big hands, white now and smooth, but still hard and strong, through his hair that was just as black and coarse and only slightly higher on the forehead.

"I ain't here to argue," she said, "but I reckon you *could* come when I need you."

"I was comin'," Buck said, impatiently.

"Maybe you were comin' when *you* got ready," his mother said. "I wanted you when *I* was ready."

"Must be important," Buck twisted his mouth.

His mother didn't speak for a second, just let her eyes rove up and down and over his shoulders and chest, thicker, and heavier, but more carefully dressed in dark plain clothes.

[164]

"You got bigger," she said, suddenly, "without gettin' a belly, too." She looked proud as her eyes went up to his hair. "You got the McPherson hair. Heavy an' black, but it'll turn. Papa never had a grey hair."

Buck snorted.

"Papa never had as much to worry over as I got either."

"Fourteen children," his mother said, jerking her head up some, "where you got one an'—" She stopped, then, and looked at the big silk knot of Buck's blue tie. "I—" she started to go on, when Buck shook his head. Buck's face scarcely seemed to have changed expression, yet there was a hardness and a whiteness near his mouth.

"Go on," Buck said, speaking low. "An' he's in Waycross, Georgia, with his mother, an' the only thing I got to do to raise him is keep sendin' that check ever' month." His shirt front moved as his chest pushed out in a long breath.

"No, son," she said, quickly, looking up now at his eyes. "I shouldn't—" She shook her head. "It's hard to watch your tongue when somethin's swellin' in your mind."

Buck didn't answer and the lids came down slowly, hiding his grey eyes. His mother sighed and straightened up and cleared her throat.

"Well, business," she said, and her smile was little and somehow sad, fading off and settling into still lines that ran from her nostrils to the corners of her lips.

"You've done mighty well," she said, and the words had a testing sound to them, as if she were feeling him with them. She looked up over his head a moment, pursing her lips.

"We had two buildin's when Papa died," she said. Buck nodded. "An' we got twelve now?" Buck let one corner of his mouth slide up but didn't answer. "We got four-five times as much farmin' land as he ever owned," she went on. "We run two stores here an' one in Georgia, a bank downtown, and my boy's the mayor."

She nodded her head approvingly and made a little sucking, squeaking sound with her lips.

"Wait a minute," Buck said, slowly, laughing a bit, "they're my stores an' my bank. You claimed too much."

She laughed with him, then, and for a second neither of them spoke. She looked up finally with something timid in her eyes.

"Remember what Papa told us?"

Buck nodded.

"You to straw-boss," she went on, "but me to ride herd an' use a check rein when I figured it was time."

Buck nodded again.

"You're thirty-eight now," she said, "an' that'd make it around ten years. In all that time, I never said whoa once."

Buck didn't move now, he just watched silently as her hands went to the hem of her handkerchief and began to pleat.

"Well, I ain't goin' to say whoa," she said, "but I've got a few things I want done." Her eyes questioned Buck's but he answered with a shrug and spread his hands out on the desk.

" 'Bout Wiley and some o' the others," she said, bluntly. "They ain't gettin' near what's their part. They need it now an' I want 'em to have it."

Buck shook his head quickly. "No," he said.

His mother sat up straighter.

"They're mine," she said, "just like you. I want 'em to have their share like your papa laid out for you to give 'em."

Buck's face settled into hard, bargaining lines and his lower lip stuck out a little and his eyes stayed still on his mother's face.

"They get their share of what he left," he said, flatly.

"I know that," Jeanie Bannon said, quickly, "but they don't get any part of what's been made with it since Papa died."

"Didn't make any of it, either," Buck said. "They laid around suckin' rum and gamblin' while some of us worked. I don't figure they ought to get a part of what somebody else makes."

"You drink as much as Wiley," she said, "an' you gamble an' do worse. Jeff an' Hearn do their share, too, though I will say Jeff ain't as bad as you and Hearn. He sidles around here, savin' string or mighty near it, an' lookin' like he's too busy to play, but—" She stopped and pulled down the corners of her mouth and looked wisely up at Buck through her lashes. "We ain't got no business in Macon, Georgia, an' the girls've been hearin' things about some diamonds an' stuff bein' bought."

Buck didn't look up or answer.

"Hearn," she went on, "he works two hours an' hunts or fishes the rest o' the day, then he dresses up like a barber off duty an' starts flashin' around like he'd done somethin'!" She shook her head warningly. "You started somethin' you can't stop with them two."

Buck's lips curled.

"Jeff an' Hearn don't drink workin'," he said. "An' they gamble on their own time with their own money. So do I." He tapped the desk. "Besides," he went on, heavily, "you an' me can't blame Hearn too much." He looked at her with meaning in his eyes.

She flushed.

"I reckon maybe we'd a'best kept our hands out o' that mess with the Tiller girl. He'd a'been better off married to her."

He didn't speak while she breathed audibly and when she spoke again her voice was strained.

"Anyhow, if they need it, I want 'em to have it. If your boy —?" She stopped quickly and looked down at the handkerchief she was twisting in her lap.

Buck swung around in his chair until he could see out the window into the late afternoon and he didn't speak for a long time. She looked up once at the back of his head, then down, as he turned around.

"I'll look into it," he said, "an' see what ought to be done."

Jeanie Bannon nodded quickly.

"Now," she said, as if she were in a hurry, "there's the baby girls."

"Babies?" Buck smiled. "Christina's fourteen."

She looked sheepish. "Don't look like I can quit callin' 'em that. An' there's Vesta an' Millie both older'n her."

"Old enough," Buck grunted, "to grab a handful o' money through the wicket down at the bank an' run like hell."

Jeanie Bannon sat up straight and her mouth shut tight.

"Ain't no use in lookin' like that, now," Buck said. "They do it all right. One of 'em gets Hearn to talkin' 'bout some girl down at one end an' the other two load up at the other end o' the counter. Hearn's lost half his salary payin' back what they steal."

His mother sat back in her chair, then relaxed again. She frowned.

"That ain't stealin'," she said, comfortably, "it's takin'. An' that's part o' what I meant to talk about." She drew a long breath.

"I want 'em to go to school. Not a school like Miz Kirkland's, but a boardin' school, one I heard about up in Tennessee. Edgemont School for Young Ladies."

"Good God," Buck said, "ain't they learnt enough to get married yet? That's all they'll do."

"They know enough to marry like the big girls did," she said, grimly, "just to be gettin' out of the house. But it takes some schoolin' to marry better'n that."

Buck snorted. "You married a dirt farmer," he said.

"Yes," she nodded, and she threw her shoulders back and her eyes flickered, "but I had my choice an' I took it. Now I want to see them able to turn down anybody they please."

"That'll cut deep into what we made this year," Buck said, warning with his eyes.

She shook her head. "Don't care," she said, stubbornly, "an' it won't hold a patch to what else I want for 'em." She looked a warning back at him. "I want 'em to have some property in their own names," she said, calmly. "A house each, built on the three corners left up on the block. I can keep an eye on them that way. Then I want you to write out some deeds, givin' each one a good enough buildin' downtown for them to draw a pretty fair sum." She nodded her head briskly, tapping down on the words. "A good house an' a little money never hurt no girl's chances to marry right," she said.

Buck closed his eyes, then opened them again.

"In the name of the Lord," he said, "what do you think'll be left? We ain't plumb rich, we're just gettin' comfortable."

"Well, if we ain't," Jeanie Bannon said, "you better let me pick out another straw boss."

Buck set his teeth tightly and his eyes narrowed.

"I'm sayin' you shouldn't give that stuff to them girls yet."

"I'm gettin' along," she said. "Now's the time."

"I won't do it," Buck said, flatly.

His mother stared at him and the color left her face. For a second, her eyes dulled, then they flared back and the lids came down over them until they were almost hidden. Her mouth drew down.

"Buck," she said, softly, "you're a big man in Aven. Mighty big for your age. But don't tell me you *won't* do somethin'.

You've come fast an' hard an' some got tromped on your way. There ain't a soul in town can tell you how to move, but I'm tellin' you now if you don't do what I say, I'll show you how you learned to ride roughshod." She breathed faster, and some of the color spotted back into her cheeks.

Buck shook his head, still staring at her. He didn't change expression.

"You didn't ask for no rulin's," she went on, "when you started out here in Aven. You made rules up after you'd done what suited you. You bought votes to get elected mayor an' you joined the biggest church in town just to get their votes. You've played big Ike with Joe Bannon's estate an' borrowed money because folks thought the estate was backin' the loan when it wasn't. An' kept the profits off the loan for yourself. Now, when I want the others to get their share, you get down in the lines an' won't move." She reached out one hand with the fist clenched tightly and laid it on Buck's desk.

"You didn't get your ways from Joe Bannon," she said, "that's pure 'n tee McPherson an' it comes straight from me."

She was quiet, then, just looking at Buck, seeing some of the blood leave his face. He lowered his head and leaned closer, staring out of the tops of his eyes.

"You through?" he said, careful to hold his voice steady.

She leaned forward, too, resting her forearms on the desk, looking directly at him and breathing evenly. Her hands were still, one lying over the other. She nodded.

"I helped make ever' dime Papa had when he died," he said, speaking low and slowly, "an' since then I've put 'em to work. I've made more cold-out dollars for that estate than Papa ever saw or heard of, an' I never asked for nor took a dime more'n my share. There ain't another'n in the family that could a' done it. You know that, mighty well."

He looked at his mother with a question in his eyes and she just lifted one corner of her mouth.

"Well," Buck went on, "that's all I got to say. I don't deny anything an' I don't admit a damned thing. Papa told me to straw-boss this outfit an' I aim to do it. He told me to advise you about the property an' I've done it. That's all."

Jeanie Bannon seemed to have shrunk in her stiff grey silk

dress and the lines of her face were deeper, but the eyes gleamed brightly, and her mouth twisted.

"You gave your advice," she said, "an' I'm turnin' it down." She sat back in her chair, slowly, and her hands worked deliberately to open her purse and drop the twisted and wadded handkerchief inside. "I could do it without you, get a lawyer, but I kinda wanted you to come in with me an' maybe help me," she said, holding her voice low. Her chin lost its squareness for a second and she looked at Buck with hope in her eyes. He didn't look up and the hardness about her mouth came back, deepening the lines. "But if you don't aim to do it easy," she went on, as if there'd been no pause, "I'll have to see if you'll do it hard."

Buck shook his head, but didn't look up. She rose from her chair and stood quietly a moment with her knuckles bracing on the desk top. She breathed heavily.

"You give me an accountin' of ever' dollar in the estate," she said, "an' I'll run it, or get it run."

Buck clenched his teeth and his jaw jutted out. His lips got white and tight and a small muscle swelled in his jaw.

"That enough to make you do it?" she said. He shook his head slowly, not taking his eyes off her face. She leaned closer over the desk as if she needed its support and her hand touched an ink bottle and made it rattle slightly in the silence. She sighed once, long and slow like it hurt her.

"All right," she said, warning bluntly, "see if this will." She tightened her lips. "That stock the estate owns in that little bank o' yours. Get ready to buy it, or see me sell control out from under you."

Buck didn't answer, but his face got whiter and his lips pulled back slightly from his teeth.

"That enough?" she said, urging him somehow with her tone, but carrying a challenge in her words.

Buck slowly shook his head.

"I'll sell it to Longshore." Her words rushed out as if she had no control over them, and her lower lip shook. Buck rose slowly until he was looking down at her and his eyes got smaller until the lid over his left eye began to tremble slightly.

"You'd sell me out to *him?*"

She couldn't speak. She nodded once.

[170]

Buck's slow smile was ugly.

"Do it, then," he said, "by God."

Jeanie Bannon's teeth clenched tightly and her bottom lip protruded as her head lowered. She looked steadily into Buck's eyes for a moment, then turned and walked with her back straight and her head high towards the door.

"Wait," Buck called. She turned back, halfway around, and watched his lips over her shoulder. He leaned forward on the desk a little.

"You can't drive me," he said. "I may come to it by myself an' do it without pushin', but I won't be whipped into it." He shook his head slowly. "Not by anybody—not even you."

It was nearing night a week later, when Buck walked slowly up the steps to his mother's home, listening as he went to the sounds within the house. He could hear a scuffling and a panting as he opened the front door and a high-pitched yell came from the room nearest him. He started down the hall towards the room. His eyes were red and puffy in the light and his face was tired with tight lines drawing down from his nostrils.

He was near the door when a small boy came slowly down the hall. Syrup dripped from a soggy hole in a biscuit held just above his mouth and the boy licked gravely at the bottom. He had bright red curly hair and his nose looked like all the Bannons'. His mouth was softer than the Bannons', though, and the lips wrinkled when his mouth was closed. Buck's eyes drew down tight, looking at the boy's pleated lips and vaguely he wondered if it were distaste he could see on the face before him. He sighed. Ernestine's oldest kid, Buck knew, but for the life of him he couldn't remember the name. Too many damned nephews.

"Where you been?" the boy asked, chewing stolidly.

Buck didn't speak at first. He looked at the boy without changing expression, then he reached out and knuckled the red head, hard, and pushed the boy away.

"You still wettin' the bed?" he said, and turned towards his mother's room. He looked back as he reached the door, and stopped to watch. The boy hadn't moved, but he had stopped chewing and his hand, holding the biscuit, came slowly down from his mouth. The wrinkles in the boy's lips disappeared but his mouth didn't open, it just straightened out and a small patch of white began to spread outward through his freckles He didn't say anything, just watched Buck's face out of china-blue eyes. Buck let his lips slide off his teeth in a small smile, then he grunted once. "Stubborn," he said, and went through the door and closed it behind him.

The high-pitched yell came again just as Buck saw his mother. He flinched at the sound.

"Good God!" he said, and frowned at his mother.

She was sitting in the very middle of the room in a rocking chair and she had a long limber buggy whip in her hand. She was turning and twisting and working her chair rockers one way and then the other trying to keep within reach of a boy about ten years old.

The boy was in the corner across from Buck, not yelling now, but breathing fast and his black eyes sparkled watchfully. He had a hand on each wall, bracing himself to run either way if she started to hit him. He wasn't crying and the way his mouth was set, Buck didn't think he was going to cry. His eyes shifted to Buck once and his grandmother slashed quickly. The boy dodged out of the corner as the tip of the whip swished down where he had stood.

"Damned old fool," he said, from near the door. He gauged the distance to the door with his eyes but she cut at him again, sideways, catching him against the flat wall and this time the lash curled around his bare brown arm. He didn't make a sound as she drew back again, but ran quickly, knowing now to stay off the face of the walls, to brace himself in a corner again.

Buck moved quickly.

"Here, Mother," he said, and walked to the center of the room. "Put that whip up." He went on over to the corner and caught the boy by one arm and pulled him nearer to his grandmother. "Tell her you're sorry, Gene," he said. His nephew shook his head.

"I ain't sorry," he said. He glared at his grandmother.

"Never is," she said. "Steal an' lie an' fight like a tiger and the only way I can whup 'im is to catch 'im heavy-bellied under that bunch o' bananas in the closet."

"He been stealin'?"

"Bananas," Jeanie Bannon said, bitterly. "Bananas."

Gene's head went up and he shook the hair out of his eyes.

"Wouldn't have to steal 'em," he said, "if you didn't lock 'em up."

Buck didn't say anything. He pulled the boy by one arm to the door and took him out into the hall. He closed the door, softly, and bent down to whisper roughly.

"By God, when you want somethin' don't steal it from kinfolks." He pushed the boy's shoulder with the palm of his hand. "Git goin'."

Then he turned and went back into the room.

"He's right," he said. "Much money as you got, looks like you'd get out o' the habit o' hidin' and lockin' up food." He crossed the room with long, quick strides and his hand jerked angrily at the door to the closet. He glanced inside and sniffed, smelling the ripeness of the bananas. Then he turned back to his mother. "Half rotten," he said, curling his lips. "I'd as soon see him steal bananas as to see them thrown away."

Jeanie Bannon's mouth shut tight.

"Now, young man," she said, "remember who you're talkin' to." She thrashed her whip on the floor, irritably. "An' where you been sleepin'?"

Buck ignored her question. He went over and sat on the edge of the bed and put his hands down on his knees, square.

"Don't look like you been sleepin' at all," she sniffed.

Buck didn't look at her.

"I'm goin' to do what you wanted done," he said, abruptly. "I'm bringin' a surveyor over tomorrow to lay off those house lots, an' I've got deeds in my pocket to three buildin's downtown."

Jeanie Bannon's eyes narrowed and one side of her mouth rose slightly. She slowly laid her whip down on the floor, then looked back up at him.

"Reckoned you'd see the light," she said.

Buck shook his head.

"You didn't make me do it," he said. "I just changed my mind. I've got the accountin', too. I aim to turn it right over to you tonight. Soon as I get these deeds signed."

[173]

His mother cleared her throat and a muscle in the side of her jaw began to twitch.

"What about the bank stock?" she said, her voice shaking a little.

"Hmph!" Buck nearly laughed. "You can sell hell out of it," he said. "I don't own the bank any more."

Jeanie Bannon sat up straighter, but didn't speak.

"You figured you'd sell control out from under me," Buck said, carefully, "so, I just turned aroun' an' sold control out from under you. An' I sold it to Longshore, lock, stock an' barrel."

Her voice was hoarse.

"That where you been this week?" she said. "Workin' on that?"

Buck nodded. "Day an' night," he said. "He bought the fanciest set o' books in the state an' if I was you, I'd sell out quick as I could. It won't be long."

His mother looked down at her hands in her lap, then back up at him.

"I might a' known it," she said, slowly, "take a McPherson to beat one." She was quiet a second, still looking at him, then she began to laugh in her chest.

Buck watched her and as her laugh grew into a full sound, he started grinning, and finally he looked down at the floor and shook his head.

She was choking a little and holding back laughter, but not making any sound, when Buck spoke again.

"Looks like we just butted each other out o' the bankin' business," he said. She nodded, but didn't answer.

"Well," Buck stood up, "let's get these things signed an' wind up."

"Wait a minute, son," Jeanie Bannon said, quickly, "let's don't fly off the handle no more. Sit down."

Buck sat down, slowly, watching her face.

"I don't want to lose a straw boss that can beat me," his mother said. She twisted her neck as if she were embarrassed. "It'd pleasure me if you'd just keep on like you was doin'. An' we can wait on givin' that stuff to the missy girls. Don't reckon I'm plumb wore out yet."

Buck sat very still a moment, then he got up slowly and walked over to the fireplace and kicked the grate to make the coals settle.

He looked down into the fire, then he spoke over his shoulder, abruptly.

"We'll let 'em have it now," he said. He waited awhile longer, twisting his neck as if it were tired, then he turned around quickly and faced her.

"It was kinda fun fixin' up to give 'em that stuff," he said, smiling somehow timidly.

Jeanie Bannon smiled, too, gently, and nodded.

"That's somethin' I've wanted you to learn."

Buck snorted.

"*Me* learn it?" He jerked his thumb over his shoulder. "Why in the devil don't you unlock your bananas?"

She didn't say anything for a moment, then they both began to laugh, and Jeanie Bannon shoved the handle of her buggy whip out from under the rocker with the toe of her soft, wrinkled, shiny black shoes.

She began to rock again.

CHAPTER SEVENTEEN

IT WAS a heavy day, a late spring day that would have been a summer day except that the sun had not yet laid a heat shimmer over the bare, sanded back yard.

Buck yawned on the porch and wondered why he yawned so late in the day. He felt lazy but good. Breakfast had been good enough to remember and dinner was cooking in the kitchen behind him. He turned his head slightly sideways and sniffed. He could smell sassafras and he could hear the low bumbling song the cook was singing:

> "Nigger an' the white man playin' seven-up,
> Nigger win the money but 'e scaired to pick it up."

Buck pushed closer to the screen. "Lay it on, Henry," he said, low and lazy in his throat so nobody could hear it.

He saw his mother in tiny squares through the screen, watching her lean forward in her rocker to pick up another lapful of peas from the basket at her feet. She dropped some emptied green strips onto a newspaper and dribbled small hard peas into the pan on her lap. She leaned far back until her face was in a spot of shade from the chinaberry tree. He opened the door. It had a weak spring and didn't slam behind him until he was down the steps and crunching across the sand towards his mother.

She looked up without surprise and took the sweet-gum brush out of her mouth with fingers that were stained green from the peas.

"Light an' set," she said, and her eyes wrinkled at the corners.

"Reckon you're dead set on bein' country," Buck said, "shellin' peas, chewin' a gum brush, and sassafras tea boilin' for a spring tonic."

She dropped her hands into her lap and rocked twice, fast.

"I am country," she said. "Your papa used to say we come from so far in the piney woods that when we rendered a hog we got as much turpentine as we did lard."

She was laughing before she had finished saying it. Buck chuckled, remembering, and leaned over to pull a single sheet of the newspaper out from under his mother's pile of pea shells. He spread it out at the foot of the chinaberry tree and straightened up to take his coat off.

"Feels good," he said, "gettin' hot."

"Soon be hot as a cob pipe," she said, then she flicked her hand out sharply two or three times, shaking a small clinging worm off onto the ground. "What you doin' home so early?"

Buck sat down and leaned back against the tree and started rolling up his sleeves. His arms looked hard and brown again and his hands curled strong when they were relaxed. He was slow answering.

"Too pretty to work. Weather like this a man ought not to be indoors."

"That little farm you're workin'," his mother said, "all of us ought to work more in the land. Be good for us. Even the girls."

"I can see them," Buck said, "and them wearin' their Edgemont bloomers." He rolled a little on the ground, reaching for his coat, and fumbling for the inside pocket. "Reminds me I got a letter here from Christina."

"Hmph!" his mother said, "funny they didn't write it to me."

"They had a reason," Buck said, "listen."

"Dear Buck:

"This is to tell you that we are all doing fine and that we liked the chicken and cake you and Mother sent. All the other girls liked it too because what the Misses Carlyle do is make everybody that gets a box open it up for everybody else. Then one of them reads to us and we all eat. As long as she's reading, Millie just sits and listens like she's got a case of heart love, but Vesta and I just eat. I know you are the one that put those pieces of country sausage in and I know they were for me. I liked them fine, but don't do it any more. Some of the girls laughed like they did when we first got here and we didn't have any toothbrushes. We bought one each, though, and some toothpaste, too, but all it does is foam and taste good.

"Vesta is doing fine with her piano lessons and the teacher says she can play good. Millie is jumping center on the basketball team but all she does is read on the window seat and faints sometimes in church. Vesta and I are both too short to play on the team but we are trying and I make good grades in mathematics.

"Well, we are all doing fine and hope you all are but, Buck, don't send us so much money. The Misses Carlyle open everybody's mail and that way the girls all know we get more money than they do and don't know how to spend it. We all bought some nightgowns that you can see through with lace because none of the other girls wore outing nightgowns, even if they were gathered at the neck. The ones we bought haven't got sleeves. Don't tell Mother.

"Well, this is all, except you can have old Pomp saddled for me on May 23rd because we'll be in on 101 right about sundown. Take care of Henry and tell him to cook a lot before we get in because what they feed a young lady here won't keep a girl going.

Your sister,
Christina."

"Well," Jeanie Bannon said, tartly, "I don't see why they wanted to hide it from me." She threw some shells carelessly onto the paper. "I don't care what kind of nightgowns they wear." She turned quickly towards Buck, hitching her chair around some.

"But there wasn't a thing wrong with the gowns they had an' as far as seein' through 'em is concerned, if they wanted to see what was underneath they could a' pulled 'em up." She sat back, then, holding herself stiff and prim.

Buck's mouth dropped open and he sat up straight, away from the tree. He looked at his mother in astonishment, then he began to laugh. He threw his head up and leaned back again and hollered at the flush on his mother's face.

He stopped quickly when he saw that she didn't laugh with him. He just lay back against the tree and watched her, wondering what was happening to her inside. The red was leaving her face and she sat very still, shelling faster, stripping peas into the pan with a quick nervous thumb.

Buck's voice was low when he spoke.

"Reckon you miss 'em pretty much."

"Plenty young 'uns in the house," she said in a flat tone.

"Huh! Too many. Two of Wiley's, three of Ernestine's, and one of—"

"They're homeless," his mother broke in, and threw a sharp glance at him out of her black eyes.

Buck sighed long and low and closed his eyes.

"I know," he said, slowly, "they don't worry me but—"

"Hmph! You don't stay here enough for them to worry you. If you ain't workin', you're gamblin' an' carousin'."

Buck looked annoyed.

"Listen, Mother," he said, patiently, "I didn't bring this up on my account. I was thinkin' about you. You ought to get away from 'em for a while."

She threw a pea shell at the newspaper with a jerk of her wrist. She didn't answer.

"Want to go see the girls?" Buck said, idly.

She stopped shelling and sat for a moment, looking curiously at the emptied shell in her hand. She was thoughtful.

"No," she said, finally. "I'll see them soon enough. I don't care 'bout visitin' much." She took her eyes off his face, and pursed her lips. "One thing I've always wanted to see, though," she said, carelessly. Then she drew a deep breath and her words rushed out. "New York!"

"New York!" Buck said. "Why in the devil?"

Jeanie flushed again and broke a thin pea into snaps with quick wasteless movements. She tossed the last of the shells on the newspaper and turned her head towards the back door.

"Henry!" she called. "Peas are ready."

She looked back at Buck, smiling a little sheepishly.

"I just want to see a bunch of Yankees all at once. An' I want to see a place big enough to hold all the people that live in New York. I want to see the Statue of Liberty an' I want to eat a lobster."

Buck slapped his hand on his knee.

"By God, we'll go," he said, then he frowned. "That is, if I can get off."

"From what?" his mother said.

Buck laughed and started getting up.

"Reckon you're right," he said. "Ain't nobody to ask but me and it looks like you made up my mind. Besides, Jeff and Tobe can do most anything I can."

He yawned wide, standing tall with his legs spread apart. The sun struck glints in his black hair and his mouth looked fuller and softer when he stopped yawning. His eyes blinked comfortably. He rubbed the back of his hand across the tip of his nose.

" 'Bout time you took a rest," his mother said. "Grey's workin' in your hair like weeds in young cotton."

"Gol dern," Buck said. "I'm ready. Soon as I get a new suit."

She stood up, too, and looked perky when she threw her head back to look up at him.

"I'm ready right now," she said, "an' if it looks like I'll need a new fascinator, I'll get it in New York."

Through the morning there had been a steady thrust against the smalls of their backs—a thrust of power, speed, excitement, and small adventures.

Now, with a shoe-box lunch nearly over, they had found black dust ground into the plush seats. Jeanie Bannon had turned her back to keep from seeing the small pool of cinders that swirled on the window ledge with every touch of wind. Buck had lifted his feet too many times away from the small cuspidor banging against the iron framework of the seat.

Buck's fingers were greasy and he pushed with his wrist against the wide stiff brim of his straw hat, shoving it onto the back of his head. He fumbled into the shoe box for a small square of un-hemmed white cloth and wiped his fingers carefully, looking out of the corner of his eyes at his mother.

She wore a hat instead of a bonnet. A black hat with a high-riding brim that drew her eyes up now and then like a magnet. Her traveling suit was dark blue and too hot for the weather but she wouldn't take the coat off because folks could see through the sleeves of her blouse. Her feet hardly reached the floor because she sat so straight and so far back in the seat.

Buck's eyes crinkled as he jerked a thumb at her shoes.

"Old Ladies' Comforts," he said.

Jeanie Bannon wiped her lips daintily and stuffed the make-shift napkin back into the shoe box, then she took a banana from a sack. She didn't even glance at her shoes.

"They'll be here when you've worn out your knob toes," she said, comfortably.

Buck looked at the toes of his shoes. He clucked his tongue, admiring them, then he sat up straighter and twitched his shoulders consciously higher into the tight-fitting dark alpaca coat. He unbuttoned the high top button and allowed more of his flowered blue silk tie to show. He relaxed some, and put his feet up in the seat opposite them.

Jeanie Bannon took the last bite of the banana, then she held the peelings upside down and let them fall back into place. She folded them neatly, once, and laid them in a corner of the shoe box. She sighed, satisfied, and looked brightly at Buck.

"Now," she said, "who was it that shouldn't a'brought a lunch?"

Buck slid down until the top of his head barely showed over the back of the plush seat.

"That eatin' made me sleepy."

"Me, too," she said, bustling around in the seat to get comfortable. "What sleepin' I did last night didn't do me any good. Felt like I could hear the clocks strikin' all over town."

"Journey proud," Buck said.

"I reckon," she said, then she sat up suddenly and began to fumble for her purse. "Stop that boy." She punched Buck with her elbow and jerked her head towards the aisle. "He gets by me ever' time."

"They call him the butcher," Buck said, and motioned for the boy to bring his tray of candies and fruits. He watched his mother out of the corner of his eye as she slowly raised herself higher and higher to see into the basket as it came closer. She leaned over Buck as the boy stopped, and poked into the basket with an inquisitive finger.

"I want one of those pistols full o' candy," she said, "this'n here." She held it up before her eyes, in a beam of sunlight coming through the window, and examined it critically. It was shiny and smooth and fat with tiny candy buckshot of different colors, mostly red. She tested the screw cap on the end of the glass barrel to see if it could be opened easily, then she ducked her head approvingly.

Buck raised himself slowly.

"What in the name of the Lord?"

Jeanie Bannon sat back, slipped the pistol into her purse, and snapped it shut.

"Well," she said, "I reckon I'd best tell you now. I wired Ivy and told her to meet the train in Waycross and bring the boy. This is for him."

Buck sat very still with his hand halfway to his mouth, and all expression washed from his face; then his eyes got black and hard. His hand moved again, automatically, and he rubbed his forefinger across his upper lip, back and forth two or three times. He looked at his mother curiously, then his eyes shifted to the small handbag on the rack above her head. He breathed deeply, once, and stood up and pulled the bag down. When he strained over her Jeanie Bannon could see thick blue veins stand out on his neck. He didn't look down until he was out in the aisle and she called to him.

"Where you goin'?"

"I ain't aimin' to jump off the train. I'm just goin' to wash up some, down in the smoker."

He walked down the aisle swaying his shoulders and hips against the lurch of the train as its wheels bit into a curve on an upgrade. He sidled his shoulders through the narrow door at the end of the car without looking back at his mother, who sighed and turned her eyes, blacker now and somehow bitter, outside onto the slanting high-branched pines, darker than green where there was no sun and greener than green when the light struck them.

The train was slowing and the pines were barely trudging by in the late afternoon when he heard the conductor.

"Waycross!" he called, at the front of the car. He came down hard on it when he said, "Way," then dribbled the "cross" into a plaintiveness that had the curl of a question on the end. He called it once and waited as if he expected an answer, then he turned quickly, leaning his head and shoulders into the smoker. "Waycross," he said again, low and flat this time, with casual crispness. He went back without coming through the car.

Buck followed the conductor's head and shoulders out of the smoker. His hair was shiny damp in front and his face was redder than it had been when he left. His shoulders swung now with a go-devil swagger that didn't come from the sway of the train. His eyes weren't hard any longer, but they shone too much and one of them didn't open as wide as the other. He walked towards his mother with his eyes on her face. He held the handle of the bag in both hands. It swung in front of him and with each step it bumped against a knee. He stopped by the seat and stood there a moment not saying anything.

"Hmph!" Jeanie Bannon said, "couldn't make it, without it?"

"I feel like I can tote the whole load now," he said, and slid the bag under the seat with his foot.

The last strength of sun was slanting under the station shed through a lazy billow of black smoke when Buck helped his mother down the steps onto the rain-warped pine platform.

They stood for a full minute, Buck with his straw hat pushed back on his head and his eyes narrowed, with both legs spread far apart. Jeanie looked around with her black eyes barely flicking the empty unpainted benches and the deserted waiting room beyond. Once she glanced quickly, anxiously back at the train as if to gauge the length of its stay in Waycross. Then she looked up at Buck with something like fear starting around her eyes.

"They'll be along in a minute," she said, nervously.

Buck didn't answer. He nodded and looked slowly around the platform.

A small, worried-looking white man with a pencil over his ear hustled by, shoving ahead of him a low-wheeled baggage truck. A tall, thin Negro slouched towards them on feet whose toes played comfortably in and out of long slashes cut along the sides of shoes too small for him. He swung a black, handmade shine box in one huge hand.

"Shine, boss?"

Buck shook his head and searched over the Negro's shoulder the empty sweep of station platform and beyond into the street. The street was empty. The Negro started back to his place against the station wall, but Buck motioned him back.

"Might as well," he muttered, glancing at his mother sideways.

She didn't say anything until one of Buck's shoes had a new gloss that spread nearly to the high top. Then she looked up at him quickly and right back down, almost timidly.

"That's what I hate about men," she said, "they always find things to do, but a woman's just got to wait it out by the hardest."

Buck didn't answer. His eyes were hard, sweeping the station again and again, then glancing quickly up the street as far as they could see. The shine boy was nearly through when Buck spoke without turning his head. His voice was low and flat.

"Better get on it," he said, "they won't hold this train."

Jeanie Bannon nodded silently. She started to say something, but shook her head and hugged her purse and turned around. She was stepping up onto the rubber mat of the red-painted box when she heard Buck laugh. She looked back.

He had just flipped a coin to the shine boy and was standing with both hands on his hips, his head thrown far back; but the laugh was short and it didn't sound like he wanted to laugh. He jerked around and walked towards the train with his shoulders swinging.

"Wait a minute, boy," he said, over his shoulder; then he spoke to his mother where she stood on the platform. "Give me that thing."

Her eyes opened wider but she didn't move. Buck held out his hand and rubbed his fingers impatiently against his thumb.

"That pistol thing."

She took it out of her purse and handed it to him, silently, then turned and walked into the car.

"Here, boy," Buck said. "Give this to one o' your young'uns."

The Negro started to reach for it, then his eyes got big and he wiped his hand on his overalls. When he held it out, his hand was a big, tender cradle of black.

"Ain't got *but* one," he said, "but this here candy gun will col' out decorate him."

He touched the tips of two fingers to his forehead and said, "Boss, I'm obliged," and for a second his face was solemn and dignified. Then, suddenly, he was smiling and the shine boy started back towards his place against the wall, strutting high-shouldered and sliding his feet, soft-shoeing a dance that was mostly inside him, to music that was all inside him.

The lines in Buck's face had deepened and locked into hardness before the train pulled out of the station. He stopped in the couplings on the square metal plate that had clanged down to cover the steps. He stood with his legs braced apart and gripped with one hand the rusty railing. He watched a sawmill fire glide by. Then he took his hand off the railing and in the dim light of the vestibule he looked at it as if he could see blood coming back into it after relaxing.

"Someday," he said, slowly, not making a sound but moving his lips, "she'll wish to God she had come."

He was just standing there, staring out at the dim lamplights shining square through the windows of the small passing houses when he felt a hand touch him lightly on the shoulder. He knew it was his mother—knew the touch and knew the smell of peppermint—so he didn't turn around.

"I didn't mention it, Buck," he heard her say, "but Mayme Foster saw the boy over here around Easter and she says he ain't got a blemish of Longshore. All Bannon."

CHAPTER EIGHTEEN

BUCK STOOD on the rear platform of the train and watched the grey-black ribbon of the roadbed shape behind him into a pattern of crossties and cinders as the wheels slipped and jolted and grunted to a stop.

He sniffed the air shortly, once, then he breathed deeply, throwing back his head and holding it a long time. He wrinkled his nose as he let the breath out.

"Well," he said, out loud, "I reckon even a pogie boat smells good to a man who calls it home, but doggone if Aven don't get right high in hot weather."

He leaned over the railing and looked forward along the train. Up ahead, the engine panted and suddenly spewed live steam into a shallow ditch. Four small Negro boys flushed out of the ditch, running, laughing, falling and rolling and laughing again.

Buck waved at them and sniffed once more as he straightened up.

"Fish at the depot," he thought. Funny about Aven. Eighty miles to salt water and none of the close-by creeks big enough to cause such a flux of fish, and still it always smelled like fish. Something from the sea the year round. Winter time, there'd be speckled trout seined from the warm-water bayous and creeks and slews where they schooled to fight the cold. Mullet in winter, too. Mullet herded with cast nets into small slews or onto the shallows. Winter time.

"Oysters," Buck said out loud and grinned to himself. Lord, the way they used to bring 'em when September rolled around. Before the new road inched through to the coast. Wagon trains with croker sack and canvas coverings wetted down at Big Creek, Spring Creek, Econfina Creek, all the streams that webbed the land and drained Alabama into the Gulf.

His mind didn't say the words, but he could see them: Apalachicola oysters with big white clean shells and a taste like they had fed on fresh water; Indian Pass oysters, small and muddy on the outside and as tight against an opening knife as a turtle's mouth, but clean inside and tasting wild with the bay and the brine; North Bay oysters, small and muddy, too, on the outside, but darker and sweeter on the inside and friendlier to the knife.

He could see in his mind the old wagons, dusty on top but dripping water underneath, rolling onto the outskirts of Aven and up Oak Street and one block east to the Wagon Yard. He could see the black dust-rimmed mouth of the wagoner yelling, "A dozen free to the first pretty girl." And he could see again, plodding along under the tail gate, the slack hound bitch that kept the cats away.

Now, though, in hot summer, with the trains on a three-hour run, he could see the huge casks, baggagemen rolling them casually on a single rim, guiding with one hand and rotating with the other until they thumped them upright into place. Now, the barrelheads with tight caulking of croker sacking dripped ice water off red snapper, that Florida fishermen had pulled out, unprotesting, often in meek clusters of three. There'd be king mackerel horsed out of the Gulf with a line as thick as a child's finger and flung over the shoulder of the fisherman to a helper who removed the fish and rebaited the hook. There'd be largemouthed bass and bream, either seined from the fresh-water creeks and lakes or dynamited, or poisoned with black walnut or limed upcreek and harvested dead downstream. And, now in summer time, there'd be smaller casks, set aside for hard-shelled crabs, red as the devil and as stubborn to crack, with a salt sweetness inside. Or there'd be shrimp, still tucking their feelers inside the curl of their bodies for protection. Or, the boneless throats and jaws of snappers, wrapped separately from fillets of mackerel or trout and sometimes pompano caught from the surf.

"Hey, Lord," Buck said, suddenly, and stretched both arms as high over his head as he could, "another mile and there it'll be, smellin' like a field hand eatin' sardines, but smellin' good to me just the same."

He turned around and went back into the car as the train began to move with deceptive slowness, seeming barely to creep at first, then rushing a little, and the breeze would bring back to the rear the hurried scuffle of the drivers.

He went easily along the aisle, barely touching with his fingers the metal corners of the plush seats, until he stood over his mother.

Jeanie Bannon wore the same dark traveling suit with the silk blouse. She sat up very straight, with her back pushed hard against the seat, but her head rolled slightly with the motion of the train and her eyes were shut.

Buck leaned over and touched her gently on the arm.

"Look out the window," he said as she opened her eyes.

Jeanie Bannon looked outside without moving her head, then she moved her eyes up at Buck and smiled slowly and sleepily.

"Acid Plant Hill," she said.

Buck's mother sniffed as she stepped off the train and then she breathed deep and slow.

"No chance of missin' Aven," she said, satisfied, "even if it was dark."

Buck didn't answer. He was looking around to locate their baggage when his mother punched him. "Jeff," she said, quickly, "he's here."

Buck turned and stuck out his hand and took a step towards Jeff, wondering queerly if two weeks could cause a change in either him or Jeff. No. Same eyes, bluer than grey, and hair neither dark nor sandy. Same nose, with a hook like Buck's but with thicker lips that came full off his teeth when he smiled. And the same pigeon-toed walk, as if there must be some show of reserve or timidity even in walking.

Buck felt Jeff's two fingers and thumb catch his palm and give it two quick shakes from side to side, then turn it loose.

"Someday," he said, "I'm goin' to grab the whole hand and look to see what's wrong with it."

Jeff's smile was shy and he flushed when he turned to kiss his mother, quickly and clumsily.

"Hearn's at the store," he said.

"Where's the rest o' the folks?" Buck asked and handed the baggage checks to a small panting white man who nodded and hurried desperately towards the front of the train. "Send 'em to the house," he called and turned back to Jeff.

"Other side o' the station," Jeff said. "I figured there wasn't no use in clutterin' up the place right when you all was comin' off the train."

"Look at her go," Buck said, jerking his thumb towards his mother's back. "She's plumb quiverin'."

They walked in silence for a moment, Buck looking from bottom to top and then back down along the tall straight-up-and-down standpipe reservoir. It still shone with newness and the small triangular plot of ground was bare again although it had been sodded with St. Augustine grass.

"Ain't as bulky as New York's," Buck said abruptly, "but man for man it'll hold as much as any in the world."

Jeff laughed.

"You must not a'liked New York," he said, "comin' home early."

Buck shook his head.

"Wasn't that," he said, then they turned the corner of the station and saw the cluster of children around Jeanie Bannon. "Let me speak to these kids," he went on, "then I'll tell you at home."

He caught Jeff's arm as they got closer to the group.

"Listen a minute," he said, and turned his head, listening and watching at the same time. The children of the family had come to the train and now they drew together in front of Jeanie Bannon, knotted tightly and pushing each other for room, all standing with open mouths and all looking up into her face except one. Only one girl could see straight into Jeanie Bannon's eyes and she stood at the back of the crowd with her hands on her hips. She was about fourteen and her red hair hung nearly to her waist in curls that fought their own weight. She was taller than her grandmother.

Buck could see his mother's face as she talked excitedly, but he could hardly hear at first. He frowned at a crew of small boys hurrying by with bundles under their arms, and moved closer, still holding to Jeff's arm.

"Well, that place was lit up as funny as anything you ever saw," Jeanie was saying. "You couldn't tell where the lights come from. It was dim, like a stump burnin' in a tie-tie on a foggy yellow night when you can see the scrub oak trunks lookin' like thin grey bones. Well, I got that lobster all right, but it wasn't as much fun as I figured it'd be. Might be just as well they ain't got 'em down here. They'd laid that critter open right down the middle and had him dressed up for eatin'. There wasn't any more fight to it than eatin' spare ribs, but a white person just don't know how to eat one of 'em. I didn't get much meat out of it and a Chinaman laughed at me. He left his lookin' like red eggshells after Easter. An' he didn't use a thing but his hands and two little sticks." She paused and breathed deeply. Then, as if she were making an announcement, she said, "He ate soup with those little sticks, too."

Buck saw the cloud of red hair slowly shake from side to side as if it didn't believe and he saw his mother glance quickly to the tall girl's face.

"Did, too," she said, quickly. "He held the sticks together with one hand and picked up all the vegetables and things that floated and ate them first. Then he drank that bowl of soup like it was coffee." She smiled triumphantly.

Buck saw the red head suddenly lift and come down in a short nod, agreeing, then he caught Jeff by the arm.

"Let's get it over with," he said. "I want to go home and start on somethin'."

Buck's big white hands were almost dainty as he ran the sharp point of a small knife through the tin foil that covered the stopper of a whiskey bottle. He and Jeff sat facing each other across the old soaped and sanded kitchen table. Buck uncorked the bottle mechanically, his eyes following Jeff's fingers as they traced the tiny raised ribs of grain that wavered down the table.

"Yessir," he said, slowly, speaking low with a current of excitement in his voice. "That buildin' caught my eye the minute I saw it. It wasn't the biggest in New York, and till you get used to it, it's kinda funny lookin'. Shaped like a sad iron. They call it the Flatiron Building. They just built it to fit what land they had and that's what I aim to do."

"You got a lot like that?" Jeff asked, reaching for a small glass and the whiskey bottle.

Buck grunted and shoved the bottle.

"Happy days," he said, and raised his glass. He drank his whiskey quickly and economically. First, he took a little water into his mouth, then he threw in the whiskey from a small glass and followed it with a long drink of plain water.

"Reckon I can find one," he said, when he had finished. He looked down at the table for a moment, then he cleared his throat and looked off as he spoke. "The city needs a new jail. Mice won't stay in that old place."

"What's that got to do with it?"

Buck was impatient.

"The lot it sits on," he said, "it's shaped like a flatiron, and it ought to sell cheap—specially since I'm the one to sell it and the one to buy it."

"I didn't know the mayor could buy land from the city," Jeff said, slowly.

"He can't," Buck said, matter-of-factly, "but the city can sell it to another fellow and the mayor can buy it from him."

Jeff's head came up quickly. "Not me," he said.

"You're too close. Have to be somebody that ain't kin to me."

"Tobe?"

"No, he's workin' for the city. Still too close."

Jeff frowned and picked at the table top with his fingernail.

"I don't like it," he said, finally. "Papa wouldn't hold with such dealin's."

"Ah, hell," Buck said, low in his throat. "Now you've started. Don't you know a man is bound to stir up some mud when he kicks off from bottom?"

"Hunh! That's it. You wouldn't have done it when you was on bottom." Jeff looked straight at Buck. "How come you'll do it now?"

For a minute, Buck didn't move. He just sat and stared at Jeff, then he wet his lips with his tongue. He pushed the bottle towards Jeff again before he spoke.

"Any change," he said, thickly, "ain't in me." Then he stood up quickly and threw down a large drink and slowly put the glass back onto the table and all the time he stood there staring at Jeff, his mind plodding carefully.

A man doesn't change, he develops. He makes, according to the things that happen to him, like a crop makes with the seasons. You can't cuss the cotton. You cuss the rain and the weevil that fester it. A man—you cuss the time he was hungry and couldn't get food or the time he wanted his wife and she—

"Jeff," he said, suddenly, "whatever I do, you know it ain't just for myself."

"I know," Jeff said, "but that still don't make it right."

"Would it make it right if it was you doin' it?"

Jeff flushed and smiled crookedly.

[191]

"Not quite," he said, "but it'd make my conscience more comfortable, anyhow."

Buck sat down and leaned across the table.

"I've laid big plans for the three of us," he said, "me, you and Hearn. Bannon Brothers, a partnership. Sounds different, huh?"

"A partnership sounds good," Jeff said. "But in what? What's the building for?"

Buck leaned back.

"A hotel," he said. "A hotel with a bathroom and a telephone in every room."

"What the hell!" Jeff said. "What makes you think a hotel'd pay here?"

"Drummers," Buck said, "they'll spend ten dollars of the company's money to make one for themselves. I found it out in New York. Give 'em a good room, a pretty good boy to wait on 'em and a fast poker game every night, and you'll see it'll take 'em two weeks to work our territory."

"Sounds all right," Jeff said, and fumbled sheepishly at his nose with a crooked finger. "And don't sound half as sharp as it did."

Buck poured carefully out of the bottle again.

"Well," he said, holding up his glass and looking judiciously at the dark line, "the Lord had pity on the gourd." He drank more slowly, now, letting the whiskey slide smoothly before following it with water. He bounced the small glass lightly on its bottom and smiled at Jeff.

"We're in the hotel business," he said.

Jeff laughed. "You talk like the scaffoldin' is all up."

"Well, it won't be so—" Buck started, then stopped and frowned as if he were remembering. He grinned suddenly and flushed. "That reminds me," he said. "That scaffoldin'. The first time I saw that buildin' was at night. It was right after the damndest thing. I was walking up there one night late and got kinda lost and I came to a street I'd never seen before. Well, I started across it. It was dark as hell and misty and I was thinkin' about somethin' else and I didn't notice where I was goin'. All of a sudden, when I got about halfway across, there came the damndest noise bearing down on me. Well, sir, I got ready to jump, looking ever' which-away for whatever it was and I'll be cussed if I could find it. The more I'd look, the louder it'd get. I still couldn't find it. I felt like if I could just get it located I would dodge it or outrun it. I was plumb crouched and ready to go one way or the other when the fool thing started shaking the ground around me and then I looked up and there it was, a damned train on stilts right over my head."

INTERLUDE

JAKE WILLIS *made an angry whimpering sound in his chest. He leaned his head against the wall next to the telephone and slowly beat his fist below the bell crank against the walnut box.*

"I'm agoin' to ring one more time," he said, "an' central better damn shore answer or I'll make kindlin' out o' this contraption."

"You're drunk, Jake." Bass Wooten spoke matter-of-factly from his seat in the window of Dean's Livery Stable office.

"I'm drunk," Jake admitted sadly, "an' it's a hell of a note when you got to get drunk to cuss out a man on the telephone."

"Aw, lay off o' Buck." Bass slid down from the window. "Let's go up to McTyre's place."

Jake shook his head and started cranking again.

"Hello," he yelled into the mouthpiece, then hurriedly, he put the receiver to his ear and listened. "Miss Edie?" he asked, then turned triumphantly to Bass. "I got her." "Look, Miss Edie," he spoke patiently into the mouthpiece, "you ought to take that switchboard to the privy with you when—" Suddenly, he jerked the receiver away from his ear. "Goddamn," he said, and glanced at Bass, then tested the receiver against his ear again. "Miss Edie. Miss Edie." He turned around and leaned his shoulder blades against the wall. "She hung up," he said, wonderingly, then slowly his eyes narrowed and his teeth clenched. With one quick movement, he jerked the receiver loose from the box and tossed it to Bass. "Hold that." He turned and locked both hands around the metal arm which stuck out of the box and ended in the mouthpiece. He pulled downward with all his weight and the box came away from the wall. Carefully, he hooked his fingers behind the box and jerked until the screws came loose. He pulled

[193]

steadily and the wires broke. He turned to face Bass and tucked the telephone box under one arm.

"Now you bring that buzzin' thing," he said, and stalked out of the office into the chill dry night. Bass shrugged his shoulders and followed.

"Six months," Jake said, mournfully, as they walked past the new triangular building that bulked large and dark between the slant of the railroad and the straight line of Main Street. "Six months I been braggin' 'bout him buildin' the first hotel—like I'd done it myself." He thumped the telephone box viciously against the new brick wall. "An' now, by God, I just find out the bastard practically stole the land from the city."

"Don't forget," Bass said, softly, "ever' time he builds somethin', Aven grows a lick."

"Goddamn that." Jake spat and stopped beside a narrow stairway which led to the second story of the sturdy wooden building flanking the new hotel structure. "I've watched 'im grow from a little chunk," he said, sadly, "to a big ol' stand-up-in-the-road that owns half them buildin's you see up the street." He paused and took one step up the stairway. "An' I've fostered him," he went on over his shoulder, "but now, if the Lord lets me, I'm agoin' to cuss him for a thievin' dog." He cleared his throat as they reached the top of the stairs. "Soon as I get a couple more drinks in me an' find a damned telephone that works."

Bass snickered, but Jake didn't notice him. He walked down the dim hall until he came to a door marked, "Aven Telephone Co." Then he held out his hand for the receiver. "Gimme that." Bass dropped it into his hand. Jake opened the door and brighter light flooded into the hall.

"Miss Edie," Jake said, with dignity, "here's number twenty-five."

He threw the telephone box and receiver into the office, then shut the door and went back down the hall with Bass following.

CHAPTER NINETEEN

BUCK WAS barely conscious of the noise going on around him. He was in the triangular lobby around which the larger triangle of the hotel was laid. Workmen passed him and hurried upstairs, trailing electric wiring, overalls pockets sagging deep with pliers and screw drivers. Buck didn't notice them. He stood on the white flaky-looking tile floor with his hands in his pockets and stared up through the stair well to the second floor, and on farther up to the railing around the third-floor passageways. He didn't know he was blocking the stairs until he heard a soft, apologetic voice behind him.

" 'Scuse me, boss."

Buck turned hurriedly and moved out of the way of two large Negroes, each carrying a side of a dresser whose mirror wobbled gently as the workmen shifted their feet.

"Here, boy," Buck said, quickly, "push me out of the way next time. It costs me a dollar ever' time you say 'scuse me."

One of the Negroes chuckled deep in his throat and the other said, "Top flo' *ex*press." Buck moved across the lobby and leaned against the leather-topped mahogany desk to watch a small harried young man with big ears stacking blotters in a desk drawer. Buck watched absently as the clerk's limp fingers flickered in and out until the drawer was full. Then he cleared his throat.

The clerk looked around and his eyes flared wide.

"Oh!" he said.

"How's it goin'?"

The clerk closed his eyes and sighed, shaking his head.

"Mr. Bannon," he said, finally, "I have worked in many a hotel and I flatter myself that I know the business, but frankly, I have never before worked in a hotel that had no name."

Buck laughed.

"Aw, don't worry," he said, "it's three weeks to the opening. We'll name it by then."

The clerk patted the desk top patiently.

"But the advertising, Mr. Bannon. There is none, has been none, and can be none until the hotel is named."

"Advertisin'? Why advertise when this is the only hotel in town?" He stood up straight and flexed his shoulder muscles. "It'll get along."

The clerk moved closer and raised his eyelids slowly to look Buck in the face.

"It ought to be named now," he said, "anything. Bannon Hotel?"

Buck frowned.

"I don't like that. Bannon Boardin'house would be about right if it was a boardin'house."

The clerk drew a deep breath. He turned and took a small mahogany name plate from one of the pigeonholes behind and blew the dust off it. He placed it at an angle on the desk, then cocked his eye at it and smiled briefly. He looked back at Buck as if he were no longer concerned with naming the hotel.

Buck glanced at the name plate, then back to the clerk.

"Had it long?"

"Ten years."

Buck touched it.

"T. H. Harrison," he read slowly. Then his lips began to slide up at the corners. He switched his eyes back to the clerk. "Harrison House," he said, deliberately, then he laughed. "That's the name. Harrison House. By God, I ought to cut your salary for namin' it after you."

The clerk's face turned red, and he snatched at the name plate on the desk and held it tightly in both hands for a moment.

"Mr. Bannon," he said, shakily, "if you think I put this thing out for—"

"Aw, hell," Buck said, curling his lips, "go back to work. I don't care how it happened, the name fits and it suits me. You quit worryin' about anything in the world but your own job and you'll do fine here." He turned abruptly and started towards the front door. Then he flung back over his shoulder, "An' I've told you my last time not to call me mister. My name's Buck."

The clerk's mouth opened and shut two or three times without making a sound. He leaned against the desk and looked blankly down at its top and shook his head. Then he looked back up and his mouth stayed partly open. He just watched Buck's back for a second, then he straightened. He reached up absently and pulled the pink elastic sleeve holder away from his upper arm and let it snap back into place. Then he nodded his head sharply.

"All right," he said, "Buck!"

Buck wasn't thinking of the clerk now. He was hurrying to open the heavy brass and beveled-glass door for Hearn who stood with an armload of bundles in the swirling gusts of wind and rain that sucked sharply into the sunken entrance. Hearn was kicking the door and Buck could see his face, pale against the shiny black of a slicker too large for him. His wide-brimmed soft hat broke sharper than ever down over his forehead and all Buck could see of his face was his nose, straighter than the other Bannons' and narrower above a mouth that was full and wide, but sensitive. His chin wasn't as square as Buck's and it had a cleft so deep that his razor usually left a few heavy reddish whiskers to gleam there if the sun struck them.

His lips were moving as Buck opened the door.

"Give me a shot quick," he said, "I think I swallowed some of that rain."

Buck took one of the packages out of Hearn's arms.

"Where's Jeff?"

"Home," Hearn said. "Still pacifyin' Mother."

Buck looked annoyed and motioned for a small colored boy who sat, proud of his white jacket, near the bottom of the central stair well, handy to the two ice chests.

"Thought I told you to stay there till she was satisfied for us to move out," he said to Hearn, then he turned without waiting for an answer and handed the bundle to the bellboy. "Room 101," he said, and fished in his pocket for a key.

Hearn walked over and eased his load down on one of the long black leather-covered tables. He jerked off his hat and whipped it against his leg and threw it on the table. He peeled the slicker off quickly and dropped it on the floor, then he swung one leg over the corner of the table and sat down.

"Phew!" he said, looking back up at Buck. "I can't do worth a cuss with her. Jeff, he can just sit still and look picked on and get what he wants. It looked like I kept her riled up so I came on down."

"Figured she wouldn't like it," Buck said, slowly, "but it still looks to me like folks ought to live in a hotel if they run it."

"Shirt sleeves to shirt sleeves," Hearn said, suddenly, without smiling. "That's what she kept saying."

Buck looked away. He stared out into the rain for a moment, feeling something familiar and old and cold as fear crawling inside his chest. His mind suddenly was back to the first night he had spent in Aven, a night when the fear had found him alone. That fear—part of the fight between man and cotton, or man and land, or man and grass. Bermuda grass, lacing a foot deep into the richest soil, holding it against the heavy washing rains and fattening the topsoil for the day when a man would need it. Bermuda grass, friendly at first, then a part of the fight, dirt banker for the man, then making him earn it, making him go in there with a steel beam and a bull-tongue scooter and a mule that was willing to burn itself out alongside of a man. He shuddered, then looked back up at Hearn.

"Shirtsleeves," he said, softly, "in three generations."

Hearn shook his head and his smile was rueful.

"She says it looks like we're fixin' to do it in one."

Buck glanced towards the desk where the clerk was idly stacking registration cards into the drawer nearest Hearn. He watched a moment, then he jerked his head impatiently towards the line of solidly built rocking chairs that backed the glass-fronted north side of the lobby. He walked over and sat down and put his feet on the new steam-heat register and leaned back while Hearn followed and sat down beside him.

"Reckon she blames it all on me," he said, bluntly.

"Says me and Jeff ain't hard to lead, though," Hearn admitted. Then he yawned. "She gave me hell. Women and whiskey. Yours was mostly women and whiskey, too, with gamblin' thrown in." He laughed. "Jeff, I reckon his main trouble is just hangin' around me and you."

Buck looked thoughtful.

"Somehow or other," he said, "when Jeff gets in a tight folks feel sorry for him and the first thing you know they're blamin' it all on the other fellow and tryin' to help Jeff out."

"I don't know what it is," Hearn said, "but it's workin'. If we stay away long enough, he'll have Mother thinkin' she figured it out for us to move to the hotel." He yawned casually and jerked his thumb towards the stairway. "I'm goin' upstairs a minute."

He started off, then hesitated and came back, looking uneasily at Buck.

"Reckon you've heard all you need about it," he said, roughly, "but she's pretty well upset about that church business, too."

Buck didn't say anything. He set his teeth and was very still, not looking at Hearn, while a cold angry hurt turned in his chest. He had a brassy taste in his mouth and he leaned over and spat into one of the huge cuspidors.

"She says movin' down here'll just make it worse," Hearn went on, doggedly, "when you ought to be doin' somethin' to stop it."

Buck stood up quickly and turned around and his eyes had narrowed and his lips had tightened until they pulled down at the corners.

"By God," he said, thickly, "I donate more'n anybody else and I go right regular. What else can I do?"

"Mother says it comes of lettin' the gamblin' joints and things stay open."

"They got schools. They got a few paved streets and the city's workin' pretty well out of debt. By God, that's more'n they deserve." He breathed raggedly for a moment, glaring at Hearn, then he turned his back again and sat down. "I'll stand on my record," he said, "an' there ain't enough churches in Jerusalem to make me change my ways."

He could feel Hearn looking at his back for a full minute, not speaking, then he heard him walk away. When Hearn got to the foot of the stairs, Buck heard him say, "Psst!" to the bellboy, and turned to see him jerk his thumb at the ice chest, then point the same thumb upstairs. "Be hasslin' when you get there, boy. I need it now."

Buck sat still, staring out at the rain again. He tasted his lips with the tip of his tongue.

"I shouldn't have snapped at Hearn like that," he thought. "Papa said there ain't but three things worth fightin' over—a land line, a baseball game, or a woman. They'll cool off. Preacher's got to say somethin' an' it can't all be good. One thing sure—they wouldn't be shootin' at me if I didn't have my head up so it could be seen. I'll worry when they stop shootin'."

He was still there when Jeff came in out of the rain, hurrying pigeon-toed, backing through the half-opened door so he could close his big black umbrella behind him. Jeff carefully leaned his umbrella against one of the six square pillars that supported the lobby ceiling, then he flicked his hands downwards two or three times, slinging a few drops of water off his fingers before sticking them into his pockets to dry them where it wouldn't show.

"Hard to tell if that rain's comin' up or down," he said.

Buck looked up at him blankly for a second.

"Huh?" he said. Then he frowned and said, "Oh." He pointed at the chair beside him. "Sit down and don't talk loud. That clerk likes to listen."

Jeff eased himself into a chair.

"Sounds like you're worried."

"No," Buck said slowly, "it just makes me fractious for folks not to understand how come I do things."

Jeff pulled his hat down low over his eyes in spite of the muggy dark that was creeping through the lobby.

"Hearn," he said, "reckon he's been talkin'. He oughtn't to say so much when he talks."

Buck suddenly stood up and turned around to face Jeff, standing with his back to the window as if he were backing up to a fire, and locked his hands behind him.

"She finally get all right?"

"'Cordin' to what you call all right," Jeff answered. "She went to eatin' just before I left and she had gotten mad instead of feelin' sorry for herself." He grinned at Buck when he went on. "But she still don't like it. Hearn must have told you some of the stuff she said, but he don't know it all. She plumb wore you out."

Buck's lips began to curl. "Women—" he started off quoting his mother, when Jeff broke in.

"Nuh-uh," he said. "She calls it 'woman.'"

The curl wiped off Buck's lips. His eyes got smaller as if the upper lids were too heavy but he didn't speak and for all Jeff knew his hands were perfectly still behind him.

"Ivy, I reckon she meant," Jeff said, and searched Buck's face with his eyes.

Buck waited a second to speak, then his voice was calm and flat.

"Well," he said, "we've worried about Mother enough. Now,

[200]

you get on upstairs and keep Hearn sober and both of you be where I can get you tomorrow morning early."

Buck didn't move until Jeff had reached the stairs, then he turned and walked slowly outside and stood as if undecided which way to go out of the small indented weather front. He hunched his big shoulders and started quickly up the street to the left, leaning close and nearly touching the walls of the buildings. The rain dripping from the eaves struck his right shoulder, but he didn't bother to move closer to the buildings and he didn't think about a raincoat or an umbrella. He just moved on, unprotected from the rain, a big man whose shoulders were getting wet, whose hands were in his pockets to keep dry, and whose dark face looked darker and harder as the dim lights of the street lamps washed over it, first pale, then bright, then pale again, and then darkness again for a few more steps. He kept thinking as he walked.

"Mother knows all right, but dammit she ought to leave me alone. The only way to get a woman out of your mind is to have her when you want her. Damn a woman, anyhow. Damn a skinny, yellow-headed woman that never made a rule in her life, and never broke one somebody else made. What I need right now is a drink."

Buck looked up as he started to step down off the curb. His eyes narrowed against the rain and he was hurrying for the shelter of the walls across the street when he noticed a man start across and then pull back into the dry spot under a canvas marquee. Buck half smiled when he recognized the small figure with its high stiff white collar and huge diamond glittering like a snake's eye in the light of the street lamp.

He stuck out his hand as he came close under the marquee.

"Back a little early, ain't you, George?" he said, shaking the cool, dry, dainty hand.

George pumped his words from a tight throat. They were strained and high and hurried, and each time he began to speak the corner of his mouth would quirk a little as if he wanted to laugh before it was time.

"Ever' time them gamblers out West would hear I was raised in Aven, they'd deal me out," he said and didn't crack a smile.

Buck laughed and caught George by the arm.

[201]

"Well, come on and tell me about it. I'm just started to the office. Got a bottle there and we can get dry."

"Not tonight," George said. "I'm workin'. But I'll tell you what. You go on an' get your bottle an' join me later on. I got a couple drummers up at Thacker's Boardin'house that feel like peepin' at the hole card."

"Good," Buck said. "Table stakes?"

George nodded. "Usual place, I reckon, but danged if I don't get tired chippin' ever' pot to that Pybus boy."

Buck snapped his fingers.

"I forgot," he said, "I got a place. Meet me at the hotel. I'll phone from the office and tell them to fix up a room and get Tobe down."

"Tobe? I didn't figure a chief o' police could—"

"Whoa-up! Don't ride Tobe about that job, George. He just took it as a favor to me."

"I get you." George rubbed his palms together. "Well, playin' in your place will mean a dollar more to the pot."

Buck shook his head and smiled.

"Unh-unh, that just means Tobe'll be chippin' the pot and passin' it to me later on."

George groaned.

"Well, I'd rather give it to a friend." He lifted a hand and started off down the street. "See you soon."

Buck moved over closer to the walls and stepped quickly towards his office in the city hall. He walked with his shoulders high and far back now and the excitement of gambling showed in his eyes. He whistled soundlessly through his teeth as he opened the front doors and left his keys hanging in the lock. He swaggered as he went through the offices, flinging a swinging door wide and walking surely in the dark until he could reach the light cord hanging in the center of his office.

He was sitting on the corner of his desk, cranking the phone to get Central, when he heard light footsteps scuffling in the dark entranceway outside. He stopped ringing and cocked his head on one side, listening for a second, then he heard Central far away saying, "Number. Number. Who do you want?" He frowned at the phone and carefully hung it up again. He leaned forward to listen and heard the scuffling steps come close to the door of his office. He moved quickly, then, and silently, tiptoeing across the office floor until he reached the door. He listened again and heard the steps, barely sounding through the door. Then, quickly, he reached out and flung it open.

"Oh, my God!"

The voice was low and breathless and wondering, but it wasn't frightened.

The girl stood with one hand upraised as if she had been going to knock. In the other hand she held a small straw valise and under one arm she carried a large leather purse. She didn't say anything else, but she dropped her arm slowly.

Buck didn't move for a moment. He held the knob of the door with his right hand and braced against the doorjamb with his left hand. He stood that way, blocking the doorway, then he let his hand drop to his sides and straightened up. He frowned slightly, noticing that she was tall, that her lips would about strike his chin. He stepped out of the doorway, and moved his eyes from her wide full mouth to the dark blue eyes that slanted slightly under heavy black brows.

"Your move," he said, suddenly.

She smiled uncertainly and quickly, barely showing teeth that were white and large and strong.

"Is this Mr. Bannon?" she said, and took a small step into the room.

Buck nodded with his eyes still on her face. He could feel but not see the cheekbones, high and prominent, and the stubborn thrust of chin inside the round face. He leaned a little closer, staring, until he saw the eyes narrow and the brows draw together, then he let his eyes fall slowly along the straight tailored lines of her blue traveling suit. Her shoulders were broad and she held them as if she knew that they were strong. Buck nodded again, automatically.

"I'm Lota Kyle," the girl said, simply. "I just got in town on the train, and I'm looking for a job teaching school. They told me you were head of the school board."

"Do you always ask for jobs at night?" Buck said.

Her lips closed a little tighter.

[203]

"I saw your lights come on as I was going by," she said. "They had told me to find you at the city hall. It was raining so I came in."

Buck looked at the wet coat and down to the hem of her dress, then he looked back at her face. He saw her breathe deeply as if she were going to sigh or yawn and her breasts showed high and small for her size and tight against the white silk of her shirtwaist.

"Come to see me tomorrow," he said, abruptly. "Here at ten o'clock."

She smiled for the first time and the smile made Buck glad he'd said it.

"I hope you can find me a place," she said.

Buck nodded.

"I think maybe I can," he said.

CHAPTER TWENTY

STILL-HEAVY drops of rain bounced the sun's rays from so many green leaves that the morning wore a tip-tilted air—an air that went right well with the fickle odor of late petunias.

Buck's eyes were lazy and nearly closed, content, looking across his desk at Lota Kyle. He turned his head and leaned it slightly backwards, breathing deeply from the breeze coming through his office window.

"Old Spang plants 'em," he said. "Janitor." He sniffed again loudly. "Can't say I like to smell 'em, but you have to sniff again to see if it's true what you smelled the first time."

Lota Kyle smiled. There was a secret wandering around behind her lips and when she raised her eyes they were laughing by themselves. She shook her head.

"Spang didn't plant petunias this late," she said. "They're volunteers."

Buck's eyebrows went up. "Volunteers?" He leaned forward. "Where'd you ever hear that?"

She leaned closer, too, as if she were going to whisper.

"Grandpa was so lazy that any crop we made was sure to be a volunteer."

"Raised on a farm?"

"Oh, yes. Just over the Georgia line. Then I went to high school in town." She spread her hands out on the desk top. "And here I am."

Buck frowned.

"No college?"

Lota suddenly wasn't smiling any more. She pulled her hands off the desk and looked down at them in her lap, then back up at him, quickly.

"I told you Grandpa was lazy," she said. "It took me until I was eighteen to finish high school, helping generally and staying out two years when Grandpa was sick."

Buck whistled soundlessly through his teeth.

"Eighteen? How old are you now?"

"Nineteen," she said, and sat up straighter. "But I'm big for my age."

Buck laughed and rocked twice in his swivel chair.

"You are big," he said, watching her face with one side of his mouth working. "Stand up," he said, not ordering or asking, just saying it. "Stand up."

The girl didn't flush or look surprised. She took her purse out of her lap and laid it carefully on Buck's desk and stood up. She didn't place one foot behind the other to rise more gracefully and her hands didn't fall into a gentle cross in front. She pushed on the arms of the chair with her hands and came up with both feet square on the floor and her arms hanging by her side. Her lips twitched once, then stopped, and she stood very still just being looked at.

Buck saw only her face. He looked as simply as a man might breathe, without any feeling that he shouldn't be staring at her high cheekbones, or letting his eyes drift too slowly down the line of her jaw to her chin. He noticed, as if it were important to him, that her eyes showed dark blue in the daylight when he had expected them to be brown or even—well, they had seemed black last night when she came asking for the job. Schoolteacher! She didn't look like a schoolteacher. They had limp hair and their clothes smelled like wet hay. They were brittle and their fingers wandered through the leaves of a book with no more rustle than a shedding snake in sage brush. This girl was—

He looked quickly down at the blotter on his desk and fumbled with the knuckle of his forefinger in the fast-spreading grey patch at his temple.

"Why do you want to teach school?"

"I don't," Lota Kyle said bluntly. Buck raised his eyes again, surprised. "Girls just teach school," she went on, patiently. "They just do it."

"Well, I'll be—" Buck sat up straighter.

"I'll teach a few years," she said without moving, "and then I'll take what I've saved and go to college. I always wanted to go to college."

"College," Buck frowned and shook his head. "My Lord, I'd forgot that." He looked away from her and spoke as if he were reading. "We decided to participate in the state educational program two years ago and our city teachers must have some college or normal school."

She didn't answer for a long time. Buck glanced at her face, then away and waited. Through the walls, he could hear the crisp rhythm of hammers driving finishing nails into the woodwork of the new police station. He didn't look around until he heard her stir.

She had moved closer and now she stood with the tips of her fingers spread out on top of his desk. She leaned forward slightly and Buck saw her fingers bend a little and saw the nails whiten, then she pulled her weight back and the blood went back into the fingernails.

"I wrote my folks last night," she said in a low voice, "that they could be coming over here pretty soon."

Buck started to speak but she went on, rushing her words.

"You said you thought maybe you could get me a job."

Buck held up his hands and let them fall back on the desk.

"Easy, easy," he said softly. "Just sit down."

She was breathing deeply, but she didn't sit down. Buck wrinkled his forehead thoughtfully and watched her bosom move with her breath and tighten against the high-buttoned front of her dress.

"You can't work for the city schools," he said, bluntly, "but if you'll sit down and quit heavin', maybe I can do something."

He reached under the edge of his desk and pushed a button. Lota Kyle moved, then, a little awkwardly, back towards the chair and fumbled for the armrest without taking her eyes off Buck.

The city clerk came in quietly. He was a tall man, very thin, with a neck so skinny his head seemed always to be keeping time with a private tune, bobbing gently as the small jar of his footsteps rippled up his body. He stopped just inside the room. One of his eyes was so nearly closed it could hardly be seen, but the other was large and bright-blue and quick-moving. It roved now, first to Lota and then to Buck. It glared.

"Don't like that goddamned bell," he said, matter-of-factly.

Buck sat up in his chair and started to say something, but the clerk stopped him.

"Soon be whupped with a piss-ellum club as be whistled in like a dog."

"Shut up," Buck said, "there's a lady in the room."

The big eye flashed once to Lota. "Howdy, Miss." Then the eye went back to Buck. "Cuss in front of my wife an' she's a lady." He shook his head sadly. "Gettin' old, though."

Buck didn't say anything. He looked at Lota. She was rubbing the back of her hand slowly across her lips, hiding her mouth, and her eyes wouldn't meet his. Buck looked back at the clerk.

"Don't say another word," he said, carefully, "until I get through." He breathed deeply and twisted in his chair, so that he wasn't looking at the clerk. "Go tell Pet Tolleson there'll be a vacancy in the county schools tomorrow. Tell him I've got a teacher for him. Tell him to see me before he hires another one." He glared at the man. "And don't tell it in the saloon before you get there."

"Hmph!" the clerk grunted. "How'd you know there'd be a vacancy?"

Buck looked down at his desk and tapped it with his fingers, patiently.

"We need a bookkeeper at the dispensary," he said. "I figured to hire one of his teachers."

The clerk wrinkled his long lips up until the top one nearly touched his nose.

"Well, then," he said, "whyn't you just—"

"Stop right now," Buck said, quickly. He stood up and placed both hands flat on his desk, leaning towards the clerk. "If you don't get out of here and do what I tell you, by God, I'll fire you and to hell with the Masonic Lodge."

The clerk's mouth opened slightly and he nodded his head once. He cleared his throat and closed his mouth.

"Just ring if you need me," he said, and started in his loping walk back through the door.

Buck sat back down slowly and let his arms fall flat on top of his desk.

"I'm—" he started to speak, then stopped to watch her.

She started laughing behind her hand, nearly choking at first, then she dropped her hands to the arm of the chair and let her head fall back against the chair. Buck started laughing, too, and watched her until she straightened up and looked back at him, chuckling inside, but not making any noise.

"Grandpa cusses powerful," she said, then her face was suddenly quiet. "Why *didn't* you just let me work at the dispensary?"

Buck smiled slowly, showing his closed teeth. He tapped the desk with a pencil while he answered.

"Well, the dispensary is right across the street. Too close. The school you'll get is about a mile out of town. Seems reasonable that I could be ridin' by some time about last bell and I *might* drive you home."

Lota Kyle looked at him with her eyes very steady.

"You might," she said, softly. "You *could*." She rubbed the back of her right hand slowly along the line of her jaw, watching Buck all the time.

The men hovered in a loose covey, not right at the small bar, but close enough for convenience and at such an angle that two or three of them could bow away from the main crowd without risk that a shepherding wife might see her own husband too often through the wide doorway between the lobby and the dining room.

Buck stood with his hands behind his back and his legs spread wide apart. He listened gravely, first to a short, thin grey man whose eyes burned and whose mouth shut hard in a straight line after each sentence. Then, turning, to the rumble from the wide satisfied mouth of a burly, youngish man whose wavy hair nearly touched the collar of a long black square-cut coat. As Buck listened, his eyes cut occasionally towards the doorway, through which he could watch the front entrance to the lobby.

"Governor," the youngish man was saying, "when Alabama first was wooed and won by the United States of America—"

"Now, by God, Tom," the thin grey man said. "The Senate can't interrupt, but I will before I'll listen to that courtship story again."

Buck laughed with the big man, watching Governor Thrasher's thin lips purse and twist with a growing thought.

"Tom," the little Governor said, throwing back his coattails and sticking his hands deep in his pockets, "you can charm the birds out of the trees, but filibusterin' is just manure on the grave of States' Rights. Forget 'em. The big fight is the Pittsburgh Plus freight rate. It'll last long enough to keep you in Washington for life."

The big man frowned and started to answer, when Buck saw Hearn bringing Lota Kyle through the main entrance to the lobby. He spoke quickly.

"Excuse me, gentlemen." He touched the Governor on the arm. "Don't whip him until I get back."

Lota was wearing Hearn's coat over her dress, and Buck could see the bold teasing smile on Hearn's face as he spoke to the girl with his lips close to her ear, then helped her off with the coat. Lota glanced over her shoulder at Hearn and said something that Buck couldn't hear, but he felt a quick lurch inside as he saw the gay smile on her lips. Unconsciously, his steps hurried.

Hearn was throwing his coat over his arm when Buck came near enough to see how Lota's eyes widened at sight of the flowers, and the bright-colored dresses milling in the lobby. Hearn suddenly looked cold and pinched around the mouth and his eyes strayed unconsciously past Buck to the bar.

Buck jerked his thumb over his shoulder.

"You got it treed," he said.

"Man, I need it," Hearn said, and nodded sideways at Lota. "Her coat wasn't the type for her dress," he said. He almost smiled. "Mine was, though." He flipped his hand good-bye and moved off towards the bar.

"No coat I ever saw would match you in that dress," Buck said softly. His eyes moved slowly from the high-piled black hair that made her look even taller, down past the tight-fitting choker collar, and on down along the close sheath of heavy white satin that ended just above the tops of her high-buttoned white shoes. He reached out and touched the simple short sleeve that banded above her elbow.

"Reckon you know you're the prettiest woman here."

Lota raised her eyebrows and flirted her wrist towards the skirt of her dress.

"I ought to be," she said. "Just look at me—brand-new."

Buck was still looking at her dress, where it fitted tight over her hips.

"First heifer I ever owned was just about that color," he said, gravely.

[210]

Lota squeezed his arm and her eyes smiled while Buck's eyes flickered around the lobby, hunting until they found his mother, watching him and pretending to listen to a group of women who sat on one of the long leather couches. His mother's eyes met his and he looked quickly back at Lota. She was gazing thoughtfully up at him.

"Mighty lucky my landlady found this material in an old trunk," she said, very low. "And right after you asked me to come with you."

Buck nodded and cleared his throat.

She looked at him sidelong. "Lucky she could sew so well, too."

Buck said, "Unh-hunh," and looked off again.

Lota caught her lower lip with her teeth. "Funny, though, everything else in that trunk smelled like mothballs."

Buck said, "Hmmm," and caught her by the arm. "Let's go introduce you to Mother." He didn't look at her as they started across the lobby but watched his mother edging over on the couch until she sat as nearly alone as she could be. She looked more comfortable than she had, listening to the reedy talk of the other women.

Buck leaned slightly over her.

"Mother," he said, "this is Lota Kyle."

Lota spoke first.

"Hello, Mrs. Bannon," she said, "I'm so glad to meet you, finally."

Jeanie Bannon looked up and smiled faintly, only with her lips.

"I'm glad to meet you, too," she said, "finally."

There was a quick silence, just among the three of them, and Lota looked jerkily away from Jeanie Bannon. She waved her hand, pointing around the lobby.

"What lovely flowers," she said. "Where *did* you get them?"

Buck was watching his mother's face with a puzzled frown.

"Rosehill Gardens," he said, absently, "Montgomery," and kept his eyes on his mother.

Jeanie Bannon's mouth had tightened down and little lines were showing from her nose out and down to the corners of her lips. She was pretending to look around the lobby, but only her head moved. Her eyes stayed on Lota, watching the girl's face move excitedly, until Lota looked brightly back down at her.

"Your dress is beautiful, Mrs. Bannon," she said. "Your hair shows up so well against that dark-blue satin."

Jeanie Bannon smiled wryly.

"Hmph! It'll show up better when it gets whiter." She lifted a finger, pointing towards Buck. "His is working along, too," she added carefully.

Buck straightened his shoulders and patted his stomach.

"No belly, though."

Lota looked up at the grey on Buck's temples.

"It won't be long," she said, then she turned swiftly as someone caught her tightly by the arm.

"Buck," the Governor said, frowning fiercely, "I've met your mother. Prettiest woman here. But you've been stingy with her closest competitor."

Lota's eyes were wide, startled, looking up at Buck. "Young woman," the Governor said, "I'm the governor you've heard cussed so much, and at my age that half-scared look in your eyes is a great compliment."

Buck laughed.

"Miss Lota Kyle, Governor."

"It's exciting to meet a governor," Lota said.

The Governor bowed slightly.

"I'm a little excited, too, Miss," he said, then turned towards Jeanie Bannon whose eyes had gone from one to the other during the introduction. "Perhaps you ladies would excuse Buck while he joins me in a short discussion of liberty at the bar."

The Governor walked energetically, talking all the time, across the lobby with Buck's elbow firmly gripped.

"Fine-looking girl. Built strong, like a first-generation woman." He glanced quickly at Buck. "Pity she can't sit with us up at the end."

"Hmm," Buck said, as they reached the bar. "Governor, a girl like her is as dangerous at your age as seven-card stud." He listened to the old man while he caught Jeff's eye and motioned for him to join them.

". . . completely backwards," Governor Thrasher was saying as Jeff sidled close, "a man can get too old to be hurt."

"Order bourbon for me, will you?" Buck said. "I want to speak to Jeff a second about some arrangements."

He drew Jeff aside and spoke in a low voice.

"The Governor wants a little switch in the seating. How about changing place cards for me. Put Lota Kyle up where Mother's place is. You take Mother by you and let Tobe take your place."

Jeff's eyebrows drew together, frowning, and he shook his head.

"Hell, Buck," he said, "Mother's expecting—"

"Good God," Buck said, "she'll be right down by the Governor's wife at the other end."

Jeff shuddered.

"Have you heard her talk? She sounds like a blowfly caught in a lamp shade."

"Better do it quick," Buck said, and he looked thoughtfully at the floor for a moment. "Tell Mother I said she was the only one I could trust to take care of the Senator and the Governor's wife and it'll be all right."

Jeff shrugged and nodded briefly. Buck went back to the bar. Governor Thrasher raised his glass, theatrically.

"To the Emancipation of Woman." He paused slightly. "Every night," he said, softly.

Buck laughed and looked at his glass.

"Last one," he said. "Supper's about ready."

They were at the banquet table before Buck saw his mother again. She was sitting at the far end of the long line of tables between the young Senator and Jeff, who was flanked by the Governor's wife. Mrs. Thrasher's voice fretted through the bustle of waiters and the treble tones of barely touched glassware. Her lifeless-looking hands fluttered occasionally up over her flat chest, as if she had slipped down inside the whalebone shell of her pale-green gown and wanted to pull back up.

Buck's eyes wandered across the faces at the other end, hurried over Tobe's face as if ashamed, and were caught by Jeanie Bannon's. She looked away and began to talk to Jeff but Buck had seen bewilderment and dark hurt in them. He closed his eyes briefly and shook his head. He muttered under his breath.

Lota Kyle's hand touched Buck lightly on his left arm.

"Quit that," she whispered and smiled up at him.

"What?"

She leaned closer.

"You said, 'To hell with 'em,' and it sounded like you meant it."

Buck quirked his lips, half bitterly.

"Right then, I did, but I don't reckon it'll last."

He looked at her sideways, watching the full curve of her lower lip until she began to suck it in self-consciously. She shook her head and looked down and began to shove her oyster fork back and forth.

Buck glanced casually down the length of the table and caught Tobe's eyes on him again. Tobe moved his eyes slowly, and without turning his head, to rest them first on Lota, then on Jeanie Bannon, who was staring steadily at Buck. His mother looked away quickly as Buck's eyes met hers.

Buck started to speak to Lota but stopped and leaned to the right to let a waiter set a platter with six oysters on half shells before him. He was straightening up when the Governor burst into laughter that was too loud.

Buck looked anxiously towards the Governor and saw the thin face split in another yell of laughter as the waiter bent over to whisper in his ear. When the waiter straightened, Buck saw the Governor slowly begin to rise to his feet, pushing backwards with his legs to slide his chair away. On his feet, the old man stood very straight, not making any motions for silence. He chuckled quietly until every head at the table turned his way and even whispers had stopped.

"Good people," he said, then, with his eyes snapping bright as a blue jay's. "Everybody in the state treats this poor official with the respect due his title—everybody but the Bannon boys. Lord bless 'em, they treat him like a man.

"Look before you, every one of you. At each place, there's fine china. Oyster plates, service plates. Maybe there'll be some more plates later on. Good heavy silver running a foot out on either side of your plates. Knowing Buck, I'd say it's the best he could get.

"Now, look at what I've got."

He reached down slowly, roving his eyes from one face to

another. Still slowly and in silence, he held up a large shiny tin plate in one hand. With the other hand, he gathered and held up for them a bone-handled knife and fork to match. Nobody laughed. The Governor shook the utensils.

"Oh, don't be polite," he said, shaking his head. "These are my badges of acceptance." He glanced towards his wife. "And, Myra, don't be afraid of any loss of dignity on my part. These boys have complimented me by remembering my raisin'."

The Governor's wife twittered nervously and glanced quickly at Jeanie Bannon. Buck's mother suddenly laughed, a full enjoying sort of laugh, and all down the table it quickly spread until the Governor smiled broadly and laid his utensils back on the table with a clatter.

"Now," he said, "I want to tell you about these boys and the honor they've done me." He held his head back and looked thoughtfully up at a corner of the room. "Back in 1906, it was. I was campaigning and, as the Senator can tell you, a campaigner is going to drift down to Buck Bannon or get detoured." Lota Kyle laughed, first, and the Governor waited until it died down.

"Well, to say the least, my campaign here was unorthodox. I didn't make a speech at the courthouse. My poor stomach was saved from drinking buttermilk on every back porch in the county. For three blessed days, the only hand I shook was that of an old colored woman. Brooksie!

"She was a cook, and still is, I hope, because I want to campaign again on a hunting and fishing trip on the banks of the Choctawhatchee. That's where they took me. And that's where I won the governorship. They humbled me, and by the time I hit the north of Alabama, I needed humility.

"Buck, here." The Governor stopped and looked severely across and down at Buck for a second in silence, then he slowly shook his head. "That deck of cards he's got fluttered 'hallelujah' every time he anted up."

Somebody at the far end of the table said, loudly, "Put his feet to the fire, Governor."

Buck flushed and glanced up at the Governor and shook his head while the crowd laughed.

"And," the Governor went on slowly, "that redheaded devil

at the far end of the table—Hearn. He stole my watch and then hired a colored boy to shoot a pistol every quarter hour so I'd know what time it was. He *found* my watch just as we were leaving."

Buck, watching Hearn, saw his eyes roll towards the ceiling without his expression changing. He switched his eyes to Jeff, who was slowly reddening as the Governor glared at him.

"That one," the Governor flicked his finger out at Jeff, "he's the timid one." His voice dropped lower. "Wouldn't figure him to be like the others. Timid, bah! He took my brag dog off the rear end of the wagon and swapped it to an old darky for a hound that was too lazy to pull his own ears off the ground. I didn't know it till we got to Aven."

He paused and wiped his mouth with his napkin.

"Well, sir, I've been a better man for it. I went through north Alabama like an angel of mercy when I had intended passing out a few thunderbolts. I laughed more. Ate better. Hmm! That reminds me, I was going to tell you about the honor they've done me."

He pointed at Buck's oysters.

"You all have got oysters fresh from Indian Pass. You'll get a wild turkey, fattened on the limb of a chinquapin tree; you'll eat quail, roasted in butter; you'll eat a steak from a bear that stole the wild tupelo honey of Dead Lakes; and some of you will finish off on a slice of peanut-fed ham. Good people, you'll eat."

He shook his head slowly.

"But not like I will. I'll eat something that was introduced to me on that camping trip. Something that has haunted my waking dreams ever since. Down there on the red mudbanks of the Choctawhatchee grow cypress trees so tall they look black up at the top. And now and then a cypress will find itself wrapped in the green and tender vines of the wild bullace—muscadine to any city-raised folks here. At this season of the year, the slightest Gulf breeze plunks a heavy purple muscadine into the water."

He paused dramatically.

"And then, ladies and gentlemen, a long, sinuous blue shape glides out from under the cypress knees, turns sideways in the water and waits patiently for the muscadine to stagger downwards, closer and closer, for he knows it can't get away.

"As I said, friends, I've been honored—because they didn't forget my tastes. Tonight, I'm going to eat a catfish—a bullace-fed blue cat, rolled in yellow, water-ground corn meal, fried in deep fat, by my personal cook of the night—Brooksie herself."

He turned to Buck, then, and spoke directly to him.

"Buck, I'm the first Governor to visit your new hotel, but I'm not the last. They'll be coming long after I'm gone and they'll be all shapes and sizes because they'll just be men, too. But none of them will ever be as glad to have you for a friend as I am tonight."

The banquet was over and Buck had sent a bellboy after Hearn's car to take Lota home, when he realized that the Governor had made his opening dinner a success, had set them laughing when it most needed it. He touched Lota lightly on the arm.

"Wait here a minute," he said, "I'll be back before the car comes."

He went quickly across the lobby towards the little Governor, who was talking with Jeanie Bannon and the Senator's dark, rather dumpy, wife.

"Governor Thrasher," he said, "I feel like I ought to—"

Jeanie Bannon broke in.

"I've already thanked him, son," she said, quietly. "I took it that most of what he said was for me anyhow."

Buck smiled gently.

"It should have been," he said, then he looked meaningfully at the Governor. "I'll save my appreciation until we get upstairs tonight."

The Governor's eyebrows rose.

"Ah, a new deck."

"Maybe you'll have a chance," Buck said. He started to turn around as the horn blew outside, then looked back. "Better bring your whole contingent fund, though. I could use some state money." He nodded good-bye and turned away, hearing his mother's voice trailing away behind him.

"Yes, I reckon nothing ever kills a mother's pride in—"

The huge, topless Great Northern touring car coughed in the cold. Gasoline fumes spurted, heavy, from its muttering exhaust, as a thin solemn colored boy jiggled the gas lever with a nonchalant wrist movement.

Buck helped Lota into the rear seat and started to get in beside her, when he heard a dull, thrumming sound behind him. He turned quickly and the thrumming stopped. Virgil was leaning against the wall of the hotel. His right hand still choked the throat of the guitar.

Buck started to reach into his trousers pocket, but stopped as Virgil began to shake his head. He raised his shoulders, then, and let them drop again.

"Still won't take it?" he said, gently, then he jerked his thumb towards the dining room. "Well, go in and tell Smiley I said to give you the best."

Virgil smiled slyly and nodded his thanks. Buck got in beside Lota and leaned forward to speak to the driver.

"Charley, you can start and stop this thing any way you want to, but be damned careful in the middle."

Lota pulled the high collar of Hearn's overcoat close around her face. She slid down in the seat until her head was comfortable against the stiff leather upholstering, and looked up at the sky as they drove off. She was humming and Buck held his head down to listen. After a minute, she closed her eyes.

Buck smiled almost secretly and they rode on in silence until the car was grinding slowly along a block from Lota's boarding-house. Then Buck leaned forward again and touched the driver on the shoulder.

"Stop here," he said. "They'll have to put better lights on these things before I feel safe at night."

The driver allowed the big machine to lurch awkwardly to a stop on the rutted road and turned around in his seat.

"You can go on back," Buck said. "I'll walk Miss Lota on home—no piece at all—then I'll walk back."

Lota stopped looking at the moon and sat up quickly.

"Oh, Buck," she said, plaintively, "my shoes."

Buck opened the door on her side and slid past her to the ground. He held out his hand.

"Come on," he said quietly, and Lota wriggled her shoulders higher into the heavy coat. Buck caught sheeny glimpses of moonlight on the satin of her new dress as she caught his hand and stepped out.

They stood still, in a steady wind, watching the dim hulk of the car lumbering off towards the lights of the business district. Lota spoke first.

"I was proud of—" She stopped then and started over. "I was glad I knew you tonight. The Governor and all."

Buck didn't answer. He looked down at her with a queer set sort of smile beginning, then quickly ending, on his lips. He rubbed the heel of his right hand against the grey of his temple. He couldn't see the white of her dress any longer, only the way the moon softened and fuzzed the lines of her face so that it blurred white against the dark collar of the coat. Buck reached out slowly and took her by one elbow. He turned her so that she faced him, then he caught her under the other elbow and gently lifted upwards. She rocked up on her toes, then back down, and he saw her smile.

"I want you to marry me," he said abruptly, and watched her face, feeling the sudden stiffening of her body through her arms, and wondered why he had said it so bluntly.

She hadn't looked at him yet. Her lips were slightly open and she was staring down at his shirt front. Suddenly, she caught his coat with both hands and laid her head forward against his chest. He could feel her hair blowing and it smelled good, not like perfume or soap, or just hair, but like something that would be there one minute and gone the next. He wondered, breathing deeply and slowly, if this odor would join the others that haunt a man.

Lota pulled her head away from his chest and held it back, holding to his coat, and looked at him with her eyes wide and her lips still apart.

"Why me?" she said, simply.

"You're the one I want."

"Do you love me?"

"Yes," Buck said quickly, and watched the curve of her lips.

"You've only known me three weeks," she said, somehow rueful, "you don't even know if you'd like to kiss me."

Buck made a small laughing sound in his chest. He caught her waist and pulled her closer. He saw her close her eyes and purse her lips. He started to smile, but his mouth thinned down almost cruelly instead. Her lips were hard against his, held too tightly. He kissed her, gently moving his lips, until he felt her mouth soften and widen and then her arms were leaving his waist and

[219]

sliding up and around onto his shoulder blades. She pulled her mouth away from his with a short gasping laughing breath and moved her arms up around his neck.

"Yes, I'll marry you," she said, and kissed him again, quick and hard. "My Lord, yes."

INTERLUDE

BASS WOOTEN *sat on the lid of a large garbage can self-consciously twisting his neck in the stiff white collar of a striped shirt. He gazed across the street at the arched entranceway of a red-brick church.*

"I'll believe it when I see 'em come out o' that church," he said to Jake Willis.

Jake shifted slightly so his shoulder would be more comfortable against the metal lamppost.

"You see 'em decoratin'," he said, tonelessly. "No, sir, Bass, when that fool makes up his mind—whew! Met her five weeks ago an' this time tomorrow I'll be supportin' another Bannon."

"Supportin' hell. You mean runnin' errands."

Jake flushed and didn't answer.

"Well, you can be glad o' one thing." Bass punched Jake in the ribs with a stubby thumb. "Old as Buck is, there ain't apt to be no more a'comin'."

Jake spat onto the brick paving and grinned sourly.

"Ain't but one thing Buck Bannon could do an' surprise me. That's to walk right up an' give me my watch back an' say I didn't owe him a dime."

CHAPTER TWENTY-ONE

Started. Walk slow now like a pallbearer, or we'll outrun that gar-mouthed kid with the ring. Somebody better watch him, by God. If he's anything like his daddy, the little bastard'll steal it, pillow and all. T. Peyton Sudduth! So damned sorry even his bees won't make honey.

Nothing to this. Easy as breaking piecrust. Look at 'em staring and listen to 'em whispering. Bragging on Lota. She does look good. Godamighty, walks down that aisle, stepping long and free from the hips down, striding pretty as a Tennessee mule. Women! Talking about that spider-web veil or wondering who's going to give her away.

Damn if there ain't Angus McTyre, solemn as if he was measuring drinks in his bar. Only reason he's here is it's free.

Stylish George, in a collar fit to choke him and a new little bristly mustache that looks like briers growing up around a lime sink. "Laughing" Bell right in front of him. I'd know his shoulders shaking anywhere, laughing, and ain't a damned-nother soul laughing. Wonder what's always so funny to him, or if it's something like hiccups that you can't stop.

The city councilmen, every one of 'em sitting in a row like deacons and every one of 'em wishing I'd drop dead so he could be mayor. Old Cap'n Bottoms, talks so soft and sweet and careful, why he even says, "Chicking" just to be sure, and he'll steal something he don't even want.

Look at 'em. Every man out there, wishing he was in my shoes for tonight and telling themselves they don't see how I did it. Let 'em wonder. By God, a blind hog gets an acorn now and then. Old wrinkled-lip sawed-off Ed Mercer, looking satisfied and secret like a kid wetting under water, and hoping I'll buy the new church chimes so he won't have to put. Brought his chew in with him and too stingy to spit. Country as nursing a baby in the wagon yard.

Go on down. Lessie Whitfield! Sitting two rows from the ribbons. By God, everybody'll think she's kin to me. Fat, and Lord I remember the first time she came in Green's store. "Don't want a thing, just show-casin'," was the way she said it. Thirty years. She wasn't so fat then but what she could get a good price at Mabe's. Looks as respectable as anybody now, though, and sits there mighty calm for a whore in church.

Getting close. Easy now. My Lord, there's Aunt Bee and Uncle Barnes come thirty-five miles. What's he turning around for? Mouth open and red like he's been eating pokeberries, and beard like cotton candy. Aunt Bee ain't turned around and she's the one I'm kin to. Reckon she won't, though. I can hear her now. "Well, we'll go, Barnes—we may be needed—but it'll mean a present, an' a weddin' now, to my mind, ain't no more fun than a cemetery hoein'." Both of 'em ought to be bored for the hollow horn.

God, look at that. Inside the ribbons. If there's anything I've got it's kinfolks. Five and a half pews of 'em. Damned if the four big girls didn't marry in, 'stead of out. Regina's! Little old black mustache and a mouth set to blow a flute. Chews the same piece of gum every day and rests it at night in a Phenolax Wafer box. Should have been killed when a grapevine would have hung him.

Almost, now. There's Jeff with Mother. She don't look so peart, but I reckon she's just worn out what with that breakfast this morning and going all day. That sawyer sweetheart of Vesta's eating last night. Every time he'd butter a biscuit somebody'd steal it. Said his piece of steak must have come from where the yoke rubbed. Well, he may be all right, but I mistrust a man that tells you he's honest. Big sucker, though. Bigger'n me. Vesta, she's too feisty for anything better, I reckon.

Whoa, now. Here we are. Preacher looks just as natural. All right, get started with us dearly beloveds. I know this thing backwards and forwards. Hell, I ought to. Same thing with Ivy. Ivy, Ivy, Ivy. Godamighty and me here marrying a girl not as old as my boy and I never saw him. Hmph! Should have invited her.

Sure, take obey to hell-and-gone out. She's going to cherish me. But if I want her to obey bad enough, she'll do it anyhow. Big wedding, church wedding, long wedding, with flowers and here comes the bride and visitors and a whippoorwill preacher. Hard-ankled Baptist. Take my money every month to get to cuss me every Sunday. Twenty-five more dollars this afternoon.

God, I ought to get a cut-rate, as many cane-bottomed chairs as I've bought for the Sunday school department.

Listen to the preacher, fool. What'd they do if I missed a question, make me stay in or start all over?

There's Tobe. Wondered when he'd slip in a side door, grinning like a mule eatin' briers, but I knew damn well what he'd be thinking. Stand off and cuss me for marrying a kid. Don't look much like I can suit me and Tobe both when it comes to picking a wife. Funny thing, he liked Ivy and he likes Lota, but he just don't want me tied up with nobody. Reckon—uh, uh. Look out, here it comes.

"I, Joseph, take—"

Hell, nobody ever called me Joseph. Ought to have been Buck. I, Buck. They'd have laughed, though. That store I, Buck, Incorporated. Unh, unh, hold it. This is a wedding and a serious thing.

That fool Hearn, said this was the kind of marriage where the bride lays her dental work over till after the wedding, so the husband would pay. Dentist, the devil. Teeth that'd crack a hicker nut. Strong enough to do it, too. Standing there now looking like she never heard what the preacher's saying before, as many times as she practiced. If that preacher wasn't on a stand, she'd have to squat to see his face. Wup!

"I will—" And that about settles it. She sounded weak on that last one. Just a kid. Wonder what she's thinking about. Me? Hell, probably Denver, Colorado. Snow, of all the God-blessed ideas. Denver, on a honeymoon. Seashore, Florida, California, New York—and damned if she didn't pick Denver in the winter because she's never seen snow.

That's it. All over now. That brat with the ring showed up all right. Turn easy and you may kiss the bride. Hell, don't I know it? That's one thing I can natchally do. Take it easy. Here, anyhow. Plenty of time. More time than a forty-eight-year-old man needs with a nineteen-year-old wife.

That's right. Close your eyes and come up on your toes. Head back. Mouth just as soft but cool and still like it couldn't forget the crowd and was saving up for later on. That's all right with me. Be careful of that damned veil back there, but I don't see why. It's the last time it'll ever be used. Might as well wear it out today. All right, breathe deep and turn around and start back. Change the music. Swing yo' partner. Listen to the fiddle and hurry down the middle.

Same people, but different now. Changed, somehow. Faces sagging a little, looks like, but maybe it's just I'm walking uphill, kinda. Hope so. Lota's quickening.

Damn glad. Last row coming. Who in hell's that woman in the sun bonnet? Can't even see her face. Like a possum in a sack. Probably stopped in to rest. Sure, that's it. Saturday afternoon and the town's full o' folks from the country. Well, I'll never know, now. Got to hurry. Sun's slanting mighty low through that vestibule window, pretty, too, all different-colored.

Let's get going. Watch the steps. Got to change clothes, tell everybody good-bye, and catch that train in an hour. Hope Jeff gets everything fixed all right. Straight Pullman and Montgomery by pure dark, then a whole damned drawing room to Denver. Hot damn. Clickety-clickety-click. Unh-unh, too fast a tune for me.

Hurry out here. Watch the steps. Damn those kids, get 'em out of the way. Better save that rice till you see how the crop comes out. By God, kissing can wait. Anybody I want kissing my wife and me knows to come on to the hotel.

Free drinks'll bring 'em. Let's go. Get in that car. I'm cold out in a rush to put some work on that Peachtree Street imported bartender myself.

Buck shook his head slightly at the bartender and looked down at the glass he was slowly turning between his fingers.

"Last one here for a while, Slappey," he said, and glanced quickly towards the door into the lobby as Hearn came through and jerked his head for Buck to come on. "Hold 'em in the road," he said, and spun the glass across the bar.

"She's coming down," Hearn said, grinning. "And, man, is she frocked out?"

Buck saw her trying to stride across the lobby, but having to take short steps in a dark-blue tailored suit with a hobble skirt. The white collar of her silk blouse was soft and not high around her neck, but was held together at the hollow of her throat with a blue polka-dot tie with flaring ends. Her shoes showed black and shiny and the buttons seemed to dance in the bright lights of the lobby.

Buck watched her for a second, and saw that the smile on her face was eager yet uncertain and that she glanced several times to the right or left, but always swinging her eyes back to him.

He turned to Hearn.

"A man can go clear to the bridge with her," he said, simply.

Hearn didn't answer for a second and Buck glanced at him. Hearn's eyes were half closed and his nostrils were flared a little. Buck felt a sudden catching in his chest and he frowned, watching his brother. A small queer smile started on Hearn's lips, then, suddenly, he opened his eyes wide and shook his head. When he turned to Buck there was no expression on his face.

"Reckon so," he said, as Lota stopped close to them, breathing fast.

"Let's go," she said.

"In a hurry?"

Lota wrinkled her nose at Hearn. "If you weren't going to drive us to the train, I'd kill you now."

Buck looked at his watch.

"Wait here just a minute, Lota," he said, and touched Hearn's arm. "I want to see Hearn over here. Won't take long."

"I'll run on out to the car," Lota said, quickly.

Buck waited until she was at the door, trying to think, wondering how he could bring it up, then suddenly knowing there was no reason for him to wonder about Hearn. No. The look on his face had come from something else—maybe he was worried about something. Maybe—

He looked at Hearn then down at his fingernails, before he spoke.

"You ain't—" He started, but stopped. "Everything all right?" he said, finally.

"Sure." Hearn's tone was irritable.

"Good." He breathed deeply. "Mother didn't seem any too chipper about this business. You notice? She left too quick."

Hearn grunted. Buck waited, but Hearn didn't say anything.

"She don't like it, does she?"

Hearn shrugged.

"You didn't ask her if she would like it before," he said, "why worry about it now?"

"Aw, I—" Buck stopped and blew out a long breath. "Hell, let's go."

Jeff was waiting at the station as the car ground over fresh grey slag. He came hurriedly over with tickets folded neatly into an envelope and his pigeon-toed walk looked more awkward and timid from the pace.

When he was shaking hands with Jeff, Buck was thinking: "This is the only man in the world that likes to buy railroad tickets. The only man alive that likes to check baggage. And, by God, he's my brother."

Buck lay staring straight up into darkness and listened to the wheels four-clicking underneath him. Now and then his body would roll slightly towards the inside or the outside of the lower berth. He'd hear the straining creak of metal, and he'd know he was one more curve farther from Montgomery.

Finally he sighed and shook his head on the pillow. He spoke out loud, deliberately.

"Well, I will be damned if I ever saw anything get too heavy as quick as her head did."

There was no answer and he turned his head to the left to listen for Lota's long, even breathing.

"Thank God she's breathing," he said, louder. "I was worried."

Lota didn't stir. Buck sighed again and tried to slide his arm gently out from under her head. Lota muttered in her sleep and moved convulsively. She threw her left arm across Buck's chest, limply, and drew her left leg up until her knee was lying heavily across Buck's thigh.

Buck reached up with his free arm and fumbled around until he found the light switch and turned on the dim undressing bulb. Then he glanced over at Lota. She was frowning in her sleep and her black hair covered part of her face, and fell down past her shoulder.

Buck spread the fingers on his right hand and gently ran them close to her scalp until he could get a handful of hair. He lifted slowly, trying to be gentle, but the train lurched and Lota's eyes opened wide.

"Quit pulling my hair," she said.

Buck turned her hair loose and her head flopped back. She yawned.

"It's too late," she said, sleepily.

Buck swung his legs off the side of the berth.

"Get up," he said. "Honeymoon or not, by God, this bed is too little."

Lota closed her eyes.

"Well, we can't help that. Let's go back to sleep."

Buck stood up and leaned over. He punched her lightly in the ribs. She opened one eye and started to yawn again. Buck motioned with his thumb towards the upper berth.

"You're moving," he said.

"Oh, Buck," Lota wailed. "You move, I've got this place just as warm."

Buck straightened up and jerked the sheet and blanket down on the upper berth; then he leaned back over and put one arm under Lota's knees and the other under her shoulders. He lifted her out and stood her on her feet. He sat down on the lower berth and laced his fingers so that his hands formed a stirrup between his knees.

"You're the youngest," he said, "and the smallest. Step up."

Lota yawned wide and shivered, standing there with her arms hugging herself in a sheer creamy nightgown with long sleeves and a high neck. One foot rubbed on top of the other, slowly, then she braced her hands on the edge of the upper and put one foot in his handmade stirrup. She waited for a second, looking up at the berth, then back down at him.

"Well, push," she said.

Buck lifted and Lota pulled until she was hanging half in and half out of the upper. Lota kicked downwards with one foot.

"You'll be sorry," she said, in a muffled voice.

Buck looked at her legs hanging down in front of him. He kissed one knee, then bit the other, lightly.

"You've got baby faces in your knees," he said.

Lota suddenly began to scramble into her berth.

Buck sat on the side of his berth for a moment longer, staring thoughtfully up at the edge of hers. He started to speak, then stopped. Suddenly her face came out and she glared down at him.

"Is the bed big enough for you now?" she said, sweetly.

"Too damned big," he said.

"Hah!" Lota said, and her head disappeared. "Good night."

Buck said, "Humph!" and sat still a minute, waiting for her head to come back out. When it didn't, he yawned and reached back of him and switched out the little light. He threw the pillows on the floor of the drawing room and lay flat on his back with his hands under his head and his last conscious thought was "Funny, I must have been wishing for her for over twenty years and didn't know it."

"I'm starving." Lota kicked her stocking feet against the side of the seat in front of her and two puffs of fine dust shot up and drifted downwards.

Buck wrinkled his nose.

"You been hungry all the way to Colorado and halfway back. Don't you think about anything but your stomach?"

"Ah," Lota rolled her eyes at him. "You ought to know."

Buck clucked his tongue and started pulling on his coat.

"Well, one thing sure. Anybody can eat a dollar steak at one sitting won't ever die of a broken heart."

Lota felt around with her feet on the floor of the drawing room, then leaned over and reached under the seat for her shoes. When she straightened up again her face was red from bending over.

"I'm making friends with my stomach for my old age," she said. "Grandma said a body gets to where there's just one pleasure left and that's eating."

"And drinking?"

Lota shuddered and blew through her lips.

"That's no pleasure. Tastes like cane skimmings and makes me act like a fool."

Buck moved over across from her and pushed her foot into one of the shoes and sat there holding her ankle in his hand.

"What'd you ask that waiter?—'Who put the bushes on that beef?'"

Lota laughed out loud, dropping her head back against the cushion.

" 'Parsley, Ma'am,' " she said in a deep voice, mocking the waiter.

Buck dropped her foot and got up and walked unsteadily over to the small washbasin in the corner. He braced his shoulder against the lurch of the train and started washing his hands.

"Well, I hope you've seen all the snow you'll ever want. Damned if that country out there is worth a shirt tail full of oats."

"I liked the snow." Lota stood up and tucked her blouse down into the band of her skirt.

Buck slung his hands to dry them a little before trying the small slick towel.

"I didn't think you liked it the first day."

"You fool." Lota caught his eye in the mirror. "How could anybody enjoy being pushed down into it right off the train and rolled over in front of everybody in Denver?"

Buck grinned at her in the mirror. She came across the room, swaying and placing her feet far apart for balance. She put both her hands on Buck's shoulders from behind.

"Did I do all right? For the first honeymoon, anyhow?"

Buck didn't speak until he had dried his hands, then he turned around and buried his fingers deep in the hair on either side of her face.

"I think I'll keep you."

"Were you proud of me, out in the hotel and all?"

Buck nodded, smiling slowly.

"You walked in like you had a first mortgage on the damned thing."

"I was shaking inside."

"Never worry about what a man thinks until he starts to do something about it."

"I was proud of you," Lota said, then suddenly she straightened up and puffed out her chest, "Congressman!"

Buck dropped his hands and closed his eyes.

"Good God, don't say that. I've told and told you that damned fool Jeff must have gone crazy, sending me a wire like that."

"I believe it," Lota said, quickly.

"Hurrying home, I believe that," Buck said, firmly, "but I've got too many enemies to believe anybody wants me to run for Congress."

Lota pushed him in the chest.

"Kill-joy." She turned away, swaggered across the drawing room, and stood by the door with one hand on her hip. "Well, I'll go to Washington without you and I'll eat nothing but fried chicken and champagne."

Buck steered her out the door into the narrow passageway and closed the door behind him.

"You'll go to Aven," he said, "and eat nothing but sowbelly and collards."

He followed her swaying hips down the aisle, watching how easily her long legs took up the small shocks of the train and how she shifted her weight with the turn of a curve.

That Jeff! Any fool ought to have known better'n to wire something I can't live up to. Dammit, I wired him plain as day that I was just tired of wearing an overcoat and drinking whiskey that ain't got the roshineers in it.

Now, by God, I've got to run for Congress and get beat, or let her find out I broke up her honeymoon before it got started good.

Aven's tiled-roof station slid slowly and smoothly past in the dark. Buck felt like it was moving and the train was still, until he felt the stumbling grind as the wheels tried to lock for the last time. His thoughts started to drift back to the first night he'd spent in Aven, sleeping in the half-finished station on a baggage truck, when he felt Lota's fingers digging into his shoulders from behind. He turned his head to look over his shoulder.

She was standing on tiptoe, pulling up on him to see over. She hugged him and shivered a little.

"I'm so excited I'm not even sleepy and it's after midnight."

"Glad to get home?" Buck said.

"Unh-hunh," she said, tapping her foot impatiently for the porter to get the doors open and the steps down. "But that's not why I'm excited." She looked up at him with wide eyes. "Buck, I just thought. If you get elected Congressman, what'll I be?"

"Just the same damned fool, I reckon," Buck said, and flinched as she dug her fingers deeper into his shoulder. "I told you, anyhow, that there's some mistake. Hell, I wouldn't have it."

"But, Jeff wired—" Lota broke off as the doors were opened.

[230]

"Oh, there's Tobe. And Hearn." She looked closer. "Hearn's drunk," she said, matter-of-factly, as she stepped off on the red box.

Hearn looked up at them from under a hat that was pulled down far on one side. He started singing loudly:

> "Said the blackbird to the crow,
> 'What makes white folks hate us so?'
> Said the eagle as he flew,
> 'If I was a young man, I'd kiss you.' "

He kissed Lota, then held her off by her shoulders and looked at her. He shook his head, then glanced at Buck.

"You look whipped down, Buck."

"Go to the devil," Buck said and shook hands with Tobe, who had come quietly from the side and was just standing there. "Tobe, couldn't you keep him sober?"

Tobe grunted.

"He just got back himself. Been gone a week nearly. Said he wanted a honeymoon, too, and from the looks of him, he took more'n one wife."

Hearn laughed and started hustling them towards his car. He started to get in the driver's seat, but Buck stopped him.

"Whoa," he said, "let Tobe steer this thing. I want to talk to him, anyhow, and you and Lota can sit in the back."

Buck leaned over closer to Tobe and spoke low, hardly above the sound of the engine.

"Where's Jeff?"

"He won't leave the hotel for nothing when you're gone."

"Why in the world didn't he send the wire I told him to?"

Tobe shook his head.

"Better wait till we get to the hotel."

Lota was upstairs and Hearn had started out again in his big red car, before Buck had another chance to mention the telegram.

"That was a hell of a note," he said, ducking under the flap and going behind the quiet darkened bar to turn on the light over the large mirror, "sending me a wire that I'd been drafted to run for Congress."

Tobe tried not to smile.

"That damned fool Hearn got your message and he wrote the answer, without saying a word to me or Jeff about it."

Buck carefully ran some water into a small glass on top of an inch of whiskey. He sipped it once, then gulped the whole drink and wiped his mouth.

"Ought to be hung by his nose with a cotton hook. Now Lota thinks I'm practically in Washington."

Tobe shrugged and reached out his hand for a glass that Buck was shoving towards him.

"You should be," he said, "but the way things are you couldn't get elected mayor again."

Buck carefully set his glass down on the bar, and his eyes narrowed suddenly.

"Something wrong?"

"Aw, Buck, you know what was happening when you left. Preachers and deacons and sisters and Epworth Leagues. Like a bunch of wood lice eating at a tree, and you can't see them until the tree falls down."

"Is it getting worse?"

Tobe nodded and lifted his glass and drank quickly.

"Buck," he said, leaning on the bar and frowning, "they started the minute you left town, working to beat hell." He began to mimic the women. "Licensed the fancy women, taxed the gamblers, graft, ungodly, drinks too much, gambles all night, and a woman ain't safe with him. Hell-fire." Tobe suddenly spat on the floor.

Buck's face relaxed.

"Nothing new in that."

"There's something new in what they're saying now and the way they're saying it. Lota. 'Married a child,' they're putting it out, 'used his position to get her job so she'd be close to him, and beholden, and the only way he could get her was to marry her.' Oh, they're laying for you now. The preachers are going to take a lick every Sunday, even wanting to change the name of the town."

Buck frowned.

"What the hell for?"

"They say Aven is a Biblical name and oughtn't to be on a town full of vice."

Buck made wet circles with his glass and looked at them thoughtfully.

"Preachers take their texts on me, hunh?"

"They don't name you," Tobe said, quickly. "They just say that the town is run by a godless man."

"Sounds like Amos Longshore started that."

"Likely," Tobe said.

Buck grunted deep in his chest and was silent for a moment. Then he shook his head.

"No way to shut 'em up. Have to figure some way to beat it."

Tobe shrugged.

"No way for us to shut 'em up," he said, "but they cold out know how over at Pinetown. They burnt a Holy Roller out, tent, seats and all."

"No, not that way," Buck shook his head and started to reach for the bottle, "that ain't how I—" His hand stopped in mid-air for a second, then went on more slowly and fumbled for a second at the neck of the bottle. He turned suddenly and his lips were twisted in a queer cruel smile. He tapped the bottle on the bar.

"Tobe," he said, softly, "there's one way I can kill this cat." He poured a drink, looking at his glass part of the time, then at Tobe, and slid the bottle over. He laughed abruptly and it sounded too loud in the empty bar-dining room, so he stopped quickly.

"We'll get a preacher for the defense," he said, and raised his glass.

CHAPTER TWENTY-TWO

A MONTH later, Buck stood on the rim of a circle drawn on the dust of a vacant lot, by the blackened and burned remains of a canvas tent. He lifted one foot carefully and looked at the blurred footprint he had left, then he deliberately and slowly placed his foot in another spot until the powdery blue-grey ashes rose over the toe. The ashes fluffed and the wind swirled them upwards towards Jeff. Jeff spat and frowned, then moved downwind from Buck.

"There's the preacher," he said, jerking his head towards the street.

Buck coughed. "Got a jaw like a Chattanooga middlebuster." He turned and watched the huge pear-shaped figure worry its way through the charred skeleton tangle of benches and tent poles and still-smoldering rope.

"Well, Preacher," he called, "lucky you didn't sleep in your tent last night."

The Reverend Agnew Huff paused with his right foot held out of the ashes and thrust his plow-like chin outwards. "That lesson came to me, son," he said, cheerfully, "during a mission through the West Florida cow country." He started towards them, keeping a stingy balance with his too-short arms held out stiff at his sides. He was talking as he walked. "Mrs. Huff saved only her hippings," he said as he stopped in front of Buck, "and they were scorched."

"Hippings?" Jeff looked bewildered.

"Hm," the preacher glanced at Jeff. "You're a youngster. Underdrawers, son."

"Where's Mrs. Huff now?"

The preacher beamed. "Down at our rooms, preparing tonight's sermon."

Buck looked sharply at him.

"Preparing tonight's—? You mean she's making up a sermon for you to say?"

The Reverend Huff nodded happily.

"She writes them all, good and bad." He jerked his head towards the charred framework of the pine pulpit. "They're always good when we give them from the ruins. Scorchers."

Buck stared thoughtfully over the Reverend Huff's shoulder, and stirred the ashes with his toe. "Uh, suppose we don't have a sermon tonight?"

"Oh, no," the Reverend said, quickly. "Tonight's the big night." He shook his head. "Of course," he went on, confidentially, "they never know that someone usually replaces our tent, but they feel sorry for us. Speaking out of our despair and all."

Buck's mouth curled as if he could taste the ashes that floated in the air.

"We're satisfied. There's enough been said and any more might backfire. I'd rather just let folks make up their minds about who burned you out."

"Ah," the Reverend Huff said, "tonight, we hope to tell them who burned the tent."

Buck lifted his head a little and looked at the preacher steadily.

"I don't want them told."

"You mean—" the preacher's rolling voice rose, then broke off suddenly. He pursed his lips and looked down at the ground blinking rapidly, then he glanced back up at Buck. "Oh," he said, and nodded his head.

"All I mean," Buck said, carefully, "is that I don't want you to preach. Even if you could find out who did it."

"Which you can't," Jeff broke in.

The preacher looked at Jeff with the lids held low over his light-blue eyes and his mouth set tighter as his long jaw pushed forward.

"I already know, young man," he said, then he turned his eyes back to Buck. "And I think I'll preach tonight."

Buck shook his head and his lower lip began to droop. He didn't speak.

"As things stand now," the preacher said, slowly, "the men I'd fought from my pulpit will carry the blame for this."

Buck didn't answer and his face didn't change.

"And the ones I didn't fight," the preacher laughed suddenly and bitterly, "wouldn't have any reason to burn me out."

Buck spoke through tight lips, tonelessly.

"You were hired to talk and given a list of names. Now your

job is over. Your new tent is on the ACL siding. Be out of town tomorrow and don't speak tonight."

"It's my duty to speak," the preacher said, mockingly.

Buck's eyelids trembled as he narrowed his eyes. He didn't speak.

"Unless," the preacher continued, slowly, with his eyes trying to hold Buck's, "we could be paid for not doing our night's work."

Buck held up his hand and stopped him.

"You're not a regular preacher, are you? Baptist or Methodist?"

The Reverend Huff showed his teeth, smiling.

"No, I'm not ordained, but I believe I'm qualified to do one thing." He paused and lowered his voice. "I can tell the good people of Aven just what kind of man they have for mayor."

"Now, by God," Buck said, harshly, "you're going to find out what kind of man I am, but I doubt if you'll be telling it." He turned carelessly to Jeff, and jerked his head towards the business district. "Go to the City Hall. Have Tobe come right up and tell him to bring Longboy."

He watched silently as Jeff turned away, then swung back to the Reverend Huff.

"Two weeks ago," he said, slowly, "the city council passed an ordinance instructing the mayor to set licenses as he sees fit for street fairs, peddlers, traveling shows, and tent revivals." He stopped and rubbed his chin with the back of his hand, watching the preacher. "You didn't pay any license at all, and you've preached a week."

The Reverend Huff's face whitened.

"No license was set," he said, stiffly.

"There is now," Buck said, then flipped his hand out. "Just two thousand dollars."

The Reverend Huff held his voice cold and hard.

"You expected trouble with me, then?"

"No, I just got ready."

"Well, I won't pay it." The Reverend Huff's voice was lower now and somewhere behind it Buck could feel the shakiness he wanted to hear.

"No," he said, "you won't pay it. You're leaving town in a few minutes, thanking the Lord for a new tent and a suspended sentence of sixty days in the city jail for failure to pay license."

The Reverend Huff was silent, but his eyes still flickered, not wavering over Buck's face.

"That is," Buck went on, "if you want to live and do well."

The Reverend's face changed then. He looked at the ground and his mouth drew down bitterly.

"Mr. Bannon," he said, softly, "I'm going to leave all right, but only because jail and hunger and manual labor are distasteful." He looked up, smiling wryly. "No threats, please. You and I are darklings, Mr. Bannon. Threats won't work."

Buck looked blankly at the preacher and started to speak.

"You don't know that word?" the preacher said. "Darklings is old folks' talk. Saints when it suits us, sinners when it doesn't, and a private devil for each of us, glad if it's right but not sorry if it isn't. No, don't threaten. You and I won't fear dying after the job of living."

Buck stared at the Reverend Huff for a moment with his eyes lowering, then he raised his hands slowly and just looked down at them.

"Get out of town," he said, thickly, and turned away without looking back. He began to pick his way carefully through the blackened poles and braces and, as he reached the sidewalk, he heard the Reverend Huff yell after him.

"Long as you live around this town, Buck Bannon, hell won't be but one foot underground."

Buck's steps grew longer. He walked faster over the sidewalk.

"God," he was thinking, "if I ever saw a one hundred per cent —" He threw his head back to look up at the silver-patched branches of the sycamores that lined the sidewalk and tried to breathe more air into his lungs. It was a warm day, almost too warm for him. He'd have liked it cold enough to make him walk faster, or freezing, to drive his thoughts onto something else.

"Wonder what it is makes me want something bad enough to deal with a crawling dog like him. I don't care that much about being mayor. Damn if I want them beating me, though, even if they did have four preachers and a newspaper. Hah! Whipped 'em with a sawdust Holy Roller. He'd a'had me hooked, though, if I hadn't figured—"

He was muttering when he saw the buggy coming towards him at a quick trot, with Jeff and Tobe in the seat and Longboy

Taylor towering behind, holding to the rear of the seat. He waved them down.

"It's all right now," he said. "He's about decided to leave."

"You must a'scared hell out of him," Tobe Parody said.

"No, I don't think he was scared one damned bit."

Tobe leaned forward with his elbows on his knees and the reins dangling loosely in his big knotted hands. He pursed his lips and spoke solemnly.

"Well, I'm mighty glad that problem's settled. It'll leave your mind free for the next one—which ain't long off."

Longboy Taylor snickered and Buck glanced sharply up at him. Tobe coughed and Jeff started climbing down out of the buggy.

"I'll walk with you," he said, "no use in foundering the city's best horse."

The chief turned his horse around in the middle of the dirt street and brought it back to the trot as Longboy lifted one thick leg and climbed over the back of the seat. Buck heard him say something to Tobe in a low voice, then he heard Tobe laugh.

"What the hell's he whoopin' about?"

Jeff glanced sideways at him, sober-faced.

"Beats me," he said, then he coughed. "Uh, Lota's got a brand-new automobile."

"I know that," Buck said, impatiently. "Told her to get one and charge it to me."

"Well, she's really got one," Jeff said, and put his hands in his pockets and started whistling softly. He didn't say anything else and Buck didn't ask any more questions, but now and then Buck would glance quickly around as if to speak and find Jeff watching him. He walked on not speaking to Jeff, but now and then raising his hand and shaking it slightly sideways to someone passing in a buggy, or touching his hat brim good evening to a hurrying woman. Jeff whistled carelessly until they reached the small fruit store just west of the hotel. He stopped and began to fumble among the oranges that slanted yellow and shiny with wax in the sun, up and down and across the square display stands in front of the store.

"Figured I'd get some of these and take 'em up to Mother," he said, but he kept glancing up the street towards the corner of

[238]

Basin and Midway where the stone bank front gleamed white except for the bronzy flash from the door hardware.

"Aw, hell," Buck said, "Mother's still hidin' fruit from the kids. She's got more'n Abe here."

Jeff stayed bent over the oranges, watching until the small knot of people standing on the bank corner began to nudge each other and crane their heads around the side of the building, then he straightened up and turned around. The quick frightened yelp of a dog cut through the jumble of little-town noises and up on the corner a small boy put two fingers in his mouth and whistled loudly. Buck raised his head as if he were looking over the shoulder of someone in front of him and watched the corner.

The hood of a huge black automobile nosed carefully around the corner, and turned down Basin Street, avoiding a deep pit where the brick paving had sunk, then straddling a patch of broken glass, until it came straight out of the turn.

Buck saw it all, then, all of it, for the first time—a long square high-built Wescott with the top down, shiny with brass over the radiator, a solid glisten from front to sweating colored boy whose right hand held the wheel and whose left hand caressed the red rubber bulb of a Klaxon horn. Buck saw the boy turn his head to speak over his shoulder, then he saw Lota.

Lota in the back seat alone—Lota lolling against the stiff black-leather cushions—Lota in a dark-green hat with a lime-colored willow plume stiffened to curl over the top of her head and on around back of her right ear to sweep over the dark-brown velvet collar of a lighter brown suit—Lota with her right arm trailing along the edge of the back door and Lota with the long strong fingers of her right hand tapping studiedly against the metal— Lota, facing three-quarters away from his side of the street, smiling slightly and nodding to an open-mouthed woman on the street—Lota!

Buck's eyes blinked, then opened wide as the car snorted and rumbled nearer. He said just one word.

"Goddamn!"

He looked around at a strangling sound and saw Jeff standing with his face to the hotel wall, leaning his head on one forearm and slowly beating the wall with the palm of his other hand.

[239]

Somebody yelled, "That's Moses drivin', Big Moses!" Quickly Buck's eyes swung to the door of the fruit stand and fastened on the fat aproned figure of its owner. The wide grin slowly faded from the Greek's face and he shrugged, seeming to shrink, and gestured towards the opened crates.

"Oranges, Mist' Buck?"

Buck's eyes flickered from the orange stand back to the car just in time to see Lota sit up straighter, recognizing him, then sink back twisting so that she favored his side of the street.

"By God, yes," he said, and stepped closer to the boxes.

He picked up three oranges in his left hand and one in his right, then he squared his feet towards the car. Lota smiled and raised her hand, fingers curled, and inclined her head slightly. Buck stepped off on his left foot and threw the first orange at Lota. It struck the windshield in front of the Negro boy. The Negro ducked and brakes began to squeal as Buck's second orange angled into the front seat. Buck saw Lota lean forward and heard her loud, "Drive faster," to the Negro. Buck threw the third orange as the automobile passed him. It knocked hat, willow plume and all, off Lota's head. She grabbed at the hat and slid down low in the seat, trying hurriedly to settle it back on her head. The Negro boy hunched lower, so only the top of his new black cap showed, and tried to get more speed out of the Wescott.

Buck didn't stop throwing. He threw oranges at the car when he couldn't see Lota or the driver, only the willow plume and black cap. Most of them missed and two kid boys with knobby knees started yelling and running after the car and scooping up oranges that hadn't smashed too much to eat. Buck kept throwing until his arm hurt and hung limply at the side.

Then he stopped and just stood there breathing and glaring after the spattered automobile, watching until he saw Lota's head come cautiously higher above the back of the seat, and she was sitting stiff-necked staring straight ahead. Then he felt the hand of the little Greek touch his arm.

He looked down as the Greek held out another orange.

"Wanna more, maka two dozen."

Buck took it automatically and stood looking blankly down at the orange, then slowly his eyes swung after the car, to see it sweep around the corner followed by a small yellow dog that scrambled frantically along snapping at one of the hard-rubber tires.

Suddenly Buck began to laugh.

Buck leaned closer to look down out of the window of his second-story room onto the rutted wagon yard just across the railroad tracks that bordered the rear of the hotel. He watched until the big black automobile lurched through the slow-gathering dusk to stop beside a telephone pole. He didn't change expression until he saw Lota hurry across the railroad tracks to the back entrance of the hotel. Then he smiled wryly and started taking off his dark coat.

"Can't wait to get at me," he said, "but didn't want to come in 'fore dark."

He tossed the coat onto the high wooden bed, then walked quickly across the room to a small leather-topped writing table and poured whiskey and water into a heavy glass. He drank it slowly, with his eyes cut sideways towards the door that led into the hall. When he heard quick footsteps in the hall, he eased his glass down and took two quiet steps and slid far down into a large high-backed leather chair. He put his feet up on the window sill. He glanced around in the darkening room as Lota opened the door, but he couldn't see her plainly.

"Light and set, stranger," he said.

Lota turned on the lights. She didn't speak and her face was expressionless as she took off the little green hat and dropped it and her leather purse on the seat of a small chair.

"Have a drink," Buck said.

Lota still didn't say anything, but her eyes didn't leave Buck as she reached out and poured whiskey into the glass Buck had left. She didn't pour much water.

"Here," Buck said as she lifted the glass, "that stuff ain't soup."

Lota drank it quickly and shuddered as she put the glass back on the table. Then she faced square around and spaced her feet apart. She put her hands deliberately on her hips, leaned over, and spoke carefully.

"You dirty bastard."

Buck raised himself slowly in his chair and his eyes opened wide in surprise. He tried not to smile.

[241]

"Outside of that I'm all right, ain't I?" he said, and dropped back into the chair.

Lota walked over to the edge of the bed and sat down without answering. She sat still for a long minute, then she spoke slowly.

"Buck, that's the first time I ever said that word. In front of anybody but Grandpa, anyhow."

"Aw, that's—" Buck started to speak, but she broke in.

"I'm not apologizing, I'm just explaining. You hurt me this afternoon."

Buck turned his chair around quickly. He searched her face with his eyes.

"Oh, you didn't bruise me. You hurt me where it'll never be seen."

"Good Lord, you're serious." Buck got up slowly and took a step towards her. Lota lay backwards on the bed and closed her eyes.

"Here," Buck said, touching her knee clumsily, "don't start—"

Lota's eyes opened quickly and they glared out at him.

"I'm not crying. You could beat me and I wouldn't cry, but I can hurt just the same."

"Hell, sugar," Buck said, holding his hands out helplessly, "I was just jokin', throwin' those damn oranges."

Lota closed her eyes again and breathed deeply.

"You joke rough."

Buck sat down on the edge of the bed and twisted so that he could look down at her face.

"Look, Lota. I'm rough all right and will be till I die, but I honestly don't want to hurt you. You're— Well, that's all I can say. I wouldn't hurt you on purpose."

Lota raised herself on one elbow and looked him in the face.

"Buck," she said, slowly, "didn't you honestly think that it might embarrass me?"

"Well, I don't say—" Buck shrugged. "I don't know."

"I think you did," Lota said, quickly, then she turned up one corner of her mouth and lay back again. She put her hands over her eyes.

"Oh, I can see why," she said, bitterly. "A country girl going hog-wild with a big new automobile and a driver, playing Mrs. God because she married the richest man in town. I had time to think about it, all right." She turned over quickly and Buck couldn't see her face any more. Her voice came muffled now. "You don't have to tell me. I know now I shouldn't have done it, but, my God, you didn't have to do it that way."

"Aw, hell," Buck said, and touched her on the back of her thigh. "It wasn't that—" He stopped and shook his head. "Yes, it was," he went on deliberately. "It was pretty bad. I've never been one to worry about what folks think, but we can't act the big dog. I don't know why not, but I reckon it's because we maybe are the big dogs."

Lota didn't answer, she just shook her head on her arms.

"It was the size of the automobile," Buck said, slowly. "That, and it was too damned shiny."

"I never want to see it again," Lota said.

Buck nodded.

"I'll send it back tomorrow."

Lota turned over quickly and sat up with her eyes stormy.

"Take it back? Are you crazy?"

Buck laughed and patted her leg.

"I thought you didn't want to—"

Lota pushed his hand away.

"Hearn's got one just as big."

"Well, Hearn's a man," Buck said, patiently, "and besides, he's not my wife."

"You bought it for him."

"I know," Buck said, "I know that, but he's my brother and still just a kid."

"Well, I don't see why—"

Buck stopped her.

"Look, sugar," he said, slowly, "let's just forget the damned automobile. You think of something else you want in the meantime, and we'll get that."

He nodded his head twice and winked at her. Lota didn't answer. She just looked at him with her eyes still narrowed, and shook her head, slowly. Buck held up his hands.

"Anything else," he said, as if he were holding a piece of candy out to tease a small boy, "just name it."

"Hmmm," Lota said, and lay back across the bed with her hands under her head. "Anything?"

Buck smiled and sighed.

"Hell, yes," he said, quickly, and slapped her on the side of her bottom. He stood up quickly and rubbed his hands together. "Now, I'm hungry. Let's pull a few quail off Hearn's string and get 'em cooked over at the Blue Bird and you can be thinking while we eat."

He started over to the writing table with its whiskey bottle and glasses, when Lota's voice stopped him.

"Buck." He turned his head and reached for the bottle without looking at the table. She spoke softly. "I heard a man say once that you'd go clear to the bridge if you'd given your word."

Buck flushed slightly.

"That's right."

Lota swung one foot slowly and pursed her lips, looking up at the ceiling.

"Are you giving your word on this?"

"Certainly," Buck said, hastily, and turned towards the table again. He stopped still with his hand outstretched for the bottle and glanced back. "That is—"

Lota quickly propped herself on one elbow, and broke in.

"If it doesn't cost as much as a car?"

Buck nodded.

"Sure," he said, carelessly, and picked up the bottle. "You think it over and let me—"

"I already know." Lota's voice was slow and soft.

"Hmmm," Buck said, measuring a drink into the small glass, so carefully that he hardly seemed to have heard her.

"I want to go to college."

Buck dropped the glass.

"Godamighty!" He looked down at the glass for a moment, then slowly set the bottle back on the table.

"You what?"

"College," Lota said, sweetly. "I've always wanted to go to college, remember? Now, I want a year at Clifton Hall."

"At Clifton—? Where's that?"

"Over in Georgia." Lota sat up quickly, all excited. "Close enough for you to come over to see me now and then. And I'll brag to the girls when you're coming, and I'll sign my test papers Mrs. Joseph Bannon, and write checks when I need money."

"Oh, my God!" Buck swept Lota's purse and hat off the little chair and sat down heavily with his hands dangling between his knees. "I figured when the girls got home that I never would have to send another woman to college."

"You said 'anything.' "

"How long would you be—?" Buck's voice sounded stupid in his own ears.

"Just nine months. And you could come over, see?"

Buck stood up. "Ahhh!" he said, as if he were disgusted, then he walked slowly over and looked down at her. Lota smiled up at him, showing her teeth, white and strong, with her eyes half closed. She was swinging one foot and it bumped Buck's leg every time it swung out. He pushed his knee closer and pinned her leg against the side of the bed and watched her eyes widen in mock surprise.

"By God," he said, slowly, "if I was ten years younger, I'd say hell no, but—"

Lota laughed low in her throat.

"You're young enough."

Buck smiled slowly down at her and pushed harder against her leg.

"You know," he said, "tomorrow when I'm holdin' court, I'll feel as old as God, but right now, I believe I'm plenty young."

CHAPTER TWENTY-THREE

Buck was in the city hall waiting for court time when Amos Longshore came in, blowing his breath on his dry hands, and rubbing them in the whispery way that Buck could remember. Buck looked down and swallowed quickly against the fullness that always came in his throat when he saw Ivy's father.

When he looked up, Buck's lips curled. "Howdy, Mr. Longshore," he said, "how's the bankin' business?"

Longshore flushed.

"So bad," he said, dryly, "that we won't be able to carry any more of the city's overdrafts."

"Aw, go on an' carry 'em," Buck said, "we'll deduct it from your taxes."

"Hmph!" Longshore grunted, sidling up to the counter. "They'll run more'n my taxes."

Buck laughed at him. "We'll raise your taxes to meet 'em," he said, and turned shortly and walked back into his private office. He jerked his head to Tobe Parody, who was talking in a low tone with one of the clerks. Tobe got up and followed him.

Buck sat for a moment after Tobe had thrown a leg over the corner of his desk, playing his fingers like a horse race on top of the arm of his chair.

"That Longshore," he said, abruptly, "he's got the city's overdrafts an' he'll spread it all over town. Be hell explainin'."

Tobe spat on the floor. "City's been in the red long as I can remember," he said. "They oughtn't to blame it on you."

"They ain't supposed to think," Buck said.

Tobe grunted. "You're the mayor. I'm just the whuppin' boy around here."

"An' chief o' police," Buck said.

Tobe nodded and his lips twisted up as if he didn't like the taste in his mouth. He got off the desk and shambled to the window and stared down the street. He looked out for a full minute, then turned back to Buck. "Anybody can whup a nigger if the nigger's scared to fight back."

Buck didn't answer. He had his head on the chair back and the light from the window cut strong across his face. His full lower lip moved once, as if he were speaking inside himself, but he didn't move or say anything out loud for a moment. When he did move, it was fast. He sat up straight and slapped his hand down on the desk.

"Tobe," he said, not frowning now, "old Longshore's got me to thinkin'."

"Unh-unh," Tobe smiled sourly.

"Come here an' sit down," Buck said, reaching for a pad and pencil. He looked up as Tobe straddled the chair in front of him.

"How many gamblin' joints in town?"

Tobe shook his head. "God knows."

"Saloons? Them that ain't licensed?"

"No tellin'."

"Whorehouses?"

"Five," Tobe said, quickly. Buck tossed his pencil on the desk.

"I want a list o' those places. Names of the owners. When you get that, we'll get together an' reckon up what each of 'em can stand in taxes."

Tobe gulped.

"Tax a gamblin' joint?"

"Hell yes," Buck said, and his eyes got to snapping with excitement. "Here we are givin' them police protection, streets, schools, an' a brand-new fire truck, an' they ain't payin' a dime. Legal places are totin' the whole load."

"Taxin' the girls don't seem right," Tobe frowned. "More like pimpin'."

"Hell, it ain't us," Buck said, "it's the city."

Tobe raised his eyebrows and stared at Buck. Slowly, his face relaxed, and he began to laugh and slap his knees. "That's the ticket," he said. "I can just see little old Ed Reddick collectin' taxes from Josie's Hollow Horn girls. Fussin' at 'em when they want him to trade it out."

"Ed ain't goin' to collect them taxes. We need a big man, an' a strong one, to start off."

Tobe's smile faded and he groaned.

Buck stood up and slapped his hands together. "We'll open a new account," he said, "private. An' stick ever' dollar we collect in it. Then we'll pay it on the city's debit till we come out."

"Oh, God," Tobe said.

"Look, Tobe," Buck said, coming around and standing in front of him. "It's a good gamble. We can pay the city out and the high cost o' livin' will run some o' the weak sisters out o' business." He roughed Tobe on the shoulder with the heel of his hand. "Lord, man," he went on, "we're cleanin' up the town. We're reformers. We'll be gettin' purity votes, an' they'll come in handy next time."

"An' I'll lose ever' friend I got," Tobe said, bitterly. "What's old C. C. goin' to say? C. C. Parish, that worked for us?"

Buck was staring at the floor.

"C. C.?" he said, slowly. "Why, he ought to be good for a hundred or more a month. See him first."

"Aaah!" Tobe leaned over and spat again. "I'd quit, if I didn't know you'd have me framed and throwed in the strong house."

"Me?" Buck looked at him and laughed. "Why, Tobe, you're my friend. Best I got."

Tobe eased off the corner of the desk. "You'd do it, though, wouldn't you?" he said, smiling crookedly.

Buck's mouth sobered quickly and he looked up at Tobe with his head on one side, frowning, with his eyes questioning.

"You're serious," he said, and he shook his head slowly. "No. I think—" He stopped and just looked at Tobe a second. "Whatever you do is all right with me," he said, gently.

Tobe spread his big hand out in front of his face and looked at it carefully, then he pressed it hard against the top of Buck's desk. He turned around without saying anything and walked to the door with his big arms swinging awkwardly, but he looked back as his hand twisted the doorknob.

"Dammit," he said, softly. "You got a way that makes folks hate to turn you down. Makes 'em want to do more for you. A feller like that can do a lot o' harm—or good." He rattled the doorknob irritably. "You—anybody like that ought to be dosed out careful."

Buck smiled slowly.

"You dose me out," he said, "but not too careful."

Tobe said, "Hmph!" then he pulled his shoulders back and looked self-conscious and spoke slowly. "Court time. Come a'runnin'."

Buck looked at the clock and frowned.

"Ah!" he said, "I'd rather be a hound under a fish wagon than a judge, even a leetle old city recorder judge."

He came fast, though, to Tobe's side and caught him by the elbow and pushed him through the door first. They walked down the short hall.

"If I was to judge 'em all from what old Longshore's done," he said, once, "I'd send 'em all to the pen. But I reckon if I judge 'em from what I've done, I'll turn 'em all loose."

Tobe was laughing when they entered the small crowded recorder's court, but he frowned for the benefit of the prisoners who sat on a long bench along one wall. Buck didn't quit smiling. He winked at one of the defendants and nodded reassuringly at the mother of a young boy.

"Howdy, Miz Peterman," he said. Mrs. Peterman ducked her head like a watering bird and smiled quickly, as if she were ashamed, but still glad that the mayor had spoken to her and to nobody else. She fumbled with gloved fingers, twisted and thin as a boxwood branch, at a bun of hair behind her ear, and Buck turned his eyes away from the tight high veins that quivered in her neck above the collar of her weightless coat.

He went on to his small oak desk, then, and squirmed sideways into the narrow space between the desk and the wall. He had trouble getting into the matching swivel chair, because it was pushed for room. The city clerk squeezed his short fat body into the chair on Buck's right, wheezing and puffing out his cheeks, and slapping the docket book down on the desk as if it were an old familiar thing to him. The city attorney bustled into the chair on Buck's left, mopping his huge bald head with a crumpled wad of handkerchief, and letting his blunt fingers ripple nervously where hair had been. He reached out with his left leg and pulled a cuspidor closer and leaned down behind the desk to spit. Then he drew his face into judicial lines and waited.

Buck glanced from right to left at his helpers, then he looked over the small crowd in the courtroom, trying as he always did to sense the temper of the people before the cases were called. It wasn't like some court days. The sounds didn't come in a low pleasantly confusing murmur, neither rising nor falling, perhaps, Buck thought, because the crowd was smaller than usual. They came instead in quick sharp spurts, and the sound of a chair scraping on the pine floor died too quickly in the sudden high of a window being lowered. Buck listened for a moment, then turned his head slowly, hunting the reason, until his eyes came to Tobe Parody, standing with his arms crossed near the close end of the prisoners' bench, leaning casually against the wall. As his eyes swept the room, Buck saw Virgil, slouching in the back and fingering his guitar. He raised his eyebrows and moved his shoulders upwards, then cleared his throat and faced the crowd.

"Let's take Widow Peterman's case first," he said, so the crowd could hear, and glanced a question at the city clerk. The clerk shook his head.

"It ain't her," he whispered loudly. "Her boy, Lige, done it, but the Killibrew boys come first on the docket."

"Hmph!" Buck grunted, then he deliberately raised his voice a little. "Miz Peterman's got to get back to her housework. Them Killibrews don't do nothin' but whittle an' they can do that here."

The crowd murmured and two or three older men in front began to laugh and nod at each other and spit secretively on the floor beside their chairs. The clerk fussed with his lips puffing in and out, but not out loud. He just flipped a page in his docket book, and called, "Lige Peterman."

The boy slouched to the desk with his hands in the pockets of his blue jeans and his thin shoulders hunched. He looked down most of the way, but when he got close, he glanced up at Buck out of small dark eyes that were deep-set in a thin sallow face. His hair was lifeless and when he looked back down at the floor, it fell over his forehead. Buck breathed deeply, as if he were sighing, then cleared his throat.

"Look up at me, boy," he said, sharply. The boy looked up and pushed some hair out of his eyes with one hand. "What you done?" The boy didn't answer.

The clerk leaned over and whispered. Buck nodded.

"Stealin' firewood?" he said, out loud, then he frowned at the boy with his head on one side. The boy gulped. Buck looked over the boy's shoulder at Mrs. Peterman.

"Your boy steal that wood?" he said. Mrs. Peterman didn't look up from her hands, working nervously at a hole in the thumb of her glove.

"From Mr. Eddins here," she said, in a low voice, and she glanced towards the bulky red-faced man on her right, then quickly back at her lap. "The last cold night we had."

Buck stood up so he could see better.

"Were you cold?"

Mrs. Peterman nodded and her eyes flickered about in the small space in front of her, but didn't try to see to her right or left.

Buck sat back down.

"Eddins," he called, "come here a minute."

The bulky man came up, his face getting redder at every step. He leaned over close and his voice was hoarse.

"Lord, Buck, I didn't mean to get all this stirred up. I just got wore out with it."

Buck nodded and winked. He looked from Eddins to the boy, who still stared at the floor, and then he rubbed the end of his thumb in the thick hair at his temple. He pursed his lips and coughed, and cleared his throat.

"Don't reckon I blame a boy for taking a little wood," he said, slowly but clearly, "if he's cold." He stopped, then, and frowned at the boy. "But," he said, loudly, "you can't just let a fellow off for stealin'." He paused and cut his eyes at the boy. The boy seemed to shrink closer within himself and his shoulders hunched more. Buck smiled a little, then. "You're sentenced to two months' hard labor," he went on, smoothly, "cuttin' wood ever' afternoon after school over at Mr. Eddins' place."

He turned to Mr. Eddins. "They ain't got much," he said, "how 'bout payin' him ever' third strand?"

Eddins breathed deeply as if he were relieved. "Haul it to his house, too," he said, quickly. Then he leaned closer, and his voice was hoarse, whispering, "Much oblige, Buck. 'F you'd a'jailed that boy I'd a'been horsewhupped 'fore dark."

Buck laughed and turned to the clerk and jerked his thumb towards the docket. The clerk turned hurriedly to a new page.

"Jonus and Arbie Killibrew," he called out, then in a lower voice, "charged with tearing down fence and stealing cattle."

Buck glanced over to the prisoners' bench without moving his head. Nobody got off the bench. Buck looked a question at Tobe Parody and Tobe moved slowly. He reached casually inside his coat on the left side with his right hand, then straightened his shoulders and leaned over to see down the bench. His right hand came out from under the coat and his fingers idled with the loose ends of his black string tie.

"Jonus and Arbie Killibrew," he said, bluntly, "get up off that bench an' drag each other up to the judge."

They got up together and shambled loose-hipped along the bench, passing close to Tobe Parody. Tobe stood straight but relaxed against the wall, a full head taller than the Killibrews.

Buck turned his face to watch as they passed Tobe and saw their light-blue eyes, red in the corners and rimmed with lashes so near the color of their dead-white skin that he could hardly see them.

"Folks call you the Cat Eatin' Killibrews, I know," he said, "but I reckon I'll have to find out which is which. Who's Jonus?"

The taller Killibrew's wet lips worked in a loose sneer, but he didn't answer and the smaller one slid his eyes up past Buck and stared at the wall. The clerk pointed at the short one.

"That's Jonus," he said. Jonus Killibrew shifted a sloping narrow shoulder, trying to keep up the strap to his faded, stringy overalls. Arbie Killibrew shuffled his feet in the silence and Buck saw that his pockets hung low and flapped as if weighted. He tried to see into their eyes, but both of them kept looking over his head with their mouths turned up at one corner.

Buck suddenly leaned over to look at the docket, then he bent closer over his desk, resting his arms on it, and looked at them from their broken-toed shoes to the tops of their heads.

"Whose cows did you all steal?" he asked, carelessly.

"B. Stringer's," Arbie said. "Nobody's," Jonus broke in quickly, then they stood as before, not looking at each other or at anything but the wall over Buck's head.

Buck sat back slowly.

"Stringer here?" he called without taking his eyes off the Killibrews.

A tall, very thin man half rose from a seat in front and nodded.

"They get 'em?" Buck asked.

Stringer ducked his head quickly, still bent over as if he wanted to sit back down, then he held up four fingers. He didn't say anything, but sat right down when Buck nodded.

Buck jerked his head towards the city attorney, and looked back at the Killibrews. "What's the limit?"

"A year, $100 fine, and costs," the lawyer said, patting the arm of his chair. "And costs," he repeated, clearing his throat.

Buck laid his hands out flat on the desk top and raced his fingers for a moment, looking at the Killibrews with his lips pulling down, before he spoke.

"You fellers 'bout to wear me out," he said, suddenly. "Been here four times this year." He shifted in his seat and rubbed his nose. "A year on the roads," he went on, "an' $100 fine each." He turned his head so the clerk would know he was speaking to him. "Costs'll be high enough to pay Stringer for them beeves." He pointed with his thumb towards the small door leading to the rear where the jail was located.

"Tobe," he said.

Jonus Killibrew shook his head suddenly, like he was throwing water off, and pinkish hair fell down over his forehead. He squinted his eyes at Buck and his lips fluttered with his breath.

"I'll see yore guts first," he said, in a trembling whine, and took a short step towards the desk, sidling with one hand reaching deep into his low-hanging pocket.

Buck stood up quickly. He felt out with his right foot, then his left, trying to push the clerk or the attorney out of his way, but he couldn't move them, and he felt the wall pressing against his shoulder blades. He didn't take his eyes off Jonus, who flipped the thin worn blade out of a shaggy-handled deerfoot knife. Far back in his mind he heard the short yelping scream of a woman, and the rushing scrabble of many feet as the crowd turned over chairs pushing backwards towards the walls. He watched Jonus and in his eyes the movements were slow and smooth as Jonus slid his thumb out along the flat of the blade to brace it against closing on his hand. But his mind saw speed as Jonus' arm flicked across the desk top in a high slash from right to left. Buck jerked his head and shoulders away from the arc of the blade, then he lunged across the desk top, pushing off from the wall, and his flailing right arm struck Jonus on the side of the head. Jonus' light body fell backwards with his feet scrambling frantically for purchase on the floor. Buck fell over onto the top of his desk from the force of his swing, but pulled up quickly in time to see Arbie Killibrew coming forward.

Arbie came on tiptoe in a small dancing kind of crouch, making a singsong noise through his nose. His knife was held low against his side for a thrust. Buck felt out again for room to move on either side, but the clerk and the attorney were frozen in their chairs, hands gripping the desk, half rising and half sitting.

Buck saw Tobe over Arbie's head. He watched Tobe's big hand come out from under his coat with a gun gripped in his fist, then he saw Tobe suddenly shove the gun back into the holster and he knew that Tobe couldn't shoot because of him. He looked back at Arbie. Arbie was coming closer. Buck suddenly put one foot on the desk and pushed up on top of it. Arbie was too close, his lips hanging loosely, and Buck jumped, throwing both feet into Arbie's chest. Arbie was flung straight backwards, but he turned like a cat to land on all fours. Buck struck the floor flat on his back. Then he turned over slowly and saw Arbie scrambling from the floor, but he couldn't move or breathe. He saw Tobe again, coming in three long strides from the side of the room. Tobe kicked Jonus Killibrew in the face as he passed. Jonus fell backwards from a sitting position, and Tobe grabbed Arbie by the shoulder from behind. He swung Arbie around, with his left hand, his right drawn back. Arbie jerked as he turned, ducking into a low crouch and his right hand stabbed forward, towards Tobe's stomach. Tobe bent over slightly, quickly, as Arbie's knife came away, and his left hand grabbed at his stomach. He pushed Arbie off with his right hand, then he backed away, reaching under his coat, still holding his stomach with his left hand. He backed slowly and Arbie followed close. Blood welled from between Tobe's fingers. His right hand came out from under his coat with a heavy short-barreled gun, and he braced it against his hip. He was turning to bring Arbie into line, when Buck dimly saw Jonus get up off the floor.

Buck fought the weakness in his legs, trying to get up, and he tried to yell to Tobe, but he couldn't draw breath into his lungs. He was on all fours, gasping, and white in the face, when Jonus took a short step towards Tobe's back.

Jonus reached over Tobe's shoulder with his knife blade choked by his thumb and hooked it across Tobe's throat. He jerked it fast, and blood spurted from a long curving slash. Tobe fell backwards, still holding his gun against his hipbone.

Buck shook his head again hard. He slowly pushed himself onto his knees, and was struggling to get to his feet as the Killibrews started towards him, one on each side, with their faces working. He stood up, finally, weaving and bent over and started towards them. He saw Tobe between and behind the Killibrews.

Tobe rose slowly on his left elbow and blood spurted faster, pouring down his chest. He raised his gun slowly, not bracing it this time, and he shot Jonus between the shoulder blades. Carefully, then, as the heavy slug knocked Jonus face forwards at Buck's feet, Tobe sighted at Arbie. Arbie turned quickly as Jonus fell, and Tobe shot him high in the chest. Arbie twisted, falling into a small knot of a body with his knees curling up towards his chest. Tobe held himself up for a moment longer. He shot twice more into the shapeless bundle of Arbie, then, straining to hold his sights in line, he emptied his gun into Jonus' body. Slowly, as if he hated to let go of something, Tobe fell backwards. The hammer of his gun clicked three more times on empty chambers.

Buck stumbled forward, holding his arm across his chest low down, and he fell on his hands and knees by Tobe. He caught him by the shoulders and tried to pull him upright, but his hands slipped in the blood and Tobe slid back down. Buck saw the gaping slash in Tobe's throat and automatically pushed the heel of his palm into the cut. He held his hand hard against it, pressing down against the collarbone, and fought for his breath.

Then he heard the crowd again, high-pitched voices, and feet shuffling, then stopping, and shuffling again slowly towards him. He looked up and focused his eyes, shaking his head, and suddenly he could breathe again. And talk.

"Get a doctor," he croaked, trying to yell. "Goddammit, do you think a man can bleed forever?"

His head dropped back down and he knelt there, waiting, with his eyes blurring on Tobe's white face, and his hand sliding in the cut in Tobe's throat, trying to hold back the gush of blood. He tried to breathe slowly, evenly, watching for movement in Tobe's face. Gradually, his eyes cleared, and he saw the lips move, mouthing, but not making any sound, then he saw a tiny crack of white and Tobe's eyes were opening into slits. Buck bent lower, turning his head sideways to listen, watching out of the corners of his eyes for a movement of the lips.

They moved and he couldn't hear. He came closer and didn't try to listen, he watched, and he saw Tobe's eyes slowly open wider. Then the lips again. They struggled to shape a word.

"Money," they formed, and then again, "money."

Buck nodded. "Money," he said, out loud.

The lips moved again, working slowly.

"Ever' month," they said. "Send—"

Buck bent closer, quickly, and put his mouth close to Tobe's ear.

"I know," he said. "I know. I'll send it ever' month, same place."

The lips closed then, loosely, and the breath that came through them fought out in quick gasps. Buck saw Tobe's eyes beginning to close.

"Ever' month till you're well again," he said, softly.

Buck thought it was quiet until he spoke.

"I reckon I died a little, too," he said, and then the quick little grass birds stopped bickering in the vacant lots. Buck stood very still, missing the sounds, and waiting with his ear cocked, while his eyes ran the darker slant of shadow cast by a telephone pole, so new that the sour smell of fresh-cut timber still hung in the air.

Then, suddenly, a rain crow begged up into the night and the birds started again, clicking their pointed wings against the dead stalks of high weeds. Abruptly, Buck began to walk, trying to hurry, but hating to reach home where there were people and loud voices, or worse, maybe voices that knew how he felt and hushed when he came near. He began to think, again.

"Got to be a reason," he thought, "for Tobe to die—not just to die like a man would die in bed—but to die like Tobe, with his throat cut trying to save me.

"Couldn't be just to get rid of Tobe. Or the Killibrew boys. It'd be easier some other way—better all the way round to let them die in their beds—unless there's a reason outside of them just dying.

"So that leaves me. The whole thing hinged on me. They came

[256]

for me. Tobe came to help me. Then they killed Tobe and he killed them. It started with me and it ended with me.

"Maybe it was just to make me die an inch or two. But that'd be mighty wasteful. It would be better business to just let me die all over instead of killing three men to whittle me down a little bit."

Buck stopped walking without meaning to, hardly knowing that he leaned his shoulder against the bole of a sycamore, and stood there a moment, pressing hard against the big silvery scales of bark. His mind picked at the thought.

"Maybe it wouldn't be wasted, or wasn't supposed to be, anyhow. Maybe it was done to make me do better, or different. But, if it was, what have I done wrong? Am I supposed to change? Now, how in the world can I just tell myself to change? I'm like I was made and it don't seem right for me to set about remaking a man, even if it is me. And how would I start? Godamighty, it's just like I furnished a farmer—gave him land to work, seed to plant, and mules and tools. He'd do the best he could, I reckon. Looks like I got furnished with whatever I am, and it's up to me to do the best I can with what I've got. I don't go behind and look up a farmer tryin' to furnish him with some more. After I've set him up, the rest is up to him."

Slowly, Buck started walking again, unconsciously holding his hands out far from his sides, still feeling somehow the stickiness that he had washed off after holding Tobe. He didn't say anything out loud, but he mumbled as he walked, looking down at the ground.

He was facing his home, looking into the lighted hall from the front yard, when his mind fastened solidly on a new thought.

"If God had figured for a man to know what God was doing, He'd have made it that way. I reckon He's able to do it, but He don't. He just sticks them here, looks like, and tells them to work it out the best they can. So that's what I'll do. I'll go along, using what tools He gave me the best I know how, and if I manage better'n some, or worse'n some, it'll be my own crop. Hell, I ain't a man to change."

He went up the steps then, slowly, still holding his hands out by his sides, but feeling in his legs as if he wanted to push on his knees to help. Out loud he said, "I talk like a damned circuit rider."

Jeanie Bannon was at the door when he opened it. She was just standing there waiting, fumbling with the curtains that hung over the glass panels on either side of the doorway.

Buck stopped before he closed the door behind him and tried to look at her eyes. There was too much pity in them. He shook his head and looked down at her hands on the curtain, and didn't say anything.

She cleared her throat and looked away, too.

"I got all the young'uns to bed early," she said, "so they wouldn't—"

Buck shook his head.

"No use," he said, "it'll come sooner or later. Questions and no answers."

She looked back at him, then, biting her lip, and started to say something. She stopped and sighed, then her jaw set slightly.

"It wasn't your fault," she said, defensively. "An' besides, Tobe wanted to do it. He'd rather have died that way."

Buck's head came slowly up and he stared at his mother's eyes for a second. He seemed to be trying to find something in them. Then, as if he were puzzled, his head dropped back down, shaking from side to side. There was a bitter look about his mouth as he spoke.

"Maybe," he said, "but it puts too big a burden on the man that's left alive."

INTERLUDE

THE TWO *mules ahead of them looked as if they were walking up a long slim blade of moon, the light was so nearly the color of the dust on the Clayhatchie road. Jake and Bass had ridden in almost total silence until the little gleams that meant Aven were hidden behind them by a rim of the shallow dimple in the land where the town was built. Dimly, far ahead of them a small light blinked once, then was lost to view again behind the bole of a large tree.*

"That's the house up ahead," Jake said in a low voice.

"I wish—" Bass started whispering fiercely, then broke off and spoke again in a louder tone. "I wish to the Lord, Buck was the kind of a man you could either hate all the time or like all the time."

"I'll shore go with you on that," Jake said, fervently. "You an' me both know who burnt that preacher out, an' I could a'stomped him a dozen times for that, then here he goes an'—"

"Damn that preacher," Bass interrupted. "I'd ruther need a preacher than have that'n."

Jake shook his head.

"Ought not to burn anybody out," he said, firmly, then his face twisted up, puzzled. "How he can do that, then turn around an' send this stuff back, durned if I can figure."

"I cain't understand 'im." Bass shook his head. "That junk in the wagon bed ain't worth no more'n the cost o' sendin' it back."

Jake laid the reins over in Bass's lap and started fumbling in his pocket. "All I know is, he sent me down to foreclose this afternoon." He scrubbed his palm over the ragged edge of a plug of tobacco. "Then, when I come back with the stuff, I just chanced to mention how the old man had died a couple days ago." He bit off a small chew and rolled it with his tongue until it was comfortable, then held the plug out to Bass. "He cussed me for a widow robber," he went on, somehow proudly, "an' made me load it again an' start right back."

Bass bit off the plug of tobacco.

"Well, sir," he said, "you cain't never tell about Buck. I didn't figure he'd ever get over Tobe Parody gettin' killed. Looked like for a long time it'd softened him, an' I guess maybe it has in the long run."

"Hell, he's always been soft 'bout women an' kids, but God help anybody like us."

Bass frowned and shook his head.

"I don't know," he said, thoughtfully, "wasn't long after them Killibrews got Tobe that Buck drifted up to the yards an' got to talkin' to me. He knowed close to the day when I'd retire from the road an' he come right out an' offered to set me up in some little café or somethin'." He wiped his mouth. "Durndest thing."

Jake turned anxious eyes towards his friend.

"Did he say anything about you signin' a mortgage?"

"Why shore." Bass looked scornful. "Nothin' but right."

Jake scowled and patted his empty watch pocket meaningfully.

"I believe in schoolin'," he said, bitterly, "but damned if I don't wish I'd never learnt to sign my name."

CHAPTER TWENTY-FOUR

FOR A FEW MINUTES, all sounds near by were the simplest kinds of sounds—early morning sounds—a sighing scrape as dirt slid off the spade, then a tearing noise as the sharp-worn lip of the spade bit again down through matted grass roots. After a while, though, Buck's breath began to hassle through his teeth and he straightened up over the shallow hole. He tossed his spade so that it stuck up in the large pile of dirt. He put both hands on the small of his back and limbered backwards and forwards, groaning.

"That's a poor make-out," he said, "but my hands never did fit a scoop too close, not at daylight anyhow."

"Your idea," Jeanie Bannon grunted. She hitched her cut-down chair closer and leaned over to look into the hole. She curled her lips. "It's just as well a man don't plan no more surprise diggings when he's got a girl nineteen tangled up in his eyes—especially if he's fifty."

"Forty-eight."

"Forty-nine."

His mother didn't even look up. She eased out of her chair and knelt down on the dew-wet grass, careful to tuck her workaday skirts under her knees. "Now, hand me that bush and we'll see if that thumb of mine is still working."

She bent far over, scraping with her fingers hooked out like rake teeth to loosen dirt down into the hole, and then she set the small bush. She was careful not to shake off any of the dirt that clung to its roots and her hands were gentle clear out to the limp and sapless white feeders that seemed to grow sparse hair that was coarse and brown, stronger than the root that fed it.

Buck sat down in the chair and crumbled clods of dirt while his breath leveled off steady but still deep and long. He tossed handfuls of leaf mold from an old rusty washtub, now and then, but he was sparing with it, as long as he could find plain dirt that he could rub in his hands and scatter loosely. He didn't speak until he had calmed his wind.

"Wonder how come it's getting hard to find these things. I can remember when everybody that was anybody had a banana shrub or a sweet shrub one. Now you've got to comb the county to buy three banana shrubs."

His mother raised her head and pushed the damp clutch of hair off her forehead with her wrist, not to get dirt on her forehead.

"Sweet shrubs is sickening. Cape jessamines, too." She patted the loose dirt down a little around the trunk of the shrub. "A colored boy about twelve got burnt up once near the old home place and there was a Cape jessamine close by." She hunched her shoulders quickly as if she shuddered. "I don't reckon anything sweetens up a place like a banana shrub, though."

Buck was silent a moment, staring into the hole his mother was slowly filling in around the trunk. He twisted his head uncomfortably. "I wish I knew how they'd like the houses."

His mother raised her head again. "They'll like them." She watched him steadily for a moment. "You've been mighty good about the houses. And thinking of the banana shrubs."

Buck didn't answer. He looked critically at the small white house set neatly in the angle of the corner lot on which they had planted the shrub, then his eyes wandered back and forth to the other two corners where houses exactly like the nearest centered corner lots that were each one-fourth of the block. He could see Jeanie Bannon's home—the first house he'd ever built—still reared two stories above the fourth corner and in his mind's eye he could see the barn and the meat house and the chicken runs and the cow lot all sprawling back to the strict edge of the parcel of land that went with the house behind her. His eyes squinted along the precise white shine of smooth sidewalk that bordered the block. He frowned at the roots of the sycamores growing between sidewalk and curb, where already big roots had pried up slabs at the foot of each tree. He followed with satisfaction, though, the same type of slabs that formed wide walkways leading up to the four green steps of each house. His upper lip curled a little as he thought about those walkways, and he hoped nobody would notice that they were made out of the same stuff and laid just exactly like those the city had used for sidewalk. He leaned over suddenly and spat for luck at the trunk of the small shrub as his mother pushed back, sighing.

"Worries me," he said, "them not having but two bedrooms."

"They'll do good to keep those clean," Jeanie Bannon said, rubbing her hands together briskly to clear them of loose dirt.

Buck pushed up with his hands on his knees. He walked over to a small hydrant that showed about a foot above ground under the edge of the house. He filled a large bucket and came back, and poured it around the trunk of the banana shrub. He didn't speak until he had laid the bucket down and glanced sideways up at the sun's rays angling through the trees across the street.

"Well, we'll know soon. About time Lota was bringing them over."

Jeanie Bannon reached up and caught him by the forearm and pulled down, raising herself from the ground. "Son, if just one of them acts like she don't like her gift house, we'll cut her throat with a salty meat knife." She straightened up, laughing a little, brushing the clinging grains of sand and grass off her long skirt. "Let's start through the back and maybe we'll meet them." She held on to his arm as they walked across the yard towards the fringe of chinaberry trees that hid from view the small outbuildings—tool sheds, farrowing pens for the few hogs she insisted on raising for winter meat, pump house—all seeming to burrow closer each year to the big home that Buck had built.

She stopped him before they had gotten halfway to her yard and pointed out a good-sized clump of mullen growing wild. "That shows you how much I notice. I've been looking for some mullen leaves to make me some tea."

Buck twisted his lips wryly. "Give me one good smooth-mouthed mule, I'd plow under every stalk of mullen in the county." He was bending over as he talked, fumbling close to the ground for the young and tender leaves that grew, light green and furry, against the larger and darker main stems. "What's ailing you, anyhow?" he said, as he straightened up. "Take a powerful hurt to make me drink that stuff."

Jeanie Bannon looked away quickly towards the tree tops, then back down at the mullen leaves in her hand, before she glanced up at Buck.

"Kinda gaspy in the stomach lately—like indigestion but worse," she said, then shrugged, "don't make much difference. I don't like what I eat any more."

Buck was looking at her with an anxious question in his eyes

[263]

when she suddenly turned her head as if to catch a faraway sound. She patted his arm.

"I hear them coming, let's go back."

He caught her under the elbow and hurried her around the new house again and they each sat on one of the small stone blocks that rose in two sections on either side of the steps.

"We ought to hide and listen," Buck said.

"Lord, son, don't ever tiptoe in on kinfolks." She pushed straggling hair out of her eyes with her wrist. "You might hear 'em cussing you and have to slip back out."

"I reckon," Buck said, "but I—"

"No," she broke in, "when you're my age you'll know it's lot of times worse for folks to criticize you to your face than behind your back."

Buck snorted. "Old folks' talk." He slid off the block and walked quickly clear of the corner of the house and stood there until Lota and the three girls started into the back yard.

"Godamighty," he said, watching them. "They're ladies."

His mother laughed out loud.

"What did you expect, field hands? You ought to have seen them get off that train last night."

"Unh-unh!" Buck shook his head. "This is the way I wanted to see them, walking across the yard with Lota, all fresh and maybe a little sleepy from getting up early, not tired and gritty from riding a train two days." He whistled through his teeth. "Lota stands near a head over Christina and Millie and they're half a head taller'n Vesta." He watched them picking their way across the newly laid out yards, mindful of the weeds that reached out for their stockings, and he heard them laughing, Lota's deep-voiced laughter trailing excitement. He wondered for a second what they were laughing at, then the wondering grew into a twinge of jealousy. Not jealousy for either one of them, but jealousy for twenty, or nineteen, or even thirty-five again. He glanced over at his mother and his lips twisted bitterly. He saw her watching his expression with a sour little perk to her lips, so he blanked his face and turned back towards the girls.

Gradually, as he watched, the jealousy left him and in its place came a slow calm surge of pride that they were his womenfolks —that Christina's long, tight-waisted blue skirt with the white peekaboo blouse could be the quality it was, and that Millie's middy blouse and skirt could replace the heavy, built-for-service clumsiness she had worn before. He was proud, too, of the high-flung chins and the two great piles of bright yellow hair that bobbed excitedly on either side of Lota's dark head. His forehead wrinkled and tightened and he didn't know exactly what he felt when he looked at Vesta. She was so small, so thin and flat-chested, with features that seemed to shrink because she was empty inside, not from sickness. Her hair was nothing to notice, neither black nor brown nor yellow, neither heavy nor thin. She was the oldest, he knew, yet something stirred inside, telling him that she was the one who was playing at grownup and feeling that the fine clothes she wore were insecure, soon to be folded carefully back into the box in the attic and replaced with stiff and scratchy garments that would hold up. Christina and Millie walked with free-swinging arms, like Lota, with their shoulders high and their small breasts pushed out as if they were proud to have them. Their high-heeled shoes flickered over the ground as if they liked it but didn't mind leaving it behind them. Vesta stepped high enough, but only as if she didn't want to dirty her shoes before they went back into the box.

Christina was first to see Buck standing at the corner of the house. She yelled, "Hey, Buck, look at me," and pulled loose from Lota. She raised her skirt nearly to her knees and began to waltz towards him over the grass, with her nose up in the air. She tripped over high grass and stumbled forward a couple of steps before she could catch her balance. "Damn those heels," she said in a loud voice, and, holding her skirt up in one hand, she ran until she could fling herself against Buck and hold so tight around his neck that her feet left the ground. "Hmm-hmmph!" she said against his shoulder, "it feels good to be home and hug somebody." Then she pulled away and looked at him with her wide mouth twisting in mock distaste. "Even if it is just your brother."

Buck laughed and pushed her away as Millie walked up, consciously swinging her hips and pointing her toes out to give better balance. She was looking down her nose at him. "You may kiss me," she said, haughtily, then she burst into delighted laughter and laid her cool hands on both sides of his head and kissed him twice on the mouth. He started to put his arms around her, but she pushed him away. "That's enough, that's enough." She followed Christina over towards her mother, looking back over her shoulder. "For just one house, anyhow," she said.

Vesta waited quietly beside Buck until he looked down at her. She just said, "Hello, Buck," and he winked at her and touched her arm. She waited for a second, hesitant, then held up her face with her mouth pinched tight. Buck touched her cheek with his lips then quickly turned to Lota.

"How 'bout you?"

Lota yawned widely, deliberately, and shook her head.

"I didn't get a house," she said, and winked at him. Vesta didn't see her wink, and turned quickly with her mouth setting so tightly that little lines showed white branching out and down from her nostrils to her lips.

"We didn't kiss him just for that," she said, tartly.

Lota's eyes opened wide and her lips parted twice before she spoke. She looked amazed.

"Didn't you?"

"*I* don't kiss for houses," Vesta said, slowly, and deliberately she added, "or marry for money."

Lota's face turned white and her eyes struck Buck's, desperate for him to know what was in them, then she turned back to Vesta. She looked slowly from Vesta's too-tiny feet, past her narrow hips, pausing at her flat bosom for a breath, then scornfully at her pinched lips.

"Or anything else," she said.

"Both of you shut up," Buck said, low and rough, "and smile, dammit, or I'll beat hell out of both of you. Vesta, if you ever speak to Lota like that again, I'll—well, by God, I just won't stop her."

Vesta switched her shoulders and walked, with her face set, right between Buck and Lota over towards her mother and the other girls.

Buck looked down into Lota's eyes for a moment and felt them begging. He smiled slowly with just one side of his mouth, then put an arm over her shoulders and pulled her closer. He said, "Shh," mostly with his lips and nodded slightly, reassuring her, then they walked over to the others.

[266]

"Well," he said, loudly, and cleared his throat, "what do you young'uns think about the houses?"

"Well, I can't beat the price," Christina said, tapping her foot and looking judicial.

Millie stood beside her mother and smiled and nodded to Buck, then she leaned down and whispered something in Jeanie Bannon's ear. Jeanie laughed and patted Millie on the thigh.

"She says she can fill it up in two years."

Millie blushed but looked defiantly at Buck. He frowned and started to shake his head, but she shook hers first.

"I'm eighteen," she said, and looked hard at Lota. Lota laughed deep in her throat and glanced up at Buck. " 'Nuff said." He shrugged and turned towards Vesta.

Vesta was looking from one house to the other with slightly narrowed, shrewd eyes. She didn't pay any attention to the others for a few seconds, then her eyes suddenly opened wide, satisfied. "I choose—" She broke off as she turned around, then her face turned red and she raised her hands palms upwards in a slight gesture. "They're mighty nice," she said, not looking at her mother.

Jeanie Bannon's voice was quiet and firm as she spoke and her eyes roved, black and shiny, from one to the other. "The deeds have already been made out. The corner back of me goes to you, Vesta. Millie gets the corner on my right and Christina gets the other one." She hesitated a moment. "Any swapping that's going to be done, you all can do among yourselves." She rose to her feet, pushing up with her hands flat on the stone block. She looked at Vesta's small satisfied mouth, then at Christina and Millie, who were looking back and forth at each other, then at their houses.

"I won't trade," Millie said, suddenly. "Me neither," Christina added quickly.

Jeanie Bannon looked at Vesta with a wry curve growing slowly along her lips.

"Well, Vesta," she said, "I hope to the Lord you haven't got too high-toned for hogs, because the only thing between me and you now is the pig pen and I don't figure to get rid of my hogs."

Vesta's lips tightened. "That was the one I wanted, Mother," she said, in a small, faintly injured tone, "to be near you."

Buck cleared his throat. They all turned to look at him.

"Well," he said, awkwardly, "I hope it works out—being so close and all." He cleared his throat. "Just one thing. Some folks build fences to keep things in and some build 'em to keep others out. You girls fence *in*, don't fence *out*."

Aven's nights were late in the dying days of June. Yet they seemed to rush, as this one did. Dusk padded over the red-clay hills that folded the Choctawhatchee River eighteen miles to the west, then it pawed through Big Tired Swamp out onto the flatlands in a hurried puny warning of night. Suddenly, darkness swooped into the streets, the churches and the saloons, into the homes and the small hidden gambling houses, and finally into the corner of the Harrison House sample room where Buck kept two or three chairs, an old scarred table, a small icebox, and called it his office.

Buck never consciously welcomed the night, yet he was always aware of the quick yeasting in his chest that was like a celebration in advance for what the night would bring. He felt it now and leaned far back in the round-backed wooden chair to free his watch from his pocket without breaking off the small gold Masonic emblem that was the facing for his black silk fob. He held the watch aslant towards the two casement windows that opened onto the railroad tracks out back of the hotel, then he yawned and shook his head and shoulders as a wet dog shakes off water.

"Wish that damned doctor would come on," he thought. "Send word he'll be here and then don't come. What in hell? Doctors make me uncomfortable, anyhow. Preachers, too. Feels like they know something I don't, something secret that I can't get my hands on, and when they talk it's with just part of their minds on it. Wonder what he wants. Going to throw the book at me, I reckon. Quit drinking. No more late hours, gambling. Cut down on my homework. Like hell I'll do that. Hate to argue with a man about drinking and things, though. Tobe was the only man ever lived I could take it from, and he's gone. Rather wait till Doc leaves for a drink, but God, the six-forty blowed long ago and my stomach itches on the inside. I don't reckon it's that. Could be he wants to buy some land or needs a house right quick. Got to be something like that. I never called him and he's got no right arguing me till I start paying him for it. Good friends as we are, anyhow, he knows damned well I ain't going to sit here strong as homemade sin and get doctored. Not and him too weak to pull a sick whore out of bed."

Buck let his feet drop from the counter in front of him and reached for the telephone on the small scarred table. He was muttering to himself and jiggling the hook when he heard the small door open quietly at the end of the sample room nearest the lobby. He hung the receiver back on the hook and stood up to turn on the overhead light. He blinked and shaded his eyes with his hand.

"That you, Ad?"

"Hello, Buck." The voice that answered was hardly large enough for even Adam Tolleson, M.D., who was already looking up towards Buck before he got near, and whose skinny shoulders sagged with the weight of the small black bag which bumped against his leg with each step. Buck watched him down the aisle between the counters. He winced at the sight of Tolleson's thin and pinched grey face and he wondered again at how patiently the grey eyes could look out at the world.

"Sit down." Buck touched the back of a small chair as if he were shoving it nearer Dr. Tolleson.

"Whew." Tolleson breathed deeply, easing into the chair. "I wish Hosea Pryde would get sent to the Federal pen. Lovely just had her fifth in five years and Hosea's already licking his lips."

"Sending Hosea off won't stop Lovely," Buck grunted.

Tolleson snorted like he wanted to laugh and ran his stubby fingers through spiky close-cut hair. He was silent for a moment, not looking at Buck, then abruptly, he said, "Got a drink?"

"Lord, yes," Buck said, quickly, and reached his hand under the dirty grey cloth covering that hung from the counter to the floor. "I'm right ready, myself." He set the whiskey bottle on the counter, then without getting out of his chair, he stretched and took a bottle of water out of the icebox. He poured drinks without speaking, then raised his glass. "Surprised but pleased."

"I like a drink," Tolleson said, wryly. "I just don't have the time."

"You're killing yourself."

Tolleson shook his head.

"*You're* killing yourself. I'm donating myself."

Buck kept his eyes on Tolleson's grave face for a long time, then he shifted his gaze to the shadows that draped the long room.

"*My* life's being thrown away, hunh?" he said, slowly.

"Not entirely," Tolleson answered quickly, and started to go on, then he hesitated and shook his head. "No, friends have no business advising each other." He looked up brightly. "One more, then I'll get down to the reason for my call."

Buck started pouring two more drinks, keeping his eyes carefully away from Tolleson's face.

"Keep on talking," he said. "It won't bother me."

Tolleson slid down lower in his chair and leaned his head back, clasping both hands behind it. He mumbled under his breath for a moment, then looked at Buck with an apologetic smile.

"Poems say it best," he said, then looked back at the ceiling.

> "All, all of a piece throughout;
> Thy chase had a beast in view;
> Thy wars brought nothing about;
> Thy lovers were all untrue."

He stopped short and waited, not looking at Buck. Buck said, "That all?" and Tolleson went on.

> " 'Tis well an old age is out;
> And time to begin a new."

Buck's lips tightened as Tolleson finished. He held out one glass. "I've heard that same thing for twenty years, sometimes in the Unknown Tongue, but damned if this ain't the first time anybody rhymed it."

Tolleson leaned forward to touch Buck's knee.

"Forget it. I shouldn't bring up those things in the little time we have together. Besides, no man ever fitted better his time or his place, or did as well with as little as you've done for yourself and your people and your town. All I say is that the rough days are going. It's time to change with the tide."

"Well," Buck said slowly, "there's one good thing. Won't nobody but me get hurt."

"Oh, no, you're wrong. What you do today will affect a child born tomorrow, just as what you did a year ago affects Lovely Pryde's new boy."

"Now, by God," Buck said, quickly, "don't go laying that to me."

Tolleson leaned back in his chair and laughed out loud, then he spoke softly, still looking up at the ceiling.

"Well, Buck, I didn't come down here to talk about you."

"Shoot," Buck said.

"It's about your mother." Tolleson's tone was blunt. "Have you noticed her lately? I mean the way she looks."

"No. She said she didn't care about eating any more," Buck said thoughtfully, "but I don't reckon I've looked close."

"You go up and look tonight, Buck. Your mother won't live much longer."

Buck's eyes half closed but his face didn't change. In the short dead silence, though, he wondered if he were really hearing the faraway baying of a train whistle, or if his mind had taken him back to the early morning when his father had died. Then, for a second, his thoughts seemed to die out in front of a flaring picture of the wheels and drivers churning furiously under a smoky engine. He shook the picture out of his head.

"How do you know?" he said, slowly.

"Cancer," Tolleson said.

Buck looked down at the floor.

"How long can she live?"

"Maybe a year."

"Isn't there—?"

"Not a thing," Tolleson frowned. "I can make her fairly comfortable now, but not for long."

"How did she take it?"

"She doesn't know it." Tolleson looked up at Buck with a quizzical pity in his eyes. "Some patients react badly when they know —give up. Some fight harder and do better. You and your folks must be the judge of that."

Buck nodded without speaking and without looking up.

"I'll be going now," Tolleson said, gently. "Call me if I can help."

Buck didn't move until Tolleson had reached the door into the lobby, then he raised his head.

"Hell of a note. First doctor she ever called for herself and he gives her a one-way ticket."

He couldn't see Tolleson in the dark near the door, but he could hear him plainly.

"She's just got a one-way fare, Buck, but she's routed right."

CHAPTER TWENTY-FIVE

THE LOBBY was painfully bright after the dimness of the sample room and Buck squinted going through. He shook his head at the limber-hipped Negro boy who strutted beside him long enough to ask if he wanted the car.

"I need the walk," he said, dully, and wondered why he thought walking would help. He took his hat off as he stepped out onto the sidewalk and walked with it swinging in his hand down a street that suppertime had stripped except for a few old-for-their-age youngsters who leaned their shoulder blades against the yellow front of Salvador's Snooker and Billiard Parlor. "God," he was thinking, "all going. First Tobe, now Mother, and first thing I know, there won't be nobody left but me." He walked on for a while with his head down, barely seeing the alternate patterns of shadow between the triangles of light cast by new metal street lamps, and he wondered again why the simple routine of step after step should smooth his heavy troublings.

His body felt dead and his mind sluggish, until he came slowly abreast of the billiard parlor, then his mind and his eyes focused quickly on a new subject. The door was suddenly flung open and a small, squarely built boy of about fourteen ran out with his ragged bowl-cut hair streaming behind. Buck stepped aside and caught the boy across the stomach with one arm, then he straightened up and held him by both shoulders.

"Whoa!" he said, roughly, and grabbed a handful of the boy's hair and jerked his head up so the dark-blue eyes could only glare up into his. The face was filthy. "What the hell's the matter with you, Smut?"

Before the boy could answer, the door opened again, the older hangers-on ducked inside, and a small very dark man came outside. His hands were folded under a long dirty white apron and he smiled, slow and shy.

"No troubles, Mist Bock. He's shoot one game, run like hell." He shrugged. "Joost one game."

Buck held onto the hair with one hand and cupped the square chin in the other.

"Boy," he said, softly, "a man might steal if he's hungry and not be bad, but a man that'll steal when he don't need it is a low-down hog." He looked sideways at the dark man. "Your spittoons clean?" Salvador dropped his head on one side and held his hands out palms upwards. Buck looked back at the boy. "You go to school today?" The boy shook his head and gasped. "No books."

"You're a liar, too. I bought books for you last month." He turned him loose and shoved him towards the poolroom. "Get in there and clean spittoons and if you ain't in school tomorrow, I'll beat your butt."

He turned back to Salvador and started to speak, but the small man broke in quickly.

"He's nice, you buy books for alla poor boys, Mist Bock."

"Never mind that," Buck said, impatiently, then his tone grew heavy. "Sally, I got you a suspended sentence for braining that cousin of yours, because I didn't see much wrong in one Greek killing another, but damned if I don't put you in the big jail next time I catch a kid boy in your joint."

A look of patient suffering came over Salvador's face, and his hands fumbled under the apron as Buck turned and started away. Buck had reached the near-by corner when he heard Salvador's soft "Mist Bock." He turned and looked back. Sally's eyes were softly anxious and almost pleading. His hands were still under the apron.

"Got new box figs from Syria," he said, haltingly. "Tella you mama I send 'em up."

Buck stood still with his back to the shadows and smiled slowly so that his teeth showed very white in the light. He nodded and winked.

Salvador breathed deeply, quickly, and made a noise like scaring a cat. He had his hands on his hips when he walked back into the poolroom and his head was held high and to the right.

Buck walked slowly on out of the business district, into the residential section, and his eyes were on the horizon, where the sky had been shredded into grey and blue tatters by longleaf pines that still spiked the slope to the west of Aven.

He thought of Sally and the other foreigners in town, and the way they'd come in with a bundle of shawls and a ragged tent and a small, almost fiercely dark wife who never learned English; and how they'd look *out* at the world even when they were standing in the sun, as if their clothes and bodies were temporary houses out of which they could look and speak but could never leave. He wondered if they were that way all the time, or if they dropped that air when the people who were foreigners to them weren't around. And he wondered what it was about them that drew his sympathy, if it were because he had come to Aven with the same set of drawbacks except for speaking the language, or if he had suddenly turned pious and felt that he was giving a gift when he accepted figs from Syria. He shuddered suddenly and shook off that thought and forced his mind quickly back to what Dr. Tolleson had told him.

"It don't seem right," he said out loud, thickly, as he started across an unpaved street. He was still saying it over and over under his breath when he stooped to throw out of the street a small round rock. Then the thought of his mother left him and he muttered, "Just the size to cripple a horse." He shook his head stubbornly and wondered why his mind would grasp at homely things and then he knew that it was like his mother whose hands never stayed still in troubled times, but drew themselves to the chores, a basket of garden peas, a churn, or the old wooden butter mold whose sides and top were pulpy from use and hot water.

"The times I've seen her, just walking in the kitchen, here and at the old place, and maybe not having any work to do, touching nearly everything she passed as if just the touching of it would make Papa strong again or even well enough so that she would be sure of him for a few more years. Like a blue-gum midwife mumbling and running her hand over the greasy little sack hanging around her neck. Kind of a juju.

"Less'n a year, the doctor said, and it feels like a lot of it is over already. Less'n a year to be good to somebody that spent a lifetime being good to you. That ain't much time. Time. Time. Time. There's never enough of it to go around. Not enough hours in the day, but when a man's young time stretches out in front forever. Then, by God, he stoops down one day to pick up a kid's ball and he comes back up panting a little and dizzy and he'd meant to holler and throw hell out of it, limber as hickory. He just rolls it back and stands there and wonders what went with time. And there's not a thing he can do but mumble in his head that it went too fast and he didn't have any warning. Warnings come every day, though. Somebody dies and another one's born. Warning enough, but there's others, too. Like Tolleson telling me it's time to change. What the hell, he may be right, but Lord which way to go? I can't change my ways in a world like this. Here I am, sitting mostly on top, and maybe I could just quit work, but that ain't my way. I got to do business with somebody. Likely it wasn't that way on purpose, but damned if it don't look like the Lord set up a class of victims like he put baby bream in a pond for the trout to feed on and like he put insects here for the birds to eat. Mighty hard not to feed on 'em, too. Dammit, you can't feed off a man bigger'n you. He's grazing, too. Anyhow, a man that ain't been tempted don't know what he'll do and he ain't in no position to criticize. Now, by God, how come I said that? I got no guilty feelings. Maybe I've squeezed a mortgage too close and maybe I've shaved off a little for myself when I bought for the city. Folks forget, anyhow. They've forgot how old Longshore's folks trafficked in slaves so they could raise him and the others in the big white house in the middle of ten thousand acres of sandy loam. Maybe forty-fifty years from now, some Bannon'll be oozin' religion at the church door and folks won't remember that Buck turned his eyes off while his hands gathered a crop they didn't make. Aw, hell! Why lie about it. It takes something like this to make a man take stock, but I reckon I been knowing that what I've done wasn't for the next generation, and it wasn't because I couldn't do it different. It was because I was scared; scared, by God, that I couldn't stand a lifetime of plowing, chopping cotton, praying for rain or screaming at a freeze. Scared, by God, that if I didn't get it one way I wouldn't be man enough to get it the other way."

Buck was still wondering when he stumbled suddenly and looked up to realize that his feet had brought him to the door of his mother's home without his knowing he was so close. He stopped at the steps for a moment, staring at the oblongs of light that came through rectangular panes of glass on either side of the front door.

"I still ain't ashamed," he said, to himself. "Ain't but one thing shames me. When Papa was dying and when Tobe had just got killed I can remember coming home this way and I'll be damned to hell if I thought about a thing but how it was going to affect me, and here I am doing it again."

His feet were heavy, going up the worn steps, and he felt a tiredness, for the first time in his life, that didn't come of labor, when he pushed the heavy door open. There was a second, as he stood inside, when he didn't hear a sound and the cool, dim, high-ceilinged hall reminded him of the caves at Marianna, Florida, with the green-patterned wallpaper of the hall mocking the solid heavy wet moss that fed off the entrance to the caves. Then, suddenly, he heard the accustomed drone of voices begin and the door at the far end of the hall, the one that led into the kitchen, opened and Millie came towards him. She was frowning as she hurried down the hall and trying to swallow while she motioned him towards the big quiet parlor with one hand and gestured for silence with the other. She walked with quick, jerky steps and her shoulders swung in a sturdy businesslike manner that Buck recognized and almost laughed to see. He could remember her as a child when she had important secrets; she always shared the secrets and always in the same manner, as if something should be done immediately and only in the way she dictated. She went into the parlor ahead of him and turned quickly as he entered the doorway.

"This is one night you could have been sober," she said, flatly, with her lip curling.

Buck scowled.

"What the hell business—?"

"Plenty," she snapped. "Dr. Tolleson told me he was going down to see you. You knew about Mother soon enough to leave off a few drinks, anyhow."

"Suppose you just tell me what you got me in here for and leave me out of the conversation."

She looked him up and down for a moment with disgust wrinkling her nose. Then she got businesslike again.

"We've decided that it's best for Mother not to know," she said in a voice that left no alternative. "So, if you can remember, don't say anything to her about it."

"Who decided?"

"Vesta, Christina, Jeff and I," she said in quick impatience that seemed to say it was unimportant, and she jerked her hand towards the kitchen. "Nobody else here."

"You could have waited," Buck said, tonelessly.

"For what?"

"The rest of us might have something to say."

"Well," she said, then put her hands on her hips, "what else could you have decided?"

Buck's eyes softened, looking down at her.

"She's got a lot of property," he said, slowly, "and folks with property have an obligation to pass it on right. Sometimes they have to know."

"Thinking about a will already?" she said, quickly, and then her eyes showed that she was sorry it came out. She bit her lower lip, looking up at him. Buck's face whitened slowly and he turned and walked out of the parlor ahead of her.

He was going down the hall towards his mother's room when she caught his arm.

"Now, don't go in there like that, dammit," she said, and her manner was a mixture of shame and defiance.

Buck moved his arm slowly from under her hand and jerked his head towards the kitchen.

"Go on back there."

He breathed deeply, trying to get his thoughts in order, and he waited until the kitchen door had shut behind Millie, before he cracked the door and looked cautiously inside.

Jeanie Bannon hurriedly pulled the front of a loose flowered wrapper together over her chest and glared at the door with her black eyes flaring wide.

"Come in or get out, one or the other," she said, tartly.

"Wanted to see if you were asleep," Buck said, and walked over to sit in the big rocker beside her bed.

"Just is dark," she said, and lay back against the two big pillows that were stuffed behind her. She reached up with a hand that trembled to pull the white ruffled cap off her head. She tossed her head vigorously as she threw the cap to the floor. "Never did like them fool things."

"Feel all right?" Buck said, casually, and leaned back in the rocker.

"How could I feel good?" she said, testily. "Fool doctor spent

[278]

a half a day browsin' around under the bedclothes. It's enough to kill a well person." Her face flushed and Buck watched the line of red creep from the high neck of her simple cotton nightgown into the roots of her nearly white hair. She didn't look at him. "Didn't mean to say that," she mumbled, then glared at him, "but it's enough to set a body off."

Buck didn't answer, but he smiled gently and leaned down to look under the bed.

"Out of snuff?" he asked as he came back up.

Jeanie Bannon pursed her lips tightly and Buck could see the deep wrinkles branching out from the corners. "Hmph!" she said, and thrashed at the pillow with her elbow. "You know I don't use it any more. Not since the girls got back from college."

Buck didn't look at her and his voice was patiently tender.

"Where is it?"

Her eyes were bright. They flashed cunningly first at him and then at the door into the hall. She looked at him finally with a partnership in her expression.

"Over yonder," she pointed, "in one of Vesta's old cold-cream jars," then she chuckled silently as Buck brought it from the dresser to her bedside. Buck turned his back as she opened the jar and walked easily over to the door into the hall and listened for a second, then he came back and sat down again.

"How's things downtown?" she asked companionably over the slight bulge in her lower lip.

Buck told her how things were downtown and they talked comfortably for a while in the manner of country folks who know each other well, making one word do for a sentence, a grunt giving the condition of the crops, or a frowning shake of the head sympathizing with cholera in the hogs. Then Buck laced the fingers of his hands behind his head and leaned back looking up at the ceiling.

"Wish Papa could see us now," he said, slowly, "making out all right, and things."

His mother sighed and the wrinkles came again around her mouth as if she primped them to keep them from trembling.

"Somehow," she said, "I been feeling him more lately. Seems as long as I can work, and June around, it ain't so bad; but the last few months I been missing him like when you was a baby

[279]

and he'd leave and go off to Eufaula to get furnishings for another year."

"Lots of times, I figure it'd be easier to join him," Buck said soberly, rocking gently.

"Me, too," she said, quickly, and stirred on the bed so the springs whined faintly. "Sometimes it seems like it'd be a blessed relief not to have to wait no longer."

Buck rocked in silence for a moment, feeling a warm choking work up towards his throat, and he hoped his voice would be steady.

"Maybe it won't be long," he said, gently.

He looked down at her as he heard the springs twang louder. She was sitting up straight now with a bright fierce questioning in her black eyes. Her hands held tight onto the sheet and pulled it taut over her legs.

"Are you trying to tell me—?" Her voice was harsh and it shook a little, so she broke off and just sat there throwing the question at him with her eyes. "Are you?" she said, low this time.

"Yes'm," Buck said and swallowed against the warmth in his throat. He gripped his knees to keep his hands quiet and watched her face.

Jeanie Bannon sat perfectly still for a moment, staring at him with eyes that didn't see him. Her lips pushed out as she tightened her jaw until it showed white and her chin turned up until the soft end of it brought out pin-point dimples that were whiter than the flesh around them. She made a small sound that was nearly a moan but was mostly a sigh, then she sank back against the pillows and looked up at the ceiling. Her hands slowly relaxed on the sheet and lay very still.

Buck leaned forward quickly to look at her face, but her low-voiced words stopped him.

"I ain't sayin' I'm not scared and I ain't sayin' I am, but it just don't seem like there ever is a convenient time for dyin'."

"It's a long time off," Buck said, hopefully.

"How long?" she asked with no tone or feeling in her voice.

" 'Bout a year." His words were so low it hardly seemed to him that she could have heard them, but she answered strongly.

"Hmph! Less'n that, I reckon."

Buck didn't answer.

"Hey," she said, sharply, "I said less'n that."

Buck still didn't answer.

"Reckon I was right, then," she said, with a creeping of triumph in her voice.

"Yes'm."

She breathed shallowly for a few moments, then turned her head so that she could see Buck.

"You told the others?"

"They know it."

"How come I'm the last to hear it? Seems like it's as much my business as anybody's."

"They didn't want to tell you."

"Lord God!" she said, "I'd rather know." She struggled up again from the pillows and narrowed her eyes in determination. "I'd a heap rather know it, so I can live out the rest o' my life like I please."

Buck breathed deeply with relief as he leaned forward to touch her hand clumsily.

"I hoped I was right," he said. "That's the way I'd want it for myself."

She moved her hand impatiently.

"Quit pattin' me," she said, and settled the fluffed sleeves around her wrists. "You better call the—" She stopped and cocked her head to one side to listen. "They're comin'," she said and her mouth pulled up grimly. She almost chuckled.

Millie came in the door first with a carefree swing to her hips that didn't go with the worried look in her eyes; then behind her, listening too interestedly to her forced chattering, crowded Vesta and Christina and Jeff. Millie suddenly stopped talking as she saw her mother, sitting upright in the bed with her hands bracing down on her knees. She started quickly towards the bed, frowning. "Now, Mother, you know," she started, then stopped and looked closely at her mother's face. Suddenly she swung to face Buck.

"You drunken dog," she said, slowly, biting into each word, and she clenched her fists tight against her hips. "I'd like to—"

"Here, now," Jeanie Bannon broke in, sharply, "stop that." Millie stared at Buck for a second, then turned to her mother as if she hated to take her eyes off Buck. "All of you sit down,"

Jeanie said calmly, "but don't sit on the bed. I never felt like saying it before, but it makes me nervous as all get out for somebody to bounce all over my bed.

"Now," she said, matter-of-factly, when they all had found chairs and pulled them closer, "this is the last time I want this mentioned by either one of you. I reckon I'll have to put up with Wiley and Suzie and all the rest slobberin' over me, but I don't intend to have it more'n once from either one of you children. I'm strong enough to know what I want and I mean to get it. I'm going to live the rest of my life doing just what I please." She stopped talking, suddenly, and sat there looking down at the foot of the bed with a puzzled wondering expression. Then she went on, "I just wish to the Lord I was forty years younger." She closed her mouth tightly and looked from one to the other of her children until her eyes fell on Vesta, whose prim pinched features were obviously suffering. "Vesta," Jeanie Bannon said, tasting her slow words, "get me a slop jar. I want to spit out my snuff."

Vesta's hands jerked and she shuddered delicately as she rose and went towards the bathroom that had been installed a few years back. Jeanie Bannon watched her out of sight with scornful eyes, then looked down the line again. "Millie," she said, sweetly, "you've got the prettiest teeth, if you haven't got the cleanest mind. I want you to chew the sweet out of a piece of gum for me and then wash it off pretty good."

Millie got up without a word and walked with her shoulders swinging defiantly through the door that led into the room that the three girls used.

The mother looked at Christina. Christina fidgeted and looked away. Jeff dropped his eyes before his mother could swing her face his way. Buck waited until her eyes struck his, then he started laughing deep in his chest.

"The rest of you just stay close by." She flounced and leaned back against the pillows, sighing gratefully, and looked up at the ceiling.

"It's a plumb shame," she said, softly, "that everybody can't afford to live all the time like they didn't have but one more day."

CHAPTER TWENTY-SIX

Two MONTHS LATER, Buck's huge black Wescott Six muttered to a jolting stop on the still-unpaved street in front of his
mother's home. Lota honked the horn twice, then slouched behind the wheel. Buck sat alone on the back seat, hating the stiff
and lumpy cushions, but glad the top was down so that the late
August breeze would dry the sweat on his forehead and maybe
get the damp lifelessness out of his hair. He held his hard straw
hat with the wide brim carefully between his knees and watched
the back of Lota's head. He heard faintly the dim drumming of
her impatient fingers on the metal door beside the driver's seat.
He watched the gently swinging curl that barely touched her
broad white collar. He couldn't feel the breeze that blew it. He
wondered, squinting at the curl, if it was the sun that gave the
curl its reddish glint and left still dark the bun from which it had
blown loose.

His mind was blank except for the curl when he heard the front
door slam and looked up to see Jeff and Millie on either side, helping Jeanie Bannon down the front steps. He looked carefully to
see if he could tell how much weight she had lost in spite of
the long tan duster she wore. Her face was still full enough, he decided, though her color was bad. Or maybe it was the color of the
driving bonnet.

"Looks pretty well," he said, and didn't know he had spoken
out loud until Lota turned around and said, "Hunh?"

"Nothing much," he said, then leaned closer and spoke in a
low voice. "Remember, now, don't mention where we're going."

Lota nodded and twisted around in the seat until she could face
Jeanie Bannon. "Need any help, there?"

"Don't need these," Jeanie snapped. "They're just trying to
inherit."

"Hell," Jeff said, and dropped her left arm. His face flushed
and he turned away quickly as if trying to hide it. He walked
awkwardly down the street towards town, and his straw hat rode
far back on his big head. He held his shoulders up straighter, but
looked more pigeon-toed from the back.

His mother shook Millie's hand off her arm.

"Here, boy," she called, "come back here."

Jeff walked on silently without looking back or breaking his stride. She called again, louder, but Jeff kept walking. She watched him with a puzzled frown on her face, then turned abruptly and got into the car without help.

"That ain't no way to talk," Buck said, roughly, as she settled down on the seat. He glanced at Millie's white, set face, then turned back as Millie swung around towards the house. He motioned for Lota to drive on before he spoke again.

"Looks to me like you're tryin' to place blame for your troubles."

"Hunh!" She just grunted and clutched the flaps of her bonnet closer together as the car grumbled going into high gear.

"No reason to hit out at the young'uns," Buck went on slowly. "Seems to me you got a responsibility to be better instead of worse."

"Sweep around your own back yard."

"What does that mean?"

She looked up, challenging him, then.

"It means if you've figured out some rules good enough for me to die by, it wouldn't hurt for you to try living by some just as good."

Buck scowled into the whip of the wind and tried to sink lower so it wouldn't strike his eyes.

"I don't want to talk about me and my sins," he said, bluntly.

"Neither do I, but somebody's got to make you see light. There's a time for everything, but the day's worn out and gone when you could allow open gambling dens and sawdust saloons and—" she glanced sharply towards Lota, "them other houses."

Buck looked up in time to see Lota's head turned slightly so that she could hear the conversation. He frowned warningly at his mother and shook his head.

"That'll be all for now," he said, flatly, then looked off to the left, watching the small shotgun houses slide by, growing scarcer and scarcer with every lurch of the car in the hard-baked ruts. He watched the empty countryside rush towards them, feeling inside a hurrying something that wanted to get outside of town, where quiet flat distances perhaps would help to ease the tension. He could still feel it, almost as if it were a strong impulse running through a wire from him to his mother, a silent tightness that he wanted to relieve but couldn't. He tried to breathe it out, or think it out, knowing all the time that only words would help, as only words could cause it. He felt it build, waiting for her to speak, because he knew he had let the tension live too long for him to break it.

"Glad it's Sunday," she said, finally, in a self-conscious voice. Buck sucked in a long breath and blew it out slowly, feeling the calmness begin as he turned his head. He smiled one-sidedly.

"Me, too," he said, and tossed his hand lazily towards the empty fields on his left. "Always makes me feel mournful to see a bunch of hands picking over a field that's already been stripped."

"Nothing like it, though, when the fields are plumb busting white, to see 'em scrambling after it while it's still heavy with dew."

Buck laughed. "I'd scramble, too, if I was picking at thirty cents a hundred."

They stopped talking, then, not deliberately, but as if the motion of riding and the cool of the wind and the countryside patterns of green and brown were satisfying enough. Lota drove slowly and Buck knew she was impatient with the roads that held her back from the smooth power she liked to feel.

Neither spoke again until they reached the shade of a small thick cypress swamp whose usually slimy wet soil was baked dry and cracked like dark-grey porcelain. The air was musty cool and the gaunt and scaly trunks of the trees seemed choked by heavy layers of dried mud that circled each, three or four feet above the ground.

"Hmm!" Jeanie Bannon said, and shivered, "it's like an old springhouse with crickets on the wall."

Buck just nodded. They were silent until Lota slowed down for a new-looking bridge across a bustling rocky little creek. Buck's voice was casual.

"Looks like pretty good land, starting at this creek."

"Got good timber, anyhow," she said, brightly. Then she suddenly pointed ahead and to the left up a long slope of hill. "Look at that. Anybody'd build a house that far from the road must have somethin' to hide."

Buck flushed and cleared his throat, watching Lota's shoulders begin to shake.

"Some folks build back to keep out of the dust."

"Hmph! Uses up too much land that ought to be growing peas and beans." She raised up higher in the seat so she could see better as the car crept over the crest of the hill. "It's a right pretty house, but it'd wear out two brush brooms a day to keep that yard swept."

Buck felt his face get redder as Lota began stopping near the front of the house, which sat about a hundred yards off the road in a large grove of oaks. He stared away from his mother, trying to keep his eyes on the red-painted metal roof, or the shiny new blades of the windmill that raised its arms above the second story, far back out of the trees. He tried to think how he could best tell her what was in his mind as the car ground slowly to a stop, but thoughts wouldn't come to him. The words in his mind kept revolving around the windmill and the new barn that was being raised across the road and down about two hundred yards. He didn't look at anybody until he heard Lota say, "Well?" then he looked up at her and frowned. He saw his mother's puzzled expression and tightened his jaw.

"Well," he said, slowly, "I reckon we can get some of the hands to keep it swept for you."

Jeanie Bannon's face whitened slowly as she stared at Buck, then she began to fumble with the latch on the door beside her. He reached over to help, but she pushed his hand away. She stood up painfully in the car before she got the door open and looked around without speaking. Buck couldn't keep his eyes off her and yet he wanted to look away. He watched her throat and saw the muscles work as if she were swallowing. Then she reached down and pulled the handle and pushed against the door with her knee until it swung open. She had stepped out on the ground before she spoke, turning slowly to face Buck before the words would come.

"You oughtn't—" She stopped and her hand came slowly up to her face. She rubbed her thumb roughly against her nose and cleared her throat. "It's mine?"

Buck nodded, keeping his eyes on Lota, who bent forward over the wheel and started clicking the ignition key on and off.

He heard his mother's steps making tiny grinding sounds in the white sand of the yard and somehow he still could feel her hands touch the car as she walked around it. She was away from the car before she spoke again.

"For a while, anyhow?" she said, in a voice that brought a question and a hurt back to Buck.

She went slowly towards the front of the house, and when she reached the steps, she bent over, clumsily, and touched the wood. She spanned with one hand the shallow depth of one step and leaned farther over to gauge its extra width. She straightened back up and walked to the side of the steps and bent over again to get a side view. Then she turned back around and jerked her chin down in a gesture of approval.

"Whoever figured out these steps," she called, slowly, "tell 'im I reckon I can make it all right."

Buck stood up and started to get out.

"Who was it?" she asked.

"Jeff," he said.

She bit her lower lip and ducked her head. She turned quickly around and walked stiffly, as fast as her uncertain legs could carry her, around the side of the house. Buck stepped out of the car and started to follow, but Lota stopped him.

"She'll be better off alone," she said.

"I don't know." He frowned and ran his hands through his thick greying hair. "Damned if it ain't got where everything I do—" His voice trailed off and he sighed and clamped his teeth tight together. He sat down on the running board of the car and crossed his legs. Lota reached over the door. She curled her long fingers against the side of his throat and patted.

"She's just mixed up, kinda. Things are coming at her too fast."

Buck rubbed his face against her hand and nodded. They waited for a long time in silence except for the creaking of the windmill and the small sounds the wind made in the big oak trees. Buck looked at his watch several times and once he wound it, thoughtfully. Finally, he stood up and tightened the muscles of his shoulders impatiently.

"I'm going after her."

Lota nodded and opened the door.

"I want to stretch, too."

They walked around the side of the house. Buck noticed as he always did that Lota's long strides made her hips sway in an easy strong movement that carried her along smoothly just a little ahead of him.

The back yard was as clean as if it had been scrubbed, except for a fringe of wild-plum trees that Buck had allowed the builders to leave, because it would be a border and a screen between the big house and the old original tenant dwelling which seemed to lean against a huge pine to take some of the load off its field-stone pillars. Jeanie Bannon wasn't in sight.

Lota twisted her head around to look over her shoulder.

"Is the house locked up?"

Buck nodded, then pointed towards the tenant house.

"Probably over there drinking out of the Misstledines' well."

Lota saw his eyes fall to her hips as she started walking again and she began to switch them elaborately, still looking back over her shoulder. Buck took two longer steps and came up close behind her. He cupped his hand and slapped her bottom. She jumped one step and whistled, then she started walking faster around the corner of the fence and its border of plum trees. Buck followed at his same deliberate pace, but his eyes stayed on her until she turned out of sight towards the tenant house. He wondered, as one step moved her out of his view, if she'd always be able to turn on a light of laughter and peace in him, or if time would surely blot out even that return from her nearness. He felt his throat thicken and he twisted his neck inside his collar. Unconsciously, he began to slide the knot of his tie down and unbutton his shirt collar as he turned into the small yard of the tenant house. He saw Lota again and stopped with his hand still at his collar. She was standing near the rickety, grey stone chimney where it leaned stubbornly away from the body of the house to leave a crack two inches wide in the unsheathed sidewall. She had one finger raised to her lips and with the other hand she motioned for softness as his shoes whispered nearer on the sand. He came closer, careful to lift his feet high from the last footstep, not to slide them, and he cocked his head on one side to listen near the crack.

"Buck's my oldest boy." Jeanie Bannon's voice came low but

strong through the thin walls. "Then came a passel o' girls. Myrt plumb littered her yard, then died after the last one. Nance, she just had three, and then their daddy died—he was way too old for her anyhow—and she moved off with his folks. Reckon she'll marry again, though. Be bad on her if she don't, young as she is, with her blood. All the rest of 'em, except the three youngest boys and the three youngest girls, have already married and done their duties. No, it's been so long, I'd almost forgot Ernestine. She left three for me to raise, but they're up so big now they're almost like mine. Vesta, one of the young'uns, is getting married next week and I reckon she won't be much out of the family way. Hey, Lord, it's a queer feeling to find yourself old and troubled and right where the string peters out, then look back and see the trail you've left. But it's a pretty good feeling in some ways— take this house and all. Buck just heard me say I wanted to get back on the farm before I died. And here I've got a thousand acres and a big white house with a dozen rooms and big stores and barns and tenant houses and folks to do my work. Poor Buck. He didn't know and I don't mean for him to ever know. What I wanted was what you've got. You got peace that can come from the things you know every day and the things you work with. The only peace I can get now is from the inside. I don't reckon that's Buck's fault. He couldn't know what I wanted. And even if he did, he couldn't give them to me. My Lord, nobody can give them to me now. The things I want wouldn't be any good to me anyhow—I'd have to be twenty again."

Her voice stopped suddenly and Buck heard a chair scrape and he heard the small ring of metal on the hearth. He knew someone had poked at the fire and in his mind he could see the blackened coffeepot set aslant on the uneven stone near fluffily whitening oak ashes. Then he heard a low murmur from another voice. He stared dully at the crack in the wall until he heard Jeanie Bannon's voice start again, prim and formal this time.

"Thank you for the coffee, Miz Misstledine." Buck could hear her straining out of the chair and he could see a low-set rocker with arms that were rubbed slick by hands that had felt them as old friends. Then she spoke again.

"I'd say you should come to see me after we've moved in, but I reckon—" She broke off as if she were confused and when her voice came again it had a new kind of wistfully hoping lift to it. "Your place is so much like the house we used to live in, maybe you'd just let me come down here to visit. Maybe I could watch you do the things I'd like to do again and maybe I could help some."

Buck straightened up beside the chimney and caught Lota by the arm. He pulled her towards the fence and gestured with his hand. They slipped out of the yard without speaking, and walked back to the car. Buck felt a dull kind of pain in his chest as he climbed into the back seat. He didn't want to talk, yet the words came in spite of him.

"Seems like everything I touch starts off all right, then all of a sudden something takes it out of my hands and twists it all wrong."

INTERLUDE

JAKE WILLIS *stood on the damp ground, far enough away from the splattering of the faucet on the back porch, and sourly watched Bass Wooten scrub his face, chest and shoulders. He waited in silence until Bass had finished washing and started drying himself off with a coarse thin towel.*

"*What the hell?*" *he said. Then,* "*I'd go with you.*"

Bass flung the towel onto an upended orange crate on which lay a slippery-looking bar of yellow soap and a dirty washcloth.

"*All right, dammit,*" *he said, peevishly,* "*but I tell you right now, I ain't got a dime.*"

Jake's eyes brightened.

"*Now, you're talkin'.*" *He pulled a small roll of bills out of his pocket and rubbed it against his nose.* "*An' I got the money.*"

"*Godamighty!*" *Bass's eyes bugged out.*

"*Sold four hogs,*" *Jake announced proudly.*

Bass suddenly halted in the middle of pulling a shirt over his shoulders.

"*Whose hogs?*" *he asked, softly.*

Jake flushed and put the money back in his pocket.

"*Mine, by God! I ain't no thief.*" *He twisted his neck back and*

[290]

forth in his collar, then blurted, "It was the litter from that sow Buck give me last year."

"Whose boar serviced her?"

Jake held out both hands, palms up, then dropped them to his side, hopelessly.

"I thought so," Bass said, and jerked his shirt irritably around so that the sides met. "Why didn't you pay Buck at least somethin' on what you owe?"

Jake stepped close up to the edge of the porch and glared up at Bass.

"Listen," he said, flatly, "if you want to go to Kilkare with me an' the Ziglar girls, come on, but don't keep arguin' at me all the time."

Bass didn't answer in words, but he mumbled under his breath as he faced the small mirror hanging on the wall and tried to make his string tie hang carelessly. When he had finished, he turned and glared back down at Jake.

"This is my last say 'fore we get the girls, but 'dogged if somebody ain't got to think about him. Tobe got killed an' that hit 'im hard. Now his ma's a'dyin'." He ran his fingers hard through his thinning hair. "Looks like some folks could at least pay their debts so he wouldn't have that—"

"Wait a minute," Jake interrupted, "who said his ma was fixin' to pass on?"

"Nobody out an' said it, but you know durn well Dr. Tolleson's been there ever' day for over two months." He leaned down close to Jake's face, and his voice grew confidential, "Where the hen scratches, there be the bug also."

Jake frowned and his eyes wandered down to the ground.

"Pore widow woman."

"Pore Buck," Bass said, flatly. "Ever'body around him droppin' out, an' his brand-new wife packin' off to boardin' school."

"Good God!" Jake's eyes were puzzled and hurt. "I didn't know all that." He glanced hopefully up at Bass. "Reckon we oughtn't to call this off an' let's—?"

"No, sir." Bass stumped heavily down the rickety back steps and took a long stride over the puddle of water. "You come over here an' get my mouth all set to nuzzle that oldest Ziglar girl, an' now I aim to nuzzle her, if Buck starves."

GLASS STARTED tinkling somewhere in the room, and Buck held his breath for a moment trying to locate it. Without touching her and without a word being spoken, he knew that Lota was lying beside him, straining to hear it more clearly. He stared up into the thick hot darkness and listened while the tinkling grew louder and more regular. Then, suddenly, his ears found the kinship between the tinkle and the far-off rumbling that came through the window behind the bed.

"The eight-ten to Hartford," he said, too lazy for his voice to show triumph.

He felt Lota's breath on his arm as she spoke.

"What did you think it was, sleigh bells?"

He slapped the side of her thigh with the back of his hand and felt the bed shake as she laughed silently. She stirred, pretending to move farther away, but not increasing the distance between them.

"Keep your hands off me," she said, and yawned luxuriously, "you've already done enough damage."

"All I'm liable to do tonight, too."

"I don't know," she drawled, and started to sit up, "I'd better not take a chance."

"Wait a minute," Buck said quickly and held his arm out into the dark. She sighed and fell back limply.

They lay still again, listening to the now faster and louder tinkle of glass and the heavy trudge of the big drive wheels as the engine pulled closer from the northeast. The glow from the big headlight came slowly, seeming to grow from nothing into a pale dusk, so smoothly it was hardly noticeable. Then, with a rush, the train was close and the light was brighter still, reflected by the mirror in the walnut dresser across the room. Suddenly, the train was almost under the window and the light was gone and it was darker than before. In the room, there was left only the tiny tinkle of glass and the grind and clash of wheels and couplings that shook the hotel like a midget earthquake. But in Buck's mind was the picture he had waited for—the sight of Lota's body, long and slim and strong, stretched full out in the shadowy light that came so slowly and left with such a rush. The dim light had blurred the rounded outline and left only a memory of a sight that was hard to recapture, like a snatch of song that comes and goes. He could sense, but not see, that her skin in the warm and hurried little twilight had a dusty glow that wasn't pink and wasn't olive, but had a tinge of both. He felt her stir slightly and knew she was going to speak.

"I know what you're thinking," she said, softly. "And I know why you made me lie back down."

"Why?"

"You knew that light was coming."

"Unh-hunh."

"How'd you know it would come, we've never been to bed this early before."

"There's a two-twenty train every morning."

Lota raised herself slowly and leaned over on one elbow. He couldn't see, but he knew that her eyes were near and dark and half closed.

"You've stayed awake, while I've been sleeping? Why? It's not just to see me."

"It's just been lately," Buck said. "I don't know why. Maybe because I knew you'd be leaving tonight. Maybe because—I don't know. I been crowded, seems like. Things coming all at once and in too much of a hurry." He rolled his head impatiently on the pillow. "Makes me feel like my score is being added up."

Lota was silent for a moment, then he could feel her breath on his cheek. Her chin burrowed gently into the hollow of his throat and when she spoke her voice was muffled.

"Buck, would it mean a lot if I didn't leave tonight? Just forgot college for another few years? I'd do it, you know."

"I thought I'd taught you better'n that," he said, roughly this time. "Never back out—always finish what you start, good or bad, because a memory of something you didn't do is as galling as a saddle sore."

He felt her breath come out slowly on his throat and knew that she was glad he wasn't going to keep her from going.

"It's so near, though," she said, "tonight at eleven. I almost hate to go, now."

"You'll go." Buck caught a handful of her hair and lifted her head and shook it slightly. "Better get up now." She sat up on the edge of the bed and he felt around with his feet to locate the sheet that was crumpled and pushed down to the foot of the bed. "Here," she said, and pulled it over him.

He could hear her quick movements in the dark and could catch the silky whisper of her slip; then he felt her lean over again. She turned on the bed lamp and he blinked up with his eyes slitted. Her hair hung down, nearly touching his mouth, and he could see her face framed in the black disordered curls. She looked sleepy and her lips were fuller than he'd ever seen them. She leaned farther over and kissed him, quickly, then straightened up and shook her head and threw the wild hair back over her shoulders. She walked over towards the bathroom with movements that quickened as she went.

"Hope to the Lord Carmen's ready," she said, briskly. "I'll bet two dollars she cries at the station."

"She'll cry," Buck said. "She's a female."

Lota turned around at the bathroom door and cocked her head. She put her hands on her hips. "I won't cry and if I'm not a female you're in a hell of a fix."

Buck laughed.

"Get on out of here," he said, and raised himself on one elbow. "When you get dressed, tell 'em down in the kitchen to have us some supper 'bout nine-thirty."

"What do you want?"

"Quail, I reckon."

"Hearn been hunting?"

Buck snorted.

"When ain't he hunting?"

Lota disappeared into the bathroom, but her voice came back, muffled by the sound of running tap water.

"When does he work? Don't look like he does a thing but spend your money." The water cut off suddenly, and her head came back around the corner of the door. Her face was wet. "He can't think about a thing but liquor and women and they cost like the devil."

Buck's lips curled and he looked her up and down as she stepped out into the room, drying her face.

"They don't cost much," he said, "and they never will cost as much as they're worth."

Lota laughed delightedly and threw the towel at him. "Fool!" She sat down to pull her shoes on. She bent over to button them. "Lord, I'm getting fat," she said, in a strained voice. "You reckon I'm going to have a baby?" She sat up straight, suddenly, with a startled look on her face. "My God, if I am it'll come right at final examinations."

Buck whooped with laughter. He balled up the damp towel and flung it back at her. "Get on out of here," he said, "and let me get dressed." He lay back down and watched her finish dressing and hurriedly pat powder on her face, then carefully rub it off.

"Lord," he was thinking as she opened the door into the hall, "I'll miss her." He hardly knew what the words meant as she leaned back through the door to call that she would have to run to the corner drugstore for shoe polish.

"It's hard to realize it," he thought, "and two weeks ago when we took Mother out to the farm, it seemed like it was way off in the future that she was leaving. Hey, Lord, don't time ever take a day off?"

He got out of bed and went into the bathroom. He threw cold water into his face and rubbed a cool damp towel over his shoulders and around his neck. He dressed slowly, in a dark-blue suit of thin silky material. His coat was loose over a white shirt with wide flat pleats and a stiff removable collar. After he was dressed, he dried his face off again and carefully smoothed Lota's chamois powder rag over his face. Then, peering into the mirror to see if he had laid it too heavily on any one spot, he rubbed both palms over his face and removed the excess powder.

Whistling softly, he turned almost unconsciously to the small table whose marble top held two bottles, both half empty, a small tub of ice, and several glasses. He picked out of the ice tub the squeezed and pulpy half of a lemon and tossed it into the small metal wastebasket. He started automatically to pour a drink, then suddenly he frowned and put the bottle down.

"Reckon Hearn'll take one with me," he muttered and went out into the hall, still frowning as he reached back of him into the room and cut off the lights. He looked critically over the halls as he reached the lighted area. The long triangle of the mezzanine floor was empty and dimly lit by small bulbs that fringed the over-hanging narrow corridor running along the three sides of the building. Some light came from the open transoms of rooms on the third floor, whose doors opened onto the banistered corridor. Other globes shone along either side of the three stairways which led from the mezzanine floor into each third-floor corner of the triangle.

"Gets dingy in no time," he said to himself as his eye caught the streaks of dust that had settled almost unnoticed on the cream-colored plaster walls. He could hear a rumble of voices from the lobby as he passed the square railing around the stair well lead-ing downwards, but the voices faded out as he neared Hearn's room. He was reaching for the doorknob when he heard low furious words coming from the open transom above him.

"Don't touch me again."

Buck's head jerked up and he stood perfectly still for a second, then he narrowed his eyes. Lota's voice! He turned his head slightly and waited.

"Here, I didn't want to fight." It was Hearn's voice, lazy and low, and Buck knew how his mouth looked when he spoke, one corner sucked far in and down and lips barely moving. "I was fix-ing to kiss you." Buck's jaw tightened and he lowered his head like a bull.

"I'm your brother's wife."

"Buck's gettin' on," Hearn said. "I just wanted to keep it in the family."

"God, what a bastard."

Hearn laughed.

"Reckon you're right, but when you're in college and get to needin'— Well, you just call on me."

Lota gasped. Buck heard her quick furious footsteps and the small rattle as her hand touched the doorknob on the inside. He listened carefully and could hear nothing, but he knew that she was just on the other side of the door, facing Hearn and trem-bling with fury. He felt muscles begin to swell in his chest, could almost hear the pound of blood in his temples and in the thick veins that began to stand out on his neck.

Then he heard her speak again, low-voiced and bitter.

[296]

"The low-down part of it is you know I won't hurt Buck by telling him."

"It was a good gamble," Hearn admitted.

"And he'll go right on loving you. He'll furnish you money for women and liquor and fine bird dogs and you'll come in now and then and leave a dozen birds and them not even gutted."

"Unh!" Hearn grunted as if she had struck him.

She shook the door. "And, by God," she went on, talking faster and faster, "when I get to where I have to be serviced like a damned brood mare, I'll get a man. It won't be a spineless dog."

She jerked the door inwards and took two steps, glaring back over her shoulder until she touched Buck's chest. Then she whipped her head around, startled, and looked up into his eyes, barely showing through the slits of his lids. His arms were braced, one hand on either side of the door, and he didn't look at Lota. His eyes didn't move from Hearn's face.

"Go downstairs, Lota," he said in a voice that was thick and strained, but gentle. "Wait for me at the table."

"Buck, I—"

"Go on, Lota, right now."

She closed her lips tightly, facing his shirt front for a second, then she turned slowly and looked at Hearn, whose face had paled and whose eyes now switched from her to Buck and then to the open mezzanine beyond.

"I can't even feel sorry for you," she said, softly. "Only for Buck."

She turned quickly and ducked under Buck's still outstretched and braced arms. Buck could hear her heels in small muffled jarrings on the carpeting. When he heard them strike the ribbed metal sheeting that protected the stairsteps he moved for the first time. He relaxed his arms and stepped without a word into the room and closed the door behind him. Hearn didn't move or speak, he stood near the bed with his arms down by his side. His eyes had stopped flickering from one spot to the other, and fastened themselves on Buck. He held his head up high, and the veins stood out tight above his open collarless shirt.

Buck didn't speak and he didn't take his eyes off Hearn. He walked slowly and heavily across to the dresser and looked down

[297]

onto its glass top. His hand trembled a little as he reached out to fumble with stiff fingers in the small pile of change, pocketknife, mismatched dice and collar buttons. He poked awkwardly with his thumb at the diamond stickpin that was thrown carelessly into the pile, then he drew his fingers slowly across the glass and made four tracks in the film of powder.

Hearn didn't move as Buck turned back from the dresser and stepped closer and his face didn't change when Buck spoke.

"I'm going to put Lota on the 11:05," Buck said in a low, strained tone. "You be gone when I get back."

"Aw, for—" Hearn started to speak and Buck slapped him hard across the mouth. Hearn closed his eyes and his lips started shaking. Buck slapped him again with his other hand and Hearn flinched but didn't move or open his eyes. He licked at the small trickle of blood from a cut on his lip.

"Words won't help," Buck said thickly. "I'd have killed any other man, maybe any other of my brothers. You'll be lucky to just walk out."

Hearn didn't answer. He sat down, slowly, on the edge of the bed and Buck heard the faint whang of the springs as he turned towards the door. He opened the door and walked out and down the stairs to the lobby. He could feel a solid hurting that seemed to have no location, no beginning and no end. The muscles in his jaws worked and he loosened them again and again, until he could walk into the lobby with his face composed, but still flushed. He nodded to one or two of the guests who clustered under the slow-turning ceiling fan, but he didn't see them plainly or hear them answer. He was nearly under the wide doors that led into the dining room before he became conscious of any of the noises around him. Then he heard the clerk.

"Mister Buck. Mister Buck."

He turned around, slowly.

"There's a note for you."

"I'll get it later."

The clerk nodded brightly and tapped a folded newspaper on his palm. He showed his teeth in his professional smile. "Cotton's up three cents," he said and winked.

Buck turned without answering to find Lota and looked towards the corner table where they usually sat. He told a passing waiter to bring him a full bottle of whiskey. Then he started walking towards her with his head down, in and out of the tables. He was thinking, "I've made three thousand dollars today, but God only knows what I've lost."

At first Buck wouldn't get out of the car at the station. He sprawled in the back seat and stared at the big silver-painted water tank whose single adornment was a small guide light, shining like a steady star at the top of the ladder. He had told Jeff and Lota to leave him alone, but to send Carmen to the car, and now he waited, wondering why whiskey had failed him. Always before, it had spread its glow swiftly, drink by drink, until he was glad out to his fingertips. He had drunk too much and he knew it, yet it laid its heat in a single spot and left him too clear-headed, with an uncomfortable lodging in his stomach. He wiped his forehead off with a heavy white linen handkerchief and breathed deeply, then stirred impatiently, wishing Ernestine's oldest girl, Carmen, would come on.

He didn't know she was near until she touched the car; she walked so lightly, even over the grey chert pebbles the railroads sprinkled on their station yards, that her steps made little or no noise.

"Uncle Buck," she said, and he turned his head to see her bright red hair gleaming in the light from the waiting rooms. He could barely make out her pretty, narrow face with its too-large brown eyes and its too-thin lips.

He touched her hand where it rested on the door of the car and turned his face so she couldn't see into his eyes.

"I made an error the other day," he said, bluntly. "I make a lot of them, somehow, lately."

She didn't answer, but her hand began to slide back and forth on the door. He knew she was embarrassed and that she'd be looking down at the ground and wishing the train would come on.

"You understood what I meant when I told you I wanted you to write me—without anybody knowing?"

"Yes, sir." Her voice was low, with a catch in it.

"It didn't make you feel any too good about getting to go to college, did it?"

She didn't answer.

"Makes you ashamed for me, doesn't it?"

"Uncle Buck, I—"

"No, wait, girl," he broke in, "this is likely the last time anybody's going to hear Buck Bannon apologize." He pulled himself upright on the edge of the seat and rubbed his handkerchief across his mouth. "I was wrong, and wrong in the worst possible way. I made you feel like a hired spy and I didn't trust my own wife." He breathed raggedly. "I'm sorry, Carmen," he added simply.

"That's all right," she said, awkwardly, but she didn't look up.

He didn't speak for a moment and she said, "Is that all?" and started to turn away.

"No, one more thing. Instead of asking Lota or writing me for money, when you want any—not when you need it, either, by God—you draw a draft on me."

Carmen gulped.

"Draft?"

Buck laughed shortly and bitterly.

"Don't worry, Lota can show you how." He fumbled for the door handle and she opened it for him, quickly, and now he looked up into her eyes and they were soft. She was biting her lips.

"Train's 'bout due," he said, and stepped cautiously out, feeling better, knowing that the whiskey was taking hold now. He started walking across the slag with Carmen beside him and suddenly he laughed out loud. "Well, you're just one more that's got something on me," he said.

"Aw, Uncle Buck, it never would—"

"Understand," he said, "that makes us partners; it don't make me a victim."

She laughed, then, and caught him by his arm. She said, "All right, partner," and swung along beside him with a gay confidence in her step he'd never seen before. It gave him a quick disturbing thought that she was an orphan and so were her brothers and they must have felt alone except for each other. He'd see what could be done for the boys, he was thinking, when he heard Lota call. He looked up and around to find her in the dark

[300]

shadows beyond the waiting rooms. He forgot the orphans and guided Carmen at an angle across the yard.

Jeff and Lota were sitting on the top of a baggage truck with their legs dangling over the edge. Buck could barely see Lota's eyes when he reached the truck, but he could see that she was sitting on a sheet of brown paper. He knew, comfortably, that Jeff had thought of the paper and that he would insist on the girls taking it along so the plush seats wouldn't dirty their clothes.

"Got any more of that paper?" he asked.

Jeff started unwrapping a piece for them off a small neat square.

"Here, make this do," Jeff said, and punched Lota with his elbow. "Move your lunch box back a little so they can sit down."

"Take care of the lunch," Buck said. He put both hands on the baggage truck and made a small turning jump. "Whup," he grunted, and held out his hand to Carmen, who shook her head and jumped up by herself.

"Damned shame, that lunch," Buck said. "They won't eat it. It'll be thrown out less'n a wagon greasing out of town. A shoe-box lunch is too country nowadays."

Lota started to protest but Jeff cut her off.

"Reckon so. Anyhow, bananas and peanuts and candy pills will be a change for them."

"Both of you go to the devil," Lota said. "I notice, anyhow, neither one of you take a lunch in a shoe box. You have it packed at the hotel in a wicker hamper with an ice container. Even if you're just going out to the farm to see Mother."

Jeff leaned forward and looked across Lota at Buck.

"Got a message for you," he said. "Tom Easton and Charley Cope are taking their game chickens to the fights in Mexico City. Say they want a good poker player to go along."

"Why don't you go?"

"They'd pick me like a robin," Jeff said. "And besides, it was you they wanted."

"Not this time." Buck shook his head. "I'm going to start campaigning pretty quick, but if you'd like the trip, why, go ahead and I'll take care of anything that comes up here."

"Hearn plays a better hand than me." Jeff shrugged. "I'd rather see him go and win than me go and lose."

Buck felt Lota move suddenly and knew that she had jabbed Jeff with her elbow. He tightened his mouth and spoke flatly. "Hearn won't be going."

Lota jumped down quickly and smoothed her hands across her hips. "Think I hear it," she said loudly and stood listening with her hands in fists at her sides. Buck was silent, listening too, and he could barely sense Carmen moving beside him.

"There she comes," he said, suddenly, and somehow felt a small gratefulness inside him that he had heard it before Jeff or Carmen.

They were waiting close to the track when the engine fussed slowly by, fretting now and then with a spiteful hiss of steam. They were standing within three feet of the car door when it opened.

"Told you it'd stop right here," Jeff said. "Does it every time."

The car door suddenly folded inward and a businesslike Negro porter in a white coat lifted the metal flange and swung it up to the side to expose the steps. Then he stepped down to the ground with consciously dignified movements. He jerked out the small red ladder step and settled it with a flourish that was almost like dusting it off, before he straightened like a ramrod.

"Board, suh," he said without smiling or looking at them.

"You a preacher, boy?" Buck handed him a dollar.

"Nossuh, ef I is anything, I reckon it's a crapshooter."

"Well, boy, you take care of my womenfolks."

"I gotcha, suh."

"And here, if they don't eat this lunch, make 'em give it to you—fried chicken and cake."

"Now you's got me, boss."

Buck turned and caught Lota by both elbows and held her away from him a moment, looking down at her. She had started to cry a little.

"Female," he said, gently, and kissed her on one of her eyes.

"What about Hearn?" she whispered, then looked down and touched the top of her head to his chest.

"I'll do something about it," he said, "that's a promise."

Her voice was muffled against his shirt front.

"He just didn't think and he couldn't know how I—" She looked up suddenly and her eyes were brighter and the tears were fewer. "You know, though, don't you?"

"Board, suh." The porter's words were a warning.

Buck winked down at her and squeezed her elbows tighter.

"Get on the train," he said, "and make this as good a year as you'll ever have."

She kissed him quickly, holding him tight around the neck, and her lips were hard and fierce against his.

Buck watched until Lota and Carmen had turned from the platform and out of sight into the car, then he touched Jeff on the arm.

"Let's go," he said, thickly. "I don't like to wave folks off."

He could feel Jeff's eyes on him as they walked across to the car and he stepped carefully, not wanting to show that the whiskey was creeping up on him. His hand missed the handle of the door as he reached out for it and he looked up to find Jeff's eyes watching him soberly.

"Hmm," he said, and felt ashamed as he settled himself in the front seat. Jeff turned the key and smiled at him.

"Got a load on, haven't you?"

"I didn't drink no more'n it took."

"No more than what took?"

Buck slid lower in the seat and pulled his hat down over his eyes. He told him about Hearn, speaking tonelessly and briefly, looking through narrowed eyes at the sky that swept back over him. When he had finished, Jeff was silent until he had eased the car into the wide parking lot across the railroad tracks back of the hotel.

"I always knew Hearn didn't think like you and me," Jeff said. Then, speaking awkwardly, "But I don't reckon I ever figured he'd go that far." He got out of the car on his side and stood silent until Buck stepped carefully out and caught his arm before starting towards the rear entrance. He spoke hesitantly. "You got anything else in mind to—"

"Nothing," Buck said, flatly. "Not another damned thing. Just let 'im root hog or die." He clamped his jaw and didn't speak again until they had reached the small corner of the sample room where he felt at home and where he kept his books. He switched on a small overhead light and sat down with a sigh into the deep ragged seat of the rocking chair.

"Let's get a bottle back here," he said, and let his head drop backwards.

"Haven't you had enough?"

Buck rolled his head from side to side against the back of the chair. "Ain't no such thing as enough."

Jeff turned towards the lobby, picking his way through scattered chairs and cots and packing crates. Buck closed his eyes and welcomed the deep creeping drunkenness that spread faster and faster outwards from his stomach. He was almost asleep when Jeff came back, but he jerked his head sharply as Jeff opened the door of the icebox.

"Pour some water in mine," he said, slowly, and was proud that his words were distinct.

"Here's a note the clerk had." Jeff held it out to him. Buck didn't even turn his head.

"You read it. I'm tired. Read it out loud."

Jeff poured a drink for Buck first and put it in his hand, then he drank quickly, and wiped his lips on his shirt sleeve. His hands were wet, so he dried them by passing his hands under his armpits. He tore the envelope open and moved closer under the light.

"Dear Daddy," he read slowly, then stopped. He glanced at Buck with both eyes opening wider. He looked quickly at the end of the page, then back at Buck. Buck's face whitened slowly, but he didn't look at Jeff. His upper lip was a thin line, but his lower lip began to protrude. His hand shook a little, but he raised his glass steadily to his lips.

"Read on."

"Mother and I got in town this afternoon. She wants to see you and so do I. It seems funny to be writing to a father I've never seen and calling him 'Daddy,' and I know it must make you feel queer to read this. We'll be here most of the next two months because Grandpa is sick and is going to be operated on. You can get in touch with us at Grandpa's house. I hope you are feeling well."

Jeff's quiet voice stopped and he tossed the note to the small table with the scarred leather top. "That's all."

"How'd he sign?"

Jeff's mouth quirked.

"Your son, Amos."

Buck drank the last drop out of his glass and set it down on the floor carefully, then he grasped both arms of the chair and lurched to his feet.

"Amos," he said, as if he were spitting. "Goddamn. His name is Joseph Amos Bannon and out of all that she had to call him Amos after Grandpa Longshore."

"Want to answer it?" Jeff asked, softly.

Buck caught the table top in both of his hands and leaned far over it to keep his balance.

"Answer it?" he said, slowly, with a note of cunning and triumph oiling his tones. "Sure, I'll answer it. The way they answered me, and me standing there like a damn fool with a little glass pistol full of red candy and had to give it to a shine boy." He swayed and shook his head roughly, trying to clear his sight. "Goddammit, yes, I'll answer it—with the loudest silence they ever heard." He stood up straight and jerked his thumb towards the telephone.

"Get me Tom Easton on the line and then run tell those bellboys to start packing me up."

"What about your campaign?"

"Damn the campaign. If they want me they can get me. That's all the running I'll do."

Jeff called a number and waited quietly with the phone in his hand, then he spoke low into the mouthpiece. "Just a minute." He motioned Buck to sit down, but Buck shook his head. He leaned over and cupped the mouthpiece in his hand but refused the earpiece.

"Tom," he said loudly, "when are we going?" He looked up at Jeff for the answer. Jeff said, "Tuesday." Buck solemnly nodded at the telephone. "That ain't soon enough, though," he said. "We'll leave tomorrow on the first train to Montgomery." He looked back up at Jeff. "Hang up." Jeff dropped the receiver on the hook.

"Man," he said, "you're drunk as a goat."

Buck relaxed into the rocker and sighed and closed his eyes.

"I'm drunk," he said, "and I'll tell you how it feels. It's like when I was a boy lying on the bank of Beulah Creek, half-nigh asleep and barefooted with an acorn hung between my toes—too damned lazy to get up and not able to flip it out with my toes."

CHAPTER TWENTY-EIGHT

"Is that thing right?" Buck pointed at the date on the half-filled page of the dirty hotel register. The clerk glanced nervously at the calendar behind him, then smiled automatically. "To the minute, sir."

"Damn," Buck muttered as he signed in his precise, straight-up-and-down handwriting. "Sixty-one whole days and God knows how many nights." He placed the pen carefully back in its wire whorl rack and twirled the book around so the clerk could read it.

"Give me about an hour," he said, glancing at the big old clock over the desk, "then, have a car down front for me."

"Sorry, sir, no cars allowed." The clerk was studying the register with a puzzled frown. "An old city ordinance," he went on slowly, "on account of the girls at the college."

"A hack'll do," Buck said, crisply, "but I want a clean one with a dressed-up driver."

"In an hour," the clerk said, then looked around the small lobby with studied interest. He coughed behind his hand. "Uh, Mrs. Bannon, sir. She'll be outside, I suppose?"

Buck tossed his room key to a hovering bellboy and pointed to his two large suitcases. "I'll take the little one myself," he said, and nudged the small alligator hide valise with his foot. He turned back to the clerk and his face was blank although his eyes were half closed to hide laughter.

"*Quién sabe?*" he said, and his shoulders went up with his eyebrows. He turned to follow the bellboy upstairs without giving the clerk time to answer.

"If he wants any more Mexican talk," he was thinking, "I'll have to order ham and eggs." He followed the bellboy down a narrow unlit hall into a room that was surprisingly large, with huge casement windows. It was musty and damply chilly. Buck could tell the windows hadn't been opened in a long time. He glanced at the small fireplace where two hickory chunks with the bark still on them lay over several lightwood knots.

"Light that fire, boy," he said, "and open some of these windows. I want this room to smell as fresh as new ground." He pulled a small neat pack of new currency from his inside coat pocket and slid one of the bills out from under the band. "Here," he said, roughly, "when you get through with me you can keep the change."

The bellboy stood on his tiptoes and hunched his shoulders. He touched the bill only with his fingertips.

"Wheeoo!" he crooned, "little bitty baby Jesus."

Buck started unbuttoning the vest of his heavy dark suit.

"Keep the fire going till I get back. Have me some supper up here about eight o'clock. Two fried chickens, hot biscuits, plenty of butter, some little potatoes baked in the jacket, and lots of coffee."

"Boss, you's hongry."

"Fix a table for two," Buck went on, and tossed his coat over on the bed. "Straighten up the room after I'm gone, with clean towels, new soap, everything. And when you see my hack hit the front of this hotel tonight, scat up here ahead of me with ice and anything else you can think of."

"They calls me Blue Darter, boss."

"That's all," Buck said, shortly, and sat down to pull his shoes off. The boy started towards the door in a small happy cakewalk, but Buck called him back. "Another thing, get me a big bunch of flowers." He frowned, holding one foot in his hand. "And a suitbox packed full of sliced pound cake, still hot if you can find it." He dropped his foot and started on the other. "Reckon you can get flowers this time of year?"

"For this much money," the boy said, fervently, "I'd rob a fresh grave."

An hour and a half later, Buck's clumsy two-seater hack rolled swiftly behind a fast-trotting team of roans, through a heavy stone arch that was covered with ivy. Its rubber-rimmed wheels ground lightly over a driveway that sounded in the dark as if it had been thickly padded throughout most of its curving passage under heavy oak limbs.

"Must have toted pine straw out of the woods," Buck thought as the carriage swept stylishly up in front of a large grey-stone building whose white-pillared porch jutted like a firm chin onto a lawn that was still green and thick. The carriage tilted far over when Buck stepped out on the narrow iron footrest and its springs creaked as if they'd never been greased.

Buck said, "Just hold your horses," to the driver and leaned over to reach inside again. He balanced the long rectangular suitbox and its load of pound cake, still smelling hot, carefully flat on one arm, while with the other hand he caught up the small bunch of flowers wrapped in thin white paper. Last, he hooked two fingers of the hand that held the flowers into the handle of the alligator valise.

His face was red from exertion and he was straining to balance the box of cake when he reached the porch and stood between the two false white columns that flanked the heavy spotless doors. He shifted his feet and frowned with concentration trying to twist the knob of the doorbell without putting down either of his burdens.

"Whew!" he said, finally, through clenched teeth, "that got it."

The narrow rectangles of glass on either side of the door suddenly flashed brighter and Buck heard quick precise steps tapping towards the entrance. He held himself very straight as he heard the hand touch the inside handle, then suddenly the wide door swung open and he faced a glare that hurt his eyes. It seemed to come from no one large light, but from many tiny bulbs contained in a single ceiling fixture. Its glass prisms tinkled drearily and danced the light around the long wide hall. He didn't see anyone at first, and leaned a little closer, ducking his head to peer down the hall at the deep blue-figured rug and the heavy old hall tree which matched every chair and small table lining the panelled walls.

"Good evening, sir." Buck started slightly. The voice had been rich and low and the pronunciation of each word was careful, as if it had been carved out of the alphabet. He glanced to the right and his eyes narrowed when he saw a small very black Negro girl of about twenty, dressed in a shiny black uniform with a white collar.

"Was that you talking?" he asked, suspiciously.

"Yes, indeed, sir."

"Hmm." Buck put his tongue in one cheek and looked her up and down carefully.

"You wanted to see someone, sir?"

"Hunh?" Buck was still staring at her shiny black face, with a puzzled frown. "Oh, yes. I'm Mr. Bannon, and I want to see Mrs. Bannon."

"I'm afraid there's no Mrs. Bannon here, sir. This hall is under the supervision of Mrs. Darby."

Buck shifted the weight of the box of cake and spoke irritably. "Well, get Mrs. Darby, then. Maybe she'll know my wife."

The black face didn't change expression. "She's at dinner, sir, but I'll find out if she can see you." The door started to close, gently. Buck pushed his shoulder against it.

"I'll wait inside," he said, and his mouth tightened as he pushed into the hall. She turned around with a shrug that was almost invisible. He watched her walk down the hall towards a double sliding door opening into a room from which came the low murmur of many voices and the subdued plink of silver striking china. He watched the trim black-clad hips switch as the maid turned into the dining room. He mumbled, "Talks like Judge Alford, but they'll never educate the wiggle out of her rear end." He took two steps nearer the room, trying to listen and perhaps pick Lota's deep tones out of the medley, then suddenly the voices stopped, as if a thread had been cut. Quickly, Buck turned towards a small table and slid the box of cake off his arm onto the marble top, careful not to disturb a clumsy-looking vase whose varied colors were nearly hidden under a sheen of lacquer. He placed his valise cautiously in the shadows behind the fancywork legs, then took off his hat and faced in the direction of the dining room with the flowers held at a stiff angle across his new high-buttoned vest. He heard a chair scrape.

He knew from the first faintness of the footsteps that they didn't belong to Lota. Lota walked with firm sureness, taking long strides to get where she was going in the easiest and shortest way. These were older steps, and slower, and there was a lisp of sound as if one foot were being dragged. He was surprised at first sight of Mrs. Darby. She was short and stout like a pouter pigeon, not the slim and elegant old lady he had expected from Lota's letter. She wore a dark-blue velvet dress that touched the floor and hid her feet. He knew suddenly that she wore the dress

[309]

long to cover her lameness. She limped just enough to give her a rolling gait, and to make her head of grey hair bob from side to side as she walked. She was smiling, faintly and politely.

"Good evening," she said, acknowledging his presence with a question tingeing her voice. Her blue eyes were blank and her round chin jutted as stubbornly as the porch.

"Didn't mean to disturb you, ma'am," he said. "I'm Buck Bannon and I've come to see my wife."

Mrs. Darby glanced back over her shoulder as if she were afraid someone would hear. When she faced around again, the smile had changed to a frown of warning and her lips were pursed in a soundless "Shhh!" She gestured towards the doors at the other side of the hall, then led the way into a small cluttered sitting room which she lighted by twisting a knob switch on the wall. She limped over to a stiff-looking chair with a needlepoint seat, then nodded to Buck.

Buck looked around for a chair large enough, then he thought of the flowers. He held them out with a small jerky bow.

"They'll look good in that shiny vase out yonder, ma'am."

"How very nice," Mrs. Darby said and took them. She fumbled around with her good foot until she found the bulge in the faded carpet and dimly Buck heard a bell ringing far back in the house. He watched her, in silence, wondering why she didn't open the paper and look at the flowers, until the little Negro maid stood stiffly beside her mistress's chair.

"Put these in the hall, please," Mrs. Darby held them out with hardly a glance at them or the maid.

The maid turned to leave and Buck glanced first at Mrs. Darby's frozen face, then at the maid's stiff-held back.

"Wait a minute," he said, abruptly, and Mrs. Darby's eyes opened wide at his tone. The maid turned around. "There's a box of cake on the table out there," he went on. "Take it in to the girls and let them finish up on it."

The maid looked at Mrs. Darby, trying to confirm the order without asking a question. Mrs. Darby nodded slightly, then turned to Buck. He sat down.

"Mr. Bannon," she said, folding her plump hands over her lap, "there are some rules here with which you are doubtless unfamiliar." She coughed as if to invite an answer.

Buck's face showed bewilderment and, finally, concern.

"Lota?" he questioned hesitantly. "I thought she was doing—"

Mrs. Darby laughed nervously. "No, no, no, Mr. Bannon. Lota is a splendid student. Rather—ah—boyish at times, but on the whole quite one of our finest young ladies."

Buck looked relieved. "Well, then," he said, and smiled broadly, "not much use in me knowing the rules, unless you're figuring to enroll me."

Mrs. Darby's face froze and her chin lifted higher. She just looked at him.

He coughed slightly and felt his face flush. "Hmm," he said.

"Mr. Bannon," she said, speaking distinctly, with tolerance, "my position is at all times one of great responsibility and trust. Now, I may say, one of my duties has become rather—ah—delicate, and I— Well, to be frank, Mr. Bannon, I find myself unable to relish instructing you as if you were one of the young men who sometimes are allowed to call."

Buck raised himself in his chair and tightened his grip on the armrests.

"Instruct me?"

Mrs. Darby drew a deep breath and closed her eyes for a second, then she shook her head and opened her eyes again. She didn't face Buck. "Our young ladies," she said, in a voice that shook a little but was growing defiant, "are allowed to have male visitors only in the presence of one of the members of the staff." She cleared her throat slightly, then went on as if she were reciting, "They will at all times conduct themselves in a manner in keeping with the highest traditions of Clifton Hall. They will not—"

"Wait a minute," Buck broke in. He pulled his chair slightly closer and spoke earnestly. "Here, I'm not going to do anything wrong. This girl's my wife."

Mrs. Darby stirred restlessly and kept her face averted.

"They will not leave Clifton Hall unless their attire is approved by faculty members," she continued doggedly. "They will not ride in automobiles under any conditions, although they may be allowed by senior faculty members to drive slowly in an approved public vehicle, driven by a servant acceptable to Clifton Hall."

She paused for breath and glanced quickly at Buck.

He sat very still, straight up in his chair, with his head cocked on one side. His eyes were narrowed and his lower lip protruded. He seemed to be considering.

"Well, that's all right," he said, quickly, and nodded. "I don't mind you being around when I see her and I've got a hack outside with a colored boy driving. Said his name was Numbers."

Mrs. Darby's face smoothed out and she looked at Buck with gratitude in her eyes.

"Numbers is well known here. He is entirely acceptable."

"Whew!" Buck breathed deeply and leaned back. "Now will you ring for Lota to come. Please," he added quickly.

Mrs. Darby smiled gently and shook her head slowly but positively.

"No student may leave the table until meals are concluded, except in cases of sickness or emergency."

Buck lifted up both hands, then let them fall on his knees.

"That's for kids," he said, and smiled with an effort. "Lota's a woman."

"Mr. Bannon!" Mrs. Darby's voice was sharp. "Our rules are for one and all and in the eyes of Clifton Hall, Lota is still a—" She broke off, and red showed spottily through the powder on her cheekbones. She looked at a point on the wall over his right shoulder and her voice was stifled. "She must wait until coffee time."

"Hmm." Buck stood up slowly and jerked his head once in exasperation. He took two quick strides towards the hall, then stopped and turned back around. "You mean—?" He came closer and bent over. "Mrs. Darby," he said carefully, "I don't know how I got mixed up with you." He heard a step behind him and whirled to see the small Negro maid. "Or her either," he went on, "but—"

"The young ladies are opening the cake," the maid said clearly and bent her knees in a modified curtsey. "They wanted it with their—"

Quick, long-striding footsteps sounded hollow coming from the big hall and Buck held up his hand for silence and cocked his head. He listened with his eyes gleaming, then turned quickly to Mrs. Darby.

"Guess who that is," he said, softly. He turned to the door as the footsteps came faster.

"Buck!" He heard her voice before he saw her and the urgently husky tones made him draw his breath in sharply.

He didn't answer, but kept looking out into the hall until she came in view. She hesitated at the door, afraid she had been mistaken, then she saw him. Her eyes opened wide at first, as if she had gasped, then they narrowed and she walked slowly towards him with her arms coming up.

"That cake," she said. "It had to be you." Her hands touched his waist and slid around under his coat, close and familiar, as if she'd never been gone. She held her face tight against his chest as he put his arms around her, and he could feel her shaking slightly. He rubbed his lips into the high-piled black hair, holding her closer and trying to smell and taste and feel her all at once. He didn't notice the silence until he heard Mrs. Darby gasp.

"Lota!" Her voice was sharp and somehow frightened. Lota didn't answer. Buck raised his head and turned it lazily to look back over his shoulder. Mrs. Darby was sitting upright in her chair, stiffly, and her face was stricken. She twisted her hands in her lap. "Lota," she said again, louder this time.

Buck held Lota's head tighter against his chest and looked Mrs. Darby in the eyes. He smiled slowly, then deliberately licked his lips. He turned his head back to Lota. He caught the knot of hair at the back of her head with one hand and pulled it back until her lips rose to meet his. Her eyes were closed. He kissed her, carefully and hard, and as her hands slid further up his back under his coat, he twisted her sideways until the side of her face was in view of Mrs. Darby.

Mrs. Darby stamped her foot.

"Lota," she ordered loudly, "open your eyes."

Buck raised his head and drew a deep breath. Lota looked up at him and her mouth was full and soft with the lips half parted. He pulled her around and started walking towards the door with his arm still around her waist. He didn't look back as Mrs. Darby scrambled to her feet with a choking sound. They walked straight towards the open-mouthed Negro maid until she stepped quickly to one side; then they turned down into the hall towards the front door.

Lota walked beside him in a musing, almost dazed silence until Buck pulled the front door inwards and the first cold breath of air struck her. Then she looked up sharply, frowning.

"Where are we going?"

"Hotel Bristol," Buck said, flatly.

Lota's eyes widened and flickered from his face over his shoulder, and Buck heard Mrs. Darby's limping footsteps come to a quick stop. In the small silence he could hear her trying to quiet her hurried breathing. He turned Lota so that she faced him, caught both of her upper arms in his hands and held her close. He stared down at the top of her head until she pulled slightly away and dropped her head back to look up at him with eyes that were puzzled and somehow begging.

"Buck, I—" She caught her lower lip in her teeth and her eyes left his face again. She looked unseeingly at the large knot of his blue tie, and her head went slightly from side to side.

"Do I have to kiss you again?" he asked, softly.

She looked back up, then, and her smile was small and rueful.

"That would do it," she said. She tightened her lips in quick decision and caught her breath sharply. She moved to one side so she could see the house mother, who waited in silence, hardly breathing.

"I'm sorry, Mrs. Darby." She touched Buck's arm. "I'll go get my coat."

"You'll be warm enough." He glanced down for the first time at her long heavy blue skirt and the severely plain white shirt-waist with black bow tie. He frowned, and she laughed at him. "Uniform," she said, and flicked the skirt with her finger.

"Lota!" Mrs. Darby's voice was warning. Lota looked up almost with surprise in her eyes at the bite in her tone. "Yes, Mrs. Darby?"

"You know our rules?" Lota glanced up at Buck, then back to Mrs. Darby. She nodded. Mrs. Darby shook her head, slowly, appealingly. "Don't go," she said simply. "Don't you see, you are the first young married—uh—lady we have allowed in Clifton Hall, and if you go like this—" She shook her head sadly.

Buck snapped his fingers. "Forgot something." He shouldered

[314]

past Lota and Mrs. Darby. "Excuse me." He started towards the small marble-topped table which now held his flowers and stooped over to feel behind it. He heard a small scuffling sound and glanced quickly down the hall. A head of bright red hair tried to pull itself back into the dining room without being seen. Suddenly, then, the red hair burst protestingly out into the hall, pushed from behind by several pairs of hands and followed by a flood of giggling laughter. Buck stood up and stared. "Well, I'll be damned, if I didn't forget my own niece," he muttered.

Carmen balanced precariously on one foot for a second, not looking at him but appealing with her eyes back towards the dining-room door. There was something wild, yet pathetically shy about her, and Buck felt the quick surge of pity he always felt for her. He began to walk towards her with the same slow deliberation he would use trying to harness an unbroken colt.

"Hello, partner," he said, and held his hand out.

Her small green eyes flared gratefully and her wide mouth relaxed its embarrassed tightness. He put his arm around her shoulders and hugged her tightly, looking distastefully down at a uniform exactly like Lota's. The laughter from the dining room stopped. He glanced up. About thirty girls tried to crowd into the doorway, all different sizes and shapes, but all disturbingly alike in their uniforms. Several of them in front were stooping so the others could see over them. Two or three were still chewing and some of their mouths were open. They were all staring at Buck. He looked down at Carmen, wondering why they stared, then suddenly he jerked his arm from around her shoulders.

"She's kinfolks," he said, quickly.

They laughed and Buck felt his face flushing. He patted Carmen on the shoulder, awkwardly. "I'll see you tomorrow," he said, and turned back towards the front door without looking at the girls.

"Hey, mister," one of them called. "Thank you for the cake."

Buck looked back over his shoulder and started to speak when two of the girls, pushed from behind, fell on their hands and knees, screaming and laughing. Then the rest of them crowded through the doorway.

"Good God," he muttered, "let me get out of this place." He hurried to the table and quickly dragged his small valise from behind it. When he looked up, Mrs. Darby was walking towards him, patting the air with her fat little hands.

"Girls, girls! Are these my young ladies?" She limped past Buck, as if she didn't see him, talking all the way. "Finger bowls, girls. Finger bowls. Come, Carmen. Stomach in, girls, walk from the hips."

Buck watched her herding them through into the dining room, then he turned quickly around to see Lota leaning against the front door jamb laughing with both hands on her hips. He went towards her with long strides, a small anticipating curve turning up his lips, and the lower lip protruding slightly.

"College," he said, disgustedly, and caught her by one arm and swung the door wide. "Let's get out of here before she remembers us." He hurried her down the wide steps, taking two at a time, and rushed her, gasping and laughing, to the hired hack.

"Here, boy," he said to the mournful Negro in the too-large black coat. "Come down from there." He slid another bill off the flat pack in his coat pocket and crammed it into the bony black hand. "I'm stealing your hack. It'll be at the Hotel Bristol, out front."

The driver started climbing slowly out, mumbling to himself.

"I knowed it, I knowed it. Minute I seed that lip hung out. I knowed it."

Buck caught Lota by the waist from behind and almost threw her up into the driver's seat. He pushed her farther over and bounced himself in with one foot on the small iron footrest. He jerked out the whip and unwrapped the reins and rattled them over the backs of the horses. The team reared a little in surprise.

"Git," he said, and slapped their rumps lightly with the whip. Then he turned to look down at Lota.

She was hunched sideways on the stiff and lumpy leather seat, staring wordlessly back towards Clifton Hall's white pillars. He felt a sudden rush of shame and reached over to put the whip back into the socket. He touched her arm, wondering why he should hesitate.

"Are you sorry?" he said, just loud enough for his words to carry over the thud of the horses' hooves and the creak of harness.

She straightened in the seat without looking at him for a moment; then, abruptly, she put both of her feet up on the dash-board's shiny rim and slid lower into the crook of his arm. She raised her head and her eyes were very large and shiny in the shadows of her lashes. She shook her head and he smiled down at her. He felt with his feet to find the little valise in the foot, then nodded downwards at it for her to look.

"If that same bunch of mullets is still playing poker next year, I'll make another trip and build you a college bigger'n this one."

CHAPTER TWENTY-NINE

W<small>INTER'S</small> <small>FINE RAIN</small> stitched the darkness of very early morning, and Buck sat quietly by the fire, wondering what it was that woke him so early nowadays. It hadn't been a noise and Lota hadn't stirred. She still slept like a tired child, asprawl on her stomach with the pillow pushed against the bedstead and her head burrowed up into its softness.

He wondered if it could be the quietness, then shook the thought away—he'd been doing it for a long time, both at home and throughout the trip to Mexico. It was like a sudden fear, waking abruptly and staring into darkness. Now it had become an old familiar feeling and was hardly fear any longer; but he never woke that way without the same wide-eyed start, almost as if he were expecting something. Something that never came.

He reached out, quietly, so as not to awaken Lota and laid a fresh pine knot on the fire. Then he hunched closer and watched the pitch ooze out, as if it were the most important thing in the world to see that first gaspy catch of flame tasting the fatness of a lightwood knot. It popped loudly and tossed a small half-red and half-grey chunk of oak heart onto the hearth near his bare feet. He jerked them back and without thinking said, "Whup!" out loud.

"Hunh?" Lota spoke sleepily with her voice muffled in the pillow. He didn't answer. He watched her, holding his breath unconsciously to help her stay asleep. She felt out dazedly with her hand, running it over the spot where he had been sleeping, until suddenly she turned her head sideways and opened her eyes. He could see them shining in the come and go of light from the fire.

"What you doing?" she mumbled.

"Mighty little a man can do alone this time of night."

She sat up slowly, yawning and pushing her hair out of her face with her wrist. She pulled her legs up and hugged her knees and tried to fix the blankets so they would cover her shoulders. Her knees made a crackling sound and she said, "Ooh! I'm getting old."

Buck grunted and spoke tonelessly.

"A little age won't hurt in the company you keep."

Lota's eyes showed quick concern and she leaned over, trying to read his face in the firelight. He kept the profile turned to her. Carefully, he dipped the pointed end of a slender too-shiny metal poker into a small boiling of black pitch on top of the fat knot. Lota's voice came hesitant and questioning.

"Buck. If you're worried about me leaving school. I mean— Well, don't. I can go back some time." She smiled ruefully. "Maybe someday when you won't be wanting me around so much."

Buck turned his face away from the fire so he could see her, and blinked away the little night of blindness that came of staring into the fire. He smiled back at her crookedly.

"It's not that. I just wake up, kinda. Got to be a right friendly feeling."

"It wasn't always that way?"

He shook his head and didn't answer.

Lota threw the blankets away from her shoulders. "Well, Buck—" she said, then stopped and swung her feet and legs off the edge of the bed. She stood up quickly, pulling her nightgown straight from where it had twisted to ride her right hip. She came closer to the fire, bringing one blanket with her, wrapping it around herself until she could sit on a small footstool beside Buck with her bare feet on the hearth that was powdery grey with ashes. She put her arm across his knees and hugged them tight without looking up. "Well," she said again, comfortably, "if it wasn't always that way, what way was it?"

Buck rumpled his hand through her hair from back to front. "Nothing for you to worry about."

She looked fiercely at him over her left shoulder and blew out of one corner of her mouth to move the hair that had fallen across her eyes.

"If I'm not a woman, dammit, take me back to school."

He slid his hand around her head and cupped her chin and pulled her head back until he could see her eyes, seeming twice as big upside down.

"You're a woman, all right, but for God's sake don't hunt trouble. It'll come."

She kept staring at him, backwards, until his eyes wouldn't

meet hers any longer. "Aw, hell," he said, and pushed her head upright so she wouldn't be looking at him.

"It makes me feel like a fool," he said, slowly, "but it started with Dr. Tolleson and a little verse he said. Something about I'd been chasing the wrong thing, that I'd wasted my good years and it was time to change. My head started working like a boiling of syrup. Sometimes I'd get a feeling like what the hell I'd had a good time, but mostly it kept saying over and over that I'd swapped years for minutes. What I thought was rich was poor and what I'd felt was good was bad and it began to eat in me like a shanker and all because of a damned little doctor that hadn't read to Salts."

Lota twisted until she was on her knees with her hands on his thighs, looking at him with puzzled watchful eyes.

"I got friendly with it, though, down in Mexico. About this time of night, I thought I could hear something I hadn't heard in thirty years. I heard the corn grow. Did you know you could hear corn growing? Just about dusk when I was a kid I used to lie out between the rows and there wouldn't be a breath of wind and I could hear it cooling off and crackling and not a blade would swish, but you'd swear you could see it stretching up and hear the ears firming and the stalks straining." He stopped as if he were embarrassed and stared into the fire for a moment, then he went on awkwardly. "I felt better after that, but I never wake up without wondering if I really have wasted all my years and all my work." He stabbed abruptly, almost viciously, into the fire with the poker. "It never does any good, though. I wouldn't know where to start if I wanted to change."

Lota's eyes were warm and wide and seemed to be staring past him. "Don't change," she said, simply. "Those pouting little men envy you straddling a whole town—and when their belled cats of women see you, they envy me. And I like it." Something sly crept into her eyes and she cut them sideways towards his face. "Besides, I know some things they don't know."

He raised his eyebrows until they came to heavy points, questioning her.

"I know about the boys you've sent to school," she said, with a veil of triumph lying over her tones. "And I know Mrs. Spooner, about them not paying you any rent for years because he's worked down, and the youngest girl never will be right."

He stirred and cleared his throat irritably.

"I know," she said, again, speaking very low, in a voice that was almost a shamed whisper, "that when you get ready you fasten your hands upon your heart."

"What kind of talk—?"

Lota laid her head down on his knee.

"That's a poem I learned this year. It fits you a whole lot better than the one the doctor said. After you figure it out."

"Say it."

She shook her head. He leaned over and pushed her away from his knee. "Stand up," he said, huskily. She stood in front of the fire with her head still inclined a little towards him so that a long heavy rope of black hair touched at the corner of one eye and hung below her shoulder. "Now, say it," he said.

She waited without looking up and he felt again an old thickness in his throat as he saw the slim curves of her strong body outlined against the fire through her thin nightgown. She raised her head and clasped her hands behind her, unconsciously, as if she were a child reciting in class. Her words came slowly at first, then faster.

> "Could man be drunk forever
> With liquor, love or fights,
> Lief should I rouse at morning
> And lief lie down of nights.
>
> "But men at whiles are sober
> And think by fits and starts,
> And if they think, they fasten
> Their hands upon their hearts." *

He didn't take his eyes off her face. Even after she had slid back again to her seat beside his knee, he tasted his memory for the sound of her voice as it had been, warm and flexible, clear as the morning call of a quail. Slowly, then, he stood up and put both hands on the mantelpiece and leaned his head between his arms, staring down at the hearth. He tried to catch the words

* From *Last Poems,* by A. E. Housman. Copyright, 1922, by Henry Holt and Company.

again, trying first one and then the other, as he had seen his mother fit bright scraps for color and shape in a quilt. Liquor, love or fights, the words would come and nothing would follow but confusing memories of corn whiskey drunk from a common dried gourd near the boiling spring with its dancing grains of sand—or Lota, and he'd grasp the mantel harder to keep from turning to touch her—or fights; that time he'd broken Coot Harper's arm. Then, timidly, the words began to shape themselves into patterns and fall away until he could get the meaning, and slowly an undertone began to beat in his brain—"they fasten their hands upon their hearts."

"There never was time before," he said, suddenly, huskily, in the silence. Lota didn't answer. He turned around and leaned his back against the mantel, feeling for it with his shoulder blades.

"Maybe that is me," he said, fiercely yet defensively. "I don't know. I never knew anything but work and scheme and try to live. Do you know what that means—what it is to never know where you quit being a boy and get to being a man? Do you know what it means, how it feels, to have so few good memories of being a boy, that the ones you do have stand out like lights on a Christmas tree? Chop cotton through the sun with a limber-handled hoe that whips and never hits the right place. Shovel manure into a wagon bed and shovel it out again on a garden that's got to be fed before it can feed you. Then plow in more of the man than the manure. Do you know what it means to take a chance and leave before your hands get crooked in a mold to fit a plow stock—to leave and not care, just because nothing can be worse than what you've got?" He was silent, breathing deeply and holding his teeth tightly together. "Never any time for anything," he went on, more calmly. "The next milestone always looks like the most important one in the world, then there's always another, and always a short cut to the next one." He smiled wryly. "The short cuts get rough sometimes, but you take them in the scramble, because you've got to get on top and stay there. By God, there just hasn't been enough time to get sober, until —" He clamped his lips together and turned quickly to face the mantel again.

"Until what?"

He breathed out slowly, trying to relax the hurt in his throat.

"Until now, I reckon." His shoulders rose in a small shrug. "Or could be, if I knew where to start. A man can't sweat and think pretty at the same time. And when those pretty thoughts finally come, he's apt to be out of practice grabbing at whatever he's going to fasten his hands on."

Lota kept her eyes on his face, and for a long moment her parted lips didn't close. "Now I feel like a fool," she said, softly. "I shouldn't have told you about it. Lord knows, I'm not fool enough to love a man for what he is and then try to change him."

He didn't turn around.

"But what if you did?" he said, urgently. "What do other men do?"

"They put chimes in a church," she said, practically.

"Hell, I've done—" He stopped and swung around quickly and stared down at her. She grinned up at him.

"That's why I said it."

"Wait a minute." He held his hand out and his brow wrinkled thoughtfully. He chewed on his lower lip, looking at her but not seeing her. He nodded slowly and stepped carefully around her and walked over to the bed and sat down on its edge. He felt under it, reaching between his widespread knees, watching her with a slightly cruel smile. He pulled out the small alligator valise and stepped back to the chair in front of the fire. He clasped the bag between his knees and started opening it.

"Know what's in here?" He laughed at her puzzled frown. "I'd have told you before but—" He winked at her. "That nightgown got my mind off my business." He jerked the bag open suddenly and turned it upside down over her lap. Small packets of green bills tumbled out, all neatly stacked and counted and wrapped around the middle. Lota gasped. She reached down and picked up one pack. She held it closer to the fire and her lips trembled reading the figures.

"Good God A'mighty!" she said, and dropped it. She stared down at the pile of currency in her lap and on the floor. Once she looked up at Buck and swallowed loudly and began to fumble blindly with the package. "Where—?" The words came feebly and she shook her head and just looked.

He laughed, fully, throwing his head back and stretching out his legs on both sides of her. "Alabama, Florida, Mississippi,

Louisiana, Texas and Mexico," he said, reciting the words, "and back again—from anybody that had more money than they had sense." He leaned over, speaking confidentially, "Why some of those fools don't know better'n to let a man study their discards."

She didn't answer, but looked back down at the money and rubbed the back of her hand across her lips, slowly. Then her head rose, quick and alert. She began to pack the money back into the bag, feverishly, counting bundles as she packed.

"I know what let's do," she said between counts. "Let's—"

"Wait a minute," he interrupted. "You'll do all right without that—and so will all the others." His voice dropped lower and his words came more slowly. "This is for something else—kind of a crutch till I can get my hands fastened where they belong."

Lota jerked her hand away from the money and her face was suddenly frightened and pained.

"Not money, Buck?"

He touched her jaw with a gentle fist.

"Not just money, but nearly everything, good or bad, costs money. This will easy build something that a lot of folks have been wanting around home."

Lota's eyes widened and she caught at his knee with strong fingers.

He nodded. "Unh-hunh. The opera house."

She pulled herself closer and higher until her forehead would rub hard against his chest and the satchel fell on the floor. Some of the money spilled out, unnoticed.

"You didn't need to change," she said with her voice muffled. She pulled herself higher against him. "Buck. Buck. Buck. I'm so proud, it's like excitement." She pulled away to look at him. "Mostly because you thought of it." She tucked her head back against his chest and for a little while she was quiet and still; then, with his hands on her sides under her arms, he could feel her body slowly stiffening and pulling away and he could tell without seeing her face that she was thinking. She looked up, thoughtfully, and her lip was caught between her teeth. "I wouldn't miss it for the world. Not even for college." She thought again, frowning, and nodded slowly with her lips curving into a smile that relished her words before she said them.

"I'm going to wear white satin, cut real low, and white gloves up past my elbows."

Buck's mouth opened slightly and he held his head on one side, puzzled.

"At the dedication," she said, patiently, "when you make the speech."

CHAPTER THIRTY

He KNEW something was wrong. He knew it by the dead
leaves rustling before the wind across the yard, scuttling on their
five-pronged legs around and over each other like lifeless and
dried brown crabs. He had felt it earlier in the day—as the small
engine first hesitated at the wooden bridge, then snorted and
trudged on across the flooding Chattahoochee. An hour's ride
from Aven, he had felt it stronger. Now, he knew it. She would
have had the sanded yard swept until nothing showed but the
short slanting scratches that followed the stroke of a homemade
yard broom. The cold warning had been in his chest during the
screaming baggage hunt at the Aven station. Throughout the
short ride out to the farm, his mind had boiled for failing to let
anyone know he was coming and his eyes had worried over Lota's
face as she drove—wondering if she felt it, too. Now, though—the
yard wasn't right, hadn't been swept since a rooster's jerky strut
had left a wake of starfish patterns in the coarse dry sand. He
could feel it stronger in the late afternoon chill—could sense
it in the lonely winter's sound of a farmer calling "Soo-pig" across
the narrow swamp that bordered the big field. Jeanie Bannon was
down and something inside said, "Soon." He could hear the
Negro hands at the cane mill near the seed house laughing and
hollering, "Look out, nigguh," and he knew there were no white
folks at the mill. Then, suddenly, a sweet and steamy fragrance
billowed around the house from the old-fashioned syrup kettle
—a homesick odor, just as train smoke and burning leaves and
ham frying far away were lonesome smells—and he could feel
it stronger.

"She's bad off," he said, hoarsely, and cleared his throat, not
looking at Lota as he stepped out of the car and started across the
yard. He heard the door open behind him and knew she was
following, but he kept his eyes on the house as if he expected it
to tell him before he could get inside.

The front door opened just before his lifted foot came down
on the step. Mr. Misstledine stepped out and shut the door behind him quickly to keep the cold from slipping in. He came
down the steps, slowly and watchfully, long and too thin in a

faded pair of overalls with the jumper buttoned high around his reddened neck. His narrow face was mournful and his eyes didn't meet Buck's.

"How is she?"

Mr. Misstledine reached inside his jumper and scratched his chest.

"Ailin'," he said, carefully.

"I don't see the doctor's car anywhere."

Mr. Misstledine shook his head slowly.

"Won't have nairn. Said she don't need no help to die."

"God Almighty!" Buck started up the steps and past the old tenant. "Have you fools run her crazy, too?"

Mr. Misstledine gulped and his Adam's apple jerked briefly into sight above his jumper collar. "She ain't in there."

Buck stopped and looked back over his shoulder with his mouth tightening and his eyes questioning.

"Naw." Mr. Misstledine shook his head. "She was out back at my place when she was took yesterday and nothin' would do but she was goin' to stay there." He twisted his neck in his collar, avoiding Buck's eyes. "Sweet Wife," he said, apologetically, "she ain't left her a minute hardly, 'cept to gether eggs, and your sister Millie's out there now. She run me up here."

Buck jumped down the steps in a hurry, talking as he went.

"The whole world's gone to hell, leaving a dying woman in a place like that."

Mr. Misstledine's watery eyes closed for a second, then he leaned over to spit in the ragged border of dead zinnias.

"Hit 'uz good enough for me an' Sweet Wife to live in," he said. He spat again, harder. "By God," he added, tersely.

Buck brushed past Lota without a word and strode quickly around the corner of the house, muttering. Lota followed him silently, watching his hands clench and unclench, until he reached the warped and weather-greyed door. He looked back over his shoulder, then, with his eyes wide, wondering and somehow hurting. He turned the knob and pushed, but the door didn't open. He rapped lightly with the tips of his fingers, holding his head close to the door, listening and looking back at Lota. He heard someone inside take two quick steps and heard the soft scrape of a chair being moved. The door opened quietly a few inches and he could see Millie's face, grave and strained, with watchful blue eyes warning him to quiet.

"Asleep?" He formed the word with his lips, and tried to peer past her into the dimness of the small room. Millie nodded and looked back over her shoulder. She opened the door wider and started to slip out.

"Who's that?" The words came suddenly, almost startling in the quiet, and the muscles in Buck's arms jerked. The voice had been thin and tired, with none of its old vibrance behind it.

"It's Buck, Mother." Millie pulled the door open for Buck and Lota to enter. Buck stooped needlessly and sidled his shoulders through the doorway, feeling cramped and too large for the cabin. He was glad to see a bright blaze sucking hungrily up the blackened and leaning chimney. It was the only light, but it rippled in waves across the room to the wide cherry-wood bed to wash the shadows away and find Jeanie Bannon's grained cheeks.

"Hey, boy," she said, and fumbled with the pillows back of her head, trying to raise herself.

Buck walked slowly over to the bed, straining to get his eyes used to the gloom, trying hard to see the old Jeanie Bannon—with black eyes snapping and firm lips pulled often enough away from fine strong teeth in a laugh that used all of her body. He couldn't find that Jeanie Bannon at first. He could see her eyes all right, still black and shining like chinquapins in moonlight, but they were bedded down in flesh that sagged and folded. He tried to keep his face from showing his thoughts, wondering with a sense of racing shock if she could have aged so much in two months. Or if she had been aging so gradually he'd never noticed until it got ahead of him while he was away. He made himself smile and pushed one of his knuckles down lightly on the back of her thin bony hand. He could feel the veins, fine and too fragile, standing out like pale-green, new-growth curls on a creeper.

"Here," he said, roughly gentle, "they said you'd got sick."

The eyes brightened and for a second her wrinkled and pursed mouth tightened as if she were going to smile. Then she slyly turned her eyes up towards him.

"Well," she said, slowly, "if I get any worse, I won't argue about it."

The eyes flared bright again as she said it and her teeth showed in a soundless chuckle.

Buck felt pride flare in his chest along with the hard ache of grief—pride that it was his mother who could poke fun at dying. He was fumbling with his mind for words when she jerked her head sideways.

"Drag up a chair."

He hooked his foot under the front rung of a light store-bought rocker and pulled it nearer. He eased into it, grateful that its low seat would bring him closer to her, but hoping the light wasn't good enough for her to read his face by. He heard Lota speak without knowing what the words were and realized that he'd forgotten her and Millie, standing by the fire. He looked up at Lota and she smiled back at him. She came over to the bed and leaned over to kiss Jeanie Bannon on the forehead.

"Hello, Mother."

"Now, they ought not to have got you home." She frowned and tossed her head fretfully. "You'll be too long out of school."

Lota laughed out loud and the sound of it shocked Buck. He looked up at her almost in anger at first, then he saw that her eyes weren't laughing, and he felt a whispering of thankfulness inside. He leaned closer to the bed and grinned at his mother.

"Lota got kicked out," he said. "For going to bed with a man."

Jeanie Bannon's brow furrowed quickly and her breath came in sharply. She looked up at Lota for a second, then she turned her eyes on Buck. They were both still laughing. Slowly the lines eased out of her frown and she nodded eagerly in understanding. She began to chuckle comfortably and wriggled her body lower in the bed.

"Tell me about it."

Buck told her the story. Millie came over and leaned against the foot of the bed and Lota moved around to stand behind Buck with her hands resting lightly on his shoulders. At first Buck kept his eyes carefully on his mother's face, straining to say words that would please her. Then, so gradually he hardly noticed it, the sickroom constraint disappeared. He could lean back in his chair and catch Lota's hand in his and cross his legs and talk easily and find again with his mother their old communion.

Jeanie Bannon finally laid her head back on the pillows and

[329]

sighed, wiping with the back of her hand at the corner of her eyes.

"Lordy," she said, glancing at Lota, "I envy you. A big strong girl and you've got a big strong man." She caught Buck's eye, and winked. "For the next few years, anyhow."

"Here," Buck said, "don't be puttin' a Jonah on me. Clean living will keep me here right on."

"Bah!" his mother said, then she moved her eyes sharply straight ahead at Millie. "That'n now. She'll never get a real man—ain't built for it."

Millie stood up straight and put her hands on her hips.

"I don't know," she said. She moved to the side so her mother could see her and pulled her long skirt up nearly to her knees. "If skirts were this short, I'd be beating them off."

"Humph! All baseball players, too."

Millie dropped her skirt and glared at her mother. She didn't say anything, and the room suddenly was very quiet.

"Baseball players?" Buck's quick words cut deliberately into the quiet. Millie nodded and her hands went back onto her hips.

"What of it?" She looked back at her mother defiantly. Lota cleared her throat to speak, but Buck squeezed her hand and stopped her.

"I never could understand," he said, thoughtfully, "how come you girls don't marry better. You're all right pretty, and I never saw either one of you with a dirty neck."

"Now, you just wait." Millie said her words slowly with a space between each. Her head went from side to side as she spoke. "As long as you've been living in Aven and running around with senators and bankers and really big men, you've never introduced either of us to a man." She stopped abruptly and clenched her teeth. "Why?"

Buck didn't answer, but he felt a flush coming up his face. He let her eyes hold his for a moment, then shifted them uneasily to his mother.

"Think that over," Millie said distinctly, and turned quickly and walked out, closing the door softly behind her.

The silence was heavy until Jeanie Bannon said, "Whew, boy, she laid it on heavy, didn't she?" She turned slightly in the bed and went on, wearily now, "Go catch her and ease her off, Lota."

Lota winked in understanding and followed Millie, leaving Buck with his eyes avoiding his mother.

"I'm glad she said that, Buck," she said, gently. "You ought to be taking some notice of your kinfolks."

"Aw, good Lord, Mother, I—"

"I needed a talk with you," she went on as if he hadn't spoken. "It won't be long before you'll be in single harness for sure—and nobody to use a check rein." The wrinkles in her lips smoothed out in a slow remembering smile. "Your Daddy, remember, gave me a job, too. Holding you down."

"Let's don't talk about it," Buck said, softly. "We've got time aplenty."

She shook her head.

"Now's the time. When we wrote my will there wasn't as much money or land as there is now. I'm leaving it up to you to see that it's split right along the same lines as the stuff we mentioned in the will."

"Hell, Mother, you know I'll—"

"Don't cuss," she said, automatically, then leaned weakly back farther into the pillows. "That's all I need to say. More, really. You know, it's only a man who's afraid of his own weakness who needs to take from those who are smaller and weaker." Her eyes opened wide and flashed a warning at him. "Look after my girls," she said, with a slight pause between each word. "Look after my girls. The boys can take care of theirselves after everything's split, but my baby girls—" She sighed. "You'll be the only solid thing they'll have left. Watch after them."

Buck leaned over earnestly, as if he wanted to answer, but she shook her head and her eyes closed again. She breathed a little faster.

"Tired," she said, "tired." She opened her eyes a small crack, and forced a tight smile to smooth out the wrinkles in her lips. Her words were soft and rueful. "Never even asked you about Mexico."

Buck touched her hand again, hesitantly.

"Better wait for that until you rest some."

Her head rolled from side to side on the pillows.

"Can't wait long." She opened her eyes wider and he could see something hungry in them. "What's it like?"

Buck closed his eyes, trying again to push away the thought of her that worked in his mind, trying to find the words that would please her, and wishing his words would come pretty, whether they were accurate or not. They didn't have to be right, but they must be words that she could roll and shape in her memory until the picture would come clear—as clear as the tiny field-stone, foot-washing pool would flash with the words, "Beulah Church."

"Waking up in Mexico," he said, slowly, feeling his way, "is like when you were a young'un, and had been a long time under a scuppernon' arbor where everything is shady and cool and speckled a kind of rusty brown and even the edges of the leaves look blurred—and all of a sudden you step out into the bright sun. Then everything sharpens. Seems like every blade of grass stands out by itself instead of being just a part of a mat, and if you look close at the scuppernon's in your hand, they aren't fuzzy any more, and every little freckle is plain and rusty brown, and where you pulled it loose, the juice doesn't leak, but kinda pouts through the hole and glitters in the sun. Down there, you can see better, or something. White gets so white it looks frosted, and red gets redder. And all the smells will mix up if you want them to, but you can pick them out one by one, like if you were feeding the hogs and wanted to, you could catch down the wind the smell of sassafras from the new clearing." He stopped talking suddenly, watching her closed eyes, trying to see if she were still awake. She didn't move. He eased out of his chair and moved softly away from the bed, watching over his shoulder. The floor creaked and her eyes opened quickly, almost startled. He smiled and stopped.

"You rest a while. I'll send Millie back in." Her eyes closed again, but she didn't speak. Buck moved towards the door again, but stopped with his hand on the knob.

"It'd be better if you'd move into the big house," he said in a low voice.

She didn't move or open her eyes.

"There ain't no stylish way to die."

Buck waved his hand from side to side in a silencing gesture, then turned and tiptoed out of the cabin. Lota and Millie were standing in the yard of the big house and he hurried towards them, knowing from the set of Millie's shoulders that she was still mad. He didn't look at her when he reached them, but he touched her with fingers that made friends with her arm.

"Why, in God's name, hasn't she got a nurse?" he asked Millie, and wondered why he still spoke in a near whisper.

Millie jerked around to face him. Her voice was tired and exasperated. "Buck, we could all have forced a nurse on her, a trained one, and kept the doctor here day and night, but she wouldn't have it. She cried." Millie bit her lip, trying to control its trembling, and shook her head. "I never saw her cry before." She held her head up high. "She wouldn't let anybody but me touch her, anyhow, when she really needed help. So that's all. The doctor left some medicine to stop the pain—dope I suppose—and he comes out every day to check up."

Buck nodded, staring at the ground, half seeing Millie's small feet set defiantly wide apart.

"Where are the others?"

"Most of them had kids to look after. Jeff had to check up at the hotel and the rest just scattered till after supper." She frowned. "No way to feed 'em all out here."

Buck glanced at Lota, then down at the ground again. He felt around in his mind for words.

"Hearn?" He questioned with a lift to his tone.

Millie looked quickly over Lota's shoulder at the big bare hickory tree.

"He's at the hotel," she said, carefully. "He's changed some and maybe—" She stopped awkwardly.

Buck coughed and didn't look at Lota.

"Unh-hunh," he said, then caught Lota by the arm. "We'd better get down and clean up."

Lota patted Millie on the arm. "We'll be back tonight," she said. "Can we bring anything?" Millie shook her head and turned without speaking and walked back towards the little cabin. Lota took a quick step after her, but Buck caught her arm. "Leave her alone. She's got guts she's never used."

They walked without speaking around the big house, and all the way something inside kept whispering urgently, "I'm alone, I'm alone." Until suddenly a thought ached in his head, and made him squirm inwardly. He was wondering again how death would

[333]

affect *him* and not his mother. He couldn't dodge it, or explain it, could only hope that everyone thought the same things in times like this. His mind was dully turning words, inspecting them, discarding them and groping stupidly for new thoughts, when they reached the car and the cold metal of the door brought him back to Lota and the clear wind-driven sounds of winter. The dreary thud of a mule's hooves endlessly circling the grinder in a hock-deep trench, never escaping the long peeled boom of the mill. Now a sudden faraway and quick-ending yelp of a feist dog chasing in the swamps something he was afraid to catch. Then the high-pitched yell of Mr. Misstledine to his wife down in the hog lot. "Turn 'em, Sweet Wife, turn 'em. Whoa-up! Head them hogs, Sweet Wife, 'fore I knock hell out of you!"

Suddenly Buck laughed out loud, in spite of the choke in his throat, and he shook his head. "Damn fool," he muttered. He glanced at Lota, who was standing quietly, watching him. He rubbed his jaw, feeling a little embarrassed and not knowing why.

"Wish she could have heard that," he said, and tossed his head back towards the cabin.

"We'll tell her tonight," she said, and reached for the ignition key. "She'll like it better if it comes from you, anyhow."

"Reckon so." He slammed the door hard and slid far down in the seat so the wind would go over his head. Lota punched him. She pointed towards the front of the car.

"Crank," she said.

"My God!" He sat up straight with a pained look on his face. "I never turned one of these things in my life." He shook his head and slid back down in the seat. "You do it."

"Now, listen here—" Lota stopped suddenly and caught his arm and held it tight, telling him to be quiet. She turned her head sideways, Buck listened, and it came again, closer this time.

"Buck!" It came from back of the house once, then it came again, closer. "Buck! Wait!" Then the sound of running footsteps. Millie, running and calling his name in a gasping scream. He looked up at Lota with his eyes flaring wide, searching and questioning, and inside him slowly built up the old dull hurting answer .

"She's gone," he said, hoarsely.

CHAPTER THIRTY-ONE

For weeks after the funeral, Buck stumbled through his days—lonely in the company of friends and feeling it an unhealthy loneliness—miserable at his work, yet doggedly studying and signing official papers at the city hall—finding dullness in the search for a proper location for his still unannounced gift of an opera house—persistently farming, renting lands and buildings, making loans and foreclosures, fighting the details of the hotel. He tried consciously to numb himself with work and most of the time he succeeded.

Only occasionally would he give up to a sweeping desire for a simpler loneliness, one that would come of being the only man in a big scope of woods, or perhaps, a deeper loneliness, standing on the edge and looking over a naked and shamed slash of land where timber had been and where the stumps of pine were fresh cut, still ugly and not yet dignified by vines or decay. Now and then he'd run into one of his tenants and force himself into bluffness. "If you ever get beef hungry, Sykes, knock one of these yearlin's in the head, but bring me a quarter so I can keep count." Mostly, though, he sank himself into the woods without company, for an hour or so, then he'd suddenly shake his head from side to side like a mired oxen and plunge back towards town and work.

He found the site for his opera house immediately after one of those silent periods on the big farm. He had walked deliberately over block after block of downtown Aven, automatically nodding, smiling, or shaking hands in spite of the fact that it wasn't election year. His eyes had seen it for years, rain-washed and rutted, so that hardly a solitary stalk of dog fennel would fight its way up through old buggy axles, tin cans, jars and bottles half full of brackish water, and his mind had only said, "That lot ought to be cleaned up." Today, though, his mind jumped at it, and he laughed inside, keeping his face expressionless and began to step it, casually, from across the street. He was seeing the first laying of the foundation, when a shaking hand touched him on the shoulder from behind.

"I've been hunting for you." The voice was very thin and high but the words marched out, slow and stately. Buck answered without turning around.

"Well, Virgil, now you've found me." His mind quickly multiplied the number of paces by three and he nodded, quickly, satisfied, and wheeled to face the familiar figure. Virgil was thinner and greyer than when Buck had last noticed him on his ceaseless and aimless patrol of the town and, as always, Buck didn't know whether to laugh at him or feel sorry for him. His high-heeled cowboy boots with castoff hickory-striped trousers tucked in, his too-small hat dented four times in a cavalry peak, his flowered vest, and his ever-present guitar were all there to laugh at. Yet Buck could never see them without remembering how his eyes wondered out at the world, vague, puzzled, and pathetically interested.

"Jeff wants you at the hotel," Virgil said, and gestured smoothly backwards with a sweep of his arm. The guitar thrummed almost soundlessly and Virgil caught its strings around the throat in gentle fingers. "Shhh!" he said.

Buck caught himself frowning at the guitar. He jerked his eyes quickly away and reached into his pocket.

"Run back down there, Virgil," he said, "and tell him I'll be along pretty soon." He held out half a dollar. Virgil shook his head and looked beyond the coin.

"I don't want another job today."

Buck laughed.

"Fifty cents."

Virgil looked over Buck's shoulder. He was patient.

"You can't hire a man who's tending his own business."

Buck flipped the coin and caught it, showing it off.

"No," Virgil said, firmly, "I have eaten today, and I'm warm."

Buck dropped the coin back into his pocket.

"Well, drop in at the hotel and eat a meal."

Virgil tipped his hat, still looking over Buck's shoulder.

"Some colder day," he said, smoothly, and nodded good-bye.

Buck watched him take a few steps up the sunny side of the street, wondering if he ever played the guitar, or if it was simply a friend whose voice he knew he could hear if he chose.

"Virgil!" he called, abruptly, hardly knowing why. Virgil

[336]

turned to face, but not see him. "You never have been crazy, have you? You've been throwing a bluff for twenty years."

"No, I'm not crazy," Virgil said and his thin lips quivered. "But my brother is. He works."

Buck laughed out loud and pushed his hand out and away from him as if to hurry Virgil off again on his leisurely visit with the town. He realized, queerly, that it was the first time he'd laughed in a long time and turned towards the hotel, walking slowly, letting his mind lumber over Virgil.

"Damn if he ain't right in one way," he thought, and tried to put it into words. "Can't sleep in but one bed at a time. Can't eat but three meals a day and be comfortable, or wear more than one suit at a time. Reckon if a fellow stretched that thinking out, he'd figure anything above what he needs is like a mill rock that he's got to drag along. If that's so, I'm toting a load."

He chuckled, opening the door to the hotel lobby, and almost spoke aloud.

"I still like money." He held the cold coins in his pocket, warming them in his hand, while he walked across the lobby, feeling pleasure as he always did in the grey-speckled marble inlay of the floor. He nodded briefly towards his right, more at the desk than at the clerk, as he opened the door and went back into the dim warmth of the sample room. He craned his neck to see over the built-in shelves bisecting the long plain room, wondering if Jeff was alone. Jeff was in a large rocking chair with a leather seat, huddling rather than sitting, with his hat pulled low over his eyes, shading them from the single overhead lamp. Another man sat with his back towards Buck, leaning over the one small table on his elbow and holding the telephone receiver to his ear. He wasn't talking, but his pudgy right hand made circular gestures in the air, waving a long unlit cigar. The bright cone of light bounced reddish gleams from short tight curls that fitted his head like an almost pink skullcap. Buck didn't change his pace when he saw him, but he smiled lopsidedly as he rounded the corner of the shelves and his eyes met Jeff's. He jerked his thumb towards the man at the telephone.

"Big business," he said, and Jeff's thicker lips curled answering the small hidden sneer in Buck's voice. "Mister Gates," Jeff said.

[337]

The man at the telephone turned quickly and almost bounced from the straight chair he was straddling. He popped his cigar hurriedly into his wide mouth and held out his right hand, still bending over slightly and holding the receiver ready.

"Hello, Buck." His voice was very deep, surprisingly deep for a man so small and so young, and it grated coarsely. His words were clipped, short but deliberately spaced, giving the impression that the next word might be very important. Buck shook the hand.

"What's up, Pearly?"

The too-soft protruding lips split in a quick grin around the cigar, showing its chewed end gripped belligerently between large, beautifully white teeth.

"The boss sent me down. Wants you to make a quick swing around your district with him."

"Hell," Buck said, lazily. "Governor's got two years to go."

The red-haired man jiggled the hook impatiently, then glanced back over his shoulder at Buck. "It's a build-up, Buck. Not for him."

"Who for?"

"I'm ready to talk, Central."

He spoke too loudly into the phone, then nodded shortly at it without answering. He shifted his chair so he could look at Buck and talk at the same time, and crossed his short legs.

"Senator Whiddon's due for a Federal job," he said. "You guess who the boss is going to appoint."

Buck felt color flooding into his face and he turned his head quickly so that shadows would fall across it. He cleared his throat and started to speak, then changed his mind. He glanced quickly up at Jeff. His brother sat quietly back in the shadows, but Buck could see the small quiet movement of his lips where the hat brim hid his eyes. He held his eyes on Jeff for a moment, frowning thoughtfully.

"Can you take care of everything?" he asked, softly.

Jeff nodded.

"Been doing it."

"Hold on a minute." Pearly Gates broke in, suddenly. He held the line in silence for a second, then said, "Hello, Governor," in his deepest and busiest voice. He listened, then nodded his head in short quick yesses before he spoke again. "Hold the phone, Governor." He moved his eyes towards Buck, questioning with them. Buck looked at Jeff, then quickly back to Gates. He nodded. Gates started talking again, but Buck didn't listen. His eyes were back on Jeff. They watched each other, each feeling the strong tide of proudness, yet trying to hide it, until Gates hung up the phone and beamed at them again.

"He'll meet us at the north end, Lee County, early tomorrow," he said.

Buck didn't answer. He got up and leaned over the telephone, bracing himself with his left elbow on the table. "Ring my room," he said, softly, and waited a moment.

"Lota," he said, then, "pack a couple of bags for me. Enough for two weeks. And drop in a couple of new packs of cards. The Governor'll be there."

Out of the corner of his eyes he could see Pearly Gates, jerking his head delightedly.

"You looks tiahed tonight, Mister Buck."

Buck eased stiffly out of the big black car in front of the hotel. He placed his hands on his hips and leaned backwards, straightening and soothing the stiffened muscles.

"Charley," he said, looking up at the hotel's unblinking front sign, "I've drunk buttermilk, seems like, in every kitchen this side of Georgia during the last ten days." He sighed and rubbed his knuckles for luck on the close-shaven head. "Here's hoping I don't have to drink any more for six years."

He glanced back at Jeff. Jeff's eyes widened, questioning. "Six years?" He whistled. "Must be a pretty sure thing."

"Within three months." Buck winked. "I'll give you the details tomorrow. Right now, I've got to get cleaned up." He grinned. "And see Lota." His face suddenly sobered and he held his head on one side, puzzled. "I still don't see what she could have had to do so she couldn't meet the train."

Jeff's face was suddenly blank and he shifted the car into gear hurriedly. "See you tomorrow," he said. Buck nodded and turned around. He hurried to the door and pushed it wide open so the bellboy would have time to sidle in behind him before the door closed again.

"Run the bags on up, Charley," he said, still frowning, "while I get my mail."

The bellboy's shoulders rose defensively as he hurried over to the row of dark chairs that made up the bell stand. "I got a rush call to Two twenty-eight, Mister Buck. Be right wid you next." He slid the bags across the polished floor and trotted up the stairs, glancing back once at the landing, then scooting faster as he saw Buck's eyes still following him.

"What the hell is this?" Buck muttered and forgot his mail. He followed the bellboy up the stairs slowly, not even stopping to speak to the small clot of drummers who were watching a domino game in the corner by the largest steam register. He wasn't listening with his mind, but his ears heard one of the players slap the table and yell loudly, "By God, you reenus me one more time and I'll hit you in the face with the double six." Buck didn't bother to look back but he laughed low in his chest and went down the long corridor towards his room, hardly realizing that his step had lengthened and quickened, or that his shoulders had gone back a notch.

He opened the door softly, holding his breath unconsciously, hoping he'd get a quick sight of her before she saw him. Dim light came through the widening crack, but he still couldn't see Lota. He pushed it wider.

"If that's my husband, quit playing around and come on in." Her voice had come with the old huskiness and with the same rough hint of laughter. He slammed the flat of his hand hard against the door and pushed it wide open. He started inside, but stopped quickly as he saw Lota, stopped and stood very still with the wide smile fading off his face. He bent his head forward slowly peering at her, and his mouth opened slightly.

"Well, I will be—" His words trailed off without finishing the sentence and his head dropped to one side, inquiringly.

She was lying in bed—in a bed he'd never seen before, a spindly and weak-looking bed whose carved footboard rose a bare few inches above the mattress. She was propped up on several shiny silk pillows, gracefully arched so that each line of her body was outlined in her pink satin wrap. The only light in the room came from a shaded bed lamp above and behind her head, but it showed her eyes, not looking at Buck but gazing at the wall above him.

"Surprised?"

Buck closed his mouth.

"That ain't the word," he said.

She reached out languidly, and flicked her long fingers, pushing aside the loose and empty paper shells that cluttered the top layer of a big box of candy beside her. She raised her other hand, quickly, and pushed aside the airy strands of a feather boa that draped her throat, then she put a whole piece of candy in her mouth. She waved one hand towards the wall, and spoke thickly, "Turn on the big light and look at the rest of it." Her eyes were watching him, anticipating, and eager for his reactions.

Buck fumbled for the switch on the wall without taking his eyes off Lota. He flipped it up and blinked his eyes in an unnaturally soft glow of light.

"Godamighty!" he said, almost whispering in awe. He let his eyes rove briefly over the pale-blue, newly painted walls and its gleaming white woodwork, until they settled on a new and fragile dressing table which stood in place of his old solid dresser. Then he walked slowly across the room towards it, letting his hand stray absently over the thin curving back of a new chair whose seat was covered with sand-colored coarse material.

He sniffed as he reached the dresser, then shook his head and blew out like a dog trying to get a feather off his nose. A strong fragrance kept floating up from the small matching set of china powder boxes, cream jars, and perfume bottles. He drew one finger lightly across the film of powder that lay over the delicate glass cover, then let his hand wander around the fluted pleats of filmy white that frocked the dresser edge.

"You must figure to quit bathing." His voice was almost toneless, but he spaced his words ominously.

"I've always had that much." Lota sat up in the bed and her words began to sharpen. He didn't answer, but fumbled beneath the dresser top. "There's no drawer," Lota said, with her voice falling low, but still edging.

"Where's my stuff?" He looked over his shoulder, wearily. Lota moved her head slightly to one side towards a small chifforobe that matched the bed and the dresser. "Some of it's in there," she said, watching him, "but I stored some you won't need till hot weather down in the sample room."

He stepped over towards the chifforobe, quicker this time, and jerked the two doors open. He stooped so he could see into it, then straightened and drew a deep breath. He slammed the doors shut, and turned towards her with his head lowering and his bottom lip beginning to protrude. Lota watched him with her eyes widening. She started to speak, then swallowed and didn't say anything.

"Where are my Goddamned shirts?"

Lota caught her breath sharply at his tone, then she wrinkled her nose and blew from between tight lips to move the floating ends of feather strands away from her mouth. She drew her shoulders up straighter and her eyes narrowed, but she worked to keep her voice patient.

"They're in a very nice chest," she said, slowly, "under the bed." She pointed downwards over the side of the bed. "It rolls on little wheels." She blew again at the feathers, angrily, and her hand reached up automatically to pull the boa to one side.

"If you think I'll break my damned—" He broke off, suddenly, and whirled around. "Where's my old chest of drawers?"

"I moved it into another room," Lota snapped, then her lips clamped tight and she began to breathe heavily. She straightened the boa again and he turned around to see one of her feet moving rhythmically under the light pink satin comfort.

He moved deliberately closer and bent over with his lips drawn down and his nose wrinkled, puzzled and a little contemptuous. He reached out, fingers curved to hold a teacup, and with thumb and middle finger, he caught the end of the boa. He pulled it slowly as if he were afraid it would break. It slithered around Lota's neck. She bit her lower lip and glared at him, but she didn't move as the other end slid off her shoulder. He held it up between his fingers, out from his body, like he would have held a wet cat. He blew his breath at it. It stirred gently. He dropped it, then wiped his fingers on his leg.

"Saw one of those once on a fish-and-bread whore," he said, conversationally, and turned his back to walk towards the bathroom.

Lota gasped and almost strangled for words.

"Now, you just—" She sputtered and stopped. He didn't look back until he reached the bathroom door, then he stopped suddenly and swung around. He jerked his thumb over his shoulder at the new full-length mirror set in the door.

"Put that pond gannet around your neck again and come look at yourself," he said, jeering.

Lota kicked the coverlet off her feet and swung her long legs off the edge of the bed. She started towards him, barefooted, holding the wrapper in a tight fist over her stomach. Her eyes were flared wide and her teeth were clenched. The feather boa lying on the floor trailed on her foot for a second, but she kicked backwards and it fell off. Her eyes were storming as she stopped in front of him, but her mouth had begun to work and she caught at her lip with her teeth. Her hand slowly unclenched from the front of her wrapper and she put both hands on her hips.

"So help me—" she started, but he broke in.

"Look at yourself." He stepped aside and inclined his head in a small bow. She started to speak again, but her eyes couldn't stay away from the mirror and she closed her mouth. She jerked her eyes away as she saw herself and fastened them on his face.

"I hoped you'd like it," she said, dully, in a low voice that didn't carry its usual huskiness. She turned around and walked back to the bed with the wrapper hanging loose and both hands limp at her sides.

Buck watched her lie face forward across the bed with her bare feet sticking out over one side and her long heavy hair falling off the other side. She didn't move or make a sound.

"Now, Goddammit, Lota," he said and stopped. He wiped his palm across his mouth, then drew the edge of his hand slowly back and forth under his nose, watching her. She didn't move or answer. He breathed out long and slow, then he walked softly towards the bed. He stood over her for a second, then pulled one of the new chairs closer, looking at it in disgust. He sat down on it and hitched it closer. He started to touch her and opened his mouth to speak. The chair creaked and leaned over to one side. He jumped up, quickly, and reached back to shake it. It rattled a little. He muttered under his breath and picked it up in one hand. The seat had sagged slightly out of line. He tossed it aside as if it were an empty bottle and it thudded on the new heavy-blue carpeting. Buck glanced down at the carpet in surprise. His face reddened slowly.

"Well, I'll be a—" He turned back towards Lota. She hadn't stirred.

"If I wasn't afraid of that bed, I'd sit on it and whip hell out of you."

She still didn't move or answer. He jerked away from her and strode heavily over to the small table that held the telephone. He started to pick it up without looking and fumbled for a second with the head and shoulders of a large French doll with flaring pink skirts.

"Hell-fire," he said, and pulled his hand away so fast he knocked it off. Doll and telephone fell to the floor. He breathed faster, staring down at the telephone and the doll cover. He just looked at it until he could faintly hear a voice repeating, "Office. Office. Your order, please." Then he suddenly bent over and scooped up the receiver and the mouthpiece.

"Harrison," he said, letting his words come slowly and painfully, "get hold of the shade-tree carpenter that did this and have him undo it. Tomorrow." He started to hang up without an answer, then put the receiver hurriedly back to his ear. "And tell Charley to take my baggage to another room and bring me the key." He slammed the receiver on the hook and set the phone back on the table. He didn't look at the doll again, but stood staring at the wall for a moment. Then he turned slowly to see Lota. She still hadn't moved or spoken. He walked over to the bed and leaned against the foot of it, gripping its curving footpiece with big white-knuckled hands.

"Lota," he said, softly, almost tonelessly, "I know why you did it. I've no wish to hurt you. The idea was good, I reckon, to surprise me and all, but—" He stopped, waiting for her to answer, but she stayed still and silent. His chin came closer to his chest and his lips pursed thoughtfully. "I heard an old colored woman say something once," he went on. "She wouldn't wash a street-walker's underwear and all she'd say was that they just 'wasn't her nation o' people.'" He loosened his grip on the bed, and straightened up. "That's the way I feel about this stuff," he said, gently.

She didn't answer. He watched her for a long moment, then turned and walked towards the door that led out into the corridor.

"I'm going into another room for the night," he said, as his hand touched the knob. "Are you coming?" His voice sounded far away in his own ears and he waited for the answer with his breath held painfully tight within him. It didn't come.

He opened the door and went out into the hall to meet the bellboy, who was coming towards him with a suitcase in each hand. He held the key in his teeth and its fibre tag dangled out of the side of his mouth.

"Right nex' do', Mist' Buck," he mumbled and slid the baggage hurriedly to the floor. He fumbled a little with the lock, then reached inside to turn on the light. "One oh two," he said, and quickly set the baggage inside. "Want me to—?"

"No," Buck broke in. "That's all." The bellboy left, with his face carefully blank.

Buck closed the door softly behind the bellboy and stood for a short while with his back pushed hard against the door facing. His hand was still on the knob. He turned it softly once, and opened the door an inch or two, then he shook his head and closed it again. He went deliberately into the bathroom and turned on the cold water and let it run for a while, then he leaned over and began to drink out of the spout. Suddenly he jerked his head away from the running water and stared up into the shaving mirror without seeing himself. His forehead creased and slowly he rubbed at his nose with his forefinger. Abruptly he turned out into the room and grabbed the telephone.

"Harrison," he said, quickly, and jiggled the hook. "Hey. If you haven't already called that contractor, hold up on it. Hunh? Yes. Now, this is what you do. Put us in Room 102 for good. Get that room cleaned up good and—" He broke off quickly and glanced at the door into the hall. It was opening slowly, an inch at a time. "Wait a minute," he said, softly, and watched the door come farther open. He waited until he caught a glimpse of Lota's hair, gleaming a little in the light from the room, pushed close to the opening. "Put it on the records as a bridal suite," he went on, speaking as much to the door as to the telephone, "and charge double our usual rates." He listened a moment, watching the door, but nodding into the telephone. "That's right," he said, crisply, and silently pulled the hook down with a crooked fore-finger. He spoke carelessly into the deadened mouthpiece.

"I'm going to see if Mrs. Bannon will do over a few more for us."

He hung up, then, and took two quick steps to the door. It tried to close, but he caught the knob and jerked it open. Lota straightened quickly and stood there in the darkening corridor with her hands behind her and a slow-gathering smile pushing a sheepish expression off her face.

"Visitin'?" He said it low, dragging it out, and his eyes laughed at her a little.

She shook her head slightly and bit her lower lip.

"Migratin'," she said.

INTERLUDE

Aven was *one of the little miracles of the past thirty years.*
"That's what it is," Bass Wooten muttered to himself, as he slowly rubbed with a damp cloth the circle a cup of coffee had left on the glassy white counter top in the B. and B. Café. "Durned little old chinquapin of a place growed up like a toad-stool after a rainy spell."

His lips moved, but he didn't make any sound as his mind went slowly over Aven. He saw the brick buildings downtown, the ones whose owners had jostled and nudged each other until their properties had met, quite often piously astride a land line whose existence had been denied in court and disproven at night with a gun or a knife.

"God, at the tripes that've been spilled over nothin' but a little spit o' dirt."

His thoughts ran on, disjointed and lazy, through the center of Aven where the symbols of the early times—overhanging bal-conies to dignify the second story of each business house—were being razed to widen the streets and sharpen the lines. And the neatly spaced street lights—nothing out of the ordinary to the traveler, but bright miracles to the old-timers, who knew it had been only a blessed whim that Aven had survived at all after the glutting labors of its birth as a sawmilling town.

Bass's wiping cloth slowed in its small circling until finally it stopped and, for a second, he stood perfectly still while his mind moved on out of the crowded business district onto the second miracle of Aven. His damp, sweaty face showed no emotion. His round shiny blue eyes were fixed vaguely on the wall across from him, but they didn't see the calendar there. They saw instead the slow picture of high-piled cotton wagons grinding slowly down Oak Street, one after the other, under the dark green of the oak limbs whose weight dragged them down into tired arcs. And they saw the now even alignment of the homes on each side of the streets as new builders took sight of their neighbors' fronts before they laid foundations for their own. And the flowers— azaleas blazing a dusty reddish orange against the white of a low fence, forsythia hedges throwing their bright yellow bells up in challenge to the sun, Cape jessamine shrubs dotting green lawns and mellowing the night, a pansy-bordered walkway dancing with velvet browns and purples and yellows, dogwood trees and redbuds teasing with white and pink petals the salty southwest wind.

"Hey, Lord," Bass muttered, and flicked his cloth sharply at a large cockroach which had come out of the hidden shelves below the level of the counter. "They're puttin' silk stockin's on a reg'lar whore of a town."

He heard the whine of the spring on the screen door as he bent his head to find the roach lying on its back and kicking. He stepped on it, quickly, feeling his lips wrinkle in distaste at the minute crushing, then the door slammed and he heard footsteps.

"Hey, Bass!" He looked up.

"Evenin', Jake." His face reddened and his eyes didn't meet Jake's.

Jake ambled slowly forward in his faded blue overalls and jumper, with his eyebrows raised high and a blandness to his face.

"Coffee," he said, and threw one leg over the oak-topped stool, then slouched comfortably with his elbows on the counter. Bass turned quickly so his eyes wouldn't be exposed to Jake's. He picked up a thick white cup from a wire rack. He blew into the cup to clear it of any soot or cinders that might have seeped through the ceiling from the bull-voiced switch engines lumbering up and down in the near-by yards.

He poured coffee from a grey-flecked enamel pot that stayed hot over a small kerosene stove. He scooped a saucer off a neat stack beside the cups and slid it across the counter towards Jake. The saucer clattered loudly. Bass put the cup of coffee into the saucer and the clattering came again. Jake didn't ask for sugar or cream or a spoon. He leaned over and looked directly down into the cup.

"Lot o' rattlin' o' the dishes for the fewness o' the victuals."

He waited without looking up, blowing into his coffee, but Bass didn't answer. Jake finally cleared his throat.

"Mighty good to see a fellow get in shape to retire."

"Go to hell."

Jake's frown was pained.

"Now, Bass, I'm just—"

"Shut up." Bass slapped viciously at a heavy-bodied, metallic fly that zoomed in over-and-under figure eights around the shaded light globe that hung close over his head. Then he leaned his elbows on the counter and stared moodily out the window towards the tiny triangle of grass which surrounded the city water tank.

"Damn pore retirin' I did," he said. "Got pensioned from the road where I worked all day, then opened a café where I work day an' night."

Jake's mood suddenly changed. He turned his head so he wouldn't see Bass and his voice lowered, became toneless and gloomy.

"You can eat when you're hungry." He scratched his head. "Me, I'm a damned mule. I just drag along, gee or haw." He slapped his hand down flat on the counter and his chin jutted. "I tell you now, there'll come a time when folks won't let a man be treated like a mule—work all day for nothin', then have some dressed-up bastard come throw him his fodder at night."

Bass shrugged.

"You can always quit."

"Mules don't quit an' they don't get fired," Jake said, bitterly. "They just die."

"I reckon," Bass said, and they fell silent, listening to the faint beginnings of a train whistle coming from so far away the sound seemed to have no direction. Jake automatically pulled his watch out of his jumper pocket and glanced at it.

"Fifty-seven's on time."

Bass chuckled at sight of the watch.

"Buck give it back too late for you to get a job with it."

Jake nodded.

"Most folks give too late." He emptied his cup. "Good Book says a man can get right in the last minute o' his life, but mostly that just makes folks wait too long."

Bass adjusted the purring flame under the coffeepot.

"Crew'll be in right soon." He turned back to Jake. "Buck ain't waitin', though. Durned if he didn't get that opera house up like the devil was after him."

"Might'a been," Jake said, sourly. "Would a'been if he'd ever found out how the city got that property."

Bass flipped his hand in a gesture of impatience.

"I don't give a damn how they got it. You can't get around that big opera house."

"Well, you shore can't get around that jail house alongside of it, or the fire station, or the trucks inside, an' the pavin', an' the danged graft on all of it."

Bass reached for Jake's cup.

"Quit gruntin'. You got to admit, his ma's been dead four-five month an' now, seems like, he's tryin' to give back what he took —if he did take it."

"Hmph!" Jake stood up and tossed a nickel on the counter. "I ain't never an' never will believe a man ought to steal a dollar so he can give back fifty cents in charity."

Out in the soft, heavy night, the train whistle came again, riding in triumph over the slamming of freight-office doors, and the creaking of trucks, and all the feverish noises that waked up the station when a train was due. The whistle boasted now, coming downhill, and Bass leaned over his counter with a faraway, wistful expression in his eyes.

"Listen to that man," he said, softly. "Hoggin' a manifest freight an' glad of it."

CHAPTER THIRTY-TWO

Buck stood on a small chair and held his arm out straight, pointing through the window of his hotel dining room, over the tops of the buildings across the street, towards a wide half moon of bright light.

"Thirty days, gentlemen. Laid the first brick a month ago, and we're opening tonight." He clenched his fist loosely and shook it from side to side close to the wind-chapped face of a heavy-set man who looked as if he would be more comfortable in railroading overalls. "That's high-ballin', Hog." He raised both hands with their palms turned towards him and motioned to pull closer the small crowd of men who were grumbling and laughing among themselves. "So, step up, friends, and shell down the corn." He jerked his thumb to the left. "My brother, Honest Jeff Bannon, has a list of your bets. He'll be glad to give you written receipts, but my advice is to take your receipts from Smiley at the bar." He raised his voice. "Smiley, free drinks to every man who pays his honest gambling debts tonight." He laid his hand on the shoulder of a man who stood close to his chair, a man whose greying hair stood up in an angry brush. "Even the ones who didn't bet any more than Angus McTyre." McTyre's mouth turned down.

"I'll drink only with my host," he said, "and I'll pay no broker." He caught Buck's arm and pulled him off the chair. "Here's my twenty-five and don't complain, only thank the Lord that a man who knows you as well as I do will still bet with you."

"Thank you, Lord," Buck said, gravely, and walked beside McTyre to the bar. "Gin for Mr. McTyre, nothing for me."

"It's been waiting." The bartender flashed a set of poorly fitted false teeth and slid a small glass of gin and a large tumbler half full of water across the bar. McTyre tilted the gin slowly into the water, then raised his glass to Buck.

"The Queen, God bless her."

"Never changes," Buck said. McTyre carefully pushed the glass back across the bar and wiped his mouth with the back of his hand. He didn't speak until the bartender had moved on down out of hearing, then he glanced sideways at Buck.

"This charity business must have gone to your head—got you on a dry drunk."

"Not exactly." Buck shook his head. "I'm waiting for— Well, you'll know in a couple of days."

McTyre questioned with his eyebrows.

Buck said, "Excuse me, Mac. Jeff's through with the boys." He moved slowly away from the bar, watching the crowd of men turn from the table where Jeff sat and hurry towards the bar, pushing ahead of them a small dusty-looking man in a crumpled grey suit who was trying to frown and failing because they were all laughing at him. "Ed wants champagne, Buck," somebody yelled, and the small man caught at Buck's arm as he was pushed past. "How much did you lose, Ed?" Buck was looking over his shoulder. The little man winced. "Five hundred." Buck laughed out loud. "Give him one bottle," he called to Smiley, "but make him drink it all himself." He went on through the crowd, nodding now and then at one man or another, until he reached Jeff at the pay-off table.

Jeff glanced up at him with a smile that disappeared as quickly as it came and finished piling the crumpled and stained bills into a neat stack. "All there," he said, and shoved the stack across the table as Buck pulled a chair closer. "Twenty-seven hundred and seventy-five." Buck rubbed the ball of his thumb slowly along the line of his jaw and frowned at the money. A queer thought seemed to click in his mind. "I ought to get a kick out of this, but I don't." He shook his head suddenly, as if to throw off a dizzy spell and blinked his eyes.

"Something wrong?" Jeff asked quickly.

Buck slowly picked up the stack of bills. "Rabbit ran over my grave." He carelessly rippled the ends of the bills until he had gone about two thirds through, then he jerked off the top layer and slid the bottom pile back across the table. "Your cut," he said.

Jeff flushed and tried not to look at the money. He left it lying and kept his eyes on Buck. "I'm not due a cut. You'd have had to take the loss."

"Take it." Buck's voice was harsh. "It's as easy to give it as it is to leave it."

"Hell," Jeff said, softly, and pulled the money towards him.

[351]

He folded it once across the middle and slid it into his hip pocket, then he buttoned the pocket. Buck stuffed his into the side pocket of his coat, watching Jeff with a half smile on his lips.

"Speakin' of leavin'," Jeff said, with his eyes over Buck's shoulder, "you never asked a word about your boy."

Buck's jaw muscles tightened and his lips thinned. He didn't say anything.

"He's a pretty good kid."

Buck only nodded and the silence that fell between them seemed even more silent for the background of laughter and talk at the bar. When Jeff finally spoke again, his words were hesitant.

"Seems like every kid ought to know his daddy, but, if he can't have that, he ought to have somethin'."

Buck's jaws relaxed suddenly and his eyes shifted down until they stared at the wrinkled tablecloth. He began to slowly trace with the end of his finger one of the old starch slicks.

"Well," Jeff said, "I don't reckon it *is* any of my business." He stood up and started towards the bar without looking at his brother.

"Wait." Jeff stopped and turned back to stand over him, looking down at Buck's head and shoulders from behind. "You're right," Buck went on without turning around. "None of it's his fault and I don't reckon they'd ever save a dime, even out of what I send them." He rolled his head on his neck, irritably, and his words came rough. "If you don't mind messing with it, draw up a new will for me. Leave him one pretty nice store building. Take it off Lota's share and I'll make it all right with her. The rest of it can ride like it is."

Jeff nodded as if Buck could see him and spoke gently. "He spent half a day just looking and feeling of that big car of yours. Maybe—"

"Enough cash for a car, too," Buck interrupted, then waved his hand to the side as if he didn't want to talk about it any more.

"I'll do it right away," Jeff said. Buck's head turned slowly, halfway around. His eyebrows had risen and he was trying to hide a smile. "No hurry that I know of," he said. Jeff came back around to his side of the table and eased into his chair. The silence built up again between them, but it was more comfortable this time. When Buck spoke, finally, his tone was offhand, just to have something to say.

"Right nice-looking building—the opera house."

"By God, that reminds me." Jeff leaned closer and spoke lower, confidentially. "I know you don't bet wild. How'd you know he could finish in thirty days?"

"He looked like a fast builder."

"Damn that." Jeff suddenly slapped his thigh. "You paid somethin' on the side."

"Nope," Buck said, in a patient voice, "but if a fellow can't figure these things out, he ought to learn, somehow." He began to tap the table for emphasis. "Remember, he's a Georgia contractor?" Jeff nodded. "Remember how long he'd been on the foundation when I placed the bets?" Jeff tried to think. "Around ten days," he said.

"That's right. Well, on that day I happened to see one of the workmen rubbing salve on a scar on his ankle." He paused. "It went all the way around his leg."

Jeff's forehead wrinkled. "Convict?" Buck nodded. "I checked up then and found out he was using convicts for common labor. Then I called Montgomery. He didn't have a license and the state won't grant one to a private contractor using convict labor." He slowly turned his hands palms upwards on the table. "That's about all."

Jeff looked bewildered.

"I told him if he wasn't finished in thirty days, he'd have to pay my bets or I'd refuse to pay him—for any reason I could think of—and make him sue me. I'd win on a technicality." He turned his hands over and rubbed the palms against the tablecloth.

"Well, I'll be Goddamned." Jeff breathed in, long and slow, and his eyes wavered away from Buck's. "Would you have held him to it?"

"I don't know," Buck said, staring at his hands and speaking slowly. "He was a crook—the worst kind I know—and if I'd caught him cutting me short on materials or something, I— Well, hell, I just don't know." He glanced quickly up at Jeff with something anxious in his eyes. "I pay my debts," he said. Jeff nodded and Buck leaned back and muttered, "Anyhow, it's a

[353]

mighty cheap way for him to learn that a crook has got to stay smart *all* the time."

Jeff opened his mouth to answer, then his eyes switched quickly above Buck's head. "What you want, boy?" Buck didn't turn his head.

The small thin colored boy stood straight, his chest pouting tight under the white coat with its faded-red Harrison House emblem. He held his hands behind his back while he announced: "Mr. Montgomery on the phone for Mr. Buck."

Buck turned half around to look at the boy, then he questioned Jeff with his eyes. "I don't know any Mr. Montgomery."

"Me neither," Jeff said.

The bellboy's chest shrank a little.

"Clerk says Mr. Montgomery callin' Mr. Buck, but it was a lady talkin'. I heerd her."

"My God!" Buck stood up quickly and started across the dining-room floor with long strides. "That'll be the capitol calling from Montgomery," he called back to Jeff. He walked fast through the lobby, motioning with an upraised, pointing finger for the clerk to have the call transferred to the phone back in the sample room. He hurriedly pulled the long switch cord of a small blue pilot light, then went surely through the dim light, in and out of the piles of packing cases and snuff cartons, until he reached the small cleared space with the old table. He reached up high and twisted the bulb that stuck out of a socket in the wall and blinked in the sudden glare. He breathed a little faster as he drew the phone towards him and reached for the receiver. It rang as his hand touched it and he jerked his hand back as if it had burned him. Then he lifted it quickly to his ear and said, "All right, sugar." His face turned slowly red as he listened, then he began to laugh. "Hello, Governor," he said when the receiver stopped rasping, "didn't know you were on the wire. What's doing?" He listened a long time with his color fading back to normal, then slowly whitening. "Who opposed it?" he asked finally, and listened some more, then he said, "You're right, it doesn't make much of a damn now." He picked the phone up and rubbed the mouthpiece across the tip of his nose while the Governor talked. "You take care o' yourself," he said when the receiver was silent, "an' I'll get it all fixed up tonight and see you tomor-

[354]

row. Good. Good." He listened again, briefly, then said, "I'll tell him. He's slipping back here now." He raised his eyes towards Jeff who had silently come around the corner of the sample rack to stand near him. "Thanks for everything," he said, still looking at Jeff. "See you later." He pulled the receiver hook gently down with his finger and leaned back in the old rocking chair with the telephone in his hands. He breathed in deeply and let it out slowly.

"What'd he say?"

"He'll be down tomorrow afternoon," Buck said, speaking almost dully, as if his mind were far away on another thought; then he shook his shoulders as if to rouse himself, and put the telephone back on the table. "Better tell Smiley to set aside a couple barrels of beer and scrape up a few cheeses and things. The old gentleman wants a trip down the river to rest." He flashed a quick smile. "He ain't feelin' so good, but he said if you had an old throwed-away girl down here to take her along for him."

Jeff scowled and spoke irritably. "What in hell did he say about the appointment?"

Buck looked at his watch. "I've got to dress," he said, and turned towards the lobby. Jeff didn't say anything as Buck took a few steps away, but his lips began to quiver when his brother stopped and looked back over his shoulder.

"Confidentially," he said, "he wants to announce it tomorrow from Aven, so don't mention it, even to Lota." Jeff's smile broke full out, but Buck's eyes began to narrow and he frowned as if he were puzzled.

"The Lieutenant Governor and that damned Black Belt bunch fought it," he said, wonderingly. "By God, here I supported him right along on the Governor's ticket, and now he says I'm apt to be crowdin' at the trough." He jerked his head up and to one side, arrogantly. "One thing's damned certain—I'll show him how quick I can fatten up the ones at the low end of the trough."

CHAPTER THIRTY-THREE

BUCK REACHED over Lota's shoulder from where he stood behind her and tilted the long mirror of the dresser so he could see his face. He straightened the knot of blue tie into his high collar, then his eyes caught Lota's frown in the lower part of the mirror. Her mouth opened, but he spoke first.

"Well, hell, you've been sitting there a full hour."

Lota's eyebrows arched higher and she reached out to push the bottom of the mirror back without taking her eyes off him.

"Was it worth it?"

His eyes went over her reflection slowly, stopping with a slight smile at the center part in her black hair, then checking from side to side to see how tightly she had drawn the hair behind her ears. He leaned backwards and touched, without ruffling, the cluster of finger puffs on the back of her head.

"Ever look down a well and see little sidelights of the moon on dark water?" Lota shook her head with her eyes still questioning him in the mirror. "That's how your hair shines back here," he went on awkwardly. "Except it's got some red darts in it." His fingers slid down her neck to her shoulder and rubbed along the white satin strap of her dress. Lota didn't say anything, but she dropped her head on one side and pushed her shoulder up until she caught his hand against her cheek. He held his hand there until she moved her head, then he leaned over and put both hands on the dresser on either side of her, staring at her reflection.

"I'm glad you didn't mind about the store," he said, "for the boy, I mean."

Lota's eyes shadowed quickly, but they rose to meet the reflection of his anxious, questioning frown. Her hands found automatically the glass stopper of a small perfume bottle. She shook the bottle once, pulled the stopper out, and gazed thoughtfully at the long glass applicator.

"If I'd been worried about money," she said, softly, "do you suppose I'd have wanted you to be building and giving away opera houses?"

Buck straightened up and let a hand touch briefly on each

of her shoulders. "This town's growing," he said, almost to himself, "and I'll build more stores and buy more land, and make more money, as long as anybody makes it." He pushed his lower lip out, reflectively. "I'll get mine all right, even if there are more face cards in the deck nowadays."

Lota touched the tip of the glass tube behind each ear, then swiftly slid it along the part in her hair, starting at the shadowy widow's peak. She held her head back to look over her shoulder.

"Why don't you quit work, Buck? Let Jeff run things?"

"Good God!" He bent over slightly to see into her eyes. "I believe you mean that." He straightened up, shaking his head slowly, and took two steps over to the window. He bent to see out under the half-drawn shade. He was silent for a moment, then he turned back to face her, leaning against the window sill with a smile beginning at the left side of his mouth. "That's my town out there. You can see the lights of the opera house spreading like just before the sun comes up." He stopped suddenly and turned back towards the window as if he didn't want her to see his face. "You can understand. I'm big winner in the game and the big winner don't quit till the others have had their chance. If I quit, somebody else will quit bucking the dice, then another one'll drop out, and first thing you know, the whole damned town'll lay down in the sun like a wormy hound." He turned his head to the right until he could see her face, testing her reaction. She didn't move or speak. He looked back out the window and stared silently a short moment longer, then swung around again and braced himself with a hand on either side of the window, spread wide. "Besides, there's always that next milepost, and the one I'm seeing now is the prettiest little thing I ever looked at."

Lota's eyes left him and she thoughtfully dipped the glass tip again and dabbed it lightly on the inner arm where it bent at the elbow. "Senator." She rolled the sounds on her tongue. "Are you sure?"

He raised his shoulders and let them fall back in a miniature shrug.

"Sure as I'll ever be. If it wasn't for the Governor, though, the Lieutenant Governor and his pressure hounds woulda beat me out."

Lota's hands were suddenly still.

"It means a lot to you, doesn't it?"

"It means as much to you."

She carefully stuck the stopper back in the bottle before answering. "Once maybe, but not now." She caught his eye and her wide mouth curved softly. "I'll settle for a retired young businessman and ex-mayor."

Buck laughed. He came quickly up behind her and reached over her shoulder. He took the stopper out of the perfume bottle. "One more place," he said, and his lower lip was sticking out farther than before, as he bent over and ran the glass tube along the satiny line of her dress, just above her breasts. "For me," he added. She shivered and pushed his hand away, smiling at him over her shoulder.

"Keep getting frisky," she said, "and we'll be late for your own speech."

"They'll wait." He glanced over his shoulder at a small clock on the bed table. "We've got thirty minutes—plenty of time."

"Oh, Lord, is that all?" She stood up and pushed him back. "Let's hurry. If you think I'm going to miss standing around in the lobby all dressed up—" She didn't finish the sentence, but frowned at her hips as she smoothed her dress down over them. "Would you care if I got fat?"

"Not if the new meat looks as good as the old."

She pulled up her skirt and leaned over to see her new silver-colored pumps, with their narrow vamps and sharply pointed toes, sticking out from under crisp white bows, whose transparent material was dotted with silver sequins. She was biting her lower lip in concentration as she glanced from her shoes to the mirror, to the dressing table, then to the bed. "You bring my wrap." She caught a pair of long white gloves from the dresser and started towards the door, drawing them up over her hands.

Buck threw the long black velvet evening wrap over his arm and arranged it so that its white silk lining would show. The left side of his mouth rode upwards as he followed Lota, watching her hips sway with her brisk, quickening stride. They were down the corridor and almost to the stairway before Lota had worked the bell-mouthed gloves above her elbows, freeing her hands through the unbuttoned slits at the wrists. The wry smile stayed on Buck's lips all through the lobby as he saw her trying to stuff the fingers of the gloves back and under just loosely enough to show that she didn't care how they looked. Out on the pavement, the reflection from the overhead Harrison House sign spread downwards in fan-shaped brightness, pointing up the reddish glints in Lota's hair. She gave the gloves a final smoothing, then threw her head back and breathed deeply.

"It's a fine night," she said. "Feels like it's just a minute before spring."

"Cool for this time of year," he answered automatically, with his eyes on the small knot of men standing under a faded canvas awning fronting the drugstore. They were laughing, and he wondered, with a sudden angry flaring of blood into his temples, if one of them had said something about Lota or him, or the two of them, to make them all laugh. Then he pulled down his shoulder muscles to relax them and his walk became more of a saunter.

"Evenin', Miz Bannon." One of them tipped his hat. "Hey, Buck." His smile and his voice were friendly and Buck lifted his hand. "Big doin's, Buck," another one called loudly, as he went past. "Gon' tell us who's the big he-coon tonight?"

Buck didn't stop. He rolled his eyes up towards the sky and tilted his chin high and to one side. "Boys, I'm going to give 'em both barrels and the breechin'."

"Tell 'em 'bout it, but don't keep us till the saloons close."

Buck swaggered a little. Then, as he reached the curb and started to step down, he heard another voice, soft and hoarse and a little sly, come from behind him.

"Goin' to tell who sold the city that land the opery house is on?"

Buck stopped still, with his hand on Lota's arm, holding her beside him for a moment without looking back or answering; then he turned slowly around.

"Festus," he said, calmly, "if you got the guts, which I doubt, I'll call on you to tell 'em yourself in open meeting."

There was no answer as he waited silently, half turned, with his hand still restraining Lota. Suddenly, one of the men jerked himself around to face the brick wall, with his back to Buck and the other men. His shoulders were squared high and his head was jutting low between them. He didn't speak. Buck smiled lopsidedly at the men who were watching, then he turned slowly around and started across the street. He heard a loud spurt of laughter behind him and knew, comfortably, that they were laughing at Festus Young. They walked in silence until they reached the street light on the other corner. Then Buck felt Lota turn towards him and he looked down to see her watching his face with narrowed, suspicious eyes. He cleared his throat and looked away, down towards the bright flare of lights from the opera house in the middle of the block. She shook his arm.

"Who owned that land?"

He cut his eye to the side to see her and she was having trouble controlling her lips. "Festus used to."

"Did you buy it from him and sell it to the city?"

"Hell no! That's illegal, me being the mayor." He rubbed his knuckles hard across the bridge of his nose, not looking at her. "Think I'm a crook?"

"Who bought it from Festus?" She spaced her words, softly and carefully.

"Well, dammit," he said, resigned, "I reckon it was Millie and Christina." He kept his face turned away, but he heard Lota catch her breath.

"Buck," she said, slowly, "you're harder to break than a suck-egg dog."

"Now, listen here—" He broke off and glared down at her until he saw her lips turning up; then he began to smile. She laughed deep in her throat, and he leaned close to her and spoke hoarsely. "By God, it's something I can't help. It just looks like a sin not to make a little profit out of something this big."

Buck's chest was tight with pride of Lota and he had a full, high excitement in his blood when they reached the front of the opera house and began to shake hands and speak in snatches to the nervous, overdressed people who crowded the lobby and eddied out onto the sidewalk.

"Hiyuh, Buck," somebody would call, and he'd throw a quick glance and a word or two, hardly seeing them, always returning his eyes to Lota whose hand was cold with excitement when he touched it but whose voice was warm and low when she spoke. A hand would slap him on the back and he'd turn hurriedly away after a quick, prideful sweep with his eyes over the dark-flecked marble of the lobby. "Scared?" A broad, friendly mouth would shape the word in the mumble of self-conscious voices, and he'd shake his head. "Scared o' what? You folks ain't goin' to eat me, I don't reckon."

And his mind running all the time: "Damn, it's crowded in here. Like fightin' through cat's-claw briers so thick you can't pucker your lips to whistle in the dogs. Hey, look out! Push that fat little wife of his much closer and I won't be responsible. Old Mrs. Lamb—Lord, I thought she was dead. That old-maid girl of hers scrubbed clean as a hound's tooth. She'll slip off from her ma one of these days and break some poor drummer's back with those thighs of hers—would have done it already if the old woman hadn't hollered sin and Leviticus when she was freshening."

His thoughts broke off as he felt Lota's hand tighten on his arm, shaking it slightly. "Uh-uh," he heard her say. "Here comes old 'High C' Sidney." He looked around until he located Mrs. H. C. Sidney trundling her heavy bosom ahead of her through the crowd, glaring intently at him out of popping, agitated eyes, and making one whole side of the lobby seem to bustle. He wanted to move away but couldn't. She was pressed so tightly against him by the crowd that he could feel with his arm the stiff whalebone of her corset. She was fighting for harsh breath close to his ear, and trying to talk.

"Well, how's the Committee on Arrangements?" he said, to help her out.

She frowned painfully and patted both ears with fat and slightly dirty hands; then she started pulling them back through the crowd towards the two wide doors that opened into the foyer separating the lobby and the three banks of orchestra seats. He followed in her wake with a helpless shrug and a glance down at Lota.

Mrs. Sidney fought her way through the doors and closed them quickly behind her. "There," she gasped, triumphantly, and pointed towards the brightly lighted stairway leading up to the balcony.

The figure at the foot of the stairs stood in silent dignity that seemed to Buck even more complete because of the costume—the same cowboy boots and wide belt, the same checked shirt and frayed, thrown-away vest, the same guitar slung by a strap over his shoulder, and the same large black hat. And a new feature —a large cardboard sign fastened across a spindly metal frame, held so that all who entered could read the sprawling red letters: "Repent ye. The number of the beast is 666."

"Virgil?" Buck walked closer, peering at the sign. "What in the devil?"

"My very thoughts," Mrs. Sidney panted indignantly from behind.

Virgil didn't answer. He pointed woodenly to his sign, then gazed with deep interest at Mrs. Sidney's pillowy bosom. She drew herself up, returning his stare, and clutched Buck's arm.

"He shouldn't be allowed to stay, to just stand there."

Buck's eyes had narrowed as if he were puzzled, staring at the sign, but when she spoke his face became bland and expressionless, and his voice softened.

"The whole town was invited and he's part of it." He ducked his head towards her in a slight bow, smiling easily. "Besides, he's carrying the gospel."

"Oh!" Mrs. Sidney gasped and closed her eyes briefly. She reached out and clutched Lota's arm. "My dear," she said, "it's time we were backstage." And she tottered away on her little splayed feet.

"Scat!" Virgil said, and reached around with his right hand and ran his fingers lightly over the strings of his guitar.

Buck winked once at Virgil and turned away. He followed Mrs. Sidney and Lota down the dim left aisle to the narrow steps which led from one side of the orchestra pit to backstage, sniffing all the while the newness of paint and pine and trying to read in the gloom the boxed advertisements on the canvas drop. "Billy Boy Flour," one sign read, under the flat picture of a chubby blond boy whose eyes had been painted impossibly blue. He stumbled slightly on the stairs, then blinked his eyes in sudden brightness as Mrs. Sidney opened the small door leading onto the left wing. He caught Lota's arm and pulled her back towards him as Mrs. Sidney rushed on tiptoe across the stage, patting the air with her hands and trying to tell a lanky colored boy where not to put a huge wicker basket of flowers.

"It doesn't look like it did yesterday, somehow," he whispered hoarsely, then cleared his throat. "What in hell am I whispering about?" Lota patted his arm. "You're scared."

"I'll be damned." Then he heard the low thunder of footsteps through the open door behind him. He shut it hurriedly, but the noise didn't stop and he knew suddenly that the doors had been opened and that the seats were filling up. He could hear some of them already stamping their feet and whistling. In a quick stab of anxiety, he clutched at his inside pocket, then breathed deeply in relief as he felt the rustle of his notes. He put his lips closer to Lota's ear.

"Does your stomach feel funny?"

Lota laughed delightedly and started pulling him towards the stage, where the members of the city council were already seating themselves in a semicircle that began at the right wing and extended almost to a similar row of seats on the left. Eight flurried women, the Committee on Arrangements, were being herded meekly into their seats by Mrs. Sidney. Buck saw them dimly as a line of faces and a blur of bodies, then Lota was pushing him down into one of the two folding chairs which had been placed slightly in front of the others, in the direct center of the stage. Lota sat beside him and busily started settling the folds of her dress over her feet and ankles. Buck stared at the blank side of the curtain ahead of him and wondered why in God's name he had said, "Sure," when they asked him to make a speech. He turned suddenly to lean over towards Angus McTyre, whose coarse brush of hair was closer to him than any of the other councilmen. He started to speak, but McTyre began to jab towards the curtain with an agitated finger and frown; then his face froze and he stared stonily ahead. Buck turned hurriedly back in time to see the curtain rise smoothly to about four feet, then halt and jerk a couple of times before going on up.

"Too late to back out now," he thought, and forced himself to look out over the three separate patches of faces below, and up into the balcony where smaller tiers of seats rose steeply on either side of a little black booth with a square hole in its front. He was vaguely conscious that McTyre had risen and gone to the front, but time had somehow slipped a cog and things were slithering past without touching him. He heard McTyre's rasping, nervous voice mention his name, and muscles jumped in his legs; then he drew a deep breath and tried to force his mind to think about what the man was saying, or anything, just to think again.

"All you got to do is just stand off and watch yourself do it and then it's easy, like most everything else I've done. Hell, I wasn't a farmer but I farmed, and I wasn't a grocery clerk but I sold a power of grits. I wasn't a politician but—"

He heard his name again, dimly, and he focused his eyes on McTyre, who had half turned from the front of the stage and was beckoning with an outstretched arm. Then he saw McTyre's smooth gesture suddenly stop and his eyes narrowed at the expression on McTyre's face. McTyre was frowning and shaking his head at the wings behind Buck and to his left. Buck glanced quickly around and saw a small, slim man in half-rolled shirt sleeves and a loose collar standing in the wings and waving a yellow sheet of paper. His mouth was working silently, shaping words, and he beckoned to Buck with one hand.

Buck started automatically to rise, pushing from the arms of his chair with hands that suddenly had grown white around the knuckles. He felt a hand lightly touch his arm. He looked around and Lota was frowning and very slightly ducking her head in warning towards the audience. He glanced helplessly towards the wings again and saw the little man almost come out onto the stage, then dart back behind the canvas as one member of the Committee on Arrangements hissed at him.

Dimly Buck could hear the audience begin to buzz with small clots of laughter and an over-all whispering, and he could feel but not see or hear Angus McTyre at the apron of the stage, still waiting with ushering arm to lead Buck before the people. Buck started to rise again and go to McTyre when he heard the loud, agonized whisper from the wings.

"Goddammit, Buck, come here."

He almost laughed out loud as he heard the strangled gasp from the members of the Committee, and as he looked down, he saw Lota's shoulders shaking while she hid her mouth with a small white handkerchief. He bent down to her.

"Hell," he whispered, "if I don't go, he'll wet his pants." He didn't look at the audience or at McTyre, but he felt his face

[364]

flush when someone in the audience yelled, "Scared, Buck?" as he walked swiftly into the wings.

He was glowering as he reached the little man and held out his hand.

"Shoes pinchin', Pettus?"

The little man gulped and worried his thick lips with fingers that still bore ink stains and smudges from carbon paper. He handed the flimsy sheet to Buck with a shaking hand.

"Governor's dead," he blurted.

Buck felt the blood leave his face in a sudden downward swoop and his throat filled with a quick thickness. He heard the sheet of paper crumpling and realized that he was wadding it into a ball with his right hand. His eyes hadn't left the little man's face.

"You said—?" He stopped because those words had come hoarsely, spaced apart, and his tongue had seemed to be in the way.

The little man nudged with his thumb towards the telegram. His head bobbed up and down excitedly and his eyes wouldn't meet Buck's.

Slowly Buck smoothed out the paper and for a moment all the sound in the back of the opera house flowed away until there was nothing left but Buck Bannon and a small square of yellow paper whose message said:

"Governor Thrasher had stroke in his office, died forty minutes. Call me tonight."

It was signed, "Gates."

Dully, unthinkingly, Buck counted the words.

"Thirteen," he muttered and carefully he began to smooth and fold the message so it would fit in his pocket. He shook his head hard, once or twice, like a man fighting for breath and lifted his chin as if his collar choked him. He didn't see the little man abruptly turn and leave him, but a second after he was gone, Buck whispered, "Thanks, Pettus," and turned blindly back towards Lota and the eight members of the Committee on Arrangements. He didn't see anything but Lota as she came on anxious tiptoe towards him across the stage, and he didn't notice the hush that suddenly swooped across the crowd out front. He waited in the wings, grateful for the thin canvas that kept the people from seeing him, touching with one hand the message in his pocket and with the other slowly rubbing the rough slats that framed the canvas.

Then Lota's hand was on his arm and her eyes were wide, going slowly over his face, searching it. She started to speak, but he stopped her.

"He's dead," he said, softly. "Governor Thrasher's dead."

Lota's teeth caught her lower lip and he heard the small whistling intake of her breath.

"Poor old man," she whispered. "I wonder what Mrs. Thrasher will do."

Buck hardly heard her. He turned blindly and started back into the darkness of the space backstage. She caught his arm.

"Where are you going?"

"Montgomery," he said, in a tight hard voice.

Her whisper came urgently.

"No, not now." She turned him until the light from the stage fell across his face. She looked up at him for a second and he stared down at her. Her lips grew softly rueful. She held him by his wrists and her voice came low but clear. "These people out front. The best you can do for him is remember him, but you've got a debt to pay out there."

Buck clamped his teeth quickly together.

"Let McTyre do it."

Lota's fingers kneaded the flesh of his wrists, working soothingly, drawing him closer towards her.

"It's not alone the opera house they want, Buck," she said, "I doubt if a one of them ever thought of it, but they all want—" She broke off and he could see the tip of her tongue between her lips as she bit it, trying to find the words she wanted. Her voice was lower, as if she were ashamed of the words when she finally spoke. "It's like every one of them wants a picture of you to take home, so later on he can say, 'I was there the night Buck gave the opera house.'" She patted his arm gently. "Come on," she said.

Buck's jaw muscles knotted.

"The people want too damned much. Always do."

Lota's lips moved in quick, almost wistful humor.

"Is that what you said when you were courtin' the people?"

Buck looked down at her with a growing astonishment in his eyes.

"Why, I never—" He stopped. "I damned shore did, too," he went on, "but you ought to know the way you look at a girl when the corn's flowering ain't always the way you're going to look at her when it's fodder." His face was still white and set.

Lota dropped her hands from his arms.

"All right," she said, softly, and stepped backwards, "if losing a government job means that much to you—"

Buck felt blood rush to his face.

"I never—" He didn't say any more. He pushed her slightly to one side and walked past her without seeing the small, quiet triumph in her eyes. He was feeling in his pocket for his notes as the bright glare of the footlights struck him, and he looked around quickly, not even knowing why, at the row of women beaming on his left, and saw Mrs. Sidney's pursy lips encourage him with a forced smile. He didn't see or hear Lota coming out behind him because by then he was turning to face the crowd and the people out front suddenly were clapping and he was walking stiffly towards the row of bright lights that bordered the stage. Somehow, McTyre had disappeared, and amazingly his hand had found the two sheets of written speech. He looked down at the words as he reached the footlights, but the lights reflected into his eyes from the bright curved metal shade. The words blurred and he cleared his throat under cover of the last small spasms of clapping. Then, suddenly, the silence came, heavy and hot, and with it the clear, wrenching thought that he was going to make a fool out of himself, that another old friend had died and that there was never a time for death, but death always found the time. His lips moved, without sound, but it was almost as if he could hear himself saying, "God Almighty, am I really marked? Is everybody I touch going to die?" He caught a quick, hard breath and let it out slowly and a despairing glance out front gave him nothing but three triangles of white and black lines. He shaded his eyes from the lights with one hand and looked down at the paper, not even thinking about the first two words he saw; then he straightened and heard his voice come dully.

"Ladies and gentlemen—" He stopped, hardly knowing why, and shaded his eyes again.

Abruptly from the audience came a single snort of laughter, cut off by a woman's sharp, loudly whispered, "Ben!"

Buck jerked his head up from his notes and began to peer in the direction of the laughter. "My Lord," he thought, "they think I'm scared. They don't know about— It's funny to them." He stared out at the blurring faces, then suddenly he felt an ease come over him. The laughter had done it, had made him remember that he was one of them. The faces cleared and he could recognize them. Down the line. Ed Jones, Mrs. Jones, Old Man Enfinger and his daughter, and, by God, Ben Echols, cringing back in his seat under the steady accusing glare of his tight-skinned little wife. Buck glared at Ben Echols in amazement and saw him look blankly back at first, then smile weakly and apologetically. Then he had forgotten everything but being where he was, and he wanted to laugh himself. He felt the sudden flood into his chest, and his blood was good again in his veins. He threw back his head and laughed, and it turned something loose inside, something that was warm and full and prancing. Then he heard another laugh, and another, and another until the whole crowd was bellowing with him and some small boys were yelling in the balcony. It was while he was laughing that the canny surge of power, of knowing what he could do with them, came curling over him, and he stopped to listen for a second, then held out his arms for silence. Carefully, with exaggerated movements, he tore the notes into small pieces and dropped them to the stage floor. He put both hands on his hips and leaned closer towards the crowd.

"I must have forgot," he said, loudly, "that you were all friends of mine." He was grateful for the small murmur of voices. "Now," he went on, "I can talk to you like I had you one at a time, like I've always done, and it feels better this way.

"I'm supposed to be formal about this—to turn over to the city a deed to this property with a lot of ceremony. Well, I don't care much about that fancy stuff. You all know, anyhow, that the deeds are already signed and delivered. So there's not much left for me to do up here. Just one thing I want to tell you all, though.

"This opera house is supposed to be a gift from me to the city and to everyone who lives in it. Well, it's not. I see it more like the repayment of a loan. And one that's long overdue. The money that built it came from Aven; it belongs in Aven. I wanted it to stay in Aven.

"This town has meant a lot to me—it's been my friend and it's been my good companion. It's given me more than a man deserves, and in giving it, it's come a long way. All the way from a cold-water spring in a grove of poplars to paved streets and a power plant. It's come to fine homes and flowers brought in from Mobile—azaleas to bring something besides work to all of us. I hope this opera house will do the same thing the flowers did for us—make us forget for a while that we're building a town and then remember stronger that we are growing with it, and be thankful to the town. I'm grateful to Aven because it took me along for the ride.

"Now, I want you all to enjoy this place. It's here for you and your children, and I hope their children. There's not anything else for me to say except—"

He heard it first out of all the crowd and his eyes shot up towards the small black booth. It crackled again, and suddenly the booth wasn't black any more. There was one blinding white flash of light and a loud "swoosh" as yellow flame and white smoke boiled out of the little window. Then a second of dead silence, and the lights in front of Buck flared brighter and went out. Buck started to open his mouth and a woman screamed in the balcony. One word: "Fire!"

Another moment of silence, and then the quick panicky scrambling of feet.

"Hold it!" Buck yelled the words. Some of the audience down in front turned back to look up at him, but up in the balcony someone started running down the steps. The crowd in the back half of the orchestra seats surged towards the lobby. Buck drew a deep breath and bellowed as loudly as he could. "Sit still!" A few more of them stopped shuffling their feet and turned back to face him.

He stepped closer to the footlights.

"Myra Echols!" The little woman jerked around and her face was working. "You and Ben open that emergency door." He pointed and saw out of the corner of his eye that some of the others had stopped. He glanced quickly up towards the booth and felt a sharp, cold clutching inside. Then he called out again.

"You, Ernest! Ernest King! Open that emergency door on your side." A huge man on the far left turned his wheyface briefly towards the stage, then plunged through the crowd to the door.

"Now, listen, everybody." Nearly every person downstairs had turned and was watching him, but he could still hear the shuffling thunder of feet on the stairs leading down from the balcony and see the milling crowd upstairs. "You folks on the right," he said, in a voice just loud enough to be heard above the growing crackle of flame, "you go out Myra and Ben's door when they get it open. You on the left can get out as soon as Ernest opens his. You in the middle just stand right still until that bunch of wild Indians clears the balcony." He put his hands together behind his back and began to walk up and down, watching the fire grow, shooting up from the booth now like first flames from a chimney on a dark night. He hollered once up at the emptying balcony, "Go slow down those stairs, you fools, or somebody'll get stomped in the rush." He could see out of the corner of his eye that Lota was still sitting calmly in her folding chair, although her bottom lip was caught tightly between her teeth. Two of the councilmen sat stolidly, with their arms folded. "Walt," Buck said in a lower voice and glanced towards the one nearest the wings. The councilman turned his eyes without moving his head. "Go call out the fire department." The man hardly moved his lips. "McTyre did it." Buck spoke to the one nearer to Lota. "Bush." The other councilman casually glanced in his direction. "God bless you and Walt." The one called Bush smiled crookedly, and Buck looked back at the fire. It was growing, all right, spreading outwards along the rows of now-emptied seats and licking into the ceiling, but he knew it was too slow to catch anyone in the balcony. "Take it easy, up there," he yelled, trying to throw his voice above the louder noises of running steps and sucking flame. "The fire won't hurt you, but you can hurt each other." Then, suddenly, he heard the loud crash and knew that someone in crazed fear had broken an upstairs window. He groaned. The fool would probably jump and kill himself, and now the place would really go, with the perfect draft from openings downstairs through the window upstairs. He felt cool air strike his face and knew without looking that Echols had opened his door. "Better hurry, you folks upstairs," he bellowed, and

[370]

knew they couldn't hear him. "Don't worry, downstairs. I'll keep you posted and you know damned well it'll be the truth because I'll be leaving, too, when it gets too close." He saw the draft hit the flame and his heart bumped once. It would be like a flue now. He glanced quickly from right to left and saw that the downstairs groups to either side were moving in orderly fashion out the opened emergency doors. The group in the middle stood very still, talking to each other with some excitement showing in the faces he could see, but with no signs of panic. He looked up into the balcony, but all he could find now was a fast-swirling current of smoke and gouts of flame, heaviest around the booth but growing thicker and faster and finally running wild tongues up the thick draperies on each wall. As he watched, he felt a hand touch his arm and he glanced down. It was Lota, pale but controlled.

"Can I do—?"

"Just stand here by—" He broke off and cocked his head to listen. No more running footsteps from the balcony. "You in the middle down there! Start moving a few at a time towards the front, but don't shove. Clear that space right under the booth first."

He watched them obey and breathed deeply with relief.

"Thank God they'll get out before that front wall falls off the booth."

Suddenly every light in the house went out. A woman screamed.

"Hold it," Buck shouted. "By God, if that fire don't give enough light, I'll build us another one on this stage."

Lota raised herself closer to his ear. "They're pretty well thinned out on the right."

"What's the matter with the damned fire department?" he said in a quick undertone, then raised his voice again. "Some of you folks in the middle can start working out the side doors."

"I heard the bell ringing just a minute ago," Lota answered.

"By God, if they don't hurry, there'll be a new crew tomorrow." An abrupt flaring of light through the deepening smoke made it easier to see the two-by-two files going out the three exits, and his breath was freer. The groups huddling and waiting had grown much smaller and the outgoing streams were steady, hurrying, but doing it calmly. The smoky gloom suddenly brightened and Buck swung his eyes up and around. Tiny snakes of flame had crept along the silk cords that looped from one set of velvet draperies to the other until three whole sets were burning on each side of the house, burning downwards, as long limp candles would burn, only faster.

"How'd it start?" Lota's voice was low and calm.

"Damned if I know." He pointed towards the boiling spot where the booth had been. "It busted out up there."

"It's through the ceiling," Lota said shakily.

Buck squinted above the balcony where the flames had been tallest and hottest.

"No," he said, slowly, "I don't— Yes, Lord, it is. Now it *will* raise hell in those plaster laths."

A new sound joined the roaring of flames, at first a coughing rumble, then a steady drumming. Buck looked up at the ceiling.

"Well, they finally got here and the first thing they can think about is wetting down a metal roof."

"Look." Lota caught his arm. "They're all out on the right."

"Left side's pretty well in shape, too." He turned to the two men who still sat calmly in their chairs. "Well, boys, the free act is about over. Let's get out of here."

They stood up, leisurely, and walked towards the front of the stage. One of them held out his hand. Buck took it, wondering.

"Buck," the man said, "you're a big man."

Buck felt heat come into his face.

"Hell, Bush," he said, awkwardly. Then he faced about suddenly and said again, "Let's go." He took Lota firmly by the arm and guided her off to the right wing towards the big sliding metal door that opened onto the back alley. "When did the others leave?" he asked over his shoulder.

Bush coughed and Walt laughed shortly.

"Mrs. Sidney fainted," he said, and threw his weight to help open the door, "and it looked like everybody but us wanted to help get her out."

Once it was started, the door slid easily along its oiled track, and the four of them slipped quickly out the opening. "Push it back," Buck said, "it'll make the fire easier to fight."

"Fight?" Bush said. "Look at that stuff coming through the roof. Won't do no good to fight this fire."

Buck looked up to see the sky lighted by a heavy column of flame just above the building, flame that was a sullen purple in the blue-grey smoke. "To hell with it, then," he said. "Let's trot on around front and see if anybody got hurt."

They stumbled at a fast walk through the littered alley between the burning opera house and the one-story building that served as city hall and police department, finally running fast into the street to escape the shower of sparks and small chunks of glowing char.

The crowd was backed off from the front of the opera house, some of them against the walls of the buildings across the street and others milling around on the brick-paved street on both sides of the fire. The fire chief and two half-dressed firemen stood out in the center of the street. Buck could see by the waving arms of one fireman that they were arguing. He motioned for Lota to cross on over with the crowd, then cut over towards the fire chief, striding angrily and letting his heels hit hard on the pavement.

"What the hell took you so long?"

The chief's face was white.

"We been here, Mr. Buck. Plenty long."

"Well, how come—?"

"Rotten hose, Goddammit!"

Buck turned in surprise to face the fireman who had spoken. He was an extremely thin boy of about twenty and his eyes were hollow and mad. "Can't do nothin' in there with a hose that's leakin' to hell.

"Somebody's in there fightin' it." Buck pointed to the single hose leading into the lobby.

The young fireman spat on the ground.

"Won't be long in there, an' as far's I'm concerned, you bastards that bought it can fight with that hose." He jerked around with contempt showing in the square, cocky angles of his shoulders, and started walking slowly away; then he tossed his head towards the lobby. "There they come now."

Three firemen came running out, clumsy in their long rubber

coats, and shiny with water. They slowed down just outside the building and came deliberately over to the chief.

"No pressure, boss," one of them panted. "Spraying us more'n the fire, and the damned thing is coming down pretty soon." He rubbed his hand hard across his blackened face. "All of it's up front, but the back's catchin' fast."

"The balcony just fell when we was in there," one of them rasped, coughing and spitting black spit.

Buck threw up both hands and let them fall limply back against his thighs.

"Well, let 'er rip, and just thank the Lord nobody got—"

The crowd behind them roared and Buck didn't finish. He wheeled to see them, mouths open and screaming, and some of them pointing upwards towards the opera house. "God Almighty," he said, low in his throat, knowing what it was before he saw it.

The figure came inching around the corner of the building with its back to the wall, cowboy boots teetering dangerously on the narrow stone ledge which ornamented the front and marked the beginning of the second floor. His hat was gone, and his long black hair hung lank and wet down over his eyes, but his checked shirt showed gay under the open vest. His right hand was splayed against the brick, never still, but working as if it were no longer a part of his body, to test and lead like a feeler on a caterpillar. His left hand was outstretched, too, holding his precious guitar. He moved painfully, hardly seeming to breathe, until he reached the center of the building, then he stopped, and Buck down below knew that his eyes had closed.

"Keep going, Virgil!" he yelled as loud as he could, but knew he couldn't be heard in the roar of flames and the high-pitched screams from the crowd. He turned quickly to the fire chief. "Get a ladder," he said, and two of the fireman ran off towards the truck. "We'll prop it right in front of him and get him down all right." He could feel the blood pounding in his ears and knew that his own breath was coming hard as if he had been running. "Up against the wall," he shouted to the firemen with the ladder, "just under his feet." He turned to the chief. "He's the one broke that window, sure as hell, and climbed out." The chief didn't answer, but shouted directions to the two firemen.

Buck watched them running awkwardly with the ladder between them, placing it carefully so that it's curved grapples caught over the ledge just beside Virgil's feet, and then he saw them dash quickly away from the wall. "Oh, my God!" He heard the screams as if they came from a thousand throats, then he saw that Virgil had moved. As if the ladder threatened him, Virgil had started once more, picking his way with his restless right hand, down the ledge. Buck groaned. "The poor fool." He touched the fire chief's arm. "You'll have to go get him." The chief shook his head. "Not me. I got kids."

Buck knew suddenly, surprised, that he had moved forward, and that he was walking slowly, almost automatically, towards the ladder.

"Hold my wife," he said, without even turning around to look back at her, and walked steadily over to the ladder. He looked up at Virgil. "Stand still," he bellowed, and Virgil stopped. He caught the ladder by its vertical sides and slid it carefully down closer to Virgil's feet. Virgil moved again and his right hand was touching the wide white stones of the corner.

Then, abruptly, Buck couldn't hear the crowd any more. It was as if everything had gone away and left only three things in the world: Virgil, a fear-crazed fool, a ladder, and himself. He began to climb the ladder as fast as he could, feeling all the way up that he moved too slowly, as if he were dreaming and trying to get to a place that kept moving away. Then his hands gripped the ledge, and he was drawing himself carefully and steadily up, feeling for and finding the fine balance that would bring him to his feet on the ledge. He stood with his feet on the ladder's top rung and held his arms wide out, with his hands flat against the brick wall, and slowly stepped up onto the ledge with first one foot—balancing a little there—then the other, and finally he was sidling towards Virgil with his face to the wall and his palms damp and sensitive, playing against the brick. And his mind moved sluggishly.

"Too damned much sand in this mortar. That Georgia crook must have slipped it in when I was asleep. It won't hold long in this heat. Move on, Virgil, around the corner, and jump over on top of the city hall. Hell, it ain't but about eight feet and a good-sized man can fall halfway. Any idiot can jump eight feet."

Virgil was closer now, almost within reach, stalled at the corner. Buck moved steadily, with his face scraping the smooth brick, trying to soothe Virgil.

"Take it easy, boy. Just turn this corner like you did the last one, then it's a short jump and we're all right." His left hand touched Virgil's. Virgil jerked convulsively and nearly fell. His guitar thumped hollowly against the wall. "Move on," Buck said, just loud enough for Virgil to hear, and he pushed gently against the outstretched hand. "Drop the guitar," he said hoarsely. Virgil closed his eyes again and Buck could see the silent lips moving, but he held on to the guitar. He pushed again, and Virgil moved. His right hand felt cautiously around the corner, then his arm followed, bending, almost fluid, around the sharp turn. "Hell, I'll buy you another one," Buck panted, but Virgil kept moving silently. His body pressed close against the brick as he inched out of sight. Buck saw the guitar last, slowly disappearing, and suddenly he wanted desperately to see Virgil again. He moved faster, until his left hand touched the corner and he could almost pull himself around, because the two sides gave him more purchase than the one flat side.

Virgil was still moving away on the ledge, with the city hall roof below and just a few feet away. "Like a horse in a burning barn," Buck thought. "No more sense—" He drew a deep breath to shout and felt his chest bump against the wall. "Jump across," he yelled. He touched the guitar with his left hand. Virgil's lips moved and Buck could hear the faint words.

"I didn't mean to do it," he screamed. "The sign. It touched something and then it just flashed."

"Easy, Virgil, easy. It's all right about that. Just you jump now. Jump! Go on and jump, you fool."

Virgil's eyes closed and his lips moved silently again.

"Dammit, jump!" Buck felt sudden movement under him and in front of him. It was as if he were lying flat on his face and the earth had moved beneath him. "Jump!" he roared, and jerked Virgil's guitar out of his hand and slung it, backhanded, across the alley.

Virgil screamed and his body leaned outwards. Then, apparently without being told, his legs bent and he gave a wild leap, sprawling in the air like an ape, to land on his stomach, half on and half off of the city hall. Buck saw him over his shoulder, scrambling like an animal up onto the roof, then scuttling across on his hands and knees, dragging the crushed guitar. Then, suddenly, his brain seemed to jar itself clear with one thought.

"How in the hell can I jump, facing the wall?" He felt the wall sway again, and started trying to turn. Suddenly, he knew he couldn't make the turn in time. The wall was leaning. No, it was bending in at the middle, crumpling. He felt the quick lurch under his feet and he leaned backwards and bent his knees, then desperately threw himself backwards, twisting in the air, trying to land on the roof like a cat, face downwards.

For a second, in mid-air, a shocking wrench of fear hit him, fear that he hadn't reached the roof. And with the thought came a blow on his right side, low on the ribs, and his fingers, clutching desperately, raked through the loosely strewn cinders that covered the city hall roof. Through the haze of pain from his side, he knew that he hung half on and half off the roof, with the upper part of his body barely balancing on the brick wall. His elbows automatically drew in and caught against the shallow rise of the coping, then he drew the first shuddering, painful breath of relief and raised his head, looking for Virgil in the smoke and the glare. He couldn't see him and then he realized that, almost without his knowing it, his feet were scraping sideways on the brick wall below him, trying to find purchase to bring him up onto the roof. And all the time there was the jumbled roar of fire from behind, and the mingling crash as walls gave way and crumpled tiredly into the alley below; and overriding all sounds, the hoarse cries of men and the high-tearing screams of women, and the smaller sound of his own breathing, more felt than heard, choking in the billows of black smoke that hid him.

"Virgil!" he tried to yell, but the sound was weak and he didn't wait for an answer. Carefully, he felt out with his hands, still holding to the coping with his elbows, but his fingers found nothing they could grasp. He closed his eyes against the smart of the smoke and deliberately forced his scrambling feet to relax against the sheer wall below. With his eyes still shut, he brought his elbows back and on top of the narrow coping and gripped with his fingers the right-angle edge. Desperately, then, he began to pull upwards with the full strength of his arms, hunching his big body up in jerks until he felt himself rise slightly, slowly, then suddenly faster, until he was resting painfully on his elbows atop the coping with his legs still hanging. He lifted one leg sideways, bending it until he could throw the knee onto the coping. Then, laboriously, he inched his body over until he lay parallel with and on top of the coping. He lifted his left leg as if he were exhausted, and rolled off the coping onto the roof and lay very still on his back, feeling with sensitive fingers the round and square and many-sided pebbles of grey slag, and in his mind worked one thought.

"I don't reckon either God or the Devil wants me today, 'cause they had a damned good chance right then."

He rolled slowly over onto his face and felt gratefully the hot scrape of the slag against his cheek. For a second his mind was almost asleep, while he sucked in short shallow breaths to keep from hurting his side. A dragging exhaustion kept holding him flat on the roof, but his mind started working again and all it said was, "Lota." He rolled his face hard against the roughness of the roof and the slight pain helped to clear his head. He raised himself up and his stomach moved in quick reaction to the raw pain in his side and the harsh ache of his muscles. He pulled himself up, inching until he felt his knees under him, then pushed up with his hands flat on the rooftop. He came to his feet and stood straight in spite of the biting stab under his ribs. His feet dragged through the slag, and the twitching of muscles in his thighs made his lower legs feel unfamiliar and shaky as he stumbled across the roof towards the front of the building. As he walked, his hands flailed against his body where huge sparks and still-glowing chunks of char were swept by the heat draft. He called out one more time, "Virgil!" but his voice still didn't come strongly enough. "Wonder if the damned fool jumped off," he thought as he reached the waist-high wall of brick which had been built up to support the front of ornamental stonework.

He leaned against the wall with his hands pushed hard against its smooth red-tile waterproofing and tried to see down into the street. The smoke hung low and thick below him and only a murk of light from the near-by street lamp glowed through. He started to turn back, when a quick gust of wind made the carpet of smoke swell upwards until an opening yawned, and for a moment he had a clear view of the street.

He caught a momentary glimpse of the crowd, surging wit-lessly back and forth, with opened mouths apparently yelling without any sound. Then, there was Lota. Lota, alone beside a telephone pole across the street, standing perfectly straight and still in her white dress, with her head thrown back and her arms straight down by her sides and hands clenched into small fists. He tried to wave at her, knowing his voice wouldn't carry over the waves of sound from below, but then the smoke closed in again and he was left with a confused memory of the crowd out in the street and the milling firemen in front of the city hall.

The thought struggled through that the firemen were below him. He stooped, holding onto the wall with one hand, and grabbed up a handful of the loose slag. When he had straightened again, he leaned far over and dropped the slag. He did it twice more before he heard a change in the sound of the crowd. Sharp, yelping commands and hoarse calls for the fire chief came floating up. Buck relaxed and let his body sag against the wall, and waited, wondering dully all the time where Virgil had gone.

Then, suddenly, he heard close-by shouts from behind, and he turned to see coming towards him across the roof two figures dimly seen in the smoke-fouled night. He pushed away from the wall, and then they had caught him by his arms and he was walk-ing slowly between them away from the front of the building. He didn't try to recognize them, or look up at their faces, but let his eyes sweep ahead of him, searching into the gloom.

"Virgil?" he questioned, hoarsely.

One of them answered.

"He's down inside, cryin' over his guitar."

"How'd he get—?" Buck stopped and his words turned into a low, hurting chuckle as he saw the yellowish square of light just below his feet. "Damn fool had more sense than me," he said. "I'd plumb forgot that trap door and I had it put there myself."

Then, in a kind of a heavy daze, he went coughing down the ladder that led from the trap door into the brightly lighted lobby of the city hall. Two other firemen, in slick wet rubber coats, looked up at him with open mouths as he made his way slowly down the ladder, but he hardly saw them and he didn't try to pick out a face.

"My wife?" he said, as his feet touched the floor.

"Good God!" a high, man's voice said. "We forgot to—"

Buck didn't turn towards the voice. He pushed straight ahead through the four men, paying no attention to the hands that reached out to hold his arms, and hardly hearing the words that came from them. When he reached the street, he was breathing easier and a swell of excitement was making his chest rise and fall so that it sharpened the probing pain in his side. He couldn't see her at first, even when he reached the cleared street in front of the burning opera house, because of the fringe of crowd which fronted the sidewalk across the street.

Then, hands he didn't know touched him and voices that sounded strange were saying, "God bless you, Buck," or just "By God, Buck, by God!" over and over, and still he didn't stop or slow down on his purposeful walk towards the telephone pole where he had seen Lota.

Abruptly, as he breached the wall of men and women, he saw her. She was still by the telephone pole and her face was still turned upwards, and her shoulders were thrown back and pulled down by the fierce strength with which she held her arms down at her sides.

"Lota," he said, softly, as he came closer. She didn't move at first, then slowly her head came around and she saw him. Her eyes closed for just a second, and her lips parted for the quick breath that he heard come between them. Her shoulders dropped and the awful tenseness went out of her arms. Then she opened her eyes again, and they were huge in the whiteness of her face. Her lips moved but made no sound and she leaned towards him as he came closer. Her hands groped upwards until they found his chest and she clutched in tight fingers the folds of his shirt. Her forehead came down on his chest and he could feel shudders running through her body as it pressed close to him. He put his left arm around her and pulled her nearer.

"Take it easy," he said, gently. She didn't lift her face and he barely heard the words.

"I thought you—" She rolled her forehead hard against his

[380]

chest, remembering, then quickly she looked up as he winced with the pain in his side.

"You're hurt!"

"Somethin' in my side." He lifted his shoulders and let them drop. "Ribs broke, I reckon."

She pulled quickly away from him and caught him by the arm.

"We're going right to the hotel and get a doctor." The fear had left her face and her forehead had drawn into an anxious frown. Buck felt her arm come around his waist as he turned and started down the street with her, and his mind said, "Give a woman somethin' to do an' she'll make out."

Dimly, still not consciously knowing them, he spoke to the men and women who pressed around them until they reached the corner and turned down towards the hotel. As they went into the dimly lighted, cool and empty street that stretched before them, he could feel strength flooding back into his body, and the weakness of thigh and calf he knew was leaving, because now he could walk heel and toe instead of dragging his feet.

They had stepped down the curb across the street from the hotel before Lota spoke again. She stopped him with pressure on his waist and turned slightly so that she looked up into his face.

"I almost hated you when you went up that ladder," she said, softly, and her lips trembled and turned up and she wouldn't meet his eyes.

He looked down at her in astonishment.

"Hated me?"

She touched her forehead back to his chest.

"Women aren't like men," she said. "A woman is apt to feel like a man hasn't got any right to risk a life that belongs to her."

Buck rubbed his fingers into the back of her hair and pulled her head back until he could look down at her.

"Now, how do you feel?"

She opened her eyes wide in surprise.

"Proud, of course. Why, everybody on the streets was saying— Why, good gracious, one man said, 'Many a man would go up that ladder for his brother, but damn few would do it for an idiot!'"

"Virgil's no idiot."

She nodded impatiently.

"I know that. But it was the things they said—"

"Aw, hell, don't believe everything you hear. What they say is just temporary."

She pulled away and looked up at him while the smile on her lips grew prouder, yet somehow sad.

"This isn't temporary," she said. "They know and I know that you're the man for this land and for this time, and they know that no other man in this country is as willing to give—and give anything he's got."

"Hmph!" Buck's lower lip stuck out. "Don't make much difference what I try to give, don't look like I can." He blinked his eyes once or twice, rapidly. "Damned funny," he muttered. "All my life, I'd figure out to skin somebody, or even work out a little graft, and spite o' me it would turn out and do some good." He paused and caught a slow breath, then went on. "Now, here I try to do somethin' specially good, all my tools seem to turn in my hand and the whole job goes wrong."

"No," Lota said, fiercely, "no matter what happens, the good you've done is done and can't be undone, be doggoned if the whole town burns up." He touched her shoulder with his hand and smiled questioningly down at her until her voice came again, softer and slower this time. "I wonder," she said, as she put her arm around his waist again and pulled him towards the hotel, "if it makes much difference after all what a man's reasons are, if good comes from a bad motive."

"I don't know," Buck said, almost absently, and his hand tightened on her shoulder. "Just one thing I know," he went on in a tight voice, "the Governor dyin' and the place burnin' and all that makes it look like I better do some thinkin'—maybe quit everything before it all goes wrong."

Lota stopped dead still and she swung around again to face him.

"Now, you listen to me," she said. "You're mine and I'm proud of you, regardless, but there's one thing that I think is true for everybody." She caught a quick breath.

"I don't believe," she said, deliberately, "that anybody can live without trouble if he has brains and a heart. And you've got plenty of both."

Buck laughed out loud, suddenly, and caught her close to him.

And again, as the first time he had held her that way, he could feel her body from shoulders to knees pressing against him and the scent of her hair came again and there was the quick, glad lightening in his veins.

He looked up, then, from the middle of the street and saw the lights of the Harrison House sign winking steadily overhead in the night, and inside through the many small squares of windowpane he could see the bellboys standing in a curious knot close to the desk where the clerk was glued to the switchboard.

He pulled slightly away and looked down at her.

"Let's go on in," he said. "As long as I've got you that close, I'll never have any trouble because, God knows, I never had much of a brain and—" He looked sideways at her. "Damned if I know what's gone with any heart I might a'had."

She laughed delightedly and held out her clenched fist, fingers upwards.

"I've got it," she said.

They went on into the Harrison House.

NOTES TO INTRODUCTION

1. See Wendell and Pamela Stepp, *Dothan: A Pictorial History* (Norfolk: Donning, 1984), pp. 8–52.

2. Ibid., p. 24.

3. Louis D. Rubin, Jr., "Fugitives as Agrarians: The Impulse Behind *I'll Take My Stand*", *William Elliot Shoots a Bear: Essays on the Southern Literary Imagination* (Baton Rouge: Louisiana State University Press, 1975), p. 149.

4. Virginia Bennett, Review of *Devil Make a Third* by Douglas Fields Bailey, *Commonweal* 22 October 1948, pp. 43–44.

5. Peggy Thompson, "Bannon's Town", Review of *Devil Make a Third* by Douglas Fields Bailey, *New York Herald Tribune Weekly Book Review* 19 September 1948, p. 10.

6. Edwin S. Mills, Jr., "Machiavelli in Alabama", Review of *Devil Make a Third* by Douglas Fields Bailey, *Saturday Review of Literature* 2 October 1948, p. 14.

ORIGINAL ENDING

Just you jump now. Jump! Go on and jump, you fool."

Virgil's eyes closed and his lips moved silently again.

"Dammit, jump!" Buck felt sudden movement under him and in front of him. It was like he was lying flat on his face and the earth had moved beneath him. "Jump!", he roared, and jerked Virgil's guitar away from the wall.

Virgil screamed and his body leaned outwards, then, apparently without being told, his legs bent and he gave a wild leap, sprawling in the air like an ape, to land on his stomach, half on and half off of the city hall. Buck saw him scrambling like an animal up onto the roof, then scuttling across on his hands and knees, dragging the crushed guitar, then suddenly his brain seemed to jar itself clear with one thought.

"How in hell can I jump, facing the wall?" He felt the wall sway again, and started trying to turn. Suddenly, he knew he couldn't make the turn in time. The wall was leaning. No, it was bending in at the middle, crumpling. He felt the quick lurch under his feet and he leaned backwards and bent his knees, then desperately threw himself backwards, twisting in the air, trying to land on the roof like a cat, face downwards. Then, suddenly, in midair, he knew he hadn't reached the roof.

"This is a hell of a ---." He was thinking when he struck the ground on his face, and then he didn't think any more, or feel anything, not even when one of the corner stones dislodged from the break above and fell on his back, then rolled and bounded out into the streets.

The next thing he felt was the cold wet scrape of brick against his mouth, and the dragging out into the street, and the next thing he tasted was the thick cloy of blood heavy in his mouth. The only thing he saw was one bright white satin shoe, spattered and wet and shedding sequins off its silver spangled bow as it struggled and jerked, apparently all by itself in the world.

"Pretty little foot," he tried to mumble, then suddenly his head had dropped and he could feel the wet paving brick of Aven against his open mouth and he had one thought.

"It don't hurt. God, I wonder if this is all folks are scared of."

He didn't think, or feel, or taste anything else.